THE RIGHTS OF RELIGIOUS PERSONS IN PUBLIC EDUCATION

THE RIGHTS
OF RELIGIOUS
PERSONS
IN PUBLIC
EDUCATION

John W. Whitehead

CROSSWAY BOOKS • WHEATON, ILLINOIS
A DIVISION OF GOOD NEWS PUBLISHERS

Library of Congress Cataloging-in-Publication Data
Whitehead, John W., 1946-
      The rights of religious persons in public education /
John W. Whitehead.
            p.   cm.
      Includes bibliographical references and index.
      1. Religion in the public schools—United States. 2. Civil rights—
Religious aspects. 3. Education—United States—Aims and objectives.
I. Title.
LC111.W47   1991   377'.14—dc20   90-19220
      ISBN 0-89107-610-7

99	98	97	96	95	94	93	92	91
15	14	13	12	11	10	9	8	7	6	5	4	3	2	1

For all those
with religious convictions who have
struggled to maintain
freedom of expression in public education.
Without you,
such expression would be
much more limited.

CONTENTS

ACKNOWLEDGMENTS

A s with any worthwhile endeavor, there are those whose assistance improves the project. Such was true with this book.

The Rutherford Institute interns of the summer of 1990 provided valuable research and editorial assistance. Thus, I express my gratitude to Sandra Gary and Chris Lilienkamp for carrying a primary oar in assisting me. Also, David Petter, Julie Steidley, and Clifford Stricklin provided valuable help. Also appreciated is Peter Gunas's assistance with some final details.

Thanks to Daniel Dreisbach for providing research and editorial assistance on chapters 12 and 16. The assistance of Alexis Crow and Tracey Beach in the final stages is also appreciated very much.

Thanks to Sally Mason for her dedication and for typing the manuscript. Also, Carol Whitehead's typing and editorial assistance, as always, helped.

PREFACE

Although several United States Supreme Court cases decided in recent years[1] better define the rights of religious persons in public education, significant confusion in this area of constitutional law remains. As a consequence, the struggle for full recognition of the constitutional rights of religious persons in the public education system continues.

Unfortunately, many believe that any mention of religion in the public education classroom and/or on the campus is unconstitutional. This erroneous belief is reinforced by the apparent puzzlement of the courts, displayed in various court decisions concerning the role religion should play in American public schools.

Fortunately, the United States Supreme Court, in its role of interpreting the Constitution, has not taken this position in its decisions. To the contrary, the Court has held that the government (which includes the public schools) must accommodate religion whenever it is constitutionally required. The Court has expressly held that religious speech enjoys the same high First Amendment protection as other speech under the Free Speech Clause in addition to its First Amendment protection under the Free Exercise Clause. Moreover, through the passage of the Equal Access Act, Congress has expressed its view that religious speech must be treated fairly and equally within the public schools. The subsequent affirmation of the Act by the Supreme Court further undergirds the constitutional guarantee of freedom of religious expression.

As the reader will no doubt realize, I do not shrink from offering forthright opinions in this book. For me, the morality of responsible scholarship contradicts the classic formula of a supposedly value-free detachment and allegedly unbiased description of the rights of religious persons in public education. "Instead such morality points to an avowal of the substantive beliefs and commitments that necessarily inform any account of constitutional arguments and conclusions."[2]

Thus, the reader will find I have taken clear positions on the most troublesome problems dealing with the rights of religious persons in public education. Because such views are openly presented and because contrary views are fairly considered, the fact that an illusory neutrality is not presented should enhance the value of this book to all readers. This is true whether the reader agrees with or dissents from any position I have taken. Also, no reader will have to guess or wonder at the values that may have influenced a particular judgment. It is my opinion that such judgments never stand solely on a neutral base anyway.

Finally, I believe that there is a great danger that, as it struggles to achieve a uniformity in educational technique and values communication, the American public education system is undermining the elements necessary for continuing freedom—that is, individualism and diversity. Therefore, this book emphasizes that the American system was intended to operate on the principles of equality and free and open communication. This, of course, includes equality and freedom in public education for religious exercise and expression. When and if free communication, religious or otherwise, is stifled, the system suffers and, along with it, the cause of freedom for all.

John W. Whitehead
Culpeper, Virginia
January, 1991

PART ONE

Problems

We have been taught that the Constitution guarantees us freedom of speech. But we feel that here we have been discriminated against, because we can picket, we can demonstrate, we can curse, we can take God's name in vain, but we cannot voluntarily get together and talk about God on any part of our campus, inside or outside of the school. We just feel frustrated because we don't feel like we are being treated equally.

—Testimony of a public school student
before the United States Senate
Committee on the Judiciary
(April 1983).

1

Public Education and Value Equanimity

The vigilant protection of the constitutional freedoms is nowhere more vital than in the community of American schools. The classroom is peculiarly the "marketplace of ideas." The Nation's future depends upon leaders trained through wide exposure to that robust exchange of ideas which discovers truth "out of a multitude of tongues," (rather) than through any kind of authoritative selection.

—Justice William Brennan,
Keyishian v. Board of Regents,
385 U.S. 589, 603 (1967).

Education, both public and private, is inevitably a system of manipulation of consciousness.[1] This manipulation of consciousness takes the form of the inculcation and indoctrination of certain ideologies and values in young minds. The very terms "inculcation" and "indoctrination" suggest a system of teaching by "frequent repetitions or admonitions" meant to imbue students with a "partisan and sectarian opinion, point of view, or principle."[2]

This fact has been recognized and accepted by the major institutions of American society, including the United States Supreme Court. In early cases, the Supreme Court had (with implications for free exercise of religion in public schools) stressed the state's lack of authority to "standardize its children by forcing them to accept instruction by public teachers only,"[3] or to "prescribe what shall be orthodox in politics, nationalism, religion, or other matters of opinion."[4]

However, the Supreme Court has more recently not only recognized that value inculcation in public schools is inherent, but has also concluded that it is desirable. In fact, the Court has stressed the public school's role as "a principal instrument in awakening the child to cultural values";[5] its legitimate function of "inculcating fundamental values necessary to the maintenance of a democratic political system";[6] and the permissibility of applying its curriculum so as to transmit "community values."[7] And as recently as 1982 in *Board of Education v. Pico*,[8] while only a plurality of the Supreme Court agreed with the holding that the First Amendment limits the authority of local school boards to remove books from high school and junior high libraries, *every* Justice who wrote an opinion endorsed public education's role as an inculcator or transmitter of values.[9]

The American judiciary's current acceptance of value inculcation in public schools can be understood against the backdrop of three basic educational philosophies that have influenced the development of Western educational ideology.[10] As discussed in chapter 7, these three philosophies may justify differing appraisals of student capacity which, in turn, would support differing conclusions concerning free exercise of religion in public schools.

ROMANTICISM

Romantic educational theorists hold that because what comes from *within* the child is the most important aspect of development, "the educational environment should be permissive enough to allow the inner 'good' . . . to unfold and the inner 'bad' to come under control."[11] Romanticism is based upon a psychological theory of development that pictures a child's cognitive development as unfolding through prepatterned stages, the variations in rate of development being largely inborn.[12]

A romantic educational philosophy has motivated development of unstructured curricula intended to allow children to learn at their own pace, such as the Montessori and "open school" methods. One psychologist's prescription for the child's happiness, written at the dawn of the 1960s, represents an extreme romanticist position:

> Abolish authority. Let the child be himself. Don't push him around. Don't teach him. Don't lecture him. Don't elevate him. Don't force him to do anything.[13]

As the social psychologist George Mead observed, romanticism is rooted in "the existence of the self as the primary fact."[14] Mead himself stressed that the individual is a conscious and individual personality "just in as far as he is a member of society."[15] This more behavioristic[16] perspective shaped the highly influential educational theorist John Dewey's critique of strong, nineteenth-century individualism and consequent "progressivist" educational philosophy, discussed below.

CULTURAL TRANSMISSION

The cultural transmission educational philosophy is rooted in the classic tradition of Western education. It is the belief that the educator's primary task is the direct transmission to the present generation of bodies of knowledge and of rules or values that the culture has collected in the past.[17]

While the romantic educational philosophy is thoroughly child-centered, cultural transmission theory is society-centered. The former stresses the child's freedom, the latter the child's perceived overriding need to learn the social order's discipline.[18]

It is an essentially cultural transmission educational philosophy that has informed the United States Supreme Court's recent deference to public education's alleged primary role as an inculcator of dominant societal values. Such deference may infringe on the free exercise of religion within public schools, especially when religiously objectionable curricula are at issue.[19]

PROGRESSIVISM

A variety of educational philosophy that has been termed "progressive" is less individualistic than romanticism:

> Unlike the romantics, the progressives do not assume that development is the unfolding of an innate pattern or that the primary aim of education is to create an unconflicted environment able to foster healthy development. Instead, they define development as a progression through invariant ordered sequential stages. The educational goal is the eventual attainment of a higher level or stage of development in adulthood, not merely the healthy functioning of the child at a present level.[20]

Instead of stressing education's role in the development of the individual child as an end in itself, progressivism holds that "education should nourish the child's natural interaction with a developing society or environment."[21]

By far the most influential progressivist educational theorist was John Dewey, a man some consider the "father" of modern American public education. His progressivism mediated between the romantic and cultural transmission educational philosophies discussed above.

Dewey dismissed the romantic educational method as "stupid" and considered the child's individuality to be not innate ("not an original possession or gift"), but rather "something to be . . . wrought out."[22] Dewey promulgated a "new individualism" to replace *both* the "prescientific, pretechnological individualism" that held sway when the church existed "to secure the salvation of the individual . . . as a soul,"[23] and nineteenth-century libertarian individualism. In response to the individualism espoused by prominent libertarian John Stuart Mill, Dewey argued that actions and passions of individuals are what they are "because of the social medium in which they live."[24]

Dewey did acknowledge that "the educative process" will be "haphazard" without insight into the individual's "psychological structure and activities."[25] However, he insisted that we do not know what the child's own "instincts and tendencies" mean "until we can translate them into their social equivalents."[26]

Concerning the cultural transmission educational philosophy, Dewey often objected to any view of education as a means of transmitting established or absolute truths, whose existence had no place within his philosophy of pragmatism,[27] which judged truth or falsity in terms of what "works" in experience. Instead of appealing to a fixed, core curriculum rooted in a given culture, Dewey proposed that the "true center of correlation" of academic subjects is "the child's own social activities."[28]

AMERICAN EDUCATIONAL HISTORY

Early America's prevalent homogeneity in value composition supported application of a cultural transmission educational philosophy within public schools. This homogeneity is reflected in state constitutional provisions recognizing religion as an aim of state-sponsored or encouraged education,[29] as well as in state supreme court rulings which upheld a religious ideal of education into the early twentieth century.[30]

This homogeneity is also embodied in the McGuffey readers, a series of readers widely used in American schools during the nineteenth and early twentieth centuries. Between 1836 and 1920, more than 120 million McGuffey readers were sold.[31]

The McGuffey readers were pervaded by moral lessons extolling piety, thrift, and industry. The following passage from the mid-nineteenth-century McGuffey guide to rhetoric represents a typical McGuffey religious lesson:

> If you can induce a community to doubt the genuineness and authenticity of the Scriptures; to question the reality, and obligations of religion; to hesitate, undeciding, whether there be any thing as virtue and vice; whether there be an eternal state of retribution beyond the grave; or whether there exists any such being as God, you have broken down the barriers of moral virtue, and hoisted the flood-gates of immorality and crime.[32]

The McGuffey readers were influenced by a conservative ideology that considered education an institution for transmitting and inculcating the virtues needed to preserve republican government.[33] They also contained passages from the classics of Western literature and created a high standard of literacy.

Various state constitutions have cited, without religious justification, the stability or preservation of a republican form of government as the reason for establishing a public school system.[34] Horace Mann, John Dewey's predecessor as America's foremost educator, also stressed (with explicit religious justification) public education's role as an inculcator of republican virtues. In an 1846 letter to Boston school children, Mann stressed the students' religious destiny.[35] He believed that if children aren't both prepared "to become good citizens," and imbued with "a reverence for all things sacred and holy," the republic "must go down to destruction."[36]

VALUE INCULCATION AS A MODERN EDUCATIONAL PROBLEM

Because of *early* America's prevalent value *homogeneity* (relative to the *current* value *diversity*), the inculcation of dominant values as practiced through the McGuffey readers was not nearly as problematic as the modern manipulation of consciousness in public schools. In fact, one Supreme Court justice has reasoned that because the Constitution's framers did not foresee the development of a comprehensive educational system controlled by public officials, eighteenth-century views are irrelevant in deciding whether value inculcation in the form of public school-sponsored prayer and Bible reading is unconstitutional as an establishment of religion.[37]

Modern American society is a collection of races, creeds, and religions not present within early American culture. Contemporary cultural diversity militates against any inculcation of "common" values. The cultural transmission educational philosophy cannot be exclusively practiced. Indeed, the courts' current appeal to public education's function of inculcating common values threatens the rights of religious people in public schools.

The present cultural diversity militates against inculcation of values by public schools for a number of reasons. First, current diversity means that *someone* would have to be granted special power to determine which value system will be the "common" value system to the exclusion of other competing value systems. Second, it necessarily follows from the current diversity that any teaching of supposed "common" values will discriminate against minority races and religions.

Finally, it follows from the current diversity that any attempts to impose (either directly or indirectly) a common value system will violate equal protection principles inherent in the American system of justice. Although some sort of "community" may be cultivated in the public schools, a problem both institutional and sociological in magnitude is created when a system of ideological indoctrination is imposed within public schools.

Some commentators see in modern public schools' dual goals of inculcating some "common core" of values and equally protecting all students' viewpoints the following sort of dilemma — the public school either grants equal time to a religious perspective on a "secular" subject, "in which case a discrimination between religions is inevitably effected"; or it limits itself to a secular frame of reference, "thereby belittling religion."[38]

An example of this is the teaching of human origins, a major area in which public schools have been criticized for not providing "equal time" for a "creationist" perspective along with teachings about evolution. The Supreme Court has found a state law requiring equal time for "creation science" whenever evolution is taught to be an establishment of religion.[39]

This dilemma of common values inculcation is thus very real. This is true, in essence, because (as explained further below) strict value-neutrality within the public schools is impossible.

Private schooling is chosen primarily on the basis of differing (and often minority) educational viewpoints. Parents who choose private education expect a certain form of indoctrination to occur in conformity with a particular point of view. This is particularly true of parents who choose private religious schools. Such indoctrination is the product of *educational choice.*

However, parents' relative lack of choice in public education is predicated on an absence of such "private" viewpoints. Indeed, a "public" viewpoint *should* prevail in public schools. This public viewpoint may be discerned by appeal to a "compelling state interest" in values education that is "necessary for the sustenance and preservation of our modern state [and] one of the bulwarks of democratic government."[40] Under such a standard, it may be taught, for example, that theft is wrong and that democracy is better than totalitarianism.

The acceptability of *some* sort of value inculcation in public schools argues against the romanticist educational philosophy. Indeed, the romantic educational philosophy is susceptible to criticism from both cultural transmission and progressivist perspectives. From the cultural transmission perspective, it could be criticized for leaving children culturally impoverished and unable to function as citizens. From the progressivist perspective, it could be criticized for patronizingly seeking only children's "happiness" while failing to make them confront genuine ethical and intellectual problems.[41]

It should be clear then that diversity in public schools cannot be accommodated through a "value-free" educational process.[42] If principles of nondiscrimination and equal protection[43] are to be followed, the "public" viewpoint that should prevail in public schools must protectively incorporate the myriad views and values within modern society. There is arguably a close relationship between the First Amendment's guarantee of free exercise of religion and the Fourteenth Amendment's Equal Protection Clause such that a public school's discrimination based on a child's or parent's views violates both constitutional provisions.[44] As we shall see, the protective incorporation of differing views must include *religious* views lest the equal protection principle be contravened.

However, there is a problem with the Supreme Court's approach to value inculcation. While the Supreme Court recognizes the danger of the inculcation of *religious* "orthodoxies" in public schools,[45] the Court has ignored the First Amendment implications "when equally basic but nonreligious values form a part of the philosophy established by a school and communicated to its students."[46]

THE "PUBLIC" FUNCTION OF PUBLIC EDUCATION

A problem inherent in public education is whether a legitimate public function requires conformity and information control. In the mid-nineteenth century, the philosopher John Stuart Mill recognized the danger of ideological control of public education:

> A general State education is a mere contrivance for moulding people to be exactly like one another: and as the mould in which it casts them is that which pleases the predominant power in the government, whether this be a monarch, a priesthood, an aristocracy, or the majority of the existing generation; in proportion as it is efficient and successful, it establishes a despotism over the mind, leading by natural tendency to one over the body.[47]

Mill's concern over the possibility of such "despotism" reflects his strong individualism, which shaped classical liberal political thought and is similar to the individualism that informs romantic educational philosophy.[48] Mill considered human nature to be "not a machine to be built after a model," but rather a "tree" that must be allowed to develop "according to the tendency of the inward forces that make it a living thing."[49]

We must remember that government, which includes public schools, exists for the benefit of the people, not the people for the benefit of government. Unfortunately, the ideological framework and value choices of the public schools are most often controlled by the political majorities or interest groups administering the educational system.[50] Such majoritarian control has been approved by the federal courts.

The ideological control of public schools that concerned Mill has been addressed by the Supreme Court. As previously noted, the Court has recognized that public schools, as indoctrinating institutions, *necessarily* foster attitudes approved by the society that operates and regulates them. However, courts have taken a step beyond this recognition to say that a "public" value system *should* be taught within public schools.[51]

For example, in *Minersville School District. v. Gobitis*[52] (which was overruled by *West Virginia Board of Education v. Barnette*[53]), Supreme Court Justice Felix Frankfurter went so far as to claim that when parentally inspired values conflict with governmental or social values, the state may in self-protection use the public schools to preserve those public values that in the state's opinion "bind men together in a comprehending loyalty, whatever may be their lesser differences and difficulties."[54] As Justice William Brennan wrote some twenty years later, public education's "uniquely *public* function" is "the training of American citizens in an atmosphere free of parochial, divisive, or separatist influences of any sort."[55] If performance of a "uniquely public function" by public schools means a state-enforced conformity of young people, then there is the possibility of the destruction of cultural diversity.

State educational systems tend toward uniformity. In the process of abolishing truly private education, Adolf Hitler, for example, declared that the "new Reich will give its youth to no one, but will itself take youth and give to youth its own education and its own upbringing."[56] To be troubled over the courts' application of the idea that public education exists to inculcate a particular value system is not to compare American courts to Hitler, but merely to point out the dangers inherent in such a philosophy of public education.

THE HIDDEN CURRICULUM

It is commonly said that by providing training in basic communicative skills and patterns of thought as well as imparting knowledge, schools are preparing young people to exercise those political freedoms basic to American democracy.[57] However, as has been stressed above, "[w]hat remains largely unconfronted is the pervasiveness of value transmission in the schools."[58]

It is widely recognized that value neutrality is impossible within the public schools. This impossibility has been credited to "the difficulty in separating facts, values, and the evaluative implications of 'facts.'"[59] It has been analogized to the way in which law also, "by its very nature, incorporates some views of morality and excludes others."[60] It has been explained by appeal to the "selectivity" inherent in "making decisions of inclusion and exclusion necessary to develop a curriculum."[61]

A public school's efforts to provide all points of view on issues in the classroom do not dismantle its system of value inculcation. What may remain unaffected is the school's "hidden curriculum," which includes "the role models teachers provide; the structure of classrooms and of teacher-student relationships; the way in which the school is governed; the ways in which the child's time is parceled out, learning subdivided and fragmented, attitudes and behaviors rewarded and punished."[62] The ranking and "tracking" of students, starting at an early age, according to perceived intellectual ability effects a fragmentation of learning that may be an especially potent part of the hidden curriculum. The effects of educational tracking have been likened to the detrimental effects of racial segregation that the Supreme Court recognized in *Brown v. Board of Education.*[63]

The hidden curriculum also affects instruction in basic skills (such as mathematics, reading, etc.). Thus:

> Even in those areas concerned with basic skills it is clear that teaching is never value-neutral, that texts, teachers, subject matter and atmosphere convey messages about approved and rewarded values and ideas.[64]

Because teachers cannot avoid engaging in value judgments and decisions, any pretense that the teacher is value-free will itself create the hidden curriculum.[65]

Indeed, the Supreme Court recognized how teachers themselves convey messages in *Meek v. Pittenger*.[66] In striking down a provision in a state law allowing religious schools to receive "auxiliary services" from state-subsidized teachers and counselors, the Court reasoned that such teachers and counselors could fail to remain religiously neutral within the religious schools and thus provoke controversies between the state and religious authorities.[67]

Some commentators note that while some children will "swallow whole" values included in the hidden curriculum, others will pretend to agree with such values as part of the prevailing orthodoxy "while suppressing internal tensions ranging from personal alienation to confusion and loss of identity."[68] As will be discussed later, such suppression can have a devastating impact on religious students in particular.

If the public schools disregard the views of one or another student minority, then the minority that is forced to remain within the public schools by both compulsory education laws and economics will in certain instances come under extreme pressure to conform.[69] This is especially true when peer pressure is taken into account. Peer pressure also operates as part of the hidden curriculum.

Mass state education has forced children into horizontal peer relationships, abrogating their traditional vertical relationships with adults (especially their parents). Public schools have assumed a major part of the socialization process that was once accomplished within the family. One author who currently contends for the view (discussed above) of education as a means of instilling republican virtues[70] reflects favorably on the demise of John Locke's "state of families," in which parents were given complete control over their children's education.[71] The reasoning is that some parents cannot be counted upon to teach their children properly.[72]

A consequence of the demise of parents' control of their children's education has been the increasing importance of peer relationships (along with all of the trappings of "peer pressure") relative to parental relationships. In fact, compulsory public education creates a peer group that occupies a place of prime importance in the student's life:

> [The] setting-apart of our children in schools — which take on ever more functions, ever more "extracurricular activities" — for an ever larger period of training has a singular impact on the child of the high-school age. He is "cut off" from the rest of society, forced inward toward his own age group, made to carry out his whole social life with others his own age. With his fellows, he comes to constitute a small society, one that has most of its important interactions *within* itself, and maintains only a few threads of connection with the outside adult society.[73]

John Dewey, true to his progressivist philosophy, commented favorably on public education's usurpation of what were primarily family functions. The development of the "ideal school," he argued, is simply a matter of doing systematically and competently what "can be done in most households only in a comparatively meager and haphazard manner."[74]

The current tendency of public schools to teach such nontraditional subjects as sex education and "values clarification"[75] may deepen the separation between home and school, prompting some parents to fear that a "monolithic educational creature" will stamp out diversity.[76] The implications of the use of possibly dangerous psychological techniques in nontraditional curricula are considered in chapter 2.

If a "monolithic educational creature" has in fact been created, the primary relationship in the student's life is not parent-child or even child-child, but child-state. The state-controlled public school system has filled the parental vacuum. Some psychologists in fact argue that a primary function of public education is to provide a "uniform orientation at the societal level."[77]

Negative effects of such "uniform orientation" include an obsessive conformity that harms parent-child relations, and stigmatization of nonconforming students. Stigmatization can have especially severe emotional effects on students when religious beliefs are involved.

EQUALITY

The answer to the problems addressed above is that the freedom of conscience and other rights of minorities, including religious minorities, be accommodated as public schools carry out their "public function" of inculcating public values. Viewpoints and ideological leanings of minorities must be afforded equal treatment if their dignity is to be preserved within public schools. This issue of how the inherent lack of neutrality in pubic schools concerning religion (as well as values in general) mandates affirmative accommodation of religious minorities within public schools is considered in chapter 5.

2

Rights and Human Dignity

*The Sacred Rights of Mankind are not to be rummaged for
among old parchments or musty records. They are written,
as with a sunbeam, in the whole of human nature, by the
Hand of Divinity itself, and can never be erased or obscured
by mortal power.*

—Alexander Hamilton,
Works, Volume II (1851)

Technological advances and the growth of the technocratic welfare state
(with its attendant public education system) have greatly increased the
ability of the modern state to manipulate its citizens. The technological and
scientific advances of recent decades have "raised the spectre of new and
frightening invasions of privacy."[1] The spectre of governmental invasions
of freedom has long disturbed many people.[2]

THE DIGNITY ISSUE

It has also long been recognized that privacy is an aspect of human *dignity*,
whether privacy is "an independent value," or "a composite of the interests
in reputation, emotional tranquility, and intangible property."[3] However,
as government has grown larger and assumed functions once performed by
such mediating institutions as the family and church, the citizen has become
fungible and insignificant.

Both religious and irreligious observers have addressed modern denial
of the notion of dignity upon which the classic conception of human rights
is based.

Considering the implications of the "progress of applied science,"
Theologian C. S. Lewis wrote: "Man's conquest of Nature turns out, in the
moment of its consummation, to be Nature's conquest of Man."[4] He concluded that this "conquest," if unchecked, "will abolish Man," producing

"the rule of the Conditioners over the conditioned material."[5] Reflecting on the loss of a Judeo–Christian consensus in the West,[6] existentialist novelist Alberto Moravia declared:

> Respect for man has disappeared. Man is no longer taboo and he has a much lower place than in the pre-Christian era when, at least within the city walls or within the tribal environment, the religions of cities and tribes guaranteed that sacred character to man which was later to be extended to all men without exception by Christianity. Christianity has evaporated, but so has the ancient anthropocentric and humanist idea that Christianity had salvaged from the ruins of the pre-Christian world.[7]

Moravia credited Christianity for its "quality of setting man as an end and not making use of him to attain that end."[8]

A number of serious scholars deny that human beings possess any intrinsic dignity such that "unalienable rights" ought to be ascribed to them. They are, therefore, prepared to countenance a disturbing degree of governmental manipulation of citizens. The behaviorist[9] psychologist B. F. Skinner, for example, writes that "an experimental analysis of human behavior" (such as he had attempted) should naturally "strip away the functions previously assigned to autonomous man and transfer them one by one to the controlling environment," leaving "less and less for autonomous man to do."[10] Skinner embraces Lewis's "abolition of man," which he interprets as the abolition of "the man defended by the literatures of freedom and dignity." He concludes: "To man *qua* man we readily say good riddance."[11] Skinner's application of his behaviorism to education is discussed below.

The framers of the American Constitution generally believed in the human freedom and dignity that Skinner and others deny. Thomas Jefferson considered it self-evident that "all [people] are created equal," being "endowed by their Creator with certain unalienable Rights," and that among these rights are "Life, Liberty, and the pursuit of Happiness."[12] Jefferson believed the concept of "rights" is by its very definition of religious origin. A religious definition of rights recognizes freedom's essence that no statist manipulation can destroy. If it is codified into law, a religious definition of rights affords the bearer of such rights great dignity.

ESSENTIAL RELIGIOUS LIBERTY

The framers of the Constitution foresaw the danger of statist domination and, therefore, provided that the First Amendment specifically limit the federal government's power concerning a person's most basic rights: the freedoms of religion, speech, press, and assembly. It was natural that religion was included among these rights. The framers understood it to be such an indispensable freedom that, in the words of James Madison, "[t]here is not a shadow of right in the general [federal] government to intermeddle with religion."[13] Madison insisted that "[t]his subject is, for the honor of America, perfectly free and unshackled. The government has no jurisdiction over it."[14]

It was recognized early in the history of the United States that if religious liberty is impaired, civil liberties will also suffer. This recognition is based on the unity and mutual dependence of basic First Amendment rights. The renowned nineteenth-century jurist James Kent remarked:

> The *free exercise and enjoyment of religious profession and worship* may be considered as one of the absolute rights of individuals, recognized in our . . . law. Civil and religious liberty generally go hand in hand, and the suppression of either one of them, for any length of time, will terminate the existence of the other.[15]

More recently, historian Roland Bainton has observed:

> [A]ll freedoms hang together. Civil liberties scarcely thrive when religious liberties are disregarded, and the reverse is equally true. Beneath them all is a philosophy of liberty which assumes a measure of variety in human behavior, honors integrity, respects the dignity of man, and seeks to exemplify the compassion of God.[16]

Bainton argued that only by operating within a framework of belief in "universal right, integrity, law, and humanity, if not in the Christian God," can people preserve the Western world's noblest achievement; that is, "the conduct of controversy without acrimony, of strife without bitterness, of criticism without loss of self-respect."[17]

To assure religious freedom, the Religion Clauses were included in the First Amendment:

> Congress shall make no law respecting an establishment of religion, or prohibiting the free exercise thereof; or abridging the freedom of speech, or of the press; or the right of the people peaceably to assemble, and to petition the Government for a redress of grievances.[18]

The Religion Clauses were meant specifically to restrain the federal government from establishing an official religion and from restricting the free exercise of religion by individuals. In its final wording, the First Amendment provided a broad range of protection from governmental intrusion.

HUMAN DIGNITY

As discussed in chapter 1, the structure and ideology of public education, which may result from misinformation and misunderstandings, often threaten the First Amendment rights of students and teachers.

Many public educators discriminate against religious students, teachers, and others because they fail to appreciate that the First Amendment is a collection of interconnected personal rights and the linchpin of a system of free expression and open political decision-making.

The various First Amendment rights all reflect a "single intent" and understanding on the part of the Constitution's framers:

> Expressed in terms of the traditional understanding of politics and personality, this conception [the framers' single intent] treated the individual as the central unit of political and social being, free to develop in his own way, to express himself and to engage in the struggle to mold social institutions and public policy without governmental interference.[19]

The First Amendment then is a statement of the dignity and worth of every individual, of the value of a "single human soul."[20] It is also evidence of how the framers envisioned that government exists for the benefit of the people, not the people for the benefit of government.

As agents of the government, public school officials must recognize (according to the First Amendment) the dignity of those who have no choice but to be educated within the public schools.[21] This recognition is necessary because, as discussed in chapter 1, public education inevitably inculcates some sort of values. When religious students and teachers are, for example, denied the right to free speech or assembly in public schools, students are taught an obvious principle of inequality and separation:[22] religious people are separated from the mainstream of society and denied rights on an equal basis with other citizens.

Many public school officials may respond by saying that they attempt in every way to recognize the rights of all students. Indeed, this goal of protecting all students' rights is behind their efforts to "protect" nonreligious students from religious inculcation.[23]

It has also been asserted that even if a public school's restriction on religious expression does in fact burden students' free exercise of religion, the school's concern that no religion be established "would still be overriding."[24] The worldview according to which religious speech is particularly "dangerous," and public schools are presumed to "endorse" all that they do not prohibit,[25] is used to justify discrimination against religious students and teachers.[26]

FORMATION OF BELIEF AND OPINION

If a full-orbed conception of the First Amendment is to be implemented within the present system of institutionalized, compulsory public education, the First Amendment must be interpreted more broadly than it has by those who countenance all manner of burdens on free exercise for the sake of avoiding "establishments" of religion in the public schools.[27] There must be an expansion of the First Amendment's "traditional protection of *expression* of belief and opinion to embrace *formation* of belief and opinion."[28] Protection of belief and opinion formation is essential because "[f]ree expression makes unfettered formulation of beliefs possible. In turn, free formulation of beliefs and opinions is a necessary precursor to freedom of expression."[29] Public schools must therefore inculcate values cautiously, guarding against violating religious students' free formation of religious opinion.

This caution must apply to all public school activities that may interfere with any previous formation of belief. As some commentators recognize:

> The more the government regulates formation of beliefs so as to interfere with personal consciousness, the fewer people can perceive contradictions between self-interest and government-sustained ideological orthodoxy. If freedom of expression protected only communication of ideas, totalitarianism and freedom of expression could be characteristics of the same society.[30]

If belief formation is not protected, all freedom is jeopardized.

Within many public schools, detrimental curricula sometimes presented under the label "values clarification" or "facilitative teaching" represent both governmental interference with belief formation by students and a disregard for the dignity of students.

FACILITATIVE TEACHING

In a book on "facilitative teaching" methods, two perfectly serious educators recommend various classroom exercises. Among the more fatuous methods is an exercise called "The Here and Now," designed to "increase awareness of the self in the here and now."[31] After being divided into small groups, students move about the classroom in a circle, each person talking in a "stream of consciousness," revealing "both physical sensations and mental feelings."[32] Any uninspired nonconformist is to be encouraged to say: "I am aware of not wanting to do this."[33]

Among the more potentially harmful suggested methods are various "fantasy and imagery" exercises,[34] in which students, starting as early as kindergarten,[35] are asked to visualize an array of fantasies, including (ironically) images of religious personages,[36] whom students are encouraged to "bring out." The most potentially manipulative of the methods are the "self-disclosure and self-awareness" and "appraisal" procedures. Students are asked, for example, to list their most important beliefs, identifying "beliefs that they hold contrary to those of their parents";[37] to list as many of the Ten Commandments as they remember, searching for "meanings behind" omissions and the order in which they are listed;[38] or to imagine the ideal family, each student being asked to discuss what his or her choices reveal about "what you may have missed in your family."[39]

In light of how many adult participants have "laid themselves open to enormous psycho-social damage" in "sensitivity training" and "encounter" groups led by untrained people, it is disturbing, as one author notes, that, "in the name of values education, the same techniques are being applied to children in the classroom, often without parents' knowledge or consent."[40] Even if no serious emotional damage is done, students' privacy may be invaded and their dignity thereby compromised.

In response to this danger, Title 20 of the United States Code has been amended to give parents the right to inspect any "instructional materials" used in the schools in connection with "any program or project in any applicable program designed to explore or develop new or unproven teaching methods or techniques."[41] Students are protected from any psychiatric or psychological testing or treatment to reveal such things as political affiliation, sex behavior and attitudes, or critical appraisals of family members.[42] The problem with these provisions is that they may not cover modern "values education" methods that are part of the *established* curriculum.

These modern "values education" methods may be seen as finding justification in B. F. Skinner's educational philosophy. Skinner argues:

> [T]he point of education can be stated in behavioral terms: a teacher arranges contingencies under which the student acquires behavior which will be useful to him under other contingencies later on.[43]

In discussing "the design of a culture," Skinner declares: "We need to design contingencies under which students acquire behavior useful to them and their culture."[44]

To Skinner, values education could not be directed toward inculcation of values considered objectively "right" according to a classic cultural transmission educational philosophy. Skinner claims that what a given group of people calls "good" is "what members of the group find reinforcing as a result of their genetic endowment and the natural and social contingencies to which they have been exposed. Each culture has its own set of goods, and what is good in one culture may not be in a another."[45] Of course, this definition of "good" is itself *not* value-neutral, for it is "an assertion about 'true' values, i.e., that they are defined by the standard of each culture."[46]

Modern "values education" methods may be considered an attempt to carry out the behaviorist educational project by arranging contingencies whereby students acquire behavior that is "useful" according to the particular culture's standard, not "good" according to an objective, distinctly moral standard. So understood, modern "values education" may fulfill the goals of either the cultural transmission[47] or the progressivist[48] educational philosophy as discussed in chapter 1.

Although he recognizes the failure of past utopian ventures,[49] Skinner imagines a utopia that is "a total social environment, and all its parts work together. The home does not conflict with the school or the street, religion does not conflict with government, and so on."[50] By subtly manipulating the consciousness of students as it replaces objective standards with criteria of cultural usefulness, modern "values education" may realize Skinner's ideal by resolving conflicts between home and school in favor of the school, and religion and government in favor of government.

Of course, public school officials often argue that, by the very nature of their task, there must be some indoctrination in values that will necessarily violate the beliefs of some students. One Supreme Court justice took this point to heart, claiming that if "everything objectionable" to any particular religious group is removed from public schools, "we will leave public education in shreds."[51]

However legitimate may be a state's interest in providing the moral and civic education necessary for good citizenship, the state's control of education must stop short of any measures that conflict with constitutional guarantees. The task of preventing such conflict appears more difficult when religious persons seek to express themselves within public schools. Not only are free speech and equal protection issues involved, but First Amendment Free Exercise and Establishment Clause provisions are implicated as well.

A state may seek to avoid Establishment Clause problems by altogether removing religious content from public school curricula and religious activities from public school premises. Yet this very removal restricts students' free exercise of religion during the time they are compelled to attend school. It seems that the reasonable approach is an intermediate one — granting students, teachers, and others periods of privacy during the school day during which they may speak with each other on subjects of their choice. Compulsory education must accommodate those who choose to develop intellectual and religious areas in their lives beyond those typically nurtured by the state-controlled curriculum.

THE RECOGNITION OF RIGHTS

During the twentieth century, problems in the area of religious freedom have often arisen along with the expansion of governmental control of education. Supreme Court cases dealing with religious exercises in public schools confirm this phenomenon.[52] Moreover, the involvement of compulsory attendance means that the recognition of students' rights within the schools is crucial. The Supreme Court has recognized that "[t]he vigilant protection of constitutional freedoms is nowhere more vital than in the community of American schools."[53]

As has been discussed, the compulsory nature of the educational process often turns students into captive audiences for government-controlled curricula. One legal commentator notes:

[E]ducation poses a constitutional problem because it has become (and was intended to become) a uniquely state activity: the state not only for-

mally educates through the public school system, but it also defines the
ends of education through its control over the curriculum and the
certification of both public and private schools.[54]

Constitutional guarantees are essential in such a setting to ensure that
First Amendment values are realized. As the Supreme Court has noted,
"state-operated schools may not be enclaves of totalitarianism . . .
[S]tudents may not be regarded as closed-circuit recipients of only that
which the State chooses to communicate."[55]

The Supreme Court has therefore recognized the constitutional rights
of the burgeoning American public school population, declaring: "Students
in school as well as out of school are 'persons' under our Constitution."[56]
The Supreme Court had already recognized the constitutional rights of children in 1967.[57] The Court held that juveniles faced with criminal commitment to state institutions are entitled, under the Fourteenth Amendment's
Due Process Clause, to written notice of the charges against them, the
charges' underlying factual bases, and their rights to receive counsel and to
confront witnesses.[58]

The constitutional rights of public school students were confirmed in
the Supreme Court's 1969 *Tinker v. Des Moines Independent Community
School District.*[59] In holding that First Amendment rights were available to
students wearing arm bands to protest the Vietnam War, the Court made
it apparent that public high school teachers and administrators no longer
have absolute control over their students.[60]

The expansion of students' constitutional rights has been accompanied
by a contraction of legally sanctioned religious influence in public schools.
The Supreme Court has ruled that mandatory prayer[61] and mandatory Bible
recitations[62] in public schools are unconstitutional as establishments of religion under the First Amendment.

Religious students in public high schools are often caught in the conflict
between these two concurrent developments in constitutional law.
Misunderstandings and misinterpretations of these developments have led
to a denial of the constitutional rights of students, teachers, and others.

3

Avoiding Religious Apartheid

[U]ntutored devotion to the concept of neutrality can lead to invocation or approval of results which partake not simply of that noninterference and noninvolvement with the religious which the Constitution commands, but of a brooding and pervasive devotion to the secular and a passive, or even active, hostility to the religious. Such results are not only not compelled by the Constitution, but, it seems to me, are prohibited by it.

—Justice Arthur Goldberg,
Abington School District v. Schempp,
374 U.S. 203, 306 (1963).

Several students at Guilderland High School, a public school in New York state, organized a group called "Students for Voluntary Prayer."[1] This group sought the principal's permission to conduct communal prayer meetings in a classroom before the start of each school day.[2] The students made it clear that they were not seeking supervision or faculty involvement,[3] and that their activities were completely voluntary and would not conflict with other school functions.[4] The school's authorities denied this request for allowance of student-initiated religious expression on public school grounds.

The Guilderland High School students filed a lawsuit seeking that this denial of their rights of free exercise of religion, free association, and equal protection be reversed.[5] The students lost their case in both the federal district court[6] and court of appeals.[7] The court of appeals, speaking through Judge Irving Kaufman, went so far as to suggest that even the appearance of government involvement with such a gathering of students "is too dangerous to permit."[8]

The attitude of some federal courts[9] and legal commentators[10] seems to imply that those who seek freedom of religious expression in the public schools somehow possess a *lower* legal status than those who seek freedom of other forms of expression. This attitude justifies a form of segregation of religious people from the "mainstream" of society that threatens the rights of an entire class of citizens.

In particular, the denial of equal access to school facilities based on the content of speech by religious students may amount to training students to live in a system of religious apartheid.[11] The effect is that religious people in public schools are denied equal treatment under the law.

Indeed, one commentator argues that such unequal treatment is constitutionally required. Stressing "the special role that public education plays in American society" and alleged dangers of "religious proselytization" in public schools, this commentator concludes that religious groups are different from other student groups "because the First Amendment religion clauses make them so."[12]

There has been much debate over the constitutionality of religious activity on the public school campus.[13] Although *state-sponsored* and *required* religious activity on the public school campus doubtless falls within the strictures of the Establishment Clause,[14] religious expression on the public school campus should be protected under the Free Speech Clause and other constitutional provisions.[15]

THE QUESTION OF HOSTILITY

There obviously has been confusion surrounding the rights of religious persons to express themselves in the universities and public schools. When such confusion so blurs reality that an American federal appeals court can claim that a gathering of religious students on a public school campus "is too dangerous to permit," we must be concerned.

While lecturing at New York University in 1960, former Supreme Court Justice Hugo Black remarked:

> Today most Americans seem to have forgotten the ancient evils which forced their ancestors to flee to this new country and to form a government stripped of old powers used to oppress them. But the Americans who supported the Revolution and the adoption of our Constitution knew firsthand the dangers of tyrannical governments. They were familiar with the long-existing practice of English persecutions of people wholly because of their religious or political beliefs. They knew that many accused of such offenses had stood, helpless to defend themselves, before biased legislators and judges.[16]

The reasoning of this portion of Justice Black's lecture reappeared a few years later in his opinion for the Supreme Court in *Engel v. Vitale*.[17] There the Court struck down the requirement of the State of New York that a prayer composed by the Board of Regents be recited in public schools. Justice Black recounted how religious persecution in England motivated many colonists to come to America, and concluded that the First Amendment was added to the Constitution as a guarantee that the federal government's power would not be wielded to burden the religion of anyone.[18]

Justice Black recognized the evil inherent in overt state persecution of people for their religious and political beliefs. The First Amendment clearly was intended to prohibit such persecution. The First Amendment Establishment and Free Exercise Clauses attempt to assure religious freedom in two respects: The Establishment Clause bars government from officially aligning with a particular religion, and the Free Exercise Clause bars government from penalizing the exercise of religion. Government, therefore, must find a middle ground, a position that is usually termed "neutrality."

However, this governmental neutrality will not be achieved if the First Amendment, specifically the Establishment Clause, is construed and applied *solely* with a view to the "evils" it was intended to prevent. The emphasis on "evils" to be avoided as a key to applying the Establishment Clause is evident in the concurrence of Justice William Brennan with the Supreme Court's ruling in *Abington School District v. Schempp*.[19] Justice Brennan reasoned that if the Court limited its use of the history of the framing of the Constitution "to broad purposes, not specific practices," it would be clear that the prayer and Bible reading in the public schools at issue sufficiently threatened "those substantive evils the fear of which called forth the Establishment Clause of the First Amendment."[20]

Justice Brennan realized the limitations of this emphasis on "substantive evils." He later reasoned that property tax exemptions for religious organizations are not such an evil. The state may encourage religious activities, Brennan noted, "because it values religion among a variety of private, nonprofit enterprises that contribute to the diversity of the nation."[21] This more flexible construction of the Establishment Clause runs counter to the judicial mind-set that may produce "religious apartheid" in the public schools.

If the courts treat the Establishment Clause in terms of evils it was meant to prevent, any accommodation of religious concerns in public schools can be considered governmental endorsement of a religion; that is, one of the "evils" the framers of the Constitution sought to avoid. The practical result of such Establishment Clause jurisprudence is hostility toward religious persons and "religious apartheid" within public schools.

To be constitutionally objectionable, religious discrimination carried out by the state need not even be intentionally or actively hostile. Mere indifference to the religious concerns of a particular group may transgress the mandate of neutrality of the First Amendment and result in religious persecution. Denial of students' rights, for example, to meet as a religious club on school premises may not constitute active hostility toward religious persons. It may, however, reach the level of passive hostility.

This need not occur if the Constitution is properly interpreted. The often-ignored historical perspective suggests that the framers of the Constitution and other founding documents would have been more permissive concerning religious expression in the public realm than many modern courts.

When discussing the rights of religious persons, it must not be forgotten that the rights of students, faculty members, administrators, and nonstudents are at stake. A clear sequence of Supreme Court cases has upheld the rights of such persons. (See the discussion of students' rights in chapter 8.) Commencing with rulings upholding the freedom of association of teachers and professors at public institutions,[22] the Supreme Court has recognized the capacity of high school students to engage in political dissent free from interference by public school officials.[23] This recognition of student and teacher rights heightens the controversy over religious expression in public education. Courts must decide whether their recognition of the maturity of students warrants freedom of religious as well as political expression by students in public schools.

While some may believe students are immature or impressionable to the extent that any mention of religion in public schools must be avoided,[24] the Supreme Court has not taken this position. The Court has held that teaching about religion in public schools is entirely permissible.[25] Declaring that "[w]e are a religious people whose institutions presuppose a Supreme Being," the Court has held that the state may, through the public schools, accommodate religion whenever it is constitutionally permissible.[26]

The Supreme Court has expressly held that religious speech enjoys the same First Amendment protection as other speech under the Free Speech Clause, in addition to its protection under the Free Exercise Clause.[27] Moreover, through the passage of the Equal Access Act (see discussion of the Act in chapter 11), Congress has stated that religious speech must be treated the same as political speech within public schools.

Such equal treatment follows the American tradition of free and open communication. If free communication is stifled through artificial segregation of religious speech from other forms of speech in the public arena, the American democratic system suffers.

PART TWO

Accommodation

When the state encourages religious instruction or cooperates with religious authorities by adjusting the schedule of public events to sectarian needs, it follows the best of our traditions. For it then respects the religious nature of our people and accommodates the public service to their spiritual needs.

—Justice William O. Douglas,
Zorach v. Clauson, 343
U.S. 306, 313-14 (1952).

4

The Historical Logic

[A] page of history is worth a volume of logic.

—Justice Oliver Wendell Holmes,
New York Trust Co. v. Eisner,
265 U.S. 345, 349 (1921).

"No provision of the Constitution," wrote Supreme Court Justice Wiley Rutledge in 1947, "is more closely tied to or given content by its generating history than the religious clause of the First Amendment."[1] The Supreme Court has more recently stressed, in a similar vein, that "the ultimate constitutional objective" as expressed by the framers and "as illuminated by history" is particularly relevant to adjudication of the First Amendment Religion Clauses.[2] The Court has warned that this constitutional objective must not be undermined by an interpretive "literalness."[3]

Some commentators have, according to an interpretive literalism, read the history surrounding the Constitution as supporting a "strict separationist" view of church and state.[4] Strict separationism is based on the idea that the First Amendment does much more than forbid establishment of a "national church." The Supreme Court has at times approached such a view of the First Amendment Establishment Clause,[5] only to qualify itself in later opinions. History, however, provides ample evidence that among the framers of America's founding documents, the universal sentiment was one of *accommodation* of religion in general and even at times encouragement of a particular religion.[6]

Whether the history surrounding the Constitution is read as supporting a strict separationist or accommodationist position, it is clear that this history cannot be disregarded.[7] In concurring with the Supreme Court's striking down of state-mandated prayer and Bible reading in public schools, Justice William Brennan argued that constitutional history is of limited use because the historical record was "ambiguous," the framers knew no system of universal public education, America has become much more religiously diverse, and because this diversity has guided the development of free public education.[8] However, Justice Brennan later in the very same concurrence appealed to history to support his interpretation of the Fourteenth Amendment.[9] He also counseled that the line to be drawn between permissible and impermissible involvements of religion in public life is "one which accords with history and faithfully reflects the understanding of the Founding Fathers."[10]

AFFIRMATIVE ACCOMMODATION

Instead of taking a position of "strict neutrality"[11] (the absolute separation of the state from religion), the Supreme Court has taken a position of "accommodation neutrality." This position holds that the First Amendment was intended to maintain a proper relationship, not absolute separation, between government and religion. Thus, although there may be a "wall of separation" between church and state, it is not a "high and impregnable" wall[12] that hermetically seals the state off from religion and religious individuals. Not all relationships between government and religion are unconstitutional. The state must affirmatively accommodate and even "aid" religion (as opposed to an institutional church or churches) in certain circumstances.

"Accommodation" is not to be equated with "tolerance" or "toleration." "Tolerance" is defined as "the act of allowing something," or "the allowable deviation from a standard."[13] However, in America the government does not "tolerate" religion or religious liberty, or "allow" them to exist. To the contrary, the First Amendment mandates that free exercise of religion in American public life is a constitutional right.

Affirmative accommodation of religion then has roots both in history and constitutional adjudication. In fact, accommodation is the essence of government neutrality toward religion as required by the Supreme Court.[14] The Constitution, as the Supreme Court has held, "affirmatively mandates accommodation, not merely tolerance, of all religions, and forbids hostility toward any."[15]

THE HISTORICAL RECORD

The Supreme Court has relied on the historic intent of the framers of the Bill of Rights to understand the Establishment Clause's meaning and scope.[16] Accommodation makes little sense apart from its historical roots.

The historical record shows that the revolutionary and founding periods of American history favored governmental accommodation of religious practice. Both Thomas Jefferson and James Madison, often cited for their disestablishmentarian views, approved numerous religious practices in public life. Indeed, they participated in legislative activities on behalf of religion that would disturb the very strict separationists who cite Jefferson and Madison in support of strict separationism.

For example, in 1785 Madison introduced into the Virginia House of Delegates five bills touching upon religion, which Jefferson had assumed the responsibility for drafting.[17] The most famous of these is Jefferson's *Bill for Establishing Religious Freedom*.[18] However, no less remarkable (in light of Jefferson's strict separationist reputation) is the third of these bills:

> On October 31, 1785, Madison introduced the third bill . . .[,] which was appropriately called "A Bill for Punishing Disturbers of Religious and Sabbath Breakers." There is strong evidence that this bill . . . was also penned by Jefferson. The bill in its essential parts exempted clergymen from arrest while performing religious services and mandated severe punishment for disturbers of public worship or citizens laboring on Sunday.[19]

Three other[20] of the five bills concerning religion contradict the common assumption that Madison and Jefferson were pure disestablishmentarians on matters of church and state.

As discussed below, contemporary theory and case law support both this historical analysis and the need to accommodate religion in American public life.

PUBLIC EDUCATION

Public education was no exception to this history of accommodation of religion. For example, the Northwest Ordinance, enacted by the Continental Congress in 1787, recognized the importance of religion in its provision setting aside federal property for schools. This section of the Ordinance provided: "*Religion*, morality, and knowledge being essential to good government and the happiness of mankind, *schools and the means of education* shall forever be encouraged."[21] This same basic educational provision was also enacted in many state constitutions.[22]

This early recognition of a relationship between religion and education indicates a clear belief that religion, instead of being strictly separated from the state, is in fact inseparable from the state. It is significant that the Congress of the newly formed federal government reenacted the Northwest Ordinance[23] in 1789 after it had agreed on the final wording of the First Amendment's Religion Clauses and other provisions of the Bill of Rights.

According to the Northwest Ordinance, religion was part of the foundation of American public schools. Although a basic Protestant religious ethic historically has been favored, in contemporary society accommodation of all religions, rather than encouragement of any particular religion, comports best with current constitutional guidelines.

The historical record reveals that religion was integrated into the early public school curriculum. Textbooks referred to God without embarrassment, and public schools considered one of their major tasks to be the development of character through the teaching of religion. For example, the *New England Primer* opened with religious admonitions followed by the Lord's

Prayer, the Apostles' Creed, the Ten Commandments, and the names of the books of the Bible.[24]

The influence of University of Virginia's Professor William Holmes McGuffey testifies to the persistence of a religious ideal of public education into the early twentieth century. The impressive sales of his *Eclectic Readers* (see discussion in chapter 1) from 1836 to 1920 (two years after Mississippi became the last state to institute a public school system) place them in a class with only the Bible and *Webster's Dictionary*.[25]

Like the Northwest Ordinance, McGuffey's readers stressed "religion, morality, and knowledge," in that order. In an introduction for a reissue of *McGuffey's Fifth Eclectic Reader*, historian Henry Steele Commager writes:

> What was the nature of the morality that permeated the *Readers?* It was deeply religious, and . . . religion then meant a Protestant Christianity. . . . The world of the *McGuffeys* was a world where no one questioned the truths of the Bible or their relevance to everyday contact. . . . The *Readers*, therefore, are filled with stories from the Bible, and tributes to its truth and beauty.[26]

McGuffey's readers were designed to inculcate the virtues necessary for the preservation of republican government. They, thus, played an important part in forging a conservative and religious synthesis identifying the legal interpretations of such jurists as James Kent and Joseph Story with "the moral order imposed by the omnipotent will of a sovereign God."[27]

JEFFERSON AND THE FRAMERS

Many of those who served as architects of the American government received the kind of education that the McGuffey readers exemplify. This type of education reinforced the spirit of affirmative accommodation toward the exercise of religion in public life that is evident in the words and deeds of those who drafted the founding documents, including the Constitution.

For example, one of the earliest acts of the first House of Representatives was to elect a chaplain and appropriate five hundred dollars from the federal treasury to pay his salary.[28] James Madison was a member of the congressional committee that recommended the chaplain system,[29] a fact that those who ascribe strict separationist views to Madison and other framers cannot easily explain. When the Nebraska legislature's practice of beginning each session with a prayer by a state-paid chaplain was recently challenged as unconstitutional, the Supreme Court appealed to the actions of the first House of Representatives in finding the practice constitutional.[30]

On September 24, 1789, Congress proposed a joint resolution intended to give the people an occasion to thank God for affording them an opportunity to establish the United States.[31] It is clear from the record that

Madison did not object to this resolution.[32] In fact, as President, Madison himself issued four prayer proclamations.[33] The joint resolution of Congress was submitted to President Washington the very day after Congress had voted to recommend to the states the final text of what has become the First Amendment.[34]

The Supreme Court has recognized that the views of Jefferson and Madison are particularly instructive in determining the meaning and scope of the First Amendment Religion Clauses. Concerning the legislative battle in Virginia that led to the disestablishment of the Anglican church, Justice Hugo Black, writing for the Supreme Court, noted:

> This court has previously recognized that the provisions of the First Amendment, in the drafting and adoption of which Madison and Jefferson played such leading roles, had the same objective and were intended to provide the same protection against governmental intrusion on religious liberty as the Virginia statute.[35]

It should be noted that even Virginia's disestablishment of the Anglican church may not support any strict separationist conclusion that Justice Black may have hoped to draw. One of the five bills concerning religion written by Jefferson and introduced by Madison into the Virginia House of Delegates was designed to protect the property rights of the Anglican church.[36]

Jefferson cannot, strictly speaking, be considered a framer of the First Amendment. Nonetheless, the Supreme Court, in its early Religion Clause cases, adopted, as one commentator states, the "pretension that the framers spoke in a wholly Jeffersonian dialect and that those who ratified [the First Amendment] fully understood that style of speech."[37] The unfortunate consequence of this Religion Clause jurisprudence is that "the Court has widened the gap between current social reality and current constitutional law."[38]

As early as 1878, the Supreme Court had "canonized" Jefferson's supposed version of the Religion Clauses, stating that "it may be accepted almost as an authoritative declaration of the scope and effect of the amendment thus secured."[39] The Court was appealing to Jefferson's statement that the Religion Clauses built "a wall of separation between church and State."[40]

Even if Jefferson's "wall of separation" metaphor implies all that strict separationists have deduced from it, it must be remembered:

> [T]he First Amendment was hardly the exclusive product of any one person. Subsequent interpretations of the Amendment should not be controlled by the singular statements of Madison [or] Jefferson. . . . An examination of the early activities of the Federal Government indicates that the people approved and welcomed its aid to church-related activi-

ties. . . . There was undoubtedly the faith that subsequent generations of Americans would be able to utilize the power of the Federal Government to promote the concurrent interests of government and religion under First Amendment norms that were reasonable, pragmatic, and just.[41]

It must not be forgotten as well that during the First Amendment's drafting and adoption, Jefferson was in France.[42] However, his influence must have been exercised to some degree through his correspondence with Madison.[43]

Reliance on Jefferson's and Madison's views on church and state should also be tempered by the realization that they were *not* representative of the views of other framers of the Constitution. One distinguishing feature of Madison and Jefferson, to which the Supreme Court has appealed on behalf of its Establishment Clause jurisprudence,[44] is their work as central figures in the fight for disestablishment of Anglicanism in Virginia. Madison's *Memorial and Remonstrance Against Religious Assessments,* written in 1785 in opposition to Virginia's proposed use of public funds for teachers of Christianity, and Jefferson's *Bill for Establishing Religious Freedom* (in Virginia), proposed in 1779 and enacted in 1786, were central documents for disestablishmentarian forces.[45]

Even these disestablishmentarian documents are animated by an overtly religious rationale. In his *Memorial and Remonstrance,* Madison appeals to Christianity's survival without the aid of "the powers of this world," "not only during the period of miraculous aid, but long after it had been left to its own evidence and the ordinary care of providence."[46] Jefferson likewise premised his *Bill for Establishing Religious Freedom* on the belief that "Almighty God hath created the mind free."[47]

These activities, however, distinguish Jefferson and Madison because not all states shared their fervor for disestablishment. The Supreme Court has recognized as "an unfortunate fact of history" that "as late as the time of the Revolutionary War, there were established churches in at least eight of the thirteen former colonies and established religions in at least four of the other five."[48] The Court claimed that by the time the Constitution was adopted, "there was widespread awareness among many Americans of the dangers of a union of church and State."[49]

This awareness of the dangers of church-state union (or even any *appearance* of governmental "aid" to religion) is often credited to Jefferson and Madison. Since their views on church and state have been considered authoritative, let us examine them in more detail.

While President, Jefferson first presented his "wall of separation" metaphor in a letter to the Danbury Baptist Association of Connecticut. Written on January 1, 1820, this letter was a carefully constructed response to those who had criticized his refusal to issue a presidential proclamation of a national day of prayer and fasting. Jefferson wrote:

Believing with you that religion is a matter which lies solely between man and his God, that he owes account to none other for his faith or his worship, that the legislative powers of government reach actions only, and not opinions, I contemplate with sovereign reverence that act of the whole American people which declared that their legislature should "make no law respecting an establishment of religion, or prohibiting the free exercise thereof," thus building a wall of separation between Church and State.[50]

Jefferson did not intend by his statement in this letter to seal religion off hermetically from governmental functions or public life. Jefferson referred to the Religion Clauses as an "expression of the supreme will of the nation on behalf of the rights of *conscience*."[51] Jefferson evidently was apparently *more* concerned about governmental control over religious persons and institutions than he was about any influence religious persons and institutions might exert upon government.

Jefferson expressed his views on church and state more clearly a few years later in his 1805 Second Inaugural Address. He said:

In matters of religion I have considered that its free exercise is placed by the Constitution independent of the powers of the general [federal] government. I have, therefore, undertaken on no occasion to prescribe the religious exercises suited to it, but have left them, as the Constitution found them, under the direction and discipline of the State or Church authorities acknowledged by the several religious societies.[52]

Jefferson thus construed the First Amendment as placing a wall of separation between the institutional church and the federal government (as represented by Congress) to protect both from any infringement of their respective spheres of authority. He and the other framers mistrusted the federal government and feared any attempt it might make to establish a national church. Religion was to be a state concern, not a federal one.[53]

Jefferson's activities in public life were consistent with his statements concerning church-state relations. Jefferson's actions as President, as well as the bills concerning religion he had written earlier for the Virginia House of Delegates, demonstrate that he did not espouse the strict separationism often attributed to him.

For example, on three separate occasions Jefferson signed into law extensions of a land grant that the federal government had given specifically to promote education and proselytism among the Indians.[54] Further, on October 31, 1803, President Jefferson proposed to the Senate a treaty with the Kaskaskian Indians that provided that federal money be used to support a Catholic priest and to build a church (a Catholic mission) for ministry to the Kaskaskian Indians.[55] The treaty, as President Jefferson requested, was ratified by Congress on December 23, 1803.[56]

It is therefore evident that even in the Jeffersonian sense, the term "establishment of religion" in the First Amendment has an *institutional* meaning. As the Supreme Court has recognized, quoting Joseph Story: "The

real object of the [First] Amendment was . . . to prevent any national eccle-
siastical establishment which should give to [a] hierarchy the exclusive
patronage of the national government."[57] The *institution* of the church was
to be isolated from the *institution* of the state.

This type of separation does not preclude governmental encouragement
of religion. The framers never intended to separate religion in general from
the federal state, much less religious individuals from any meaningful activity within the state and society at large. At the time that the Constitution
was framed, it would have been unthinkable to exclude citizens from prac-
ticing their religious principles except within their homes and places of worship. As Judge Thomas Cooley wrote in his influential *Principles of
Constitutional Law*:

> It was never intended by the Constitution that the government should be
> prohibited from recognizing religion, or that religious worship should
> never be provided for in cases where a proper recognition of Divine
> Providence in the working of government might seem to require it, and
> where it might be done without drawing any invidious distinctions
> between different religious beliefs, organizations, or sects. The Christian
> religion was always recognized in the administration of the common law;
> and so far as that law continues to be the law of the land, the fundamental
> principles of that religion must continue to be recognized in the same
> cases and to the same extent as formerly.[58]

To support his argument, Cooley appealed to the practices of governmental sponsorship of congressional and military chaplains and criminal prosecution of blasphemy.[59]

After analyzing the genuine implications of Jefferson's "wall of separation" metaphor, one historian has stated:

> To Jefferson, the "wall of separation" did not mean the complete and
> absolute separation of church and state such that no religion or religious
> influence was to be permitted in state-sponsored activities and laws. His
> chief aim was not the erection of an impenetrable wall of separation.
> Rather, it was the protection of free expression of one's religious beliefs
> and opinions. And if that goal was best achieved through statutory coop-
> eration between church and state, Jefferson appeared willing to endorse
> it.[60]

It is unfortunate that in its seminal modern statement on church-state
relations, both in the public schools and society at large, the Supreme Court
omitted from its version of history Jefferson's many actions that contradict
his strict separationist reputation. Focusing on the image of a "high and
impregnable wall" between church and state,[61] the Court in *Everson v.
Board of Education*[62] went so far as to claim that the First Amendment
means "at least" that, among other things, neither a state nor the federal

government can pass laws that "aid all religions."[63] The modern Supreme Court has, however, upheld affirmative accommodation of religion only by recognizing that the "wall of separation" metaphor "is not a wholly accurate description of the practical aspects of the relationship that in fact exists between church and state."[64]

JEFFERSON ON RELIGION AND EDUCATION

The compatibility of accommodation of religious expression with Thomas Jefferson's "separationism" is particularly evident in Jefferson's work in the field of education.

Jefferson was the founder of the University of Virginia. From its inception in 1819, the school was governed, managed, and controlled by the Commonwealth of Virginia. After the question of what place Christianity would have at the university was put to him, Jefferson, as the university's rector, expounded his views on religion and education in his annual report to the president and directors of the literary fund.

Simply put, Jefferson was not opposed to religious worship and study being conducted on the premises of a public educational institution. To the contrary, in order to accommodate and perpetuate the religious beliefs and practices of students at the university, he recommended that students be allowed to meet on the campus to pray, worship, and receive religious instruction, or, if necessary, to meet and pray with their professors.[65] Jefferson even provided in his regulations for the university that the main rotunda be used "for religious worship, under the regulations allowed to be prescribed by law."[66]

When Congress initially authorized the public schools for the nation's capital, the first president of the Washington, D.C., school board was Jefferson himself.[67] In fact, he "was the chief author of the first plan of public education adopted for the city of Washington."[68] The first official report on file indicates that the Bible and the *Watts Hymnal* were the principal, if not the only, books then in use for reading by the Washington, D.C., public school students.[69]

Jefferson's actions in the field of education reveal that he wanted only to exclude the public authorities from the domain of religious expression — that is, to prevent government from controlling or prohibiting religious expression.[70] This is evident in his 1779 *Bill for Establishing Religious Freedom*, in which Jefferson opposed teaching sectarian doctrines in public schools. He argued that "to compel a man to furnish contributions of money for the propagation of opinions which he disbelieves and abhors, is sinful and tyrannical."[71] These words ring even truer today, now that the greatly increased religious diversity would render any effort to teach religious doctrines in public schools far more troublesome than in Jefferson's day.

However, Jefferson's disdain for sectarian teaching in public schools was complemented by his appreciation of the need to accommodate religious beliefs and practices within those schools. He proposed that "no religious reading, instruction or exercise, shall be prescribed or practiced inconsistent with the tenets of any religious sect or denomination."[72]

Jefferson, however, did not envision public education as a means of forcibly inculcating an array of supposed "common values" as is emphasized by modern educational theorists. Instead, Jefferson prescribed that the majority of children (the "laboring" class[73]) would receive education only up to the elementary level[74] as a basic literacy requirement for citizenship.[75] Jefferson, therefore, did not believe education must be compulsory. He believed it is better to "tolerate the rare instance" of parents refusing to let their children be educated, than to "shock the common feeling and ideas" through forcible education of children against their parents' will.[76]

LESSONS OF HISTORY

History clearly teaches that from America's inception, the prevailing mood toward religion has been one of affirmative accommodation. The framers and those who taught in the public schools throughout the nineteenth century defended and perpetuated this accommodation.

If this lesson concerning accommodation is forgotten, the freedom of expression of those in the religious minority could very well be severely restricted. As James Madison once told Congress, the Bill of Rights points "sometimes against the abuse of executive power, sometimes against the legislative, and, in some cases, against the community itself; or, in other words, against the majority in favor of the minority."[77] In this respect, in ruling that a religious minority's children cannot be forced to receive all of the education the state required, the Supreme Court recognized a need to protect religious minorities in public education.[78]

As it relates to religious expression in public schools, this history of accommodation indicates:

> [T]he framers would have heartily endorsed the concept of equal access for voluntary religious speech in a public school forum. The framers would have celebrated robust and uninhibited discussion of religious and political subjects in the marketplace of ideas where truth, in Jefferson's words, "will prevail if left to herself."[79]

5

Affirmative Accommodation

[T]he Constitution [does not] require complete separation of church and state; it affirmatively mandates accommodation, not merely tolerance, of all religions, and forbids hostility toward any.

—Chief Justice Warren Burger,
Lynch v. Donnelly,
465 U.S. 668, 673 (1984).

The requirement of the First Amendment Religion Clauses that the state (which includes public schools) must "make no law respecting an establishment of religion, or prohibiting the free exercise thereof"[1] means that the state: (1) may not establish one religion over others, and (2) must allow for the freedom of citizens to exercise their religion. As interpreted by the Supreme Court, this essentially means that the state must remain neutral in matters of religion such that it does not prefer one religion over others.[2] It also means that government must not be hostile toward one or all religions.[3]

ACCOMMODATING NEUTRALITY AND A UNIFIED VIEW OF THE RELIGION CLAUSES

The First Amendment Religion Clauses assure both free exercise and non-establishment of religion. The Free Exercise Clause (guaranteeing freedom *of* religion) envisions public and private spheres in which individuals may freely cultivate and exercise religious beliefs.[4] The Establishment Clause (guaranteeing freedom *from* state-imposed religion) envisions a public sphere free from state sponsorship of religion.[5]

The Supreme Court has at times claimed that these two clauses are inherently in conflict.[6] An artificial[7] "tension" between these two clauses is indeed generated if either is seriously misconstrued, being applied without regard to the other. As one commentator states:

> Through excessive solicitude for religious exercise, government may run afoul of the Establishment Clause. Conversely, too stringent application of the nonestablishment mandate may violate the free exercise guarantee.[8]

The expansion of the welfare state since World War II has intensified this conceptual tension,[9] for much Religion Clauses litigation has concerned applications of general welfare legislation[10] that have the effect of either benefiting religious institutions[11] or facilitating free exercise of religion by individuals.[12] Compulsory education laws and the development of the massive modern public education system have created new situations in which the beliefs and practices of individuals must be accommodated.[13]

This conflict generated between the Religion Clauses is embodied in their classic confrontation in *Walz v. Tax Commission*.[14] In this ruling, the Supreme Court sustained a state tax exemption for real or personal property used exclusively for religious purposes. On its face, this case presents a conflict between the clauses. For example, an exemption would *reduce* the tax burden on holders of religious property while *increasing* the tax burden on others, arguably "establishing" religion. A denial of the exemption interferes with the free exercise of religion by requiring the state to assess religiously affiliated property, creating the possibility of governmental "entanglement" with religion.

The Supreme Court in *Walz* conceded that "[t]he course of constitutional neutrality in this area cannot be a straight line."[15] Taking a narrower view of what constitutes an "establishment" of religion than it had earlier intimated,[16] the Court upheld the state tax exemption statute by leaving room for "benevolent neutrality."[17]

Allowance of "benevolent neutrality" toward the religious practices of individuals calls for a better understanding of the Religion Clauses of the First Amendment than that which follows from the absolutist interpretation of the Establishment Clause yielding an artificial tension between the clauses. Many commentators have argued,[18] and several Supreme Court justices have recognized,[19] that the Religion Clauses are in fact *united* by a single historic purpose.

Although the Establishment Clause is cast in absolute terms — "Congress shall make no law respecting an establishment of religion" — government has in fact long accommodated religion.[20] The Supreme Court has adopted a posture of "accommodating neutrality" rather than strict or complete neutrality.[21] Several theories concerning the "unity" of the Religion Clauses justify this approach.

Constitutional scholar Laurence Tribe has proposed one theory for understanding the unity of the Religion Clauses. This is the bifurcated definition of "religion": "religion" should be defined *broadly* (covering anything "arguably religious") in cases in which the Free Exercise Clause applies, and *narrowly* (covering anything "arguably nonreligious") in cases in which the Establishment Clause applies. Tribe reasoned that "a less expansive notion of religion was required for Establishment Clause purposes lest all 'humane' programs of government be deemed constitutionally suspect."[22]

This theory of the Religion Clauses' unity appeals to those who prefer to see the Free Exercise Clause as a charter for personal autonomy in matters of ultimately held belief, and the Establishment Clause as asserting interests that are "not so much individual as social and group oriented."[23] A definition of religion (for Free Exercise Clause purposes) in terms of not just formal creeds but also the "ultimate concerns" of individuals may support the affirmative accommodation of parents who seek to protect their children against the value inculcation that inevitably occurs through the overt and hidden curricula of public schools when it undermines their deeply held beliefs.[24]

However, this theory is open to serious criticism, and Professor Tribe himself has recently retreated from it.[25] Tribe now prefers to say that in some cases in which the Free Exercise and Establishment Clauses "intersect," the Free Exercise Clause "dominates the intersection," carving out a "zone of permissible accommodation" of religious interests.[26] This theory still has the disadvantage of assuming some sort of natural antagonism between the clauses. Moreover, in light of the evidence (see discussion in chapter 4) that the framers of the Constitution desired affirmative accommodation of religion,[27] both courts[28] and commentators[29] have correctly criticized this theory for *unnecessarily* introducing a distinction alien to the text of the Constitution.

Another more promising theory of unity of the Religion Clauses considers the clauses as "two sides of the same coin":

[T]he establishment clause protects *religious liberty;* it safeguards much the same interests as the free exercise clause, but in a slightly different way. The free exercise clause defines the important individual liberty of religious freedom while the establishment clause addresses *the limits of allowable state classifications affecting this liberty.*[30]

In defining religious liberty, the Free Exercise clause may be said to be "pro-minority"; in defining the limits of state classification affecting this liberty, the Establishment Clause may be said to be "anti-majority."[31]

The Religion Clauses may thus be applied according to their relationship of logical priority:

[T]he free exercise issue must be addressed *prior* to the establishment issue because the former involves questions of purpose and effect that are central to reaching conclusions about the latter. Stated simply, government efforts to remedy a burden it has placed on the free exercise of a "minority" religion cannot realistically be viewed as having the purpose or primary effect of attempting to establish religion.[32]

The Religion Clauses, properly understood, are not in conflict. Rather, "the free exercise principle defines the limits of the anti-establishment principle. One begins where the other ends."[33]

If the free exercise principle is in fact applied as regulating the anti-establishment principle, government will express toward the free exercise of religion the favor or amiableness that the term "accommodation" connotes.[34] The approach to the Establishment Clause prescribed by the "unity of the clauses" theory outlined above justifies the "accommodation to and preferment of religion" that the American government has at times effected by statutory and other means "in order to safeguard free exercise values."[35]

Under contemporary Religion Clause adjudication, this accommodating neutrality means government conduct that "neither encourages nor discourages religious belief or practice" is clearly constitutional.[36] Such accommodating neutrality also affects First Amendment Free Speech Clause adjudication in that government must remain neutral concerning religion in its own speech, "and it must treat *religious speech by private speakers* exactly like secular speech by private speakers."[37]

The consequence of these requirements is that *accommodation* of religion is mandated. The Supreme Court made this clear in 1984 in *Lynch v. Donnelly.*[38] There the Court held:

> [T]he Constitution [does not] require complete separation of church and state; it affirmatively mandates accommodation, not merely tolerance, of all religions, and forbids hostility toward any. . . . Anything less would require the "callous indifference" we have said was never intended by the Establishment Clause. Indeed, we have observed, such hostility would bring us into "war with our national tradition as embodied in the First Amendment's guaranty of the free exercise of religion."[39]

The *Lynch* Court upheld a municipal creche display because the creche in question, which was surrounded by other, undeniably secular Christmas symbols, was judged not to be an *endorsement* (as opposed to an accommodation) of a religion.[40]

In some situations, the Supreme Court has stressed the need for a more reserved accommodation of religion. In *Wallace v. Jaffree,*[41] for example, the Court held that Alabama's allowance of a period of silence for meditation or voluntary prayer in public schools violated the Establishment Clause. Although the Court restricted the neutrality concept, the decisive factor in the Court's analysis was the avowed legislative *intent* underlying the statute. The Court determined that the Alabama statute was meant to revive "voluntary prayer . . . as a step in the right direction."[42] The Court judged that, based on this manifest state intent, it could reasonably foresee attempts to *advance* religion, not merely to accommodate it. The facts thus required the Supreme Court to issue an aberrational ruling on accommodating neutrality in public schools.

The affirmative accommodation of religion is then the *general essence* of the Supreme Court's position on neutrality toward religion. State indifference toward religion, however, is not the Court's definition of neutrality. Justice William O. Douglas wrote for the Court that state indifference toward religion "would be preferring those who believe in no religion over those who do believe. . . . [W]e find no constitutional requirement that makes it necessary for government to be hostile to religion and to throw its weight against efforts to widen the effective scope of religious influence."[43] The Court has recognized that such indifference is a subtle form of hostility.

The Supreme Court has in numerous decisions[44] endorsed the approach of accommodating neutrality. The "benevolent neutrality" of which Chief Justice Burger spoke in *Walz* is intended to "permit religious exercise to exist without sponsorship and without interference."[45]

The Supreme Court has also recognized that the supposed separation of church and state, which is so often uncritically defined in terms of Thomas Jefferson's misunderstood "wall of separation" metaphor (see discussion of Jefferson in chapter 4), is no barrier to such accommodation. Justice Blackmun wrote for the Court that:

> [The] Court has enforced a scrupulous neutrality by the State, as among religions and also as between religious and other activities, but a *hermetic separation of the two is an impossibility it has never required.*[46]

Even a judge who espouses "strict neutrality," a somewhat unarticulated form of which provided the *Everson* Court's rationale for claiming the state may not even act to "aid all religions,"[47] should realize that "strict separation" is an illusion. Some courts have concluded from the impossibility of strict separation that there must be some accommodation of religion in public schools.[48]

"AFFIRMATIVE" AND "REQUIRED" VERSUS "PERMISSIVE" ACCOMMODATION

"Required accommodation" is governmental action mandated by the Free Exercise Clause. This has alternatively been termed "benign neutrality." Such neutrality is embodied in one common type of required accommodation, "religious *exemptions* from otherwise valid legislation."[49] Concerning such exemptions, one commentator writes:

> The approach reflected in exemption doctrine can be characterized as benign neutrality. In situations where government must choose between infringing upon or facilitating religious exercise, the free exercise clause

requires that, absent an overriding governmental interest, government [must] choose the latter course.[50]

State-provided fire and police protection at a parochial school is an example of affirmative accommodation that the Free Exercise Clause would require. Parents would be reluctant to send their children to a school if these vital services were withheld.[51] Denial of such protection would be what the Supreme Court has defined as a "direct" burden on free exercise of religion,[52] one that must yield to the constitutional guarantee.

However, government may affirmatively accommodate religion *beyond* the Free Exercise Clause mandate, as long as the Establishment Clause is not violated. Laurence Tribe labels such accommodation "permissive."[53]

Everson v. Board of Education[54] provides an example of permissive accommodation. The Supreme Court allowed government funding of buses ·that transported students to parochial schools. If the Court had denied reimbursement to parents, it is doubtful that the Free Exercise Clause would have been implicated. Yet, although the state subsidy was not *mandated* by the Free Exercise Clause, it was *permissible* because it did not violate the Establishment Clause. As Justice Black wrote for the Court:

> The State contributes no money to the [parochial] schools. It does not support them. Its legislation, as applied, does no more than provide a general program to help parents get their children, regardless of their religion, safely and expeditiously to and from accredited schools.[55]

Because the Free Exercise Clause does not mandate it, permissive accommodation is discretionary — the government can either act or refrain from acting without violating the Religion Clauses.

Accommodation has been widely accepted by commentators[56] as well as by the courts. The Religion Clauses do not demand, nor has the Supreme Court accepted, that the government must remain "strictly neutral" in dealing with religious individuals or organizations. Rather, the Supreme Court "has regularly construed the free exercise clause to exempt religious exercise from burdensome legislation even though such exemptions in some sense benefit religion."[57]

THE *LEMON* TEST

In the context of accommodating neutrality, the Supreme Court has formulated a three-part test to determine whether the Establishment Clause has been violated. This determination is a court's crucial first step in deciding whether permissive accommodation may be exercised in the case before it.

The test, as stated by the Supreme Court in *Lemon v. Kurtzman*,[58] is as follows:

First, the statute must have a secular legislative purpose; second, its *principal* or *primary* effect must be one that neither advances nor inhibits religion . . . ; finally, the statute must not foster "an excessive government entanglement with religion."[59]

Keeping in mind the Court's position on accommodation of religion, it is little wonder that the key phrases in this test are "principal or primary effect" and "excessive government entanglement." Therefore, if a particular religious practice at issue in any given case no more than "incidentally" benefits religion, it passes the Supreme Court's muster. As Justice Harry Blackmun stated for the Court:

> *Everson* and *Allen* put to rest any argument that the State may never act in such a way that has the *incidental effect of facilitating religious activity.* . . . If this were impermissible . . . a church could not be protected by the police and fire department, or have its public sidewalk kept in repair. The Court has never held that religious activities must be discriminated against in this way.[60]

A basic problem with the *Lemon* test is that it affords the courts much leeway in evaluating law and government activities that may affect religion. Initially formulated to address questions of government funding to religious schools, it has been used to evaluate other situations, including those involving religious expression in public schools. As such, the *Lemon* test has been questioned in recent Supreme Court cases.[61]

The *Lemon* test is also open to criticism for generating the "tension" between the Religion Clauses. One commentator who argues that both clauses "directly protect religious liberty" criticizes the test for substituting a misleading formula and subsidiary, instrumental values (especially the separation of church and state) in place of the central value of religious liberty.[62]

ENDORSEMENT

In *Lynch v. Donnelly*,[63] Justice Sandra Day O'Connor proposed an alternative to the *Lemon* test. It is commonly called the "endorsement" test.[64]

This test states that a governmental action is invalid if it creates a *perception* that the government is endorsing or disapproving a religion.[65] The fundamental concern is whether the challenged governmental activity conveys "a message to nonadherents that they are outsiders, not full members of the political community, and an accompanying message to adherents that they are insiders, favored members of the political community."[66]

Like the *Lemon* test, the endorsement test also affords courts great interpretive flexibility. A law or activity that does not, in the Supreme Court's view, create a *perception* of endorsement could be upheld even though it in fact has a "primary effect" of advancing or inhibiting religion.[67]

Similarly, a law or activity that creates a perception of endorsement would be unconstitutional even if it in fact neither advances nor inhibits religion.[68]

Under Justice O'Connor's test, the relevant perception is that of an objective observer familiar with the text, legislative history, and implementation of the law in question.[69] Generally, a court or particular judge serves as the "objective observer" in analyzing situations where governmental endorsement is alleged.

Such an "objective observer" approach to the law, however, has as little explanatory power as similar "ideal observer" arguments in moral philosophy. The qualities attributed to the "objective observer" who will determine whether an impermissible "endorsement" has occurred (for example, familiarity with the law at issue) are simply those of the judges or justices who hear the case. It is therefore not likely that application of the "endorsement" test will change the outcome of any case. This test is rightly criticized as introducing "further ambiguities" into Establishment Clause doctrine.[70]

Various lower courts have followed Justice O'Connor's "endorsement" test.[71] Some commentators argue that the Supreme Court "treats the 'no endorsement test' as an occasional supplement to the reigning *Lemon* test, but not as a successor to, or even a definite refinement of, that test."[72] However, in some cases[73] the Court has used the test to decide the Establishment Clause issues involved.

For example, in writing for a plurality of the Supreme Court in *County of Allegheny v. American Civil Liberties Union*,[74] Justice Blackmun used the "endorsement" test to disallow a creche placed inside a county courthouse, while allowing a Hanukkah menorah placed outside the same courthouse. Blackmun held that the creche was an unconstitutional endorsement of religion,[75] while the menorah was "not an endorsement of religious faith but simply a recognition of cultural diversity."[76] His distinction demonstrates the kind of discretion the "endorsement" test grants to courts.

Justice Blackmun claimed that the "endorsement" test is merely an articulation of principles already underlying the Supreme Court's Establishment Clause adjudication:

> In recent years, we have paid particularly close attention to whether the challenged governmental practice either has the purpose or effect of "endorsing" religion, a concern that has long had a place in our Establishment Clause jurisprudence.[77]

Blackmun further stated that the word *endorsement* no more than rephrases Supreme Court decisions prohibiting "favoritism" toward or "promotion"[78] of any religion. The "endorsement" test still realizes the venerable principle that government must remain neutral by not taking a position on questions of religion.

The "endorsement" test, therefore, does not alter the Supreme Court's position that the Constitution mandates governmental accommodation of religion. Indeed, government does not necessarily *endorse* the religious expression that it *accommodates.*[79]

ACCOMMODATION AND THE PUBLIC EDUCATION SYSTEM

Problems in the area of religious freedom in the public schools have arisen along with the expansion of governmental control over education. The *compulsory* nature of school attendance makes the protection of the constitutional freedoms of students, which will often require the accommodation of their religious beliefs and practices, especially important. The Supreme Court has therefore recognized the constitutional rights of America's public student population.[80]

As discussed previously, the expansion of the constitutional rights of students has been accompanied by a decline of religious influence in the public school system. The decline of religious influence occurred as a result of the secularization of public education (often assisted by court rulings).[81]

Religious students, parents, teachers, and administrators are caught in the tension between the Free Exercise and Establishment Clauses. The courts have had a difficult time as well in distinguishing state involvement with religious symbols and activities within public schools from free expression initiated by students, teachers, and others.

This difficulty stems in part from the modern notion that public education in a secular state can somehow be valueless and thus "religion-less." Some commentators cling to the notion that the secular orientation of public schools is itself not at all religious.[82]

However, the orientation of public education has never been truly valueless or "religion-less." It has been observed that the state's preference "of a purely secular curriculum represents, in establishment terms, a choice of general anti-religionism as an evil lesser than the alternative of discrimination between religions."[83]

If education is vocational, then it deals with one's "calling," which is an essentially religious concept. John Dewey (see discussion of his educational philosophy in chapter 1) recognized this when he declared: "It is the business of the school to deepen and extend [the student's] sense of the values bound up in his home life."[84] Dewey went as far as to say that by fulfilling his "calling" as "a social servant set apart for the maintenance of proper social order," the teacher is "the prophet of the true God and the usherer in of the true kingdom of God."[85] Philosopher Alfred North Whitehead shared this sentiment in observing: "The essence of education is that it be religious."[86]

One of the historical functions of public education, as discussed earlier, has been to teach children the values, traditions, and rituals of society.[87] Secularization has meant that nontheistic values and traditions have replaced religious ones. Such values as civic tolerance and pluralism are now the predominant values inculcated in the public school system. One federal court has said that even if such values as "independent thought," "tolerance of diverse views," and "self-reliance" are in fact consistent with an alleged religion of "secular humanism," public schools may inculcate such values because they are "necessary to the maintenance of a democratic political system."[88]

The Supreme Court has long viewed public education as a unifying factor in developing citizens. Concurring in the Court's *McCollum v. Board of Education*[89] ruling prohibiting "released-time" programs for religious education within public school buildings, Justice Felix Frankfurter said:

> The nonsectarian or secular public schools were the means of reconciling freedom in general with religious freedom. Designed to serve as perhaps the most powerful agency for promoting cohesion among a heterogeneous democratic people, the public school must keep scrupulously free from entanglement in the strife of sects.[90]

The Court had, in its landmark *Brown v. Board of Education*[91] decision, earlier called public education under compulsory attendance laws "the very foundation of good citizenship," and "a principal instrument in awakening the child to cultural values."[92] A problem with judicial notice of public education's role in inculcating "democratic values" is that the vague "democratic ideal" has been considered incompatible with any absolutist religions, such as Judaism or Christianity. In his book *A Common Faith*, John Dewey stated:

> I cannot understand how any realization of the democratic ideal as a vital moral and spiritual ideal in human affairs is possible without surrender of the conception of the basic division to which supernatural Christianity is committed.[93]

The "division" to which Dewey referred is the absolutist religious concept whereby "those outside the fold of the church and those who do not rely upon belief in the supernatural have been regarded as only potential brothers."[94] In its place, Dewey proposed the "elimination of the supernatural," and he hoped for the development of "a religious faith that shall not be confined to sect, class, or race."[95]

The Supreme Court may have at least approached Dewey's view of religion within the context of public education in some of its rulings. For instance, in *McCollum*, the Court proclaimed:

> The public school is at once the symbol of our democracy and the most pervasive means for promoting our common destiny. In no activity of the State is it more vital to keep out divisive forces than in its schools, to avoid confusing, not to say fusing, what the Constitution sought to keep strictly apart.[96]

Likewise, in his *Everson* dissent, Justice Robert Jackson stated:

Our public school is organized on the premise that secular education can be isolated from all religious teaching so that the school can inculcate all needed temporal knowledge and also maintain a strict and lofty neutrality as to religion.[97]

Justice Jackson reasoned that the individual instructed in worldly wisdom "will be better fitted to choose his religion."[98] It is questionable whether this is a judgment courts should make on behalf of students.

In accordance with this emphasis on the potential "divisiveness" of religions, federal courts have held that when the *religious* expression of students is at issue, the case should be decided *not* according to a principle of affirmative accommodation, but rather by a "balancing" of students' right of expression against the school's interest in avoiding "disruption."[99] Fortunately, the Supreme Court has stated that the mere fact of political divisiveness resulting from the accommodation of religious expression cannot "serve to invalidate otherwise permissible conduct."[100] Given the Court's recognition of the capacity of students (see discussion of student capacity in chapter 7) to engage in serious debate, there is no legitimate reason for religious expression to be discriminated against based on its content.

While courts may single out religious expression as "divisive," the Supreme Court has held only six specific *practices* to be unconstitutional as *establishments* of religion in the public schools. These are: (1) state-directed and required on-premises religious training, in *McCollum v. Board of Education;*[101] (2) state-directed and required prayer, in *Engel v. Vitale;*[102] (3) state-directed and required Bible reading, in *Abington School District v. Schempp;*[103] (4) state-directed and required posting of the Ten Commandments, in *Stone v. Graham;*[104] (5) state-directed and authorized "periods of silence" for meditation and voluntary prayer, in *Wallace v. Jaffree;*[105] (6) state-directed and required teaching of scientific creationism, in *Edwards v. Aguillard.*[106] The records of these six cases show that government sponsored and was actively involved in the religious activities at issue.[107]

Unfortunately, many public school administrators have misinterpreted these cases as deciding that any religious expression within public schools is unconstitutional. Overly sweeping interpretations of the Supreme Court's rulings prompted Justice Tom Clark, author of the *Schempp* decision, to remark: "Most commentators suggested that the court had outlawed religious observances in public schools when, in fact, the court did nothing of the kind."[108]

In fact, the *Schempp* Court stressed that religion can be taught within the public schools if it is taught *objectively.*[109] In his *Schempp* concurrence, Justice William Brennan explained what it means to teach religion "objectively" when he stated that "teaching *about* the Holy Scriptures" does not violate the Constitution.[110]

The Supreme Court has stressed the difference between *communication* and *indoctrination* in the public school system: While communication is simply a transfer of information, indoctrination offers no option or alternative point of view.

AVOIDING HOSTILITY

The Supreme Court has warned that what may appear to be an indifferent neutrality may in some instances actually be a form of impermissible hostility toward religion. In his *Schempp* concurrence, Justice Arthur Goldberg noted:

> [U]ntutored devotion to the concept of neutrality can lead to invocation or approval of results which partake not simply of that noninterference and noninvolvement with the religious which the Constitution commands, but of a brooding and pervasive devotion to the secular and a passive, or even active, hostility to the religious. Such results are not only not compelled by the Constitution, but, it seems to me, are prohibited by it.[111]

One of the most subtle forms of hostility in the public realm is *marginalization* of religion. Marginalization emphasizes that religion and religious practice have minor social consequences and, for this reason, it should be permitted.[112] Justice Goldberg, however, warned that the Court must realize "that a vast portion of our people believe in and worship God and that many of our legal, political, and personal values derive historically from religious teachings."[113]

To avoid such subtle hostility, the Supreme Court has assumed a position of accommodating neutrality. Justice Douglas predicted the result if accommodating neutrality were not the Court's position:

> Prayers in our legislative halls; the appeals to the Almighty in the messages of the Chief Executive; the proclamations making Thanksgiving Day a holiday; "so help me God" in our courtroom oaths — these and all other references to the Almighty that run through our laws, our public rituals, our ceremonies would be flouting the First Amendment. A fastidious atheist or agnostic could even object to the supplication with which the Court opens each session: "God save the United States and this Honorable Court."[114]

Engel, Schempp, and other cases emphasize that the Supreme Court has not abandoned accommodating neutrality. By rejecting such practices as mandatory prayer and Bible reading in public schools, the Court has merely defined some of the limits of this doctrine. Since the state has entered the precinct of religion through the public schools, it is not constitutionally permissible for government fanatically to seal off religious expression from its public educational institutions.[115] Such a secularization would amount to a preference of nonbelief over belief, which the Supreme Court has condemned.[116]

Regardless of the legitimacy of a state's interest in assuring the moral and civic education necessary for good citizenship, the state's control of education must stop short of any measures that conflict with the Religion Clauses of the First Amendment. It is more likely that one of the clauses will be violated as long as the clauses are interpreted in a manner that generates an artificial tension between them.

A state, for example, may seek to avoid Establishment Clause problems by removing religious activities from public school curricula. Yet this very act restricts the free exercise rights of religious students during the time they are compelled to attend school.

The reasonable solution to such problems is an intermediate approach of granting students a niche of privacy during the school day during which they may communicate with each other on subjects of their choice. In other words, compulsory education must accommodate those who choose to develop religious and intellectual areas in their lives beyond what the state-controlled curriculum would typically nurture.

This kind of accommodation can occur if, as suggested above, the Free Exercise Clause concern is addressed *before* the Establishment Clause concern, so that the religious freedom, which is the goal of *both* clauses, may be realized. Too often, public school officials impose prior restraints on the religious expression of students because the Establishment Clause concern is addressed first; the Establishment Clause itself is often construed as advocating the elimination of any governmental facilitation of religious practice.

However, as the Supreme Court has recognized, governmental actions that are "simply a tolerable acknowledgment of beliefs widely held" are not per se establishments of religion.[117] The Supreme Court has made it equally clear that:

> [The] limits of permissible state accommodation to religion are by no means co-extensive with the noninterference mandated by the free exercise clause. To equate the two would be to deny a national heritage with roots in the Revolution itself.[118]

Therefore, "there is room for play in the joints productive of benevolent neutrality" toward religion.[119] This benevolence is affirmatively mandated when student-initiated religious expression is at issue.

It is especially crucial that affirmative accommodation of religious expression be mandated in public schools. Just as state-prescribed religious exercises could convey — indeed inculcate — doctrines contrary to the views of students and their parents, governmental disapproval and hostility toward a young religious adherent for freely holding and expressing religious views would be equally inappropriate.

The Supreme Court has in the past sought to "sponsor an attitude on the part of government that shows no partiality to any one group and that lets each flourish according to the zeal of its adherents and the appeal of its dogma."[120] Nothing more than this would be undertaken in permitting religious expression on an equal basis with other forms of expression in public schools and universities.

THE RELIGION OF SECULARISM

Recognizing the possibility of hostility toward religion within an increasingly secularistic society, Justice Clark, in *Schempp*, wrote:

> [T]he State may not establish a "religion of secularism" in the sense of affirmatively opposing or showing hostility to religion, thus "preferring those who believe in no religion over those who do believe."[121]

This prohibition was strengthened in *Torcaso v. Watkins*,[122] where the Supreme Court held that the First Amendment grants the same protections to and imposes the same limitations on secular or humanistic religions as it does theistic religion.[123]

It logically follows from the *Torcaso* reasoning that the government may not establish nontheistic or secular ideologies in the public schools, just as it may not establish theistic practices.[124] As one legal commentator has written:

> [I]f the total impact of a school value program is to promote a humanistic ideology, or if it utilizes the practices of a humanistic religion, it may be held that the state is aiding and preferring a secular religion.[125]

One aspect of "value programs" of public schools that has been challenged particularly often is sex education. Courts have been reluctant to find that sex education programs in fact establish a religion of secularism.[126] Courts have been motivated by a fear that "any group of parents or students [could] create chaos in the school system" by trying to enjoin any religiously offensive portion of the curriculum.[127]

While it may be wise for courts to refrain from applying to public school curricula more control than is already being exerted by other branches of government, it is clear that a religion of secularism is established, and courts must intervene, whenever public school officials deny the rights of students and teachers the freedom of religious expression within the schools. While greater regulation of school curricula may not promote the free marketplace of ideas that so many claim as their goal, mandated accommodation of religious expression most certainly will.

To avoid establishing a religion of secularism, public school authorities must accommodate students who desire to express their religious faiths. Moreover, public school authorities should cooperate with attempts by faculty members and students to open their classrooms and student organizations to off-campus speakers who may speak on religious topics or address secular subjects from a religious perspective.

Not only would these practices on the part of public school officials permissibly accommodate the religious needs of faculty and students, but they also would prevent acts hostile to religion and contrary to the Constitution. As Justice Douglas states so well:

> When the state encourages religious instruction or cooperates with religious authorities by adjusting the schedule of public events to sectarian needs, it follows the best of our traditions. For it then respects the religious nature of our people and accommodates the public service to our spiritual needs.[128]

PART THREE

Rights

In our system, state-operated schools may not be enclaves of totalitarianism. School officials do not possess authority over their students. Students in school as well as out of school are "persons" under our Constitution. They are possessed of fundamental rights which the state must respect. . . . In our system, students may not be regarded as closed-circuit recipients of only that which the State chooses to communicate.

—Justice Abe Fortas,
Tinker v. Des Moines Independent Community School District
393 U.S. 503, 511 (1969).

6

Public Forum Issues

Once the state has created a forum, it may not . . . close the
forum solely because it disagrees with the message being
communicated in it.

—Circuit Judge Juan R. Torruella,
Student Government Association v.
Board of Trustees of the
University of Massachusetts,
868 F. 2d 473, 480 (1st Cir. 1989).

The First Amendment to the United States Constitution guarantees freedom of speech. This provision includes not only the right to speak, but also the right to express oneself in nonverbal, symbolic speech, including peaceful picketing,[1] flag burning,[2] and wearing arm bands for purposes of religious protest in public schools.[3]

A frequent controversy surrounding the rights of religious persons is whether or not the public schools are proper forums for such speech activities. At one time, this issue was unsettled. However, it is now clear that public schools are a proper forum for free speech activity and, as such, the rights of religious persons to express themselves there is constitutionally protected.

The "public forum" doctrine determines the level of protection which will be given to the speech, without regard to its content, when it is made on public property.[4] The doctrine balances the individual's right to speak while on public property against the state's interest in restricting the property for specific uses. The doctrine is based on the recognition that an individual does not have an absolute right to exercise his or her First Amendment freedoms on public property.[5]

An analysis of free speech rights on public property (which includes public schools) is governed by the type of forum in which the expression takes place. The extent of the First Amendment protection given to the individual will vary with the character of the property to which the speaker desires access.[6] In this respect, the Supreme Court has classified publicly owned property into at least three types of forums:[7] (1) traditional public forums; (2) limited public forums; and (3) nonpublic forums. These apply not only to buildings or property — like a street or park—but also to any medium through which ideas are communicated.[8]

TRADITIONAL PUBLIC FORUMS

The first type of forum is the traditional public forum. These are "streets, sidewalks, parks, and other similar public places" that have, "by long tradition or government fiat,"[9] become the "natural and proper places"[10] "for the purpose of assembly, communicating thoughts between citizens, and discussing public questions."[11] These forums are "so historically associated with the exercise of First Amendment rights that access to them for the purpose of exercising such rights cannot constitutionally be denied broadly [or] absolutely."[12] "The rights of the State to limit expressive activities [in such public forums] are sharply circumscribed."[13]

The standard of review for state regulation or exclusion of speech for *content-based* reasons in a traditional public forum is one of the most exacting scrutiny. For the State to exclude speech on the basis of content, "it must show that its regulation is: (1) necessary to serve a compelling state interest, and (2) narrowly drawn to achieve that end."[14]

For example, an ordinance which banned picketing in front of a school, except for "labor dispute" picketing, would be unconstitutional. Such an ordinance would discriminate between groups of picketers based on the content of their speech without demonstrating that nonlabor picketing is more disruptive than labor picketing.[15]

The state may enforce reasonable *content-neutral* regulations as to the time, place, and manner of the speech. However, these regulations must: (1) be "narrowly tailored to serve a significant government interest," and (2) "leave open ample alternative channels of communication."[16]

For example, a time, place, and manner regulation which would prohibit noisy demonstrations on streets adjoining schools while school is in session seemingly would be a constitutional city ordinance.[17] Such an ordinance would apply regardless of the subject matter and thus would be content-neutral. A significant government interest would be served by preventing disruption of classes. Also, there would be ample alternatives of communication because nondisruptive protests would be allowed.

LIMITED PUBLIC FORUMS

A second type of forum consists of public property that is not traditionally a public forum, but has been opened by the State for use by the public as a place for expressive activity.[18] Places opened for limited kinds of expressive activity have included municipal theaters,[19] library auditoriums,[20] stadiums[21] and public college campuses.[22]

These forums must be opened by *intentional* government action, not merely by inaction or by permitting limited discourse.[23] "Intentional" governmental action is determined by reference to (1) government policy, (2) government practice, (3) the nature of the property, and (4) the compatibility of the forum with the expressive activity to be conducted there.[24]

Unlike the traditional public forums, in a limited public forum the government is *not required* to open the limited public forum in the first place but does so on its own discretion.[25] On the other hand, once the government has opened a forum for expressive activity, government officials are "bound by the same exacting standards as apply in a traditional public forum."[26]

Reasonable regulations concerning time, place, and manner of expression are permissible, provided they are content-neutral, narrowly tailored to serve a compelling state interest, and leave open alternative channels of communication.[27] The Supreme Court has held that content-based regulations must "serve a compelling state interest and must be narrowly drawn to achieve that end."[28]

Limited public forums differ from traditional public forums in two additional ways.

First, the State is not required to retain the character of the designated or limited public forum indefinitely.[29] Although the State is proscribed from exercising its authority to close the limited public forum merely to censor certain views, the government can redefine a limited public forum and close it. As one federal appellate court has held: "Once the state has created a forum, it may not . . . close the forum solely because it disagrees with the message being communicated in it."[30]

Second, a forum may be created for specific purposes.[31] For example, the forum may be limited to the discussions of certain subjects or to certain speakers. This is well illustrated in *Widmar v. Vincent*.[32] There the Supreme Court held that a public university campus had become a limited public forum *for student groups*. Although a public university campus is not a traditional public forum, by permitting some student organizations to use its facilities, the university in *Widmar* had created a limited public forum for all student groups.

NONPUBLIC FORUMS

The third type of forum is what is traditionally known as the nonpublic forum. It comprises all public property that is neither a traditional forum nor a limited forum.[33] It is generally incompatible with unrestrained expressive activities and is closed by its nature or government fiat to free speech activities.[34] For example, places such as prisons, military bases, and buses have aptly been categorized as nonpublic forums.

The nonpublic forum doctrine recognizes that the First Amendment "does not guarantee access to property simply because it is owned or controlled by the government."[35] The Supreme Court has held that this doctrine grants "[t]he State, no less than a private owner of property, ... power to preserve the property under its control for the use to which it is lawfully dedicated."[36] Therefore, government has considerable power to control expressive activity within the nonpublic forum.

The government, the Supreme Court has noted, "may regulate the content of expression to reserve the forum *for its intended purposes,* communicative or otherwise, as long as the regulation of speech is reasonable."[37] While viewpoint discrimination is prohibited, speech can be subjected to discrimination on the basis of subject matter and speaker identity.[38] Although this type of regulation would be unconstitutional in a traditional public forum, it is "inherent and inescapable in the process of limiting a nonpublic forum to activities compatible with the intended purpose of the property."[39]

The government may exercise its power to control expressive activities in a nonpublic forum in two ways. First, the government may decide to preserve the power to control the content of the expressive activities. For example, military officers may invite civilians to speak on subjects such as business management or drug control on the military base,[40] while banning political speakers. The use of these selected civilian speakers supports the operation of the military base, while the use of political speakers would not. Therefore, discrimination between the political and other types of speech is permissible in the nonpublic forum of the military base.

On the other hand, the military officers could not allow particular political speakers (for example, those supportive of the military), while barring others (for example, political speakers supportive of military cuts). This would unconstitutionally suppress expression based on opposition to the speakers' views.[41]

Second, the government could control expressive activities by creating a "limited public forum" within a nonpublic forum. When a specified portion of a nonpublic forum has been *deliberately* opened for certain expressive activities, the forum becomes accessible to "other entities of similar character."[42] For example, if a public school grants access to the school's mailing system (traditionally a nonpublic forum) to the Girl Scouts, the YMCA, and the 4-H Club, it has created a limited public forum which is opened to organizations which provide activities for children.[43] While this forum extends to other organizations of similar character, it does *not* extend to all other existing organizations.

Similarly, "[n]onpublic enclaves may exist within a limited public forum."[44] For example, while a public college campus may be found to be a limited public forum, the private office of the president of the college would be a nonpublic forum within the limited forum of the campus.

The broadness with which various forum channels are defined is significant in determining what group of people will possess rights to free expression in any particular forum. For example, if a school mail system (a nonpublic forum) is opened only to organizations which currently have official business with teachers, only a union representing teachers will have access to the mail system. A union seeking to represent teachers will not have similar access, even though both organizations fall under the category of "teachers' union."

"UNPROTECTED" SPEECH

While the government must meet one of the various standards outlined above in order to restrict free expression on government property, there are enumerated categories of speech which are *not* protected by the First Amendment. These categories include obscene speech,[45] speech which advocates illegal action,[46] libel or defamation,[47] false or misleading commercial speech,[48] and child pornography.[49] If the speech fits into one of these categories, the government can impose upon it any reasonable restrictions, and the speaker can be subject to punishment.[50]

SUMMARY

The constitutionality of government regulation of speech-related activity is thus governed by the type of forum in which the expression takes place. The nature and use of the government property in question must be examined to determine the extent to which government may regulate speech. In traditional and designated public forums, government is strictly limited in the regulations it may impose. In a nonpublic forum, government may impose more encompassing regulations of expressive activity.

In conclusion, a disturbing result of this three-category formulation must be noted. The second category, the limited public forum, is modeled in such a way that it provides little protection for speech. Although a compelling interest test is applied to a limited public forum, the government may convert a limited public forum to a nonpublic forum almost without any reason. Once converted to a nonpublic forum, exclusion of speech need only be reasonable and not motivated by hostility to the view expressed. As one commentator notes, it makes little sense to apply a strict standard to the government's ability to regulate speech in one forum category and then let the government opt out of that forum category at will.[51]

7

Student Capacity

Student maturity goes to whether the school should create an open forum in the first place. It cannot justify excluding religion from a forum that a school voluntarily creates.

—Professor Douglas Laycock,
*Equal Access and Moments of Silence:
The Equal Status of Religious Speech
by Private Speakers,*
81 Northwestern University
Law Review 1, 52 (1986).

The United States Supreme Court has found an Establishment Clause violation in every case in which it has ruled on state-required and/or directed religious activity within public schools. In his treatise on constitutional law, Harvard law professor Laurence Tribe articulates the familiar rationale underlying this line of cases:

[Public schools are] the facilities through which basic norms are transmitted to the young. It is thus unsurprising that no major religious activity, however "voluntary," has been allowed to take place in the facilities through which we inculcate values for the future.[1]

Tribe's reasoning reflects the "cultural transmission" educational philosophy discussed in chapter 1. In all of the Supreme Court cases concerning state-sponsored religious activities, the public schools were indeed functioning in an *inculcative* capacity.[2] The religious activities occurred in the classroom during mandatory instructional periods while the teacher was at least present and, in most cases, actually participating in or leading the activities.

However, as the Supreme Court has repeatedly recognized, the public school system is to serve a dual role — not only to inculcate majoritarian values deemed necessary for "meaningful" citizenship, but also to provide a "marketplace of ideas," stimulating free inquiry.[3] Recognition by the Supreme Court of the public school's role in providing a marketplace of ideas stems from its McCarthy-era rulings striking down "loyalty oaths."[4] In the first such rulings, the Court struck down a state law requiring all state officers and employees (which included a public university professor charged under the statute) to take an oath swearing that they belonged to no "communist front" or "subversive" organizations.[5] In his concurrence, Justice Felix Frankfurter stressed that loyalty oaths affect *students* as well as teachers:

> Such unwarranted inhibition upon the free spirit of teachers affects not only those who, like the appellants, are immediately before the Court. It has an unmistakable tendency to chill that free play of the spirit which all teachers ought especially to *cultivate* and practice; it makes for caution and timidity in their associations by *potential teachers.*[6]

In stating that free thought is something teachers must be able to "cultivate," Justice Frankfurter implied that the freedom of thought that teachers possess within public education ought also to be enjoyed by students. Several years later, the Supreme Court stated in a similar vein that if teachers and students are not free to inquire, "our civilization will stagnate and die."[7]

The Supreme Court issued its classic statement concerning public education as a marketplace of ideas in *Keyishian v. Board of Regents,*[8] one of its last rulings striking down a loyalty oath as applied to a public university professor. Appealing to its earlier declaration that "protection of constitutional freedoms is nowhere more vital than in the community of American schools,"[9] the Court said:

> [The First Amendment] does not tolerate laws that cast a pall of orthodoxy over the classroom. . . . The classroom is peculiarly the "marketplace of ideas." The Nation's future depends upon leaders trained through wide exposure to that robust exchange of ideas which discovers truth "out of a multitude of tongues, [rather] than through any kind of authoritative selection."[10]

The Court's language echoes John Milton's classic rhetoric on behalf of a free press.[11]

In *Tinker v. Des Moines Independent School District,*[12] its ruling upholding the right of high school students to engage in political protest that does not substantially interfere with school discipline, the Supreme Court appealed to the *Keyishian* marketplace concept,[13] and enlarged upon it:

Students in school as well as out of school are "persons" under our Constitution. . . . In our system, students may not be regarded as closed-circuit recipients of only that which the State chooses to communicate.[14]

The special significance of *Tinker* is that it explicitly applied to *high schools* a marketplace concept that had earlier been applied to *colleges*.

Federal court rulings since *Tinker* have explicitly or implicitly applied the marketplace concept to uphold free *political* expression within the general curricula[15] and libraries[16] of public schools, as well as to resolve conflicts arising from students'[17] and teachers'[18] political activity and from outside speakers.[19]

In implementing and maintaining a system of free student inquiry where student-initiated religious expression is permitted on an equal basis with other student speech, a school would be functioning primarily in its noninculcative, intellectual marketplace role. New York University law professor Nadine Strossen notes:

[T]he establishment clause concerns that prompted the Court's invalidation of public school religious expression when the school was acting as inculcator would not necessarily justify the invalidation of such expression when the school is serving as a marketplace of ideas.[20]

Student-initiated religious activity may include any traditional free speech activities, speeches, conversations, literature distribution, and meetings that would not be questioned except for their purported religious content. To exclude such expression from the school's marketplace of ideas would at least appear to discriminate against religious students.

STUDENT MATURITY AND IMPRESSIONABILITY

The judiciary's concerns over impressionability of young students are rooted in long-standing legal distinctions between minors and adults. The Supreme Court has ruled that restrictions on obscene or offensive speech that would not apply to adults may apply to minors both inside[21] and outside[22] of school. The Court has similarly held that *Tinker's* recognition of the authority of school officials "to prescribe and control conduct in the schools" consistent with constitutional safeguards[23] leaves public schools free to apply corporal punishment.[24] Federal courts have thus upheld efforts of public schools to control various destructive forms of student behavior,[25] or to prevent invasions of students' privacy in especially sensitive areas of their personal lives.[26]

While courts have granted school officials rather broad powers to protect students from harmful behavior, the assumptions of student immaturity that apply in protecting students from, for example, drugs or obscenity should not be applied to insulate students from any political and religious expression that could be considered controversial. Because of the First

Amendment values implicated whenever school officials seek to censor such expression, the Supreme Court in *Tinker* insisted that school officials may suppress *only* political expression that "would substantially interfere with the work of the school or impinge upon the rights of other students."[27]

One of the Supreme Court's chief concerns about religion in the public school system involves situations in which First Amendment values of free speech and free exercise of religion are *not* implicated. These are situations in which the state has *mandated* and *directed* religious activity. The Court has been concerned that, in these situations, students could perceive the school as supporting and/or endorsing religion.

More than once, the Supreme Court has expressed a concern that because of the particular *impressionability* of young people, they may be more likely than adults to perceive any religious expression on school premises as indicating sponsorship or endorsement of religion by the schools. Justice Frankfurter noted as early as 1948:

> That a child is offered an alternative may reduce the constraint; it does not eliminate the operation of influence by the school. . . . The law of imitation operates, and nonconformity is not an outstanding characteristic of children.[28]

The Supreme Court has also expressed concern that, as a result of such appearance of sponsorship or endorsement, "students adhering to a minority religion or no religion might feel more alienated or be more susceptible to indoctrination than adults would be."[29]

This susceptibility to indoctrination is, as the Court notes, especially characteristic of very young children. As Justice Brennan recognized in a 1985 ruling:

> The symbolism of a union between church and state is most likely to influence children of tender years, whose experience is limited and whose beliefs consequently are the function of environment as much as of free and voluntary choice.[30]

Federal courts have often similarly been concerned with the impressionability of students when limiting *religious* expression within public schools.[31] The Supreme Court's decision in *Mergens v. Board of Education of the Westside Community Schools*[32] may have marked a retreat from this assumption that students are especially "impressionable" when religious expression is at issue.[33]

Correspondingly, the Supreme Court has long insulated public school students from any direct governmental support or endorsement of religion.[34] This is reflected in many cases previously discussed.

The concern that students are especially impressionable even with regard to *student-initiated* religious expression is articulated by such commentators as Professor Tribe:

Young students are likely to be vulnerable to coercion and intimidation. Although student-initiated coercion is not state action, the state nonetheless must anticipate it and respond to it where the coercion results directly and foreseeably from a state program. No less important is the risk that younger children may see endorsement in the school's otherwise-permissible accommodation.[35]

Tribe's reasoning here may reflect an argument made by other commentators[36] that student impressionability with regard to *religious* speech may simply be assumed; private religious and political speech may therefore be treated *differently* even if the school has created an open forum for *political* speech.

University of Texas law professor Douglas Laycock, whose scholarship concerning equal access to public high schools for student religious groups influenced the Supreme Court's decision in *Mergens*,[37] disagrees with this reasoning. Laycock argues:

[W]hen a junior high or elementary school does create an open forum, there is no reason to distinguish it from a high school. Exclusion of religious speech is still discriminatory and hostile to religion. The argument for exclusion still depends on the premise that government approves of everything it does not censor. . . . Student maturity goes to whether the school should create an open forum in the first place. It cannot justify excluding religion from a forum that a school voluntarily creates.[38]

Laycock's reasoning is also closely followed in the concurrence of Justice Thurgood Marshall in *Mergens*. Conceding that the tendency of high schools "to emphasize student autonomy less than universities" may mean that high school administrators perceive that their students are less mature than college students, Justice Marshall concludes that "the school's *behavior*, not the *purported immaturity* of high school students, is dispositive."[39] The Supreme Court appears now to be much more interested in what *actions* of school officials imply about their students' capacity to engage in serious political and religious discussion than in any "foreseeable dangers" of religious expression.

Courts had resisted applying to public *high school* students the principle enunciated by the Supreme Court in *Widmar v. Vincent*.[40] There the Court stated that public *college* students are mature enough not to infer state endorsement from giving student religious groups equal access.[41] Federal courts had assumed that there is a difference between the maturity of public high school students and public university students that is of legal significance in equal access cases.[42]

However, the Supreme Court has now accepted the reasoning of Justice Lewis Powell's dissent in a pre-*Mergens* Supreme Court case[43] upholding denial of equal access to student religious groups in public high schools. Justice Powell argued that because we live in an age of "massive media information," the "few years difference in age between high school and college students" does not justify a refusal to apply the *Widmar v. Vincent* reasoning to public high school students.[44] The *Mergens* court cited Justice Powell's reasoning in support of the proposition "that schools do not endorse everything they fail to censor."[45]

The facts of modern life, as well as developments in child and adolescent psychology, indicate that the Supreme Court was wise to follow Justice Powell's reasoning. For example, New York University professor Neil Postman argues that through the development of mass electronic news and entertainment media, by around 1950 "childhood became obsolete at the same time that it was perceived as a permanent fixture."[46] Postman concludes that through television in particular "the historic basis for a dividing line between childhood and adulthood is being unmistakably eroded."[47]

In the modern age, young people are continuously confronted with a myriad of choices not available to past generations. Their choices range from whether to have an abortion to whether they should file lawsuits against their parents, teachers, or schools. These experiences necessarily force children to mature more quickly.[48]

Much current child psychology indicates that the protection from the appearance of state endorsement of religion that courts had applied to public high school students would be more suitable (if at all) for children less than twelve years old.[49] Psychologist Jean Piaget's work on how children perceive rules suggests that while children aged four to seven "do not follow rules but merely insist that they do," children aged seven to eleven play games that "acquire a genuinely social character. There is a fascination with rules."[50] *By age eleven*, "Children come to an understanding about rules, even invent their own. They use rules, rather than being used by them."[51]

Piaget's findings have been borne out in a study of children's understanding of religious differences. Psychologist David Elkind applied Piaget's contention "that concepts develop in discernible stages that follow a regular sequence related to age" to a survey designed to show what children understand of their religious identities. He found that children develop differentiated and abstract concepts of religious differences by age ten to twelve.[52] These findings indicate that by about age eleven, students are mature enough to conduct free religious expression without disturbing the educational process, and without inferring state endorsement when such expression occurs in the public schools.

As could be expected, academic studies based on these findings support the conclusion that high school students have the cognitive ability to understand that in a free and pluralistic society, toleration of speech and ideas in the open forum of public schools does not imply state endorsement or sponsorship. For example, Dr. David Moshman, an expert in the development of cognitive reasoning and intellectual development in children, surveyed the empirical research on deductive reasoning. Dr. Moshman applied this research specifically to the issue of equal access in public secondary schools for student religious expression and concluded:

These considerations support the Supreme Court's conclusion that most college students will understand the voluntary nature of student groups and will not perceive an establishment of religion. The evidence reviewed . . . suggests that high school students, and probably junior high school students as well, cannot be sharply distinguished from college students. There is no reason to think that secondary students will naively assume that all groups meeting in a school are thereby endorsed by the school or that they are encouraged to join all such groups. On the contrary, it seems likely that a prominent sign associated with notices of student activities would be sufficient for adolescents to grasp the voluntary nature of the activities.[53]

Dr. Moshman states as a general principle that children "may be deprived of certain rights if—and only if—they fail to meet criteria (such as rationality) directly relevant to the rights in question."[54]

One legal commentator, relying upon research in the field of adolescent psychology, concludes that high school students are capable of critical inquiry.[55] Based on the ability of adolescents to engage in complex legal functions, question authority figures and peers, and form personal ideals and values, this commentator concludes that "high school may in fact be a time when the distinction between tolerance based on mutual respect and explicit approval of student expression is particularly clear."[56]

The Supreme Court has also recognized students' ability to make adequate distinctions. Consequently, many Supreme Court Justices who joined in decisions finding state-mandated religious activity in public schools unconstitutional have concluded that primary and secondary school students may, despite their relative impressionability or immaturity, "understand the distinction between a school's endorsement of religious expression and its neutral provision of an opportunity during which students may choose to engage in such expression. These Justices evidently regard students as capable of distinguishing between the school's inculcative and non-inculcative functions."[57]

This necessarily means students can recognize that a public school policy that excludes religious expression discriminates against religion. As has been noted, such exclusion and discrimination against religion contradict First Amendment values.

EDUCATIONAL PHILOSOPHY AND STUDENT CAPACITY

The three educational philosophies discussed in chapter 1 may shape differing conceptions of student capacity. It may appear at first blush that of these three educational philosophies, "romanticism" would most emphasize the capacity of students to think for themselves and that "cultural transmission" would most emphasize the impressionability of students and consequent susceptibility to and need for inculcation of societal values by public schools. Indeed, one legal commentator who believes that children lack "that full capacity for individual choice which is the presupposition of First Amendment guarantees" criticizes the view stated by romanticist educator A. S. Neill that the child is "innately wise and realistic."[58]

Court decisions that rule against students' freedom of expression and right to be exposed to new ideas do in fact often appeal to a cultural transmission or inculcative model of public education.[59] Such decisions may also cite Dewey's progressivist doctrines (see chapter 1) of the function of education as a force that "shapes" students' experience and the "prophetic" role of public school teachers.[60]

However, as mentioned in chapter 1, romanticism may be criticized from both cultural transmission and progressivist perspectives for either leaving children culturally impoverished or patronizingly seeking only their "happiness." These criticisms may well be borne out in the views of the original educational theorist, Jean-Jacques Rousseau, on childhood:

> Childhood has its ways of seeing, thinking, and feeling which are proper to it. Nothing is less sensible than to want to substitute ours for theirs, and I would like as little to insist that a ten-year-old be five feet tall as that he possess judgment. Actually, what would reason do for him at that age? It is the bridle of strength, and the child does not need this bridle.[61]

Not only does the psychological research discussed above show that children by at least age eleven (if not earlier) *do in fact* possess judgment, the facts of modern life *require* that they *exercise* this judgment in more and more situations. A romantic educational theory could justify censorship of religious expression in public school on grounds that students' exposure to different views at a "tender" age would "unnaturally" force them to make decisions they both cannot and should not make.

As proposed in chapter 1, both cultural transmission and progressivist educational philosophies may be implemented in public schools *to the extent that* a "public" viewpoint *should* prevail in public schools. This viewpoint may be discerned by consideration of the state's legitimate interest in inculcating values necessary for the preservation of democracy.[62] Indeed, a few courts have applied a cultural transmission philosophy in *support* of ability of public high school students to deal with controversy and the right to academic freedom.[63] If religious students are granted the same expressive freedom as other students, the public schools will indeed transmit values necessary for preservation of our democracy.

8

The Rights of Students

All ideas having even the slightest redeeming social impor-
tance—unorthodox ideas, controversial ideas, even ideas
hateful to the prevailing climate of opinion—have the full
protection of the [First Amendment].

—Justice William J. Brennan,
Roth v. United States,
354 U.S. 476, 484 (1957).

There was a time in American history when doubt existed as to whether minors, and secondary high school students in particular, were protected by the United States Constitution. As previously discussed, that doubt has now been removed.[1]

In many varied contexts, the Supreme Court and numerous lesser tribunals have declared that minors have constitutional rights comparable to those of adults. For example, the Supreme Court, in considering the rights of juvenile criminal offenders, held that the Constitution is not for adults alone.[2]

Although juvenile rights have been the subject of much litigation in the area of criminal law, the most litigious area with regard to minors' rights has been in the context of education and the public school community. Not surprisingly, the rights of minor students have been broadened and have been more clearly defined as a result.

FREE SPEECH

The Free Speech Clause of the First Amendment was applied to public school students by the United States Supreme Court in *West Virginia State Board of Education v. Barnette.*[3] In *Barnette*, a school board adopted a resolution making the flag salute mandatory in the public schools.[4] This was challenged by Jehovah's Witnesses who maintained that the mandatory salute violated their freedoms of speech and religion as guaranteed by the First Amendment.

In deciding the case on the free speech issue, the Supreme Court found that the free speech rights of the Jehovah's Witnesses had been unconstitutionally violated.[5] The Court held that the First Amendment limitation on the government's ability to regulate or restrict speech applied to the public schools,[6] and that students have a First Amendment right "to be free from ideological indoctrination."[7]

Several decades later, the Supreme Court affirmed the First Amendment right of public school students to freedom of expression in *Tinker v. Des Moines Independent Community School District.*[8] The Court stated that "students do not shed their constitutional rights to freedom of speech or expression at the schoolhouse gate."[9] First Amendment rights, applied in light of the special characteristics of the school environment, are available to teachers *and* students.[10]

In *Tinker*, two students wore black arm bands to school in protest of the Vietnam war. The school had adopted a policy prohibiting the wearing of such arm bands and suspended those students who refused to remove them. The Supreme Court in response held that wearing the arm bands was "closely akin to 'pure speech'" and that it was protected under the First Amendment.[11]

Although school officials and the State are empowered with the authority to prescribe and regulate the students' conduct in the schools,[12] their authority over students cannot be absolute.[13] The *Tinker* Court noted that in "the absence of a specific showing of constitutionally valid reasons to regulate their speech, students are entitled to freedom of expression of their views."[14] Just as a student must respect his or her obligations to the school, the school must respect the fundamental rights of the student.[15] This is because students have been recognized as persons under the Constitution, both in and out of the school,[16] and adolescent constitutional protection extends to fundamental rights in the Constitution.[17]

As such, school authorities must show that their prohibition of a student's speech is based on more than just a desire to avoid possible "discomfort and unpleasantness" accompanying a viewpoint.[18] "Undifferentiated fear or apprehension of disturbance," the *Tinker* Court recognized, "is *not* enough to overcome the right of free expression."[19] The Supreme Court has clearly declared that the protection of freedom of expression is "nowhere more vital than in the community of the American schools."[20]

In *Tinker*, the Court formulated a two-pronged test to define what would constitute a "constitutionally valid"[21] reason for regulating students' free expression. A student's freedom of expression is guaranteed on the public high school campus if it does not: (1) *materially* and *substantially* interfere with the requirements of appropriate discipline in the operation of the school; and, (2) *invade* or *collide* with the rights of others.[22] If student expression meets these two requirements, then any prohibition of student expression *is constitutionally suspect.*

Under *Tinker*, any regulations restricting or enjoining speech must be *content neutral*. Once school officials allow some students to speak, a *limited public forum* has been created and *all* students must be allowed to speak, at least in a similar manner. The *Tinker* Court held that school officials cannot use the restrictions to suppress "expressions of feelings with which they do not wish to contend."[23]

RELIGIOUS EXPRESSION

Given the *Tinker* holding and its affirmation in later decisions, the right to the *freedom of religious expression* must be protected by public school authorities to the same extent as freedom of nonreligious expression. To prohibit the expression of one particular opinion (religious) would "strike at the very core of first amendment values."[24] Therefore, "it is apparent that religious students not only *may* but *must* be granted the right to free expression" within the confines of the two-part *Tinker* test.[25]

In fact, public schools should make adjustments to accommodate the students' religious needs.[26] The Supreme Court has held "there is room for play in the joints productive of a benevolent neutrality which will permit religious exercises to exist without sponsorship and without interference."[27] To hold otherwise, it would be necessary to read into the Bill of Rights a "hostility to religion."[28]

Public schools may fear that accommodating the religious needs of students will violate the First Amendment's prohibition of the establishment of religion. However, the Establishment Clause is, as one federal court has held, a limitation on the power of governments, not a restriction on the rights of individuals.[29] Moreover, mere apprehension by school officials that they might contravene the Establishment Clause is not enough to exclude student-initiated activity from the public school forum.[30]

On the other hand, banning or prohibiting student-initiated religious expression in public schools has significant "chilling effects" on First Amendment rights of students.[31] First, it prefers those who believe in no religion over those who believe.[32] Second, it subjugates the Free Speech and Exercise Clauses to Establishment Clause interests,[33] creating an inconsistency within the First Amendment. This gives the Establishment Clause interests precedence over Free Speech and Exercise interests and allows the school to repress students' Free Speech and Exercise rights.[34]

STUDENT RELIGIOUS ORGANIZATIONS

In *Widmar v. Vincent*,[35] the Supreme Court found that prohibiting student religious activity on school premises on the basis of Establishment Clause concerns was an unconstitutional discriminatory action on the part of a public university. The university had denied a student religious club access to university meeting facilities available to other student organizations.[36]

The Court found that the university had created a public forum by its general accommodation of student meetings and that the exclusion of *religious speech* from that forum violated the First Amendment's free speech provision. This reaffirmed the principle that religious speech is entitled to *all* the protection provided under the First Amendment Free Speech Clause.

In sum, the Court established at least two propositions regarding public schools and religious speech. First, the creation of an open forum in no way commits the educational institution to the goals of religious students who use that forum. Second, the fact that a forum benefits both religious and nonreligious persons can be used to negate any inference of state approval of the religious activity.[37]

The dissent in *Widmar* made the argument that religious groups should not be allowed to meet for the purpose of religious worship even though religious speech is permissible.[38] However, the Court's majority found that for three reasons this distinction lacked "intelligible content."[39] First, worship is a state of mind more than a category of speech. Second, even if there was a distinction, the government is ill-equipped to make it,[40] and doing so would involve unnecessary entanglement of government with religion. Third, there is no reason for distinguishing religious worship from other religious speech.[41]

WIDMAR EXTENDED TO SECONDARY SCHOOLS

In 1984, Congress extended the reasoning of *Widmar* to public secondary schools through the Equal Access Act. Under the Act, "a public secondary school with a 'limited open forum' is prohibited from discriminating against students who wish to conduct a meeting within that forum on the basis of the '*religious,* political, philosophical, or other content of the speech at such meetings.'"[42]

Some lower courts had questioned the constitutionality of the Equal Access Act on the basis of Establishment Clause violations. However, in *Mergens v. Board of Education of the Westside Community Schools,*[43] the Supreme Court overwhelmingly concluded that the Act was constitutional.

Mergens involved an attempt by a group of students to form the "Christian Bible Study Club" at Westside High School in Omaha, Nebraska. Students at this particular high school were allowed to become members of various student groups and clubs, all of which met after school hours on public school grounds. The students were allowed to choose from approximately thirty different groups and clubs on a strictly voluntary basis. The various clubs included the Chess Club, Zonta and Interact, Subsurfers, and the like. All of the clubs had faculty sponsors.[44]

Westside High School had no written policy concerning the formation of clubs. When the students attempted to form the Bible study club, they were denied access to the school by school officials.[45] After appeals to the school superintendent were denied, the students filed a lawsuit maintaining their freedom of speech, freedom of association, and freedom to exercise their religion had been violated by school officials as well as their rights under the Equal Access Act.[46]

The Supreme Court concluded that Westside High School had created a "limited open forum" by allowing a number of "noncurriculum related student groups" to meet and was thus subject to the Equal Access Act.[47] The school was found to be in violation of the Act for basing their refusal to allow the Bible study club on the religious content of its meetings.

The Supreme Court rejected the argument that high school students are likely to confuse an equal access policy with state sponsorship of religion. The Court found that "secondary school students are mature enough and are likely to understand that a school does not endorse speech that it merely permits."[48] This fact had been recognized when Congress was considering the Equal Access Act:

[S]tudents below the college level are capable of distinguishing between State-initiated, school sponsored, or teacher-led religious speech on the one hand and student-initiated, student-led religious speech on the other.[49]

Furthermore, the school itself has control over any impressions it gives its students.

Since the Equal Access Act was found to be constitutional and the school had violated the Act, it was not necessary for the *Mergens* Court to decide on the free speech and free exercise issues. The rights of religious student groups to use school facilities for meetings under the Equal Access Act is discussed in more detail in chapter 11.

Some public school authorities have suggested that while a complete ban on political and religious speech might be unconstitutional, a school policy that merely bans "proselytizing" religious or political beliefs is well within constitutional parameters. Apart from the fact that the term "proselytizing" is unconstitutionally vague, there is no authority for the proposition that the First Amendment protects the right to speak, but not the right to persuade (that is, proselytize).[50] The Supreme Court has held that speech calculated to persuade, advocate, or proselytize implicates the very reasons the First Amendment was adopted.[51]

FREE EXPRESSION IN THE CLASSROOM

While the First Amendment Free Speech Clause is designed to guarantee the free exchange of ideas in the general marketplace,[52] communication in the classroom should be protected as a "special marketplace of ideas."[53] "The purpose of education is to spread, not stifle, ideas and views."[54] As one federal appellate court has stated:

Ideas in their pure and pristine form, touching only the minds and hearts of school children, must be freed from despotic dispensation by all men, be they robed as academicians or judges or citizen members of a board of education.[55]

Therefore, students must be free to "express controversial and political viewpoints without fear of punishment."[56]

Student expression should not be confined to viewpoints that are officially approved.[57] This would, as the Supreme Court noted in *Tinker*, make schools "enclaves of totalitarianism," where students are "regarded as closed-circuit recipients of only that which the State chooses to communicate."[58] In the classroom, student expression relevant to the subject matter should be protected.[59]

Schools, which are designed to prepare students for citizenship, more effectively carry out this goal by exposing students to a "multitude of tongues" rather than "authoritative selection."[60] This teaches students to "respect the diversity of ideas that is fundamental to the American system"[61] and leaves them better equipped to participate in the political process as adults.

PRIOR RESTRAINTS ON FREE SPEECH

Any ban on free speech by students must also be analyzed in light of the Supreme Court's directive against any prior restraints on free speech. A prior restraint on free speech occurs when state officials attempt to, or do in fact, suppress speech *before* it is uttered. It is clear that the Court has chosen to respond strongly against any prior-in-form governmental encroachment on free expression.[62]

The *Tinker* Court held that prior restraints on student expression would be permissible only in the presence of "facts which might reasonably have led school authorities to forecast substantial disruption of or material interference with school activities."[63] School authorities are not "at liberty to suppress or punish speech simply because they disagree with it, or because it takes a political or social viewpoint different from theirs."[64] In *Gay Students Organization of the University of New Hampshire v. Bonner*,[65] a federal court of appeals affirmed a lower court decision granting a gay student organization the right to meet on a state university campus. An ongoing program of student organizations existed at the state university, but university officials had restrained the gay organization from holding social functions on campus.

The court in *Gay Students Organization* found it "immaterial whether the beliefs sought to be advanced by associations pertain to political, economic, *religious* or cultural matters."[66] The fact that the Gay Student Organization alone was made subject to the regulation indicated that the regulation was an unconstitutional prior restraint based on content.

FREEDOM OF ASSOCIATION

The Supreme Court stated that "[i]t is beyond debate that freedom to engage in association for the advancement of beliefs and ideas is an inseparable aspect of the 'liberty' assured by the Due Process Clause of the Fourteenth Amendment which embraces freedom of speech."[67] What was originally called the freedom of assembly has in recent years been extended to students.

In *Healy v. James*,[68] the Supreme Court held unanimously that any limitation or denial of the freedom of speech or association by a state on the basis of subject matter that is neither slanderous nor obscene is violative of students' First Amendment rights. *Healy* concerned a group of student activists, the Students for a Democratic Society, which sought and was denied recognition as a student organization at a Connecticut state college.[69]

Healy recognized an inherent general freedom of association within the First Amendment and explained that colleges and universities are not immune to the amendment's sweep.[70] The court held the college's denial of recognition to be a prior restraint on the First Amendment freedom of association. Although this particular decision involved students at a state university, the same rule applies at the public high school level.[71] This is especially so since *Mergens*, where the Supreme Court held that "the logic of *Widmar* applies with equal force to the Equal Access Act."[72] The Equal Access Act, of course, applies to secondary school students.

Tinker also helped to determine the extent to which a high school student's freedom of association comes within the scope of constitutional protection. The Supreme Court in *Tinker* specifically stated that the "principal use to which the schools are dedicated is to accommodate students during prescribed hours for the purpose of certain types of activities. Among those activities is personal intercommunication among the students."[73]

DISTRIBUTION OF LITERATURE

One other issue which has frequently surfaced is the freedom of students to distribute literature on state university or public school campuses. As a consequence of the various court decisions, it is evident that literature which is "libelous, obscene, disruptive of school activities, or likely to create substantial disorder, or which invades the rights of others" may be suppressed by public school officials.[74] However, when no such conditions exist, and particularly when the literature is not (1) sponsored by the school district, (2) represented as an official school paper, (3) financed by public funds, (4) or supervised by school faculty, school administrators have no authority to suppress its distribution.[75] Clearly then, students are protected by the First Amendment and are permitted to distribute publications on campus unless school authorities "can reasonably 'forecast substantial disruption of or material interference with school activities' on account of distribution of such material."[76]

School authorities are, therefore, forbidden arbitrarily to ban publications from the school campus. For example, in *Quarterman v. Byrd*,[77] a federal court of appeals ruled that a public school regulation prohibiting students from distributing printed material without express permission from the administration prior to its distribution was an improper prior restraint. Such a rule or regulation is invalid on its face.

At a minimum, there should be a *written* policy containing criteria to be followed by school officials when determining whether or not to permit the distribution of literature. Also, procedural safeguards (hearing, notice of charges, etc.) should be established to permit review of a denial.

Many of the above principles were applied in *Rivera v. East Otero School District*.[78] In *Rivera*, an official school policy defined various forms of "unacceptable," noncurricula materials which could not be distributed on the public high school campus.[79] "Included in the 'unacceptable' categories was [m]aterial that proselytizes a particular religion or political belief."[80]

Two students were suspended for distributing "a free nonstudent newspaper" that mainly contained religious articles.[81] The students subsequently filed suit in federal district court alleging that their First Amendment free speech rights (as well as other constitutional rights) were violated by the school policy.[82] The court applied the *Tinker* two-part test and invalidated the school policy.[83]

Although high school officials argued that the First Amendment Establishment Clause prohibited the school from allowing students to distribute an unofficial religious newspaper, the court proclaimed: "The Establishment Clause is a limitation on the power of governments: it is not a restriction on the rights of individuals acting in their private lives."[84] This crucial distinction was also made by Justice O'Connor in *Mergens*: "[T]here is a crucial difference between *government* speech endorsing religion, which the Establishment Clause forbids, and *private* speech endorsing religion, which the Free Speech and Free Exercise Clauses protect."[85] Furthermore, as the *Rivera* court noted:

> It is clear that the mere fact that student speech occurs on school property does not make it government supported. It is undisputed in this case that the students are not government actors, are not acting in concert with the government, and do not seek school cooperation or assistance with their speech. Accordingly, the Establishment Clause simply is not implicated.[86]

RIGHT TO KNOW

The Constitution does not expressly recognize a *right to know* or to receive information. However, the right to know is by implication essential to ensure the validity of the First Amendment right to freedom of expression. The Supreme Court has identified it as an "inherent corollary of the right of free speech."[87]

In fact, the Supreme Court has recognized that "[t]he right to receive ideas is a necessary predicate to the recipient's [student's] meaningful exercise of his or her own right of speech."[88] This is particularly important for the student who is soon to be an adult member of society.[89] As the Supreme Court notes: "Just as access to ideas makes it possible for citizens generally to exercise their rights of free speech and press in a meaningful manner, such access prepares students for active and effective participation in the pluralistic, often contentious society in which they will soon be adult members."[90]

Textbook publishers or outside "speakers" may not have a right to compel school officials to expose students to their particular works. However, "[students] have a fundamental interest in maintaining a free and open educational system that provides for the acquisition of useful knowledge."[91]

In *Board of Education, Island Trees Union Free School District No. 26 v. Pico*,[92] the Supreme Court ruled on the validity of a school board's authority to remove books from the library. Concluding that a number of books in their senior and junior high school libraries were objectionable, school board officials had directed removal of the books. A group of students filed suit, challenging the board's action as a violation of the students' First Amendment rights. The Court ruled in favor of the students.

The Supreme Court found that the motives of the school board in removing the books were essential in determining the validity of their actions.[93] The Court resolved that the school board could not remove books from the library simply because they disliked their content and sought by their removal to "prescribe what shall be orthodox in politics, nationalism, religion, or other matters of opinion."[94] However, the school board could remove books if the books lacked "educational suitability" or if they contained "pervasiv[e] vulgar[ity]."[95]

The decision in *Pico*, however, was limited in its future application. First, it applied only to the *removal* of library books, not to the *selection* of them. School authorities still possess considerable discretion in choosing the contents of libraries.[96] Second, the rights of the students were not extended into the classroom.[97] Therefore, school authorities still have considerable control in the classroom.

However, in *Roberts v. Madigan*,[98] the conclusions reached in *Pico* were used to prohibit the removal of the Bible from a public school library. The federal court held:

> In this age of enlightenment, it is inconceivable that the Bible should be excluded from a school library. The Bible is regarded by many to be a major work of literature, history, ethics, theology, and philosophy. . . . To deprive a public school library's collection of the Bible would, in the

language of Justice Robert Jackson, render the educational process "eccentric" and incomplete.[99]

In matters of *curriculum*, the school board has almost absolute discretion based on their perceived "duty to inculcate community values."[100] Because of the magnitude of the government interest at stake, courts have tended to be very deferential to the school authorities. As a result, student First Amendment challenges to the school curriculum have almost always failed.

An exception is found in *Pratt v. Independent School District*.[101] In *Pratt*, the public school board removed a film from its English curriculum. The students asserted that this burdened their right to receive information. The federal appellate court found that the "students had a right to be free from official conduct that was intended to suppress the ideas expressed in the films."[102]

The *Pratt* court stated that what was at stake was "the right to receive information and to be exposed to controversial ideas — a fundamental first amendment right."[103] They went on to say that a school board must establish that a "substantial and reasonable government interest exists for interfering with the student's right to receive information to show that they acted constitutionally."[104]

However, the court in *Pratt* took into account the motives of the school board to suppress any classroom instruction that opposed their traditional orthodox views. Also, since *Pratt* involved a film as opposed to a traditional curriculum resource such as a textbook, it may not apply to other cases involving challenges to the traditional curriculum. As a general rule, courts will find that the school has a substantial interest in controlling the curriculum.

EXCUSAL ON RELIGIOUS GROUNDS

The Supreme Court has not yet ruled on whether children may be excused from attending specific courses or using specific course materials which the parents and children find burdensome to their free exercise of religion. Although the excusal issue is discussed in detail in chapter 14, it is important in the context of a student rights discussion. Among the recent lower court cases, there have been mixed results.

In *Mozert v. Hawkins County Board of Education*,[105] fundamentalist Christian school children and their parents maintained that certain public school textbooks contained themes that directly contradicted their basic beliefs and thus violated their rights under the Free Exercise Clause.[106] They requested that the school accommodate their religious beliefs by allowing the children to "opt-out" of the school's reading program and receive reading instruction from their parents at home.

The federal court held that mere exposure to religiously objectionable material does not burden a student's free exercise rights.[107] The court found that unless the student is compelled to act pursuant to the viewpoints presented, or to affirm or disaffirm those beliefs, there is no unconstitutional burden on their free exercise of religion.[108]

Other courts have viewed the rights of religious people more favorably. For example, in *Spence v. Bailey*,[109] a public high school student was allowed to "opt-out" of a compulsory Reserve Officer Training Corps program (R.O.T.C.) based on his religious convictions. The state law required that every student complete either a year of physical education or R.O.T.C. Since this student attended a school which did not have a physical education class, he would have been forced either to participate in R.O.T.C. or forfeit his diploma. The court rightly concluded that this was a choice he should not be forced to make.

Also, in *Moody v. Cronin*,[110] students were allowed to "opt-out" of a coed gym class based on their religious beliefs. The students' religious beliefs mandated that they not be exposed to members of the opposite sex while wearing immodest attire and, therefore, they could not attend the class. The federal court found that the state's interest in requiring the children to participate in the gym classes did not outweigh the free exercise rights of either the children or their parents.

FORUM ANALYSIS

The type of forum in which a student's speech is made is critical in determining the outcome of any given case. School authorities have differing degrees of control over a student's speech based on the forum involved. The more authority school officials have in a given forum, the less free expression a student will have.

The two types of forums which currently exist in public schools are limited public and nonpublic forums. The student's right to free expression is significantly greater in a limited public forum than in a nonpublic forum. In a limited public forum, school officials must justify any decision to punish or prohibit student speech based on the *Tinker* two-part analysis.[111] In a nonpublic forum, school authorities have considerable discretion in controlling students' speech. It is, as the Supreme Court noted in *Hazelwood School District v. Kuhlmeier*,[112] the students in a nonpublic forum who must prove that the restraint on their speech is invalid.[113]

To ascertain under which forum any particular student expression falls, it must be determined whether the school is merely "tolerating" the student speech or is affirmatively "promoting" the speech.[114] A school "tolerates" speech when it is a student's personal expression which happens to occur on the school premises,[115] or when the student's personal speech occurs in a limited public forum which the school has "by policy or by practice" created.[116] A school "promotes" speech when it occurs in "school-sponsored publications, theatrical productions, and other expressive activities that students, parents, and members of the public might reasonably perceive to bear the imprimatur of the school."[117]

In addition to "bearing the imprimatur of the school," a school-sponsored expressive activity should be considered "part of the school curriculum."[118] This pertains to activities which "are supervised by faculty members and [are] designed to impart particular knowledge or skills to student participants and audiences."[119] It is not restricted to activities which occur in the traditional classroom setting.[120]

LIMITED PUBLIC FORUM

The *Tinker* standards for regulating speech are applicable to public forums which a school creates.[121] Student-initiated speech which happens to occur on the school premises is also within *Tinker's* protection.[122] School authorities can only silence the student's expression if it constitutes a material disruption or invades the rights of others.[123]

"The mere fact that student speech occurs on school property does not make it government supported."[124] Students, who are required to be in school, have the protection of the First Amendment while they are lawfully in attendance. The Supreme Court in *Tinker* noted that whether "in the cafeteria, or on the playing field, or on the campus during the authorized hours, a student may express his or her opinions."[125]

When a public school has created a limited public forum by opening it up to some individuals or groups, the school cannot prohibit others from speaking based on the content of their speech.[126] However, the school can require that the speaker be a member of the class of speakers for whose benefit the forum was created:[127] there must be an "equality of status in the field of ideas."[128] Without this, the school would be free to create forums open only to favored ideas.

If discussions which occur in a limited forum arouse emotions, the speaker (student) should still be constitutionally protected.[129] Although the school administrator has a right to maintain order, this should be done by quieting those who are interfering with the speaker's right to speak.[130] The speaker should not be compelled to be silent.[131]

Religious expression should especially be protected. The Supreme Court has long held that schools are supposed to teach "tolerance of divergent political and *religious* views."[132] For a school not to tolerate a student's religious expression because of possible dissension among students would be a blatant infringement on the student's guaranteed First Amendment rights.

NONPUBLIC FORUM

Restrictions on student speech which occurs in a school-sponsored activity is considered self-restraint on the part of the school.[133] To hold otherwise would be allowing the school to exercise prior restraint on student speech.[134] Since free speech is protected from prior restraint, this would be constitutionally impermissible.[135]

Educators have authority over school-sponsored expressive activities of students that *first*, "might reasonably [be] perceive[d] to bear the imprimatur of the school";[136] and, *second*, are considered part of the school curriculum ("whether or not they occur in a traditional classroom setting") so long as "they are supervised by faculty members and [are] designed to impart particular knowledge or skills to student participants and audiences."[137]

When a public school contributes its name and resources to an activity, the Supreme Court has held it is important the school have sufficient control over that activity.[138] The Supreme Court has mandated that a school needs to be able to ensure that: (1) the students learn the necessary lessons, (2) readers and listeners are not exposed to material that may be inappropriate for their level of maturity, and, (3) the public does not mistakenly attribute a student's views to the school.[139]

However, it is essential that a school avoid the appearance of having created a public forum for student expression when in fact it has not.[140] This could easily lead the audience to conclude erroneously that *all* student ideas have been presented.[141] In addition, the school would be transmitting a powerful message that the omitted ideas are not important.[142]

In determining the degree of control which a school has over a student's speech, the Supreme Court has noted that a balance must be struck between the student's right to convey his or her message and the recipient's environment.[143] While the school may not suppress a specific point of view, it may regulate the form of that speech in light of the environment.[144] This is primarily to avoid having the student speech be conveyed in an indecent or other inappropriate manner.

An example of this is found in *Bethel School District No. 403 v. Fraser*.[145] In *Fraser*, a student was suspended after delivering a speech at a school assembly nominating another student for elective office. During the entire speech, the student referred to his candidate "in terms of an elaborate, graphic, and explicit sexual metaphor."[146] The Supreme Court found that the speech created a substantial disruption of the school-sponsored student assembly.

If there is a captive or juvenile audience present, the school authorities may control the content of the student's speech in a school-sponsored activity. The restrictions must be "reasonably related to a legitimate pedagogical concern."[147] For example, a school may restrict speech which is aimed at inciting violence toward a particular minority.

The public school's regulations must be a reasonable exercise of the school official's discretion.[148] When considering whether the school's reason for censoring a student's speech is a legitimate pedagogical concern, the courts will generally give deference to school authorities.[149] However, this deference ends when the school's restrictions "directly and sharply implicate basic constitutional values"[150] such as freedom of speech and the free exercise of religion.

Although school authorities have a legitimate interest in regulating student activities which "bear the imprimatur" of the school, a school may restrict student religious speech *only* if the speech will be attributed to the school, resulting in an Establishment Clause violation. Since, as the Supreme Court recognized in *Mergens,* high school students are able to distinguish personal from school-sponsored expression,[151] personal student religious speech which occurs in an official forum should be protected. Any apprehension which the school might have regarding the Establishment Clause can easily be overcome by the school putting a disclaimer on the student's speech.[152] However, it must be emphasized that such a disclaimer can create an atmosphere and perception of inequality and can result in a discriminatory attitude by public school officials against certain students.

9

The Rights of Faculty

*It can hardly be argued either that students or teachers shed
their constitutional rights . . . at the schoolhouse gate.*

—Justice Abe Fortas,
*Tinker v. Des Moines Independent
School District,*
393 U.S. 503, 506 (1969).

The First Amendment, as interpreted and defined by the United States
Supreme Court, means that the government (and, therefore, the public
school) has no authority to restrict expression because of "its message, its
ideas, its subject matter, or its content."[1] As the Supreme Court has said:

> It is the purpose of the First Amendment to preserve an uninhibited mar-
> ketplace of ideas in which truth will ultimately prevail, rather than to
> countenance monopolization of that market, whether it be by the gov-
> ernment itself or a private license.[2]

By limiting the governmental interference with freedom of speech,
inquiry, and association (thereby necessitating freedom of expression), the
Constitution protects *all* persons, no matter what their calling—including
public school *teachers*. As Justice William O. Douglas once said:

> [T]he counselor, whether priest, parent, or *teacher*, no matter how small
> his audience—these too are beneficiaries of freedom of expression.[3]

The Supreme Court has also stated: "Any inhibition of freedom of
thought, and of action upon thought in the case of teachers brings the safeguards of those amendments [First and Fourteenth] vividly into operation."[4]
Teachers need always to be "free to inquire, to study and to evaluate, to gain
new maturity and understanding."[5] This is part and parcel of the nation's

deep commitment to "safeguarding academic freedom" in the public schools, or what the Supreme Court has called the "marketplace of ideas."[6]

ACADEMIC FREEDOM: THE FREEDOM TO TEACH

The Supreme Court has referred with approval to academic freedom as "the principle that individual instructors are at liberty to teach that which they deem to be appropriate in the exercise of their professional judgment."[7] Interpreted broadly, this freedom involves and protects both students and faculty. It is the collective freedom of the faculty member to teach free from pressure, penalties, or other threats by authorities or other persons inside or outside their institutions of learning. It is the freedom of the student to be taught by unrestrained teachers and to have access to all available data pertinent to the subject of study at an appropriate educational level.[8]

Although the Supreme Court has not directly ruled on whether public school teachers possess academic freedom, the Supreme Court has noted that academic freedom is "a special concern of the First Amendment."[9] In interpreting this, most lower courts have determined that public school teachers are vested with academic freedom in the classroom.[10] As one federal appellate court stated: "[Teachers] cannot be made to simply read from a script prepared or approved by the [school] board."[11]

This right, however, is not absolute. It must be balanced against the interest of school authorities in protecting what they consider are the "impressionable" minds of young people from any form of propagandism in the classroom.[12] This does not apply to the *dissemination of information* to students, but rather to the *indoctrination* of the students by the teacher.[13] For example, if a teacher attempts to use the classroom as a platform to advocate beliefs which undermine basic school principles, school authorities would be justified in placing restrictions on that teacher.

A teacher will rarely be discharged for exercising his or her academic freedom. The academic freedom would have to be carried to such a point that the teacher is clearly no longer useful as an instructor.[14] This might occur if the teacher uses excessive class time to discuss topics unrelated to the subject matter[15] and neglects to communicate to the students a substantial portion of the subject matter which the teacher has been assigned to teach.

Any restrictions on a teacher's academic freedom should have clear guidelines which the teacher can follow. One federal court notes: "When a teacher is forced to speculate as to what conduct is permissible and what conduct is proscribed, he is apt to be overly cautious and reserved in the classroom. Such a reluctance on the part of the teacher to investigate and experiment with new and different ideas is anathema to the entire concept of academic freedom."[16]

For instance, an order by public school authorities for a teacher to cease from discussing all religion in the classroom might violate the constitutional freedom of the teacher. It would be an unconstitutional inhibition of religion and a form of hostility not permitted. (See the discussion of inhibition and hostility in chapter 3.) An example of this would be forbidding a teacher to include relevant historical facts that pertain to the subject matter merely because of the religious nature of such facts.

Allowing school officials to exclude completely a particular idea or ideology from the classroom runs the risk of "cast[ing] a pall of orthodoxy over the classroom."[17] Various federal courts have held that administrative censorship "has an unmistakable tendency to chill that free play of the spirit which all teachers ought especially to cultivate and practice."[18] In this respect, the Supreme Court has warned that the danger of a "chilling effect upon the exercise of vital First Amendment rights must be guarded against by sensitive tools which clearly inform teachers what is being proscribed."[19]

FREEDOM OF EXPRESSION

In *Tinker v. Des Moines Independent School District*,[20] the Supreme Court stated that free expression is guaranteed in the public schools where it (1) does not materially and substantially interfere with the requirements of appropriate discipline in the operation of the school, and (2) does not invade the rights of others.[21] Although the Supreme Court in *Tinker* spoke directly to the rights of students, the Supreme Court indirectly recognized the rights of faculty.[22] This fact has been recognized by some lower federal courts.[23]

Following the decision in *Tinker* (see chapter 8), a federal appeals court in *James v. Board of Education*[24] applied the *Tinker* test to a high school teacher's freedom of expression as guaranteed in the First Amendment.[25] In *James*, a high school teacher wore a black arm band into the classroom to protest the Vietnam War. The teacher's action, like the actions of the students in *Tinker*, was religiously motivated.[26]

The court concluded that the teacher's conduct was a permissible form of symbolic speech. First, the expression passed the two-part *Tinker* test because it did not materially and substantially jeopardize the maintenance of order and discipline in the school, and it did not invade the rights of others. Second, the expression did not interfere with the teacher's obligations to teach. Although the teacher had more persuasive influence over a "captive" student audience than would another student, the teacher was not coercive and did not "arbitrarily inculcate doctrinaire views in the minds of students."[27] The high school students were able to distinguish between a teacher's personal views and those of the school board.[28]

For school authorities to restrict a teacher's speech, they must demonstrate a "reasonable" basis for concluding that the teacher's speech threatens to impair the interests of the school.[29] The *James* court held: "Unfettered discretion to violate [the teacher's] fundamental constitutional rights cannot be given to the school board."[30] Unfettered discretion could lead to suppression of a teacher's speech by school authorities based upon the prejudices of the particular community.[31]

Even if school authorities disagree with a teacher's philosophies, the teacher's constitutional right to free speech is protected. As the Supreme Court has made very clear, "the vigilant protection of constitutional freedoms is nowhere more vital than in the community of American schools."[32] Under the First Amendment, school officials, as the Supreme Court in *Tinker* held, cannot suppress expression of beliefs and feelings with which they do not wish to contend.[33] Also, school officials cannot constitutionally abridge freedom of speech to obviate slight inconveniences or annoyances.[34]

WEARING RELIGIOUS GARB

One form of expression which has from time to time been brought before the courts has been the wearing of religious garb by teachers in the classroom.[35] Religious garb refers to any dress, mark, emblem, or insignia indicating that a teacher is a member or follower of any religious order, sect, or denomination.

Generally, a teacher has been allowed to wear religious garb because it merely announces that the wearer holds a particular religious belief without proselytizing to that belief.[36] A teacher cannot be excluded from teaching based solely on his or her religious beliefs. Therefore, wearing religious garb alone is not sufficient to exclude a teacher from teaching.[37]

Where the state or school board has expressly chosen to restrict the wearing of religious garb, the courts will usually uphold the restriction.[38] However, the state generally only restricts the wearing of religious dress as a regular or frequently repeated practice.[39] Occasional wearing of religious dress is permissible under most circumstances, especially if it is part of a seasonal ceremonial recognition.

CURRICULUM

School boards are generally given considerable discretion to establish the content of courses taught in public schools.[40] This arrangement is based on the magnitude of the government interest at stake. Public high school teachers generally cannot override the authority of the school board by selecting the content of their instructional programs or by omitting items from the prescribed course content.[41]

A number of reasons have been put forth to support the absolute discretion of school officials in matters of curriculum. The Supreme Court has found that this discretion is necessary because of the school's "duty to inculcate community values."[42] Another reason is that state laws often impose very intricate standards for curriculum and course offerings which the local school boards must follow.[43] Courses, curricula, and textbooks are at the core of any educational program and are the chief instruments used in educating students.

Although the government has the prerogative of prescribing the curriculum for the public schools, it may not, as the Supreme Court has held, "impose upon the teachers in its schools *any* conditions that it chooses, however restrictive they may be of constitutional guarantees."[44] Teachers are not able to carry out their task of educating the youth if the conditions necessary for the development of responsible and critical minds are suppressed.[45] For example, the Supreme Court has indicated that it would not be constitutionally permissible to punish a teacher for informing students that there are other approaches to a given subject.[46]

Teachers are at liberty to utilize appropriate methods and means in teaching the curricular subject matter.[47] The courts have generally held that high school and university teachers have broad discretion in choosing study materials, even to the point of defying higher school authorities.[48] Because of their unique relationship to a class of students, teachers are in a superior position to know what methods will be most effective with each particular class.

Teachers who are conscientiously opposed to giving certain types of instruction based on their *religious* beliefs should be accommodated.[49] The Supreme Court has held that one cannot be forced to forsake or alter religious beliefs in order to secure a state benefit.[50] Therefore, a teacher should not be forced to violate his or her religious beliefs in order to receive the benefit of employment in the public school system. However, the state can override the teacher's religious rights if the state has a "compelling interest" in the instruction being given and the state pursues this interest by the "least restrictive means."

The school board may have a strong interest in having a teacher instruct students on the assigned curriculum. However, an objecting teacher can easily be accommodated by exchanging assignments with a nonobjecting teacher.[51]

RELIGIOUS INSTRUCTION

The Supreme Court has found both the study of the Bible and the study of comparative religion to be consistent with the First Amendment.[52] In *Abington School District v. Schempp,*[53] the Court expressly acknowledged that the Bible could certainly be "worthy of study for its literary and historic qualities" and that "it might well be said that one's education is not complete without a study of comparative religion or the history of religion and its relationship to the advancement of civilization."[54]

While courses on religion are seldom offered in the public elementary and secondary schools, it is often important for a teacher to illustrate to students how religion affects other subject matter. Indeed, it becomes increasingly difficult to respect a system of education that leaves students ignorant of the currents of religious thought that move not only their own country, but world societies as well.[55]

The religious matters which a teacher discusses should be reasonably related to the subject being taught. Once objective criteria are set out by the school authorities, any expression that is pertinent to the subject is protected unless the government can justify the suppression.[56] According to case law, references to religious matters in the public schools are permissible if (1) they are presented objectively; (2) no disruption occurs; and, (3) they are relevant to the subject matter.[57] Relevancy is rarely a problem if what is being communicated relates to curriculum material.

Teachers, however, cannot engage in religious indoctrination or proselytizing,[58] nor can they introduce religious activities into the class.[59] Public school teachers instead must take a position of neutrality regarding religion, and they must abide by the Establishment Clause principles discussed in previous chapters. For example, if a teacher attempted to distribute Bibles, this would most likely show favoritism of one religion over another, and it would violate the First Amendment.[60]

One federal district court has recommended guidelines for schools that decide to implement a comparative religion or Bible study class. These are: (1) the school board should have complete control of curriculum materials and instructors; (2) the board should hire certified and qualified teachers with no inquiry made as to their religious views; (3) the board should offer the course as an elective; and, (4) the board should ensure that instruction is objective.[61]

THE NONSTUDENT MEDIUM OF TEACHING

In the seminal case of *Wilson v. Chancellor,*[62] the issues concerning the access of nonstudents to the public high school campus were addressed. In this case, a federal district court held that a public high school board of education order banning "all political speakers" from access to the school campus was unconstitutional because the order infringed on the students' "right to hear."[63] Most importantly, however, the court ruled that the order was violative of the teacher's freedom of expression by affecting his use of speakers as a medium of teaching.[64] Furthermore, the court ruled that the order violated the teacher's Fourteenth Amendment right to equal protection of the laws and that the order existed to silence an unpopular viewpoint (in this case, the communist viewpoint).[65]

The decision in *Wilson* recognizes that the *methods and medium* utilized to teach a course are included within the teacher's right to academic freedom.[66] The court stated:

> The act of teaching is a form of expression, and the methods used in teaching are media. Wilson's [the teacher] use of . . . speakers was his medium for teaching.[67]

The *Wilson* court applied the two-part *Tinker* test to the situation where a teacher invites an off-campus speaker into the classroom. After careful analysis, the court found no material disruptions in classroom work or invasions of the rights of others.[68] The court held that simply espousing an unpopular viewpoint was no reason to restrict a speaker from the classroom.[69] The court said:

> [N]either fear of voter reaction nor personal disagreement with views to be expressed justifies a suppression of free expression of material and substantial interference with the educational process.[70]

TEACHER ACTION AS STATE ACTION

For the religious expression of a public school teacher to violate the First Amendment's prohibition against the establishment of religion, the teacher's expression must constitute "state action." State action exists when the state sponsors or mandates religion.[71] For example, state action would exist where the school *requires* daily Bible readings by all teachers.

Although a teacher is an employee of the public school, this does not mean that all expression by the teacher has been sponsored or mandated by the school. The school's interest must be balanced against the teacher's individual right to academic freedom and free expression in both public and private speech.[72]

In *Breen v. Runkel*,[73] a federal district court found that when teachers are acting in their capacity as classroom teachers, they are "state actors" for purposes of Establishment Clause analysis.[74] In *Breen*, the teachers were praying in their classrooms, reading from the Bible, and telling stories that had a biblical basis. The court found these activities to be an Establishment Clause violation. They reasoned that "Establishment Clause limitations placed on public schools outweigh whatever free speech or free exercise claims could have been asserted by individual teachers."[75]

However, not all expression made by teachers while teaching in the classroom is "state action." In *James v. Board of Education*,[76] the federal appellate court found the teacher's act of wearing an arm band in religious protest while *in the classroom* during regular classroom hours to be a form of personal expression.[77] In *James*, the court upheld the teacher's right to wear the arm band in direct opposition to the request by the school that he remove it.

The doctrine of academic freedom also negates the argument that a public school teacher is always an agent of the state for the purposes of implicating Establishment Clause concerns. Since academic freedom allows the teacher discretion within the classroom to express himself or herself and to plan the medium through which to teach the class, the conclusion is that such expression on the part of the teacher is technically "private" action, not state action. Therefore, teacher action which is protected under academic freedom does not necessarily implicate the state in such a way as to constitute "state action."

In *Williams v. Eaton*,[78] the federal appellate court held that "teacher action" can only be "state action" "if the State has been significantly involved by [the teacher's] actions."[79] A school is not significantly involved by a teacher's personal freedom of expression or a teacher's expression which results from the doctrine of academic freedom. Therefore, "teacher action" is pure "state action" only when the teacher is conveying to the students information which the school specifically mandates the teacher to convey.

INFORMAL DISCUSSIONS ABOUT RELIGION WITH STUDENTS

Teachers may discuss religious matters with their students on an *individual* basis. In *Roman v. Appleby*,[80] a federal district court found that a public school guidance counselor had a First Amendment right to discuss religion as well as other sensitive topics with a student. Since teachers have the same First Amendment rights as counselors, they have the same rights in regard to students.

Roman held that the only restrictions on the discussions are that the student initiate the topic and that the student not be compelled or forced to discuss the subject or to accept the teacher's views.[81] This is to eliminate the possibility of a teacher using his or her position to coerce an otherwise unwilling student into a conversation on religion.

The ability of the school district to restrict a teacher's right to freedom of expression also varies with the circumstances under which the expression is made.[82] In *Texas State Teachers Association v. Garland Independent School District*,[83] a federal court of appeals, making a distinction between classroom instructional time and "contract time," concluded that teachers have more leeway to discuss religion with other teachers during "contract time."[84] (Contract time is the time when a teacher is required to be on the school premises but is not involved in classroom instruction.) This, coupled with the fact that a teacher has a "captive" student audience during classroom time, leads to the conclusion that teachers will also have more freedom to discuss religion with students during "contract" time.

RIGHTS OF TEACHERS TO HOLD RELIGIOUS MEETINGS ON CAMPUS

A school district cannot prohibit discussions promoting religion or that are proselytizing in nature among teachers when they are not involved in actual classroom instruction.[85] However, the school board may prohibit teachers from holding organized meetings on campus for religious purposes if the school's general policy does not allow teachers to meet except for school business.[86]

For teachers to conduct religious meetings on the school campus, the school must have created a limited public forum. (See the discussion of a limited public forum in chapter 6.) To create this forum, the school must only allow teachers to conduct meetings unrelated to school business on the school premises. Once this forum has been created, the school cannot then discriminate against use of the building on the basis of religion.[87]

RELIGIOUS ACTIVITIES OUTSIDE THE SCHOOL ENVIRONMENT

The Supreme Court has spoken clearly in defense of the First Amendment rights of public school teachers outside the classroom. The teacher's freedom of association and the right to speak freely outside the classroom are securely established.[88] The court decisions indicate that teachers may only be terminated from their jobs for exercising their constitutional rights outside the school premises when the school administration can show that the teacher's expression has either (1) substantially interfered with the teacher's ability to perform his or her duties in the classroom, or (2) interfered with the regular operation of the school.[89]

In making the showing, the administration must rely on reasonable inferences drawn from solid facts, not on the mere apprehension or speculation that commotion or interferences will occur. There must be actual disciplinary problems in the classroom or a blatant disrespect for the teacher which interferes with the learning process.[90] An adverse attitude toward the teacher by parents is not sufficient.[91]

Since teachers have the same rights of association and of free speech as everyone else away from the school environment, it follows that they have the same rights to religious expression as well. Therefore, a teacher should be able to exercise his or her constitutional right, for example, to attend church or lead an off-campus Bible study, even in the presence of a student.

FREE EXPRESSION AND DISCHARGE SITUATIONS

The Supreme Court has clearly held that a public high school or university teacher has a First Amendment right to express views on matters of public concern.[92] To determine whether a teacher's view pertains to a public issue, a court will consider the content, form, and context of the speech.[93] One federal court of appeals has held: "The focus is on the role the employee has assumed in advancing the particular expressions: That of a concerned public citizen, informing the public that the state institution is not properly discharging its duties, or engaged in some way in misfeasance, malfeasance or nonfeasance; or merely as an employee, concerned only with internal policies or practices which are of relevance only to the employees of that institution."[94]

Courts have generally concluded that comments related to political advocacy,[95] collective bargaining,[96] and school policies regarding the welfare of the school and student body[97] are issues of public interest. However, complaints about individual work assignments,[98] personal attacks on superiors,[99] and private employment disputes[100] have not been considered issues of public interest.

If it is found that the teacher's speech is on a matter of public concern, the teacher's right to free expression will be balanced against the asserted interest of the school in controlling the workplace.[101] The state bears the burden of demonstrating that the teacher's discharge was based on legitimate grounds.[102] As the Supreme Court has stated:

> Vigilance is necessary to ensure that public employers do not use authority over employees to silence discourse, not because it hampers public functions but simply because superiors disagree with the content of the employees' speech.[103]

The teacher may voice a public concern even if it involves the administration of the school. The relationship between the teacher and principal is not "of such a personal and intimate nature that certain forms of criticism of the superior by the subordinate would seriously undermine the effectiveness of the working relationship between them."[104]

Teachers should be able to speak on issues relating to religious expression in the public schools and universities and not lose their jobs. Two examples might be: (1) a teacher criticizing a school for not allowing a student-initiated group to meet on campus, or (2) a teacher publicizing the fact that either the school or individual teachers are involved in religious indoctrination, such as meditation or visualization.

10

The Rights of Nonstudents

Once a forum is opened up to assembly or speaking by some groups, government may not prohibit others from assembling or speaking on the basis of what they intend to say.

—Justice Thurgood Marshall,
Police Department of Chicago v. Mosely,
408 U.S. 92, 96 (1972).

Although nonstudents' rights of access to the university or public school campus are intertwined with the rights of students and faculty, nonstudents possess rights independent of these two classes of persons.

FORUM ANALYSIS AND PUBLIC SCHOOLS

In resolving the issue of access to public school campuses by nonstudents, it is necessary to determine whether a school has created a forum, and if so, what type. The Supreme Court has identified three types of forums (see discussion of public forum issues in chapter 6): the traditional public forum, the limited public forum (created by government designation), and the nonpublic forum.[1] Each type of forum carries its own standards and regulations as to what constitutes legitimate communication within it.

"Traditional public forums are those places which 'by long tradition or by government fiat have been devoted to assembly and debate.'"[2] In traditional public forums, the state may enforce a content-based exclusion of a communicative activity if it shows "that its regulation is necessary to serve a compelling state interest and that it is narrowly drawn to achieve that end."[3]

> The State may also enforce regulations of the time, place, and manner of expression which are content-neutral, are narrowly tailored to serve a significant government interest, and leave open ample alternative channels of communication.[4]

A second type of public forum consists of public property which the state has opened for use by the public as a place for expressive activity.[5] A public forum may be created for a limited purpose such as use by certain groups or for the discussion of certain subjects.[6] As long as the state retains the open character of the facility, it is bound by the same standards which apply in a traditional public forum.[7]

Public property which is not a traditional or limited forum for public communication represents the third type of forum. "In addition to time, place, and manner regulations, the State may reserve the [nonpublic] forum for its intended purposes, communicative or otherwise, as long as the regulation on speech is reasonable and not an effort to suppress expression merely because public officials oppose the speaker's view."[8]

Public schools are classified under either the public forum or nonpublic forum category. "The public schools do not possess all of the attributes of streets, parks, and other traditional public forums that 'time out of mind, have been used for purposes of assembly, communicating thoughts between citizens, and discussing public questions.'"[9] A public school may, however, be a public forum for its students and teachers.[10] Moreover, if a public school is opened to the community for meetings and discussions, then it may become a public forum for the community as well.[11]

To determine the type of forum existing at a public school and its accompanying regulations, the practice and policy of the school district must be examined with regard to communicative use of the public school facilities. The Supreme Court has noted: "The government [for example, a public school district] does not create a public forum by inaction or by permitting limited discourse, but only by intentionally opening a nontraditional forum for public discourse."[12] Public school facilities may be deemed a limited public forum if school district practice or policy has opened the facilities for indiscriminate use by the general public, or by some segment of the public, such as student organizations.[13] If school authorities have instead reserved public school facilities for other intended purposes, "'communicative or otherwise,' then no public forum has been created, and school officials may impose reasonable restrictions on the speech of students, teachers, and other members of the school community."[14]

FREEDOM OF A PUBLIC FORUM AND NONPUBLIC FORUM

The freedom of a public forum and the nonpublic forum affords and opens, to some extent, the university or public campus to nonstudents or off-campus speakers. First Amendment freedoms, however, are not absolute. The Supreme Court has held that protected speech is not equally permissible in all places and at all times.[15] At the same time, the Supreme Court has mandated that even on public property which is not by tradition or designation a forum for public communication, regulation of speech must be reasonable and not an effort to suppress expression merely because public officials oppose the speaker's view.[16]

Any state statute or ordinance affecting the precious right of free speech must be narrowly tailored to its legitimate objective so as not to infringe upon protected rights.[17] The First Amendment does not permit the state to restrict the speech of some elements or classes of society in order to enhance the relative voices of others.[18] As the Supreme Court recognizes: "[T]he First Amendment means that government has no power to restrict expression because of its message, its ideas, its subject matter, or its content."[19] Indeed, discriminatory exclusion of an individual, individuals, or organization from a public forum on a university or public school campus based on the content of the intended speech is unconstitutional without a showing that such regulation is necessary to serve a compelling state interest and is narrowly drawn to achieve that end.[20]

In *Widmar v. Vincent*,[21] a university claimed that a compelling interest existed in its denial of the right of a religious student organization to meet on campus. The university argued that in complying with its duty to avoid establishing a religion, it had to deny campus access to religious organizations, even those that were student-sponsored.[22] The Supreme Court rebuffed this argument by stating: "It does not follow . . . that an 'equal access' policy would be incompatible with this Court's Establishment Clause cases."[23] Furthermore, the Court stated:

> The University has opened its facilities for use by student groups, and the question is whether it can now exclude groups because of the content of their speech. In this context we are unpersuaded that the primary effect of the public forum, open to all forms of discourses, would be to advance religion.[24]

Once the state (in the form of a public university or school system) opens its facilities to certain individuals or groups, it cannot *arbitrarily* prevent any members of the public from holding such meetings.[25] A federal district court in *Vail v. Board of Education*,[26] held that if a public high school provides a forum:

> [I]t must do so in a manner consistent with constitutional principles. Access to the podium must be permitted without discrimination. It is not for the school to control the influence of a public forum by censoring the ideas, the proponents, or the audience. The right of the student to hear a speaker cannot be left to the discretion of school authorities on a pick and choose basis.[27]

If *one* outside group or *one* outside speaker is regularly allowed onto the campus to speak on a noncurricular issue in classrooms or to assembled students, then the campus becomes a limited public forum for the discussion of that issue. As the Supreme Court has held: "To permit one side of a debatable public question to have a monopoly in expressing its views . . . is the antithesis of constitutional guarantees."[28] Once a school district determines that certain speech is appropriate for its students, "it may not discriminate between speakers who will speak on the topic merely because it disagrees with their views."[29]

Two related federal court cases[30] required a public school system to grant to a peace advocacy organization access similar to that granted to military recruiters. The peace organization sought an opportunity equal to that afforded military recruiters to place their literature on school bulletin boards and in the offices of school guidance officers and to participate in school "Career Days" and "Youth Motivation Days."[31]

In *Searcey v. Crim*,[32] a federal district court held that the peace organization must be allowed to utilize the limited public forum created in the guidance offices and bulletin boards.[33] The court noted that the policy and practice regarding the guidance offices and bulletin boards had been to hold them generally open to all groups and individuals that wished to offer students career, education, scholarship, or vocational information.[34] Therefore, the public school was required to allow students to have *all* available information to assist them in making valid career and post-secondary choices.

In *Searcey v. Harris*,[35] a federal appeals court ruled that a public school district policy governing participation in the "Career Day" program for students, which effectively barred the peace organization from participating along with military recruiters, was unconstitutional viewpoint discrimination. The school district had required participants in the career day to have "direct knowledge" of the career opportunities about which they spoke, to have "present affiliation" with the subject of the presentation, and to refrain from criticism of the career opportunities provided by other participants.[36] The court modified the no-criticism rule to permit school administrators to ban speech that would discourage students from entering a specific career by denigrating the nature or purpose of that career.[37] However, the federal court held that the regulations were unduly restrictive, perceiving that the regulations were designed either to deny directly or indirectly the participation of the peace organization in the forum.[38]

There are cases that have presented a more restrictive view of the creation of a public forum. For example, a federal appeals court held that the use of a public high school athletic field for Memorial Day services, a Special Olympics, and a "Bike Hike" to benefit the mentally retarded did not create a limited public forum for First Amendment activities.[39] Another federal court has noted: "Occasional use by outsiders . . . is not enough to make a college art gallery a public forum."[40] Moreover, in *May v. Evansville-Vanderburgh School Corporation*,[41] a federal appeals court remarked: "A college classroom (and *a fortiori* an elementary school classroom) does not become a public forum because a guest lecturer from the outside is invited to talk to the class."[42] However, regular access by nonstudent groups or individuals to public schools is a strong indication of the existence of a public forum.

In a nonpublic forum, the courts have routinely recognized that once a "school board determines that certain speech is appropriate for its students, it may not discriminate between speakers who will speak on the topic merely because it disagrees with their views."[43] In a nonpublic forum, the government enjoys considerably more power over the use of its property. However, the Supreme Court has noted that the state may not impose *content-based* restrictions which are unreasonable or which suppress expression merely because public officials oppose the speaker's viewpoints.[44]

For example, in *Gay Student Services v. Texas A&M University*,[45] a federal appeals court ordered a public university to recognize officially a gay student organization regardless of the type of forum in existence at the university. The university contended it had neither created a generally open forum for First Amendment expression nor a forum open to fraternal or social groups.[46] The university, however, admitted allowing other views of homosexuality to be presented on its campus.[47] Further, the record showed that the university recognized other groups that sought acceptance and integration of their particular lifestyle into the university community.[48] Therefore, in reaching its decision the court stated:

> We think that the denial of recognition to a student group wishing to express its own views on the same or similar subjects is clearly the sort of viewpoint based discrimination forbidden by *Perry [Education Association v. Perry Local Educators' Association]* in *any* type of public forum.[49]

The court thus highlighted the restriction placed on the government by the Constitution from suppressing free speech rights merely to oppose a speaker's viewpoint (regardless of the forum).

In *Greer v. Spock*,[50] the Supreme Court upheld the denial of access to two political candidates to distribute campaign literature and to hold a political meeting on a federal military reservation. The Court stated: "The fact that other civilian speakers and entertainers had sometimes been invited to appear at [the base] did not of itself serve to convert [the base] into a public forum or confer upon political candidates a First or Fifth Amendment right to conduct their campaigns there."[51] However, the Court noted that "there [was] no claim that the military authorities discriminated in any way among candidates for political office based upon the candidates' supposed political views."[52] The Court implied that if the base had previously allowed other political candidates on the base, denial of requests for similar access by subsequent politicians would have indicated viewpoint discrimination.[53] The principle articulated by the Supreme Court in *Greer* is that, even though a military reservation could impose content-based restrictions against political candidates, it could not suppress expression merely to oppose politicians' viewpoints.

It cannot be denied that public school officials must operate their schools in orderly fashion and must avoid substantial disruption of the educational process. However, as Supreme Court Justice Lewis Powell stated in *Healy v. James*:[54]

> Yet, the precedents of this court leave no room for the view that, because of the acknowledged need for order, First Amendment protections should apply with less force on the college campuses than in the community at large. Quite to the contrary, "[t]he vigilant protection of constitutional freedoms is nowhere more vital than in the community of American schools."[55]

However, public schools have certain authority to regulate speech as to time, place, and manner. Even in a public forum the government may .impose reasonable restrictions on the time, place, or manner of protected speech, provided the restrictions "are justified without reference to the content of the regulated speech, that they are narrowly tailored to serve a significant governmental interest, and that they leave open ample alternative channels for communication of the information."[56] For example, in *Texas Review Society v. Cunningham*,[57] a public university required that student newspapers containing ads by third parties be distributed from unmanned stands instead of in areas where student organizations maintained tables for distribution of literature. A federal district court held that this was a reasonable time, place, and manner regulation to ensure that the university be kept free from commercial hawkers and solicitations.[58] But the court also found that the regulation provided the students with two alternatives: (1) to remove the advertising and continue hand-to-hand distribution, or (2) to maintain the ads and distribute the paper from an unmanned receptacle, while keeping a copy of the paper at an organizational table and referring interested parties to the designated rack.[59] Thus, the students were left with ample alternative channels of distribution for their newspaper.

Public school authorities may as well impose prior restraints, to a limited extent, on the freedom of expression of off-campus speakers. The Supreme Court has held that a state may act to prohibit speech directed toward inciting or producing imminent lawless action and which is likely to accomplish that objective.[60] However, in the public school context, the Supreme Court has recognized that "undifferentiated fear or apprehension of disturbance is not enough to overcome the right to freedom of expression."[61] Absent a substantial constitutional reason for doing so, school authorities simply cannot censor and restrain speech as to content before there is a chance for expression.[62]

EQUAL PROTECTION

Although the constitutional right to freedom of a public forum has equal protection overtones, there are also cases which reach the same conclusion entirely upon Equal Protection Clause principles. The Fourteenth

Amendment Equal Protection Clause provides that persons must be treated equally under the law.

This constitutional principle was specifically applied by a federal district court in *Stacy v. Williams*[63] to campus student groups who invited outside speakers to lecture on *religious* subjects. This particular court reversed all the regulations of the University of Mississippi related to outside speakers on campus. Among the regulations considered by the court was one which provided that the facilities of the school could not be made available for public religious meetings or gatherings to off-campus persons or groups of person. The court invalidated this regulation by stating:

> But as this regulation can reasonably be construed to mean that no student religious group may invite outside speakers on religious topics, which prohibition would conflict with the Equal Protection Clause, it must be rejected.[64]

The federal court in *Stacy v. Williams* stated that if school officials are concerned that a lecture by an outside speaker might create the impression that the school system endorses his message, then the school can remedy this situation by requiring that before and after the speaker's presentation an announcement be made that the school does not endorse the speaker's statements.[65]

Stacy v. Williams thus clearly illustrates that "religion" is not a reasonable classification and that a state may not use the unreasonable classification of "religion" as a basis for exclusion from its public education facilities. To do so violates the rights of nonstudents to access to a public forum and equal protection under the law.

THE FREEDOM TO SPEAK

The freedom of nonstudent or off-campus speakers to utilize public and nonpublic forums in university or public school campuses is limited, as specifically noted in the Equal Access Act. (See the discussion of the Equal Access Act and nonstudents in chapter 11.) However, public school authorities cannot arbitrarily prevent members of the public from addressing student audiences. A public forum is created for outside speakers to speak on an issue in a public school if one outside group or one outside speaker is regularly allowed onto the campus to speak on a noncurricular issue. Therefore, in a nonpublic forum, school authorities may not impose content-based restrictions on expression merely to oppose the viewpoint of an outside speaker.

PART FOUR

Equal Access

[I]f a State refused to let religious groups use facilities open to others, then it would demonstrate not neutrality but hostility toward religion.

—Justice Sandra Day O'Connor,
*Mergens v. Board of Education
of the Westside Community Schools,*
110 S. Ct. 2356, 2371 (1990).

11

The Equal Access Act

[The Equal Access Act] means the school will have the [same] regulations for a religious club as for any other club, no more, no less.

—Senator Mark Hatfield

On August 11, 1984, President Reagan signed the Equal Access Act into law. The Act establishes a policy of nondiscrimination in the treatment of student groups which wish to meet during noninstructional time at public secondary schools. It was designed by Congress to clarify and confirm the rights of free speech, freedom of association, and the free exercise of religion, as well as other constitutional rights that accrue to public secondary school students.[1]

The Equal Access Act resulted from an outcry of public school students who were denied their right to free speech on a religious basis. Congress intended that the Act would restrain public school officials from this discriminatory censorship of religious speech. As Senator Jeremiah Denton declared: "We cannot permit the existence of policies or practices which single out religious students for invidious discrimination which makes [sic] them second-class citizens."[2]

Senator Denton went on to say that the Act had become necessary since school administrators felt constrained to prohibit and had canceled voluntary student meetings because of their religious content.[3] Similar sentiments were echoed by Senator Orrin Hatch who noted that "religious students are being told they cannot meet on the same basis as other clubs."[4] Senator Mark Hatfield, as well, affirmed the principle of equal treatment, stating that equal access "means the school will have the [same] regulations for a religious club as for any other club, no more, no less."[5]

The equal access principle, as originally conceptualized, resolved that public school policies should be content-neutral—that is, discrimination based on content of speech (even religious speech) would be prohibited.

Under the Act then, school officials are required to afford equal rights not only to traditional student groups (such as the chess club, drama club, science club, etc.), but also to students desiring to form clubs with religious themes or content.

School officials, of course, retain the authority to establish reasonable time, place, and manner restrictions on student activities. The Equal Access Act simply requires a nondiscriminatory application of the rules.[6]

THE HOSTILITY PROBLEM

During committee hearings on equal access, Congress heard testimony, by secondary school students from various states, that evidenced a pattern of hostility toward and discrimination against those who would exercise their constitutional rights in the public school context. Lisa Bender, named plaintiff in *Bender v. Williamsport Area School District*,[7] submitted to the Senate Judiciary Committee a letter from her high school's school board. That letter denied the right of a voluntary student club, "Petros," to meet on an equal basis with other student groups. Her response was: "[W]e saw in the Constitution that our freedom of speech was being denied us."[8]

Judy Jankowski of St. Paul, Minnesota, also testified:

A few years ago, I visited Poland with my family. We stayed with a family that had [sic] five children in school. I observed how restricted they were to express themselves politically and religiously, and I was thankful that I lived in the United States and that I had the freedom to express myself and share political and religious beliefs with others.

Now, just a few years later, I see the same restrictions put on me and my fellow classmates that are on the students in Poland, and I find this very disturbing.[9]

Bonnie Bailey of Lubbock, Texas, explained her feelings to the committee by stating:

We have been taught that the Constitution guarantees us freedom of speech. But we feel that here we have been discriminated against, because we can picket, we can demonstrate, we can curse, we can take God's name in vain, but we cannot voluntarily get together and talk about God on any part of our campus, inside or out of the school.

We just feel frustrated because we don't feel like we are being treated equally.[10]

Stuart McKinney from an Atlanta, Georgia, suburb explained that at North Clayton Junior High School, only religious clubs were singled out for discrimination although there were many other clubs:

North Clayton Junior High School offers students a wide range of extracurricular activities. These include the drama club, the beta club, FHA, math and science club, newspaper staff, student council, letterman's clubs, language clubs, chess club, plus a wide variety of sports related activities.

Membership in all of these clubs are [sic] . . . voluntary, yet none of the clubs were . . . affected as the Youth for Christ Club.[11]

Bonnie Bailey added:

At Monterey High School in Lubbock, Texas, for example, neither Y-Teens, an organization sponsored by Y.W.C.A. and opened to all girls regardless of their religious beliefs, nor Tri-H-Y, which is sponsored by Y.M.C.A., can hold any activities on school grounds, including benefit dances for the American Cancer Society.[12]

Prior to passage of the Equal Access Act, students such as these faced three important hurdles in their attempt to enjoy full protection of their First Amendment rights under the Constitution. First, there was the discretion exercised by school administrators who are often confused concerning the rights of religious students and requests for equal treatment. Students and parents often felt helpless as they petitioned school board attorneys who were either uninformed about the First Amendment or who, fearing costly litigation from interest groups opposed to free religious expression in the public schools, were overly conservative in their interpretation of the law.

Ultimately, the lengths to which school administrators had gone in order to avoid lawsuits became absurd. For example, one school district told its students that two or more of them could not sit together for the purpose of religious discussion.[13] Another school district prohibited students from praying together in a car in the school parking lot.[14] And in Washington, an assembly featuring professional athletes speaking about an important part of their lives, what made them successful, was not permitted because it was believed, *not* by the school board *but* by the American Civil Liberties Union (ACLU), to be too religious to be held during school hours.[15]

The activities of such groups as the ACLU, coupled with a confused and sometimes hostile school administration, often proved insurmountable to an unprotected student with limited resources. Even school boards favorable to religious student rights are persuaded by tight budgets and other tensions to relent to pressures from interest groups. In short, it was easier to be negative toward the students.

Second, students and their parents, as novices in civil rights matters, often faced the difficult, if not impossible, task of locating attorneys to defend religious student rights. Equal Access legislation was originally designed to solve this problem by encouraging United States attorneys to assist indigent students where a genuine case developed.[16]

Third, even when students find competent attorneys, there are conflicting federal circuit decisions on various aspects of the equal access question, some of which take a narrow view of the First Amendment rights of students.

Congress sought to overcome these hurdles through the Equal Access Act by codifying constitutional rights and by placing remedial measures within the student's reach.

THE EQUAL ACCESS ACT

In light of the problems discussed above, it is appropriate to examine the Equal Access Act. The following is a succinct sectional analysis.

TITLE 20—EDUCATION
SUBCHAPTER VIII—EQUAL ACCESS

§ 4071. DENIAL OF EQUAL ACCESS PROHIBITED

(a) Restriction of limited open forum on basis of religious, political, philosphical, or other speech content prohibited
   It shall be unlawful for any public secondary school which receives Federal financial assistance and which has a limited open forum to deny equal access or a fair opportunity to, or discriminate against, any students who wish to conduct a meeting within that limited open forum on the basis of the religious, political, philosophical, or other content of the speech at such meetings.

(b) "Limited open forum" defined
   A public secondary school has a limited open forum whenever such school grants an offering to or opportunity for one or more noncurriculum related student groups to meet on school premises during noninstructional time.

This section of the Act sets forth the fundamental equal treatment requirement that the Act places on public secondary schools. The Act is limited to those public secondary schools which receive federal financial assistance. There are very few, if any, public secondary schools which do not receive such assistance. Thus, the Act applies to virtually all such schools.

The Act leaves the definition of "secondary schools" to the state. Generally, secondary schools are comprised of grades nine through twelve, although some states define such schools as being grades seven through twelve or ten through twelve.

The phrase "to deny equal access or a fair opportunity to, or discriminate against" means that within the "limited open forum" the meeting rights of all students should be handled on an equal basis. This includes the meeting rights of religious students.

The phrase "conduct a meeting" is broad. The phrase recognizes that whatever is actually permitted by schools should pertain to student groups equally. The Supreme Court held in *Mergens v. Board of Education of the Westside Community Schools*[17] that the phrase means that student groups covered in the Act have equal access to *all* forums which other "noncurriculum related student groups" have access to, including *student newspapers, bulletin boards, public address systems,* and *annual school events.* It is *not* limited to meeting rooms.[18]

The last phrase of section 4071(a) ("on the basis of the religious, political, philosophical, or other content of speech at such meetings") includes not only religious speech, but applies to all speech content. This conforms with the Supreme Court's decision in *Widmar v. Vincent,*[19] which indicated that religious speech, including worship, has the same status as other types of speech.

One of the most important provisions of the Act is the concept of the limited open forum. A limited open forum is established both by what the school does in its practices as well as its policies. However, the Act may restrict the constitutional rights and freedoms of secondary school students more than the Constitution or cases such as *Tinker*[20] allow.

The existence and status of a limited open forum depends on the phrase in section 4071(b) which states, "whenever such a school grants" such a forum. The public secondary school decides whether or not it will have a limited open forum. Thus, a school is ostensibly free to adjust its forum to where it will not permit any limited open forums. However, in *Tinker* the students were essentially granted a forum by their mere presence in the school. They were restricted only if they exercised their freedom of expression in a way which materially or substantially disrupted or infringed on the rights of others.[21]

Section 4071(b) defines a limited open forum as existing when the school allows "one or more noncurriculum related student groups to meet on school premises during noninstructional time." Therefore, if the equal access principle of the Act is to apply, the student groups must be *unrelated* to the curriculum.

The phrase "noncurriculum related student groups" is left undefined in the Act. However, the Supreme Court in *Mergens,*[22] in upholding the constitutionality of the Act, concluded that the phrase "'noncurriculum related student groups' is best interpreted broadly to mean *any* student group that does not *directly* relate to the body of courses offered by the school."[23] This definition provides a low threshold for triggering the Act's requirements and is consistent with congressional intent to end the widespread discrimination against religious speech by students in the public school.[24]

"Noncurriculum related" does not refer *only* to organizations whose purpose is the advocacy of partisan theological, political, or ethical views.[25] Nor does it apply *only* to subjects that "cannot properly be included in a public school curriculum."[26] This would trigger the Act only if the school permitted "controversial" or "distasteful" groups to use its facilities.[27]

A student group will be found to relate directly to the school's curriculum if: (1) the subject matter of the group is actually taught, or will soon be taught, in a regularly offered course; (2) the subject matter of the group concerns the body of courses as a whole; (3) participation in the group is required for a particular course; or (4) participation in the group results in academic credit.[28]

For example, a French club would directly relate to the curriculum if French were included in the courses regularly offered by the school or if it would be offered in the near future. A school's student government would generally relate directly to the curriculum to the degree that it addresses concerns, solicits opinions, and formulates proposals concerning the body of courses offered by the school. If participation in a school's band were required for band class or resulted in academic credit, then it would also directly relate to the curriculum. These types of groups would not trigger the obligations of the Act.[29]

On the other hand, groups such as a stamp collecting club, a surfing club, a chess club, or a community service club will be considered "noncurriculum related student groups" for purposes of the Act, unless a school can show that such groups fall within the description of groups that directly relate to the curriculum. The existence of such groups creates a limited open forum and prohibits the school from denying equal access to other student groups on the basis of the content of their speech.[30]

A club is not "curriculum related" by being "remotely related to an abstract educational goal."[31] The *Mergens* Court held: "A curriculum-related student group is one that has more than just a tangential or attenuated relationship to courses offered by the school."[32] Otherwise, a school could circumvent the Act's requirements simply by describing all existing student groups as curriculum related.[33] Moreover, although the descriptions a school gives to the student activities should be considered, complete deference will *not* be given to the school in determining what activities are curriculum related.

The limited open forum concept appears to apply only to "noninstructional time." This is defined in section 4072(4) of the Act to mean "time set aside by the school before actual classroom instruction begins or after classroom instruction ends." Thus, any time during noninstructional hours (before or after school, lunch time, free periods, study halls, etc.), the student should be free to choose to participate in extracurricular activities—even if such activities have religious content.

It must be emphasized that on the question of whether religious groups (or other groups) may meet in a limited open forum during the school day, supporters of the Act were openly divided. However, from the face of the Act, it seems that such meetings should be allowed. Obviously, a court decision in favor of allowing such activities during the school day would be more consistent with the ultimate equal access principle of the Act.

(c) Fair opportunity criteria

Schools shall be deemed to offer a fair opportunity to students who wish to conduct a meeting within its limited open forum if such school uniformly provides that—

(1) the meeting is voluntary and student-initiated;

(2) there is no sponsorship of the meeting by the school, the government, or its agents or employees;

(3) employees or agents of the school or government are present at religious meetings only in a nonparticipatory capacity;

(4) the meeting does not materially and substantially interfere with the orderly conduct of educational activities within the school; and

(5) nonschool persons may not direct, conduct, control, or regularly attend activities of student groups.

These restrictions were designed to guarantee equal access to students while avoiding Establishment Clause problems for the school. As long as a school adopts an extracurricular program which implements these restrictions, the school comes within the "safe harbor" of the Act and should be protected against litigation.[34]

The "fair opportunity" requirement of section 4071(a) is mandatory if the Act is to be applied within a limited open forum to a particular school. If any of the five subparagraphs of section 4071(c) are *not* provided for by the school, then a fair opportunity does not exist, and the school is in violation of the Act.

Under sections 4071(c)(1) and (2), the meeting must be voluntary, student-initiated, with no "sponsorship" by "the school, the government, or its agents or employees." Moreover, section 4071(c)(3) mandates that employees or agents of the school (or government) may be present at "religious meetings only in a nonparticipatory capacity."

Sponsorship is defined in section 4072(2) as including "the act of promoting, leading, or participating in a meeting." The school must require that no school or government official promote, lead, or participate in any student meeting in the school's limited open forum.[35] However, the paragraph does not prohibit the presence of a teacher or other school employee at meetings to keep order. Section 4072(2) expressly allows such presence for "*custodial purposes.*"[36]

This requirement should not prohibit a school from announcing the meetings being held. If announcements are made for other extracurricular activities, then the principle of equal access, as the *Mergens* Court held, should mandate that announcements be made for all.[37]

Under section 4071(c)(3), employees or agents of the school or government may be present at religious meetings "only in a nonparticipatory capacity." Although the Act permits "[t]he assignment of a teacher, administrator, or other school employee to the meeting for monitoring purposes," this is merely to ensure good order and the protection of school property.

Section 4071(c)(4) provides that the meeting must not "materially and substantially interfere with the orderly conduct of educational activities within the school." The language of this section is adopted from the Supreme Court's 1969 decision in *Tinker v. Des Moines Independent Community School District.*[38]

In *Tinker,* the Supreme Court held that high school students may express themselves throughout the school day, even on controversial issues, as long as the expression does not "materially and substantially interfer[e] with the requirements of appropriate discipline in the operation of the school."[39] Therefore, the Equal Access Act does not seek to expand the scope of students' free speech rights any further than the limits previously established by the Supreme Court.

Section 4071(c)(5) provides that "nonschool persons may not direct, conduct, control, or regularly attend activities of student groups." Nonschool persons can mean various categories of nonstudents including youth workers, parents, and students from schools other than the school in which a student group is meeting. This requirement is an attempt to ensure that student groups be initiated, directed, conducted, and controlled by local students only.

(d) Construction of subchapter with respect to certain rights

Nothing in this subchapter shall be construed to authorize the United States or any State or political subdivision thereof—

(1) to influence the form or content of any prayer or other religious activity;

(2) to require any person to participate in prayer or other religious activity;

(3) to expend public funds beyond the incidental cost of providing the space for student-initiated meetings;

(4) to compel any school agent or employee to attend a school meeting if the content of the speech at the meeting is contrary to the beliefs of the agent or employee;

(5) to sanction meetings that are otherwise unlawful;

(6) to limit the rights of groups of students which are not of a specified numerical size; or

(7) to abridge the constitutional rights of any person.

This section of the Equal Access Act disclaims statutory authorization for certain activities by the government. However, the Act does not specifically prohibit the activities set forth in section 4071(d). The congressional concerns aired in this section are rather straightforward. The key words may be *require, compel, unlawful, limit, abridge,* and so on.

Two principles then emerge from this section. The first is the need to protect the rights of all, students and nonstudents alike, within the corridors of the public schools. Thus, all the meetings contemplated under the Act must be voluntary and without coercion by school authorities or the government. The second is the need to avoid state sponsorship while providing equal access. Finally, the Act protects voluntary student-initiated activity where students are seeking to meet with other students. As such, the Act should not be interpreted to violate or curtail the constitutional rights of students below the secondary level or the rights of teachers or nonstudents.

(e) Federal financial assistance to schools unaffected
Notwithstanding the availability of any other remedy under the Constitution or the laws of the United States, nothing in this title shall be construed to authorize the United States to deny or withhold Federal financial assistance to any school.

(f) Authority of schools with respect to order, discipline, well-being, and attendance concerns
Nothing in this subchapter shall be construed to limit the authority of the school, its agents or employees, to maintain order and discipline on school premises, to protect the well-being of students and faculty, and to assure that attendance of students at meetings is voluntary.

(Pub. L. 98-377, title VIII, § 802, Aug. 11, 1984, 98 Stat. 1302.)

SHORT TITLE
Section 801 of title VIII of Pub. L. 98-377 provided that: "This title [enacting this subchapter] may be cited as 'The Equal Access Act'."

The Equal Access Act does not authorize the withholding or denial of federal financial assistance to any public school. The loss of this important legal leverage means that persons with grievances under the Act must seek redress from the courts in actions for damages or injunctions based upon violations of the Act itself and/or related constitutional rights.

Section 4071(e) makes it clear that Congress was not attempting by way of the Act to diminish the role of the schools "to maintain order and discipline" and to protect students and teachers. Schools continue to maintain their conventional privileges of: (1) determining appropriate subjects of instruction, (2) prohibiting meetings that would "materially and substantially interfere with the orderly conduct of educational activities in the school," (3) avoiding the limitations of the Act by foregoing federal financial assistance.[40]

§ 4072. *Definitions*
As used in this subchapter—
(1) The term "secondary school" means a public school which provides secondary education as determined by State law.
(2) The term "sponsorship" includes the act of promoting, leading, or participating in a meeting. The assignment of a teacher, administrator, or other school employee to a meeting for custodial purposes does not constitute sponsorship of the meeting.
(3) The term "meeting" includes those activities of student groups

which are permitted under a school's limited open forum and are not directly related to the school curriculum.

(4) The term "noninstructional time" means time set aside by the school before actual classroom instruction begins or after actual classroom instruction ends.

(Pub. L. 98-377, title VIII, § 803, Aug. 11, 1984, 98 Stat. 1303.)

§ 4073. Severability

If any provision of this subchapter or the application thereof to any person or circumstances is judicially determined to be invalid, the provisions of the remainder of the subchapter and the application to other persons or circumstances shall not be affected thereby.

(Pub. L. 98-377, title VIII, § 804, Aug. 11, 1984, 98 Stat. 1304.)

§ 4074. Construction

The provisions of this subchapter shall supersede all other provisions of Federal law that are inconsistent with the provisions of this subchapter.

(Pub. L. 98-377, title VIII, § 805, Aug. 11, 1984, 98 Stat. 1304.)

These remaining sections are self-explanatory and were discussed earlier as appropriate.

CONSTITUTIONALITY OF THE EQUAL ACCESS ACT

In *Mergens v. Board of Education of the Westside Community Schools*,[41] the Supreme Court concluded that the Equal Access Act does not violate the Establishment Clause of the First Amendment. The Court decided this issue by an overwhelming majority of eight to one, leaving little doubt as to the rights of student religious groups in the public schools.

In *Mergens*, a group of high school students requested permission from school authorities to form a Christian club at the school. The proposed club would have the same privileges and meet on the same terms and conditions as other existing student groups, except that it would not have a faculty sponsor. The students' requests were denied by school officials.

The school officials concluded that a religious club at the school could only be mandated by the Equal Access Act, and that the Equal Access Act violated the Establishment Clause since it required schools to recognize religious clubs. The Court determined that the Equal Access Act did not violate the Establishment Clause and that the students were entitled to form a Christian club at Westside High School on the basis of the Act.

In determining the constitutionality of the Equal Access Act, the Court applied the *Lemon v. Kurtzman*[42] tripartite test. Under *Lemon*, the criteria for determining whether governmental action which involves religion is constitutional are: "First, the statute must have a secular legislative purpose;

second, its *principal* or *primary* effect must be one that neither advances nor inhibits religion; finally, the statute must not foster 'an excessive government entanglement with religion.'"[43]

First, the legislative purpose of the Equal Access Act—to prevent discrimination against religious *and* "political, philosophical, or other" speech—is indisputably secular.[44] Because the Act on its face evenhandedly grants equal access to both secular and religious speech, it is clear that the Act was not designed to "endorse or disapprove of religion."[45]

Moreover, allowing student-initiated religious expression in order to avoid discriminating against religion and to comply with both the Free Speech and Free Exercise clauses is a secular purpose. "[S]tate efforts to alleviate discriminatory or state-imposed burdens on religious exercise [expression] are consistent with neutrality, even though any such effort, considered in isolation, will appear to aid religion."[46]

Second, the Act's principal or primary effect is not that of advancing or inhibiting religion. The *Mergens* Court recognized that there is a critical difference between "government endorsed" student religion, which is forbidden, and private endorsed student religion, which is protected.[47] Justice O'Connor in *Mergens* also recognized that secondary students are mature enough not to attribute official school endorsement to student religious groups merely because the school permits the groups to meet.[48] Indeed, the school itself can protect against this by not giving students the impression that it is endorsing the religious groups.[49] This may be effectuated by way of disclaimers. Disclaimers by school officials regarding religious student groups may, however, imply an unequality concept and, thus, may be violative of equal protection principles.

Additionally, the government itself must be advancing the religion through its *own* activities and influences in order for an impermissible "primary effect" of advancing religion to be found.[50] The Act protects against this by limiting the participation of school officials to that of a custodial role and by requiring that the meetings take place during noninstructional time.

Furthermore, the benefits of using the school building, including the heat, light, and classrooms, would be no more than incidental benefits to religion. The expense of the monitors would not be relevant, since they are required by the school, not requested by the students.

Third, the Act does not foster an excessive entanglement between government and religion. The *Mergens* Court held that custodial oversight of the student groups does not involve the school in the day-to-day "surveillance or administration of religious activities."[51] It is merely to ensure order and good behavior, and does not allow faculty monitors to participate in the religious meetings.

In fact, the *Mergens* Court indicated that a denial of equal access to religious speech might create a greater entanglement problem for the school.[52] Distinguishing religious from secular messages for purposes of censoring meetings of student groups requires excessive entanglement. The *Mergens*

Court recognized that monitoring the meetings where religious speech might occur would involve an ongoing school inquisition.[53]

CONCLUSION

Obviously, those interested in promoting and preserving freedom of religious expression in public secondary schools should familiarize themselves with the Act.

Students and others interested in meeting as a group on school premises should determine whether the school has a limited open forum. If the school does not have a limited open forum, the Act does not apply.

If the school has a limited open forum, school officials should be contacted to find out what written procedures are a prerequisite to meeting. If there are no written procedures, inquire as to the school's past practices. If .the procedures are reasonably within the parameters of the Act and do not violate the Constitution, then steps should be taken to comply with them.

Unfortunately, following the *Mergens* decision, various public schools, in order to avoid allowing religious clubs to meet, have decided to eliminate all noncurricular student organizations.[54] This is obviously an attempt to circumvent the Act as well as the Supreme Court's decision in *Mergens*.[55] In some schools officials may violate the Act by doing this.

If it is clear that school officials are violating both the Constitution and the Act, they should be notified. And if, upon notice of violations, they refuse to follow the mandates of the law, then legal action should be considered.

It is important to appeal injustice. Sometimes appeal is *necessary* to ensure liberty and preserve an open and free society.

12

Use of Public School Facilities by Churches and Religious Organizations

The equal access policy would at most only make available to all community groups the benefits of School District facilities regardless of the religious nature of their speech.

—District Judge Dale Saffels,
*Country Hills Christian Church v.
Unified School District No. 512,*
560 F. Supp. 1207, 1218
(D. Kan. 1983).

The use of public school facilities by religious groups, on the same terms and conditions as other community groups, is a long-standing tradition in most American jurisdictions.[1] Access to school facilities is particularly vital in many urban settings and other communities where the price of real estate and commercial rental rates make it difficult for small or new congregations to purchase or rent their own meeting houses. In such instances, access to public facilities may be essential for a religious organization to meet.

Many states and school boards have adopted policies that authorize the broad use of all public school facilities and grounds for public and community use whenever such use does not interfere with the normal operation and mission of the school. Community use, of course, must not disrupt student instruction and must be consistent with the proper preservation and care of school property.[2] Accordingly, public school facilities in many jurisdictions are routinely available during nonschool hours for electoral registration and voting, political conventions and precinct meetings, and use by recognized community organizations (including religious organizations) reflecting a wide range of educational, cultural, political, and recreational interests.

The use of public school facilities by religious organizations during noninstructional periods is a different situation from the access of public school *students*, acting on their own initiative or in concert with a teacher or nonschool personnel, to public school facilities before, during, or after the *school day* for a religious meeting.[3] (See the discussion of the Equal Access Act in chapter 11.) Compulsory religious exercises[4] or the teaching and inculcating of religion through the medium of the public school system[5] are not at issue here. Moreover, the activity in question does not involve use of school premises *during* normal school hours where members of the student body would be the exclusive or principal audience or where school administrators and teachers would be present in an official capacity.

To the contrary, the situation under discussion is an activity of a non-school-related, outside community group long after the school has dismissed its pupils (such as on a weekend). The anticipated audience includes members of the general public. In many situations, no school personnel other than custodial employees, if any, are present.[6] Clearly, the semblance of official sponsorship, a valid Establishment Clause concern, is much less evident where a school facility is used on a temporary basis at night or on the weekend under a program that grants equal access to a variety of community groups.[7]

THE PUBLIC FORUM ISSUE

An analysis of free speech rights on public property is governed by the type of forum in which the expression takes place. A forum is not only buildings or property—like a street or park—but also any medium through which ideas are communicated.[8] In order to define free speech rights on government property, the Supreme Court has classified publicly owned property into at least three types of forums.[9] (See the discussion of the public forum issue in chapter 6.)

"Traditional public forums" are places devoted to speech and assembly "by long tradition or by government fiat."[10] Speakers can be excluded from traditional public forums (for example, streets and parks) "only when the exclusion is necessary to serve a compelling state interest and the exclusion is narrowly drawn to achieve that interest."[11]

"Limited public forums" are forums designated by government "for use by the public at large for assembly and speech, for use by certain speakers, or for the discussion of certain subjects."[12] The existence of a limited public forum depends "on the government's intention to create it, and the designation of a limited public forum is revocable. But while the limited forum exists, only a compelling state interest can justify the exclusion of speakers who fall within the group for whom the forum exists and who wish to address a topic for which the forum exists."[13]

Places opened for limited kinds of expressive activity have included municipal theaters,[14] library auditoriums,[15] and stadiums.[16] In *Widmar v. Vincent*,[17] the Supreme Court held that a public university campus had been designated a limited public forum. A state university denied a student religious group permission to conduct its meetings in university facilities because to do otherwise, school officials believed, would constitute an unconstitutional establishment of religion. Although a public university campus is not a traditional public forum, the Supreme Court held that if the university permits its facilities to be used for meetings of student organizations, it has created a limited public forum. Once it has created a public forum, the university may not exclude a student group from that forum on the basis of the *content* of its speech or views.

Any other government property or channel of communication is a "nonpublic forum."[18] The government can exclude speakers from nonpublic forums so long as the restrictions are "reasonable and not an effort to suppress expression merely because public officials oppose the speaker's view."[19]

PUBLIC SCHOOL AS A PUBLIC FORUM

Public school grounds are not a traditional public forum. In *Grayned v. City of Rockford*,[20] the Supreme Court noted that the Constitution has never been so broadly interpreted as to suggest that "students, teachers, or anyone else has an absolute constitutional right to use all parts of a school building or its immediate environs for . . . unlimited expressive purposes."[21] The school board, no less than any owner of private property, "has power to preserve the property under its control for the use to which it is lawfully dedicated."[22]

Although a public school is not a traditional public forum, it is well-established that virtually all government property, including public school facilities, can become a public forum if the government officially opens or designates the property for First Amendment activity.[23] The school board is not required to open its property to the public for expressive activity, but, once it does, school authorities may not exclude outside groups from the forum based on the content of the group's intended expression.[24]

A public school becomes a public forum for the community if it is opened by policy or practice to outside community groups for meetings or discussions during nonschool hours. Whether or not a school board has created a public forum is often an issue in dispute. A federal court of appeals has held that "[a] determination of the State's intent in creating a forum is a fact-oriented inquiry. . . and the past practice of the School Board in regard to its use of the property at issue is a proper consideration in that inquiry."[25]

The designation of school facilities as a public forum for community groups makes the school "virtually the same, in concept, as streets and parks as far as the First Amendment is concerned."[26] This does not mean, however, that school facilities cannot be regulated to a greater degree than parks and streets. The Supreme Court has recognized that First Amendment rights must be analyzed "in light of the special characteristics of the school environment."[27] The Supreme Court similarly argued in *Widmar*:

> A university differs in significant respects from public forums such as streets or parks or even municipal theaters. A university's mission is education, and decisions of this Court have never denied a university's authority to impose reasonable regulations compatible with that mission upon the use of its campus and facilities. We have not held, for example, that a campus must make all of its facilities equally available to students and nonstudents alike, or that a university must grant free access to all of its grounds or buildings.[28]

Therefore, the nature of public school facilities, their function in the community, and the activities normally conducted in them dictate that reasonable content-neutral time, place, and manner regulations of their use by community organizations may be imposed.[29]

A school board thus has several options concerning the use of its facilities. First, it could prohibit all use of school facilities by outside groups, thereby declining to open the forum. Such a policy is, of course, inconsistent with the practice and tradition of many school districts.

Second, the school board could preserve the status of the school as a nonpublic forum but carve out a limited public forum within the nonpublic forum. This option is not well developed doctrinally,[30] and the precise scope of a school board's authority to establish the parameters of a limited public forum is uncertain. A school board, pursuant to this option, may possibly restrict use of school facilities by outside groups to nonschool activities that have a direct educational purpose and serve the mission and purposes of the school. The school, it would seem, may also implement reasonable distinctions, compatible with the purposes of the forum, between groups which may or may not use school facilities. For example, the school board could restrict use to "nonprofit" groups or "recognized community groups." However, distinctions must be reasonable and applied evenhandedly to similar groups. Moreover, objective criteria should be promulgated so all groups are evaluated by the same standard.[31] The school board, therefore, may create a "limited forum" for particular groups or specific activities. However, it may not exclude expression which is within the limits it has established, nor may it exclude a group which is otherwise entitled to use the facilities in accordance with the standards set.[32]

Third, a school board may create a limited public forum by opening school facilities to use during nonschool hours by *any* public or private organization. If a school board creates a limited public forum, it may impose reasonable content-neutral time, place, and manner regulations which are narrowly tailored to serve a compelling governmental interest and which leave open alternative channels of communication.

However, a school board may not adopt content-based regulations or discriminate among groups on the basis of their views. One commentator notes the following examples of permissible time, place, and manner regulations:

(1) The school board may adopt regulations that give school activities and school groups first priority in use of the facility so that the school facility may serve its prime function. (2) The board may designate which part of the facility is available for use as a public forum. For example, it may make the auditorium, gymnasium, or cafeteria available to outside groups but not classrooms. The fact that one part of a facility is used as a public forum does not require that all parts of the facility be available for that purpose. (3) The board may adopt regulations pertaining to safety. For example, if a school auditorium seats a maximum of 250, the board may deny use of the auditorium for meetings that are expected to draw more than that number. It may also ban uses that violate health or fire safety codes and regulations. For example, regulations may require that fire escape routes not be locked or blocked by furniture, stage props, etc. (4) School boards may ban use of the facility for illegal purposes. For example, a board need not rent a school facility to a group that wants to protest marijuana laws by holding a marijuana "smoke-in." (5) To protect school property from misuse, the board may require groups that have damaged school property in the past to pay a deposit or deny them rental privileges. (6) To promote orderly scheduling, the board may require groups to apply in advance for permission to use the facility. (7) The board may ban noisy meetings or rallies during the school day.[33]

The principle is that the First Amendment does not give any individual or group the right to use public school facilities as a speech forum unless the facilities have already been opened by school practice or policy granting access to individuals or groups of similar character.

ESTABLISHMENT CLAUSE CONCERNS

Use of public school facilities by religious groups implicates the First Amendment Establishment Clause.[34] It is frequently argued that the use of school buildings by religious groups, free speech rights notwithstanding, raises a symbolic inference of impermissible state support for religion. The courts have consistently held that the Establishment Clause must be applied with special sensitivity in the public school context.[35]

As discussed above, a school board need not open its facilities during noninstructional hours to community groups unrelated to school business or the school curriculum. If a school preserves its nonpublic forum status, religious groups cannot compel school districts to open their doors during noninstructional periods for religious discourse.[36] However, if school board policy or practice opens school property to the public during nonschool hours for expressive activity, pursuant to free speech and association rights, religious groups are entitled to protection even if such expressive activity includes religious subjects.

EQUAL ACCESS

It is frequently argued that school boards have a compelling reason to exclude *religious* speech from a public forum they have created because permitting religious speech would violate the Establishment Clause. This argument has been rejected by the Supreme Court in *Widmar v. Vincent*[37] and *Mergens v. Board of Education of the Westside Community Schools*.[38] In fact, the *Widmar* Court articulated pertinent rules of law on Establishment Clause concerns and the public forum issue.[39]

In *Mergens* the Supreme Court upheld the Equal Access Act[40] in the face of an Establishment Clause challenge. The Act (see chapter 11) makes it unlawful for any public secondary school which receives federal financial assistance and which has a limited open forum to deny equal access to students to meet on the basis of the *religious*, political, philosophical, or other content of the meeting. Such groups must be noncurriculum related and meet on school premises during noninstructional time.

Justice O'Connor, speaking for the Court in *Mergens*, indicated that "the logic of *Widmar* applies with equal force to the Equal Access Act."[41] In *Widmar*, the Supreme Court upheld the right of equal access to a university campus for a religious group. There the Court concluded that "an open-forum policy, including nondiscrimination against religious speech, would have a secular purpose."[42] Such a policy would in fact avoid entanglement with religion.[43] The Court in *Widmar* also found that although incidental benefits accrued to religious groups that used university facilities, such did not amount to an Establishment Clause violation.

Widmar and *Mergens* are direct authority that permitting religious speech on an *equal* basis with other speech in an open forum does not violate the Establishment Clause. The contention that *Widmar*'s holding was narrow and limited to a university setting was rejected by the Supreme Court in *Mergens* and in other cases. For example, in *Mueller v. Allen*,[44] the Court stated:

> As *Widmar* and our other decisions indicate, a program . . . that neutrally provides state assistance to a broad spectrum of citizens [i.e., religious and nonreligious] is not readily subject to challenge under the Establishment Clause.[45]

Several lower federal courts, applying *Widmar*, have concluded that official school board policies have converted a school to a public forum for First Amendment purposes. For example, in *Country Hills Christian Church v. Unified School District No. 512*,[46] a church was denied use of school facilities for Sunday services. There a federal district court found that the school district created a First Amendment public forum when it adopted a policy opening its buildings to "recognized community groups."[47] This made the school buildings "virtually the same, in concept, as streets and parks as far as the First Amendment is concerned."[48]

In *Gregoire v. Centennial School District*,[49] which involved the attempt by a religious group to rent a school auditorium for a magician's performance that included a religious message, the school district enforced a policy stating that Pennsylvania law specifically prohibited use of school facilities for any religious activities. Nevertheless, a federal appellate court found that an open forum was created because the school district had opened school facilities for general use by community groups.[50] The court further held, "[i]t is no defense that the facility was not required to be open in the first place because the Constitution forbids a state to enforce unconstitutional exclusions from a forum generally open to the public, even though the forum was not required to be open in the first place."[51]

This equal access, public forum rule is so logical and compelling that it was frequently followed by federal courts even before the Supreme Court's decision in *Widmar*. Pursuant to this rule, courts have directed school boards to make school facilities available to outside groups during nonschool hours even though the boards considered the groups reprehensible.[52]

In the context of the issue discussed in this chapter, it is occasionally argued that religious speech in general, or religious worship in particular, is somehow a second-class form of speech and, therefore, is not entitled to full protection from content-based discrimination in a public forum. This argument has been consistently rejected by courts that have considered it. The Supreme Court ruled in *Widmar* that "religious worship and discussion . . . are forms of speech and association protected by the First Amendment."[53]

It is important to recognize that the *Widmar* Court held that both religious worship *and* religious speech are entitled to full First Amendment protection. In *Widmar*, the religious students held meetings that typically included praying, hymn singing, and Bible reading—activities fairly characterized as worship. The majority opinion specifically considered and rejected the lone dissenter's objection that religious worship is somehow not a species of protected religious speech or free speech:

[T]he dissent fails to establish that the distinction has intelligible content. There is no indication when "singing hymns, reading scripture, and teaching biblical principles" . . . cease to be "singing, teaching, and reading"— all apparently forms of "speech," despite their religious subject matter—and become unprotected "worship."

Second, even if the distinction drew an arguably principled line, it is highly doubtful that it would lie within the judicial competence to administer. . . . Merely to draw the distinction would require the university— and ultimately the courts—to inquire into the significance of words and practices to different religious faiths, and in varying circumstances by the same faith. Such inquiries would tend inevitably to entangle the State with religion in a manner forbidden by our cases. . . .

Finally, the dissent fails to establish the *relevance* of the distinction [between speech and worship].[54]

Accordingly, there is no merit to the argument that the use of school facilities for religious speech or worship by a community group is entitled to less than the full measure of First Amendment protection.

In summary, by allowing and encouraging a broad range of community groups to use its facilities and then barring all *religious* speakers or worshippers from the open public forum, a school district violates the free speech and equal protection rights of religious individuals and groups. The Supreme Court counseled in *Widmar* that "'[w]here the State has opened a forum for direct citizen involvement,' exclusions bear a heavy burden of justification."[55] The Supreme Court, therefore, has held that there is no justification for the claimed distinction between speech and worship.

THE *LEMON* TEST

In *Widmar*, the Supreme Court held that affording religious groups access to the public forum on the same terms offered other community groups is not equivalent to an establishment of religion.[56] The Court there evaluated the constitutionality of an "equal access" policy under the tripartite test it enunciated in *Lemon v. Kurtzman*.[57] If a statute or, as in this case, a school board policy conforms to all three prongs of the test, then such does not violate the Establishment Clause. (See also the discussion of the endorsement test in chapters 5 and 11.)

Secular Purpose

The first prong is the requirement of a secular purpose. Such a purpose for an equal access policy exists in that it promotes public use of school facilities for the common benefit of the residents of the community,[58] and an open forum by definition implements the fundamental secular purpose of equal treatment of all groups in society. A secular purpose for an equal access policy is also found in facilitating the free exchange of ideas and the right of association by all members of the general public.

Moreover, it cannot legitimately be argued that use of school facilities for *religious* worship undermines an equal access policy's *secular* aims. Such an argument was considered and expressly rejected by the *Widmar* Court: "[B]y creating a forum the University does not thereby endorse or promote any of the particular ideas aired there. Undoubtedly, many views are advocated in the forum with which the University desires no association."[59]

Indeed, two federal appellate courts have held that permitting groups such as the Nazi party and the Ku Klux Klan to use school facilities does not convey any state endorsement of their views or ideologies.[60] Nor does endorsement occur when the speech involved is religious.[61] In fact, Justice O'Connor in *Mergens* noted that "[t]he proposition that schools do not endorse everything they fail to censor is not complicated."[62] Justice O'Connor also noted that the mistaken inference of endorsement of school officials is largely self-imposed since the school itself has control over any impressions it gives to students.[63]

Therefore, to the extent the school makes it clear that it is not endorsing the views of certain student meetings, students will reasonably understand that official recognition by the school evinces neutrality rather than endorsement of religious speech.[64] The simple fact is, as Harvard Professor Laurence Tribe has stated, "[p]ermitting a religious group to use school facilities during non-school hours . . . conveys no message of endorsement [of religion]."[65]

Primary Effect

The second inquiry under the *Lemon* tripartite test concerns whether an equal access policy has the "primary effect" of advancing religion. The *Widmar* Court held that an equal access policy would not impermissibly benefit or advance religion. The Court recognized that religious groups, like all other groups, would benefit from access to the school facilities. However, the benefit to religion was merely "incidental," not primary.[66]

The students in *Widmar* were not seeking a religious forum (that is, exclusive use of the forum for religious purposes), but merely access to university facilities on equal terms with other student groups. The forum was available to a "broad class" of nonreligious speakers, which "is an important index of secular effect."[67]

In addition, the *Widmar* Court found that an open forum at the university would not confer any imprimatur of state approval on religious sects or practices. The Supreme Court stated that an equal access policy "'would no more commit the University . . . to religious goals' than it is 'now committed to the goals of the Students for a Democratic Society, the Young Socialist Alliance,' or any other group eligible to use its facilities."[68]

An equal access policy does not have the primary effect of advancing religion. Although some religious groups might benefit from use of school facilities, such benefit is already available to a wide variety of community groups if the school board has generally opened its forum. The benefits accruing to such a broad class of nonreligious groups ensures that the effect of equal access, as in *Widmar*, is secular and not *primarily* to advance religion.[69] The federal district court in *Country Hills Christian Church* stated the matter succinctly:

> The equal access policy would at most only make available to all community groups the benefits of School District facilities regardless of the religious nature of their speech. The benefit flows to each group generally, religious or not, but not to religion or any religious group specially.

See Board of Education v. Allen, 392 U.S. 236, 244 (1968). Religious groups share benefits with all other community groups. *If religious groups benefit, it is in spite of, rather than because of, their religious character.* This is not a violation of the Establishment Clause.[70]

It is for this basic reason—that the support of religion is only incidental and *not* primary—that courts have held that equal access to public forums by religious groups does not violate the Establishment Clause.[71]

The second prong of the *Lemon* test, that the primary effect of a state regulation or action must neither advance nor inhibit religion, is often overlooked. The primary effect of singling out religious users for special discrimination is to *inhibit* religion. As Professor Tribe has pointed out, "[a] message of *exclusion* . . . is conveyed where the state refuses to let religious groups use facilities that are open to other groups."[72] Accordingly, a discriminatory rule does not prevent a violation of the Establishment Clause, and it fails to satisfy the Establishment Clause requirement that government remain *neutral* toward religion.

Misconceptions of Establishment Clause requirements have often led to official hostility toward religion. The First Amendment does not require governmental hostility toward religion.

On the contrary, the Constitution, as the Supreme Court has held, "affirmatively mandates accommodation, not merely tolerance, of all religions and forbids hostility toward any."[73] Critics of an equal access policy often fail to grasp the constitutionally significant distinction between governmental *advancement* and governmental *accommodation* of religion. It is only when the state places its *official approval* on a religious practice, such as state-adopted and teacher-led school prayers,[74] that the result is an unconstitutional advancement of religion. However, equal use of state facilities by nonreligious and religious groups places no such official approval on religion, and instead merely *accommodates* religious practice. Any benefit thereby accruing to religion is incidental and merely results from accommodation of religion which, the Supreme Court has said, is in accordance with the best of American traditions.[75]

Access to a school's open forum cannot, therefore, be denied a religious group on the basis of the Establishment Clause. A discriminatory denial of equal access, moreover, violates the rights of free speech and equal protection and unconstitutionally inhibits religion in violation of the First Amendment.

It is often argued that use of school facilities by community groups is a *financial* benefit[76] that, when extended to religious groups, constitutes the appropriation of taxpayer funds to promote religion in violation of the Establishment Clause. Pursuant to a pure public forum analysis, no Establishment Clause violation arises if religious groups have access to school facilities on the *same* terms and conditions (including same rental rates) as nonreligious groups.

In several state court cases decided on Establishment Clause rather than public forum grounds, it has been determined that any Establishment Clause problem would be resolved by imposing a rent schedule based on the actual out-of-pocket costs of utilities, administrative, and custodial services.[77] One court, it should be noted, expressly held that school boards are *not* required by the Establishment Clause to compel religious groups to pay a "commercial rental rate."[78] Another court further rejected the argument that use of school buildings by religious groups is something of value and that the wear and tear on school property (that is, depreciation) is an indirect contribution to religion from the public treasury.[79]

Most courts which have suggested that religious groups must pay all actual out-of-pocket expenses arising from use of public facilities in order to avoid Establishment Clause challenges have issued their opinions prior to *Widmar, Mergens,* and recent Supreme Court pronouncements on the public forum, equal access doctrine. The public forum rule requires only that religious groups pay the *same* rental rates as nonreligious groups using the facilities during nonschool hours.

It is also argued that there is another sense in which the benefit derived from an equal access policy results in the primary, not incidental, advancement of religion. It is contended that, since school children are impressionable and easily confused, children who attend Sunday school in the same building as their public school classes may assume that the school district endorses their church, while children who meet at another location may believe that the school district disapproves of their church because another sect is permitted to rent the school building during nonschool hours.[80] Students reading notices of church meetings in a public school or observing such meetings, it is suggested, may believe that an imprimatur of state approval is placed upon the religious body.[81]

Widmar, prior to *Mergens,* could be used to distinguish the university setting from the elementary and secondary school setting on the maturity issue.[82] However, Justice O'Connor in *Mergens* noted that any reference of endorsement is largely self-imposed by the school.[83] To remedy this, the school can make it clear that it is not endorsing the views of those religious organizations using school facilities.[84] Such disclaimers, however, may raise other constitutional issues, such as a denial of equal treatment for religious organizations.

The contention that public school students are more impressionable than university students, however, is irrelevant to public forum analysis. Although such observation would perhaps have relevance if a school permitted outside groups to conduct religious activities in school facilities *during* class hours, it has no relevance to an equal access policy governing off-hours use of school facilities by community groups.

It is only when the mission and authority of the school are involved (that is, when teachers and students must be present for pedagogical purposes) that religious activities on school grounds raise special Establishment Clause concerns. An open forum in school facilities during off-hours does not, however, implicate the educational mission of the public school.

During these off-hours, school-sponsored teaching of "impressionable" students does not occur, and teachers and students are not required to be present.[85]

Concerns about student "impressionability" are not, therefore, constitutionally relevant to activities conducted at times when students are not required to be present or when the educational mission of the school is not implicated. During these off-hours, the empty school building differs little, if at all, in character from any other unused government property.[86] Once these empty facilities have become an open forum through general community group use, they are, at law, like any other public forum, and religious speech must be provided the same constitutional protection as any other speech.[87]

When reduced to its essence, concern over religious indoctrination of impressionable public school students often amounts to an unsubstantiated fear that students will mistakenly conclude that the government endorses everything it does not censor.[88] In fact, the Supreme Court in *Mergens* indicated that "[t]he proposition that schools do not endorse everything they fail to censor is not complicated."[89]

In any case, concerns about the impressionability of students must be balanced with the free speech, association, religious exercise, and equal protection rights of individuals and groups seeking equal access to a public forum intentionally created by school board policy or practice. Impressionability concerns are substantially weakened when expressive activity takes place at times when students are not required to be present and the educational mission of the school is not implicated.[90]

Excessive Entanglement

The third prong of the *Lemon* test concerns whether an equal access policy in the public forum will promote excessive entanglement between church and state. "Entanglement" refers not only to the day-to-day interaction between government and religion, but also to the effect on religion of state policies toward religion. Ultimately, the test for unconstitutional entanglement is one of degree.[91] The question is whether or not government policy necessitates "official and continuing surveillance" of or excessive government involvement in the affairs of religious organizations.[92]

Use of school facilities by religious groups during noninstructional hours on an equal basis with similar community groups does not require surveillance by school authorities beyond the routine security and maintenance functions the school performs with all uses of its facilities. No significant administrative function need be involved. As one court has held: "The processing of an application by a clerk is hardly an act of excessive entanglement. Moreover, inasmuch as no use of school premises is made during regular school hours, there is no need of supervision to ensure that no religion seeps into secular instruction."[93]

In *Widmar*, the Supreme Court found the entanglement prong easily satisfied because an equal access policy actually helps to avoid government entanglement with religious matters. A governmental body risks greater entanglement by attempting to enforce an exclusion of religious speech than by simply allowing all speech on an equal basis.[94] The Court noted, among other things, that "[t]here would also be a continuing need to monitor various group meetings to ensure compliance with the rule" against use for religious purposes.[95] To hold otherwise, the Court observed, would require the governmental institution to decide which words and practices were "religious" and which were not.[96] This constitutes impermissible "monitoring" and presents "an impossible task in an age where many and various beliefs meet the constitutional definition of religion."[97]

The practical difficulties raised by attempting to enforce an exclusion of religious worship from school facilities are illustrated in *Country Hills Christian Church.*[98] In that case, not only had the policy been applied inconsistently, but also no principled basis existed—or was conceivable—for determining whether, for example, singing of Christmas carols or saying a prayer before a chili supper at the school might or might not be forbidden. It is precisely these kinds of vaguely guided inquiries into religious matters that create the government entanglement with religion barred by the third prong of the *Lemon* test. Such entanglement problems are avoided by allowing *all* groups, religious and nonreligious, equal access to school facilities which have been opened for general community use.

In *Resnick v. East Brunswick Township Board of Education,*[99] the Supreme Court of New Jersey opined that entanglement concerns might also arise from prolonged, indefinite use of school premises by some religious group.[100] This concern has typically arisen in the context of a narrow Establishment Clause inquiry as opposed to a public forum analysis. Again, pursuant to the free speech/public forum doctrine, religious groups do not claim an unlimited right to use public facilities. Rather, religious groups seek to use school premises on the *same* terms and conditions as other community groups. If a school district permits community groups to use its facilities on an indefinite basis, religious groups are entitled to like treatment. If a school district imposes durational or similar requirements on community groups, religious groups should be subject to the same. Religious groups are entitled to *nondiscriminatory* treatment.

The apparent concern of the *Resnick* court is that if a church becomes permanently institutionalized within public school facilities, rendering a public school as its permanent place of worship, the school district will be implicated in the promotion of religion. The *Resnick* court relied on express *dictum* from the decision of the Florida Supreme Court in *Southside Estates Baptist Church v. Board of Trustees:*[101]

[I]f the use of the school buildings were permitted for prolonged periods of time, absent evidence of an immediate intention on the part of the Church to construct its own building, we think it could hardly be contemplated that the public school system or its property could be employed in the permanent promotion of any particular sect or denomination. Such, however, is not the case here.[102]

The *Resnick* and *Southside Estates* courts declined to place a strict temporal limitation on the use of school facilities. It was left to the trial court to draw lines in this area.[103] The *Resnick* court indicated, however, that continued use of one facility for five years "is approaching the outer bounds of reasonable time and nearing the point of prohibited entanglement."[104] If a religious group is diligently striving toward the procurement of its own house of worship (for example, the church is looking to purchase a building or property on which to construct a church building), this indicates no intention of permanent use.[105] It must be emphasized that these comments were *dictum* issued by a state court engaged in an Establishment Clause analysis without the benefit of recent Supreme Court pronouncements on the free speech/public forum doctrine.

STATE CONSTITUTIONS AND STATUTES

It is often argued that while federal constitutional pronouncements may not provide compelling reasons to exclude religious speech from a public forum, state constitutional or statutory provisions often require a more exacting separation of church and state. Thus, it is argued, use of school facilities by religious groups during noninstructional times may be unlawful under state law.

Whatever a state constitution or statute may be construed to require, the Supremacy Clause[106] of the United States Constitution controls state law, especially any state constitutional provision that conflicts with a federal constitutional right. Thus, even if a state had a statute or constitutional nonestablishment provision which stated, in essence, that any school district could establish a public forum open to community groups generally but from which religious groups could be barred, that provision would be without force or effect in the face of the contrary requirement of the First Amendment Free Speech Clause and the Fourteenth Amendment Equal Protection Clause.

In fact, the Supreme Court in *Widmar* held that it did not have to decide whether the Missouri courts might impose a stricter nonestablishment rule than the federal rule. No matter what interpretation Missouri made of its own laws, that result was limited and controlled by both the Free Exercise and Free Speech Clauses of the First Amendment. The Court said:

> [T]he state interest asserted here—in achieving greater separation of church and State than is already ensured under the Establishment Clause of the Federal Constitution—is limited by the Free Exercise Clause and in this case by the Free Speech Clause as well. In this constitutional context, we are unable to recognize the State's interest [in avoiding a violation of its own constitution] as sufficiently "compelling" to justify content-based discrimination against . . . religious speech.[107]

Similarly, in *McDaniel v. Paty*,[108] the Supreme Court *unanimously* struck down both a Tennessee statute and a provision of the Tennessee constitution that were directly and unambiguously on point—but which conflicted with the federal constitutional rights of religious ministers. The justices disagreed about which provision of the federal Constitution was controlling, but not one of them even thought it necessary to state, much less justify, the assumption that the federal Constitution was supreme.

Few have seriously contended that the Supremacy Clause does not include the supremacy of all United States Supreme Court interpretations of the United States Constitution. Obviously, a state constitutional nonestablishment provision should not take precedence over the federal constitutional rights of free speech and equal protection which prohibit the discriminatory exclusion of religious speech from a public forum.

NONDISCRIMINATORY EQUAL ACCESS

Public school facilities are not a traditional public forum, and a school board is not required to open its property to the public during noninstructional periods for expressive activity. However, once a school board designates its facilities as a public forum by policy or practice permitting use of the facilities by outside groups during nonschool hours, the forum is governed by the same strict standards that apply to a traditional public forum, and the school board may not prohibit groups from assembling or speaking on the basis of what they intend to say. While reasonable regulations concerning time, place, and manner of expression are permissible, all restrictions must be neutral regarding the content or viewpoint of speech, narrowly tailored to serve a compelling state interest, and leave open alternative channels of communication.

A policy granting religious groups access to public school facilities on the same terms and conditions as other community groups does not violate the Establishment Clause. Although religious groups arguably benefit from use of school facilities, such benefits are already available to a diverse group of outside organizations if the school board has generally opened its forum. Any benefit accruing to religion is incidental and merely results from accommodation of religion which, the Supreme Court has said, is in accordance with the best of American traditions. The fact that benefits flow to such a broad class of groups—religious and nonreligious alike—ensures that the effect of an equal access policy is secular and not primarily to advance religion. Therefore, if religious groups benefit, it is in spite of, rather than because of, their religious character. This is not a violation of the Establishment Clause.[109]

It would arguably be impermissible for one church or religious group to monopolize school facilities, preventing other community groups from using the facilities during noninstructional times.[110] If demand for use of facilities exceeds availability, a reasonable and nondiscriminatory policy governing the distribution of available time slots, such as a content-neutral "first-come, first-served" policy, would be appropriate. Such a policy must be applied evenhandedly without discrimination based on the content or viewpoint of speech. The policy must show no preference to one group over another. Nonreligious groups may not be preferred over religious groups, and one religious denomination may not be preferred over another.[111]

Religious groups, of course, may not have unrestrained use of public property. They may only use those facilities designated part of the public forum and only when such use will not preempt school-related activities or otherwise interfere with the fundamental mission and operation of the school system. They may not meet when another organization has already scheduled use of the facility.[112]

It has been suggested by several state courts that religious groups may use public facilities only on a "temporary" basis and must pay all actual out-of-pocket expenses arising from such use in order to avoid an Establishment Clause violation. These concerns have typically arisen in state court opinions based narrowly on Establishment Clause considerations prior to *Widmar*, *Mergens*, and other Supreme Court pronouncements on the public forum/equal access doctrine.

Pursuant to the free speech/public forum doctrine, most religious groups do not claim an unlimited right to use public facilities. Rather, they seek to use school facilities on the *same terms and conditions* as all other outside community organizations. If a school district permits community groups to use its facilities on an indefinite basis and at less than fair rental rates, religious groups are entitled to identical treatment. If a school district imposes durational requirements or rental rates on nonreligious community groups, religious groups should be subject to the same. Religious groups are entitled to nondiscriminatory treatment, no more and no less.

PART FIVE

Excusal and Parents' Rights

The fundamental theory of liberty upon which all governments in this Union repose excludes any general power of the State to standardize its children by forcing them to accept instruction from public teachers only.

—Justice James C. McReynolds,
Pierce v. Society of Sisters,
268 U.S. 510, 535 (1925).

13

The Rights of Parents

The child is not the mere creature of the State; those who nurture him and direct his destiny have the right coupled with the high duty, to recognize and prepare him for additional obligations.

—Justice James C. McReynolds,
Pierce v. Society of Sisters,
268 U.S. 510, 535 (1925).

The early New England colonists could have established schools for the education of their own children, but they did not. These colonists believed in and consistently maintained "the centrality of the household as the primary agency of human association and education."[1] The Puritan parents provided religious and moral training for their own children, taught them to read and write at a very early age,[2] and trained them in a "lawful" calling or occupation.[3]

However, not all the parents of Puritan New England were capable of teaching their children reading and writing. To aid these parents in fulfilling their responsibilities,[4] the Massachusetts Bay Colony enacted the School Law of 1647 (commonly called "The Old Deluder Act") which provided that a school be established in every town of over fifty households, with the teacher being paid wages by the parents of those children who used the school.[5] And in towns of over one hundred households, they also "shall set up a grammar schoole," in order to "instruct youth so farr as they shall be fitted for ye university."[6] Because the duty to provide and direct the child's education was seen as completely under the authority of parents, attendance at such schools was on a purely *voluntary* basis.[7] However, even with the establishment of town schools, households were so prominently involved in the education process that it was often difficult to distinguish home from school.[8]

This belief in the importance of the family continued unchallenged through eighteenth and early nineteenth century America.[9] Life was, as it had been from the early beginnings, home-centered, with parental authority over children unopposed.[10]

The general consensus was that education was "the concern of the individual family" and "the private function of the parent, with any state interference unjustified in terms of individual rights."[11] As a result, state involvement was generally limited to providing for the education of indigent children.[12]

George Washington believed that it was the personal duty of a parent or guardian to provide a child's education.[13] Thomas Jefferson upheld the rights of parents in rejecting the notion of compulsion in education.[14]

In other words, education, no matter how important to the well-being of the nation, was not to be placed above parental rights and traditional family moral concerns. It may thus be concluded from the records of American history that the right of parents to guide the education of their children is "an enduring American tradition, at the very heart of the precepts of our county."[15]

A FUNDAMENTAL LIBERTY

Courts in this country have historically supported this American tradition by concluding that "the natural love and affection of parents for their children would impel them . . . [to give their children] an education suitable to their station in life."[16] Great deference has been given to parents in determining how best to prepare their children "for the discharge of their duties in the after life."[17] As long as parental choice did not "affect the government of the school or incommode the other students or the teachers,"[18] parental choice in directing the education of their children has been upheld.

Through the Due Process Clause of the Fourteenth Amendment,[19] parents have been guaranteed the "liberty" to direct the education and upbringing of children under their control.[20] This is reflected in various Supreme Court cases.

In 1923, for example, the Supreme Court affirmed that the Constitution even protected the cultural preferences of parents over those of the state. The Court invalidated a state law prohibiting foreign language instruction to young school children; the state law did not "promote" education, but arbitrarily and unreasonably interfered with "the natural duty of the parent to give his children education suitable to their station in life."[21]

Shortly thereafter, the Supreme Court struck down an Oregon compulsory education law which, in effect, required attendance of all children between the ages of eight and sixteen at public schools.[22] The Court said:

> The fundamental theory of liberty upon which all governments in this Union repose excludes any general power of the State to standardize its children by forcing them to accept instruction from public teachers only.

The child is not the mere creature of the State; those who nurture him and direct his destiny have the right coupled with the high duty, to recognize and prepare him for additional obligations.[23]

In an important 1972 case, the Supreme Court upheld parental demands, based upon grounds of both parental rights and religious freedom, for exemption of children beyond the eighth grade from state compulsory education laws.[24]

THE SHIFT OF DEFERENCE

One legal commentator notes: "The role of parents as arbiters of their children's education has undergone significant redefinition over the past half-century, partly reflecting greater judicial deference to the role of the state (and their agents, local school districts) in a broad range of education areas. . . . The role of parents has reflected changing concepts in eduction: development of students' rights; the function of the schools as inculcators of values; and the broadening of school board discretion to impose requirements on students."[25]

Recent court decisions affecting parents' rights to educate their children focus on the reasonableness of school board actions[26] and the failure of parents to show an abuse of discretion by the school board or a violation of their constitutional rights.[27]

Parents must now demonstrate more than an asserted right of common law parental control over a child's education in order to challenge the actions of public school authorities.[28] Unless parents can show either a clear abuse of school board discretion[29] or a violation of constitutional rights,[30] it is likely today that the courts will direct the parents to seek redress through board of education proceedings or ultimately at the polls on election day.[31]

The courts have also begun to create rights for students that are separate from the rights of parents in the educational process.[32] The Supreme Court has also recently directed the lower courts to show deference to the judgments of school boards when considering board policies or practices.[33] As the Supreme Court has stated:

Absent any suggestion [that a school board's rule] violates a substantive constitutional guarantee, the courts should, as a general matter, defer to [the school board's] judgment [that specifies which conduct is destructive of school order or of a proper educational environment] and refrain from attempting to distinguish between rules that are important to the preservation of order in schools and rules that are not.[34]

It may be concluded that, as one considers the changing nature of American society (which includes the troubled family as a social structure and the accompanying student discipline problems), the expansion of the rights of students by the courts, and judicial deference to discretion of school boards and administrators, the rights of parents of children in the public education system are more equivocal than in the past.

EXEMPTION FROM PUBLIC SCHOOLS

As mentioned earlier, home education was one of the major forms, if not the predominant form, of education from the founding of the original colonies of Puritan New England until the early years following the adoption of the Constitution.

Indeed, many of the framers of the American founding documents received all or a substantial part of their education in the home. This includes George Washington,[35] Thomas Jefferson,[36] Patrick Henry,[37] James Madison,[38] and Benjamin Franklin.[39]

Consistent with this country's history and tradition, the Supreme Court established, in *Pierce v. Society of Sisters,*[40] that parents have an *absolute* right to withdraw their children from public school and place them in a parochial or private school. The Court found that the parental right to direct the education of their children "excludes any general power of the state to standardize its children."[41]

Although the state has an interest in inspecting, supervising and examining schools, and requiring that all children at certain age limits attend, that teachers be moral and patriotic, and that studies promote good citizenship and avoid conflict with public policy,[42] the state cannot require that all education be provided in public schools.[43] Allowing the state to do so would impinge on the right of parents to guide the education of their children.[44]

The extent of parental rights to guide their children's education has been considered further by the courts. For example, in *Meyer v. Nebraska,*[45] the Court found that for a state to deny parents their wish to have their children taught a foreign language violated the rights of the parents in the upbringing of their children.[46] And, in *Farrington v. Tokushige,*[47] the Court found that a state statute which regulated the use of textbooks, teacher qualifications, curriculum, language used, and entrance and attendance requirements in private schools violated the right of parents to control the education of their children.

In *Wisconsin v. Yoder,*[48] the Court took the rights of parents a step further. Despite compulsory attendance laws, the Court exempted Amish children from attending school beyond the eighth grade. In *Yoder,* the religious beliefs of the Amish parents required them to keep their children at home in order to teach them practical skills such as farming.[49]

The Court gave great weight to the claim of the Amish parents since it was based on religious, rather than secular or personal beliefs.[50] In freedom of religion claims, only a state interest of the highest order can overcome the individual's claims, and the state must employ the least restrictive means.[51] The Court found that the state's interest in preparing the children for effective participation in the political system was not compelling enough to override the religious rights of the Amish parents.

Since a number of families are neither Amish nor able to afford private education, a viable alternative to families opposed to various educational programs in the public schools is home education for their children. Provided the parents have sufficient time to devote to the necessary planning and instructional time, there is, for example, a myriad of instructional material available for home schooling. Although some courts have held that there is no constitutional right to home educate,[52] Most states recognize home education either by statute or case law.[53] Some states require teacher certification of the parents.[54]

VALUE INCULCATION

An express objective of public education is the inculcation of community values that will enable children to participate in the American political and social process when they reach adulthood. On the other hand, provided the inculcation does not offend the best interests of their children or society, courts have upheld the rights of parents to inculcate their own values into their children.[55] It would seem inevitable that, at some point, parental interests and the state interests may conflict.[56]

Protecting the rights of parents to inculcate their own values into their children is necessary in order to prevent the state from creating an indoctrinative monopoly.[57] If schools are granted unrestricted control over the subject matter and mode of value inculcation in public schools, the danger of impinging upon the rights of parents is disturbingly great.[58] The unique characteristics of the school make young children susceptible to persuasion by the state. Children are a captive audience in the public school setting and frequently lack the emotional maturity to evaluate the state's message in light of the values they are taught at home.

FREE EXERCISE RIGHTS

Because educational programs involve instruction in value systems that may offend religious beliefs, the danger of infringement on the free exercise rights of parents to direct their children's education is evident.[59] Although several courts have addressed this issue, the extent to which parents' free exercise rights can affect school operations is unclear.[60]

The Free Exercise Clause of the First Amendment confers a fundamental right upon parents to direct the religious upbringing of their children.[61] Any activity in the public education process that interferes with the parent's religious upbringing of the child may be subject to examination under the Free Exercise Clause.[62]

The Supreme Court has held that one cannot be forced to alter or forsake religious beliefs in order to secure a state benefit, unless the state has a compelling interest that overrides the religious right and the state pursues that interest by the least restrictive means.[63]

A public education is a benefit provided by the state which can have a tremendous value and significance in a child's upbringing. Furthermore, either a public education or a private education is compulsory.[64] Therefore, the freedom of religion of families should not be infringed upon by the state without a compelling interest. Even then, the infringement must be performed through the least restrictive means.

For a religious claim of parents against a school to prevail, several criteria must be met. First, the religious belief must be sincerely held. If the claim is clearly nonreligious in motivation, it will not be given protection under the Free Exercise Clause.[65] Second, the belief should be an essential and basic doctrine of the religion.[66] Marginal or secondary claims will not be upheld. Third, the state's activity or demand must create a substantial burden for the claimant.[67] Activities or demands which are truly offensive to and irreconcilable with the beliefs of the parents will not prevail, while those which are simply distasteful to the parents may prevail.[68] Fourth, the parents must demonstrate that the activity or demand of the school authorities does not represent a compelling state interest,[69] such as maintenance of public safety, order, peace, or health.[70]

CURRICULUM

Great deference has been given to public school authorities in determining the composition of the school curriculum for a variety of reasons.[71] First, the state has a recognized interest in introducing students to a diversity of ideas.[72] Second, the state arguably has an interest in ensuring that students achieve a minimum level of literacy in order to secure employment upon graduation and to avoid placing welfare burdens on the public.[73] Third, the state asserts that it must prepare students to make intelligent choices regarding political candidates when the students become adults.[74]

Free exercise claims of parents requesting changes in texts and courses which offend their religious beliefs have generally been denied.[75] This has happened for three reasons. First, since these claims would entail extensive involvement by the courts in the intricacies of course and text details, the courts have concluded that the claims are not well suited for the judicial process. Second, substantial burdens would be placed on school authorities, teachers, and nonobjecting students. Third, excusal from the offensive materials would be far less disruptive and almost as satisfactory to the aggrieved parents.

Nonetheless, the composition of public school curriculum has great potential for burdening religious beliefs as a result of the value-inculcation function of the public school system. Young children, in particular, may have substantial difficulty in reconciling contradictions between the religious beliefs of their parents and the secular concepts they learn in school.[76] Although mere exposure may not induce the child to disaffirm his religious beliefs, it may plant seeds of doubt which could cause him to be an apathetic believer,[77] thus undermining the rights of the parents in the education of their children.[78]

EXCUSAL

Parents have been allowed in some instances to have their children excused (see detailed discussion in chapter 14) from instruction the parents found offensive, as long as it did not affect the efficiency of the school, interfere with the rights of other students, or create disorder.[79] Although compulsory education has diluted the almost complete deference to parents,[80] the basic presumption favoring parental control is not entirely diminished.[81]

The Supreme Court has not yet ruled on whether parents have a right to have their children excused from attending certain classes or from using certain course materials the parents find burdensome on their free exercise of religion. Among recent lower court cases, the results have been mixed.[82]

In *Mozert v. Hawkins County Board of Education*,[83] Christian parents and their children claimed that specific public school texts contained themes offensive to their religious beliefs and thus violated their free exercise rights.[84] The parents did not seek to have the books removed from the curriculum, but rather to have their children excused from the classes using the offensive books.[85]

The court concluded in *Mozert* that mandatory use of religiously offensive textbooks did not burden the claimants' free exercise of religion. The court held that mere exposure to objectionable material is not sufficient to place a burden on the free exercise rights of individuals.[86] Unless the individual is required to affirm or disaffirm a particular religious practice or belief, no burden exists.[87]

However, in *Moody v. Cronin*,[88] the court was more sympathetic to the desire of parents to have their children excused from an offensive class. In *Moody*, the parents were opposed, on the basis of their religion, to having their children attend a coed gym class; a fundamental tenet of their religion mandated that the children not be exposed to members of the opposite sex wearing immodest attire.[89]

The court found that the state's interest in requiring the children's attendance did not outweigh the free exercise rights of the parents.[90] Furthermore, the state had not attempted to provide the children with a daily program of physical education in a manner that was least restrictive of the parents' rights; for example,[91] the state could have provided the options of sex-segregated or individual physical education or of exemption.[92]

In the area of sex education, some courts have ruled that excuses must be granted,[93] and others have upheld sex education partially because a provision has been made for excuses.[94] However, some courts have rejected objections to sex education courses without considering the availability of excuses.[95]

NO MERE CREATURE

The Supreme Court has held that, in respecting the rights of parents, the child cannot be considered a mere creature of the state. In terms of education, great deference must be given to parents to guide and direct their children in important areas as parents see fit. With the cooperation of public school authorities, the rights of parents can continue to be assured.

14

Excusal: Alleviating the Tension

The essence of all that has been said and written on the sub-
ject is that only those interests of the highest order and those
not otherwise served can overbalance legitimate claims to the
free exercise of religion.

—Chief Justice Warren Burger,
Wisconsin v. Yoder,
406 U.S. 205, 215 (1972).

In 1987, parents of a child enrolled in a Tennessee public elementary school objected to the required reading of a basic reader series chosen by school authorities.[1] The parents sued, alleging their child's right to free exercise of religion was violated when the school compelled the child to read the material and to hear other students' interpretations of it. A federal appeals court dismissed the case, ruling the required reading did not create an impermissible burden on the student's free exercise of religion. In its reasoning, the court emphasized there was no proof in the record that any students were ever coerced "to affirm or deny a belief or engage or refrain from engaging in a practice prohibited or required by their religion."[2]

The conflict described above represents but one of innumerable examples where parents of public school children object to certain curricula or practices in the public schools. One attempted solution to this conflict is "exemption," also referred to as a "policy of excusal." Such a policy stands as a legitimate and practical method for alleviating the tension created by objections in the public school system.

CAPTIVE AUDIENCE, THE EDUCATIONAL SYSTEM, PARENTS' RIGHTS

It has been repeatedly declared that the public school system provides a captive audience of impressionable young minds to which the state and local governments can deliver potentially objectionable educational messages.[3] The Supreme Court has recognized that public school children require special protection because they are a captive, supervised audience of an impressionable age.[4] Captive audience members, however, have a particularly important interest in avoiding exposure to expressions of beliefs, ideas, or words that they consider offensive.[5] As discussed in detail in chapter 1, those who teach public school curriculum and practices have the ability to violate this interest in communicating offensive materials or practices to students through the "system of rewards and punishments"[6] that operates within the public schools.

The involvement of the public school system in communicating values inevitably leads to conflict with those parents and children who disagree with the selected values. However, the Supreme Court has stated:

> [L]ocal school boards must be permitted "to establish and apply their curriculum in such a way as to transmit community values," and "there is a legitimate and substantial community interest in promoting respect for authority and traditional values be they social, moral or political."[7]

Because there are practical obstacles to giving attention in the classroom to all views on an issue,[8] state and local governments are selective in the values they teach. Moreover, even by ignoring certain values in education, public schools transmit a powerful message that omitted values are not important.[9] Obviously, not all will agree with the selections or omissions.

Also, objections to public school curricula and practices arise when a state's interest in universal education appears to violate the parents' right to direct "the religious and educational upbringing of their children."[10] Although parents have no constitutional right to deprive their children of an education or to prevent the state from assuring children adequate preparation for the privileges and obligations of citizens,[11] "the child is not a mere creature of the state."[12] Parents have a right and duty to nurture and direct the destiny of their children.[13] When the state interferes with this parental right, tension occurs.

STATES' INTERESTS

Parental objections might be quickly accommodated if states' interests were to be ignored. However, education of citizens has been reserved by the Supreme Court as one of the most important functions of state and local governments.[14] Though no consensus exists on how far this interest goes,[15] the Supreme Court has said that "[t]here is no doubt as to the power of a state . . . to impose reasonable regulations for the control and duration of basic education."[16] In addition to providing basic instruction such as reading, writing, and arithmetic, state and local governments often have interests in teaching values, in promoting health awareness, or simply in operating an efficient educational system.

As previously noted, public schools provide a captive audience to which educators may communicate values. For example, public schools teach the fundamental values "essential to a democratic society." The Supreme Court has noted that these values "include tolerance of divergent political and religious views" while taking into account "consideration of the sensibilities of others."[17] Through cultivating these certain values in children, public schools help preserve the foundation on which society rests.[18]

Further, the courts have held that state and local governments have interests in promoting public health through the educational process. Some federal courts have stated that the object of the protection of public health is a compelling state interest.[19] The Supreme Court stated in *Wisconsin v. Yoder:*

> To be sure, the power of the parent, even when linked to a free exercise claim, may be subject to limitation . . . if it appears that parental decisions will jeopardize the health or safety of the child, or have a potential for significant social burdens.[20]

Courts have used a compelling state interest argument in the promotion of public health to justify sex education and family life curricula,[21] alcohol and drug abuse programs,[22] and courses in the prevention of the transmission of AIDS.[23]

On a more pragmatic level, state and local governments have an interest in operating an efficient educational system. This interest emerges from the Supreme Court's warning that the "First Amendment does not permit the State to require that teaching and learning must be tailored to the principles or prohibitions of any religious sect or dogma."[24] Underlying this concern is the need to foster an academic environment where academics are not burdened by innumerable accommodations of an unspecified variety of views. Hence, the courts have recognized that the government has a definable interest in maintaining an efficient general scheme of instruction while respecting the requests for accommodation by religious objectors.[25]

Thus, tension is created when attempts to accommodate objections to the public school curriculum and practices are offset by the interests of state and local governments in the education of citizens. Possible remedies must be considered in an effort to alleviate this tension. The excusal of public school children from school curriculum and practices affords a legitimate remedy.

THE DEFICIENCIES OF OTHER REMEDIES

Examination of the deficiencies of other remedies reveals a need for a more legitimate alternative. The right of parents in many states to send their children to private schools that meet prescribed standards does not solve the tension in the public schools. First, the importance of quality education makes the choice of a private school difficult.[26] The private school may be inferior to the public school.

Second, some parents cannot afford to send their children to private schools. Often, the poor and working class are presented with schooling options they do not control and do not like.[27] The Supreme Court has stated: "[F]reedom of speech, freedom of the press, freedom of religion are available to all, not merely to those who can pay their own way."[28] Thus, First Amendment rights should not be conditioned on the ability to pay for private education.[29]

Finally, parents who can afford to pay for private schooling may not have a private school facility available.[30] Moreover, even if access to a private education is available, the private school may not provide an escape from an objectionable curriculum requirement.[31]

Another option of parents, home schooling, also does not provide a solution to the tension in public schools. In fact, there are four arguments against the position that home schooling does resolve this tension:[32] (1) "Although the direct cost may be smaller than private schooling, for many parents home teaching would require the costly decision to forego employment"; (2) "Special facilities and equipment . . . are impossible with home teaching"; (3) "The pleasure and skills acquired from interacting with other children are lost"; and (4) "If parents are not qualified to home school, such an option may contravene the state's compelling interest in requiring a basic education for all children."[33]

A third alternative, "the norm of neutrality or 'balanced presentation of views,'" fails realistically to provide a remedy to the tension in the public schools.[34] Although the neutrality of public school curricula and officials is assumed to be required,[35] implementation presents considerable problems. Time constraints prevent presentation of all views on every issue. Some views will receive more attention than others because of greater complexity or more student questions. A teacher's method or tone of presentation will affect the neutrality of the messages and, in turn, affect the students' judgment about the respective views presented.[36]

EXCUSAL: A LEGITIMATE ALTERNATIVE

To examine every conceivable remedy to this tension in the public schools would be beyond the scope of this book. However, an examination of excusal policies reveals that they are a legitimate alternative.

Excusal itself encompasses a variety of means of accommodation, some more legitimate than others. Total exemption and partial exemption from attending a course or participating in a practice are two related excusal policies.[37]

Release time programs, as discussed in chapter 15, is another excusal remedy which allows children to be released from regular public school classes to receive outside sectarian education.[38] The public school itself can provide alternative instruction for objecting students.[39] The school can likewise make an offensive class or practice elective. However, of all excusal policies, partial exemption (or partial excusal) most legitimately offers an alleviation of the tension.

A key objection to excusal is that withdrawal from a class draws attention to the child's nonconformity and may invite ridicule from other children.[40] Partial excusal, if properly handled, lessens the attention-drawing impact of total withdrawal. (For religious objectors, such peer opinion is often important.) Students may simply be absent on those days when offensive material will be covered, but still remain a part of the regular program.

Partial excusal respects the need for efficient and effective scheduling decisions. Often, curriculum decisions are made by educators before they learn which courses are sensitive (so as to make such courses elective).[41] Partial excusal allows accommodation of religious objections without subsequently rearranging the instructional process.

While the excusal policy of release time programs has been held constitutional by the Supreme Court,[42] such programs have been criticized for, in effect, creating a detention situation in a school building. As such, in many release time programs, secular instruction has been suspended, thus, in one commentator's view, imposing a penalty on the students not taking religious instruction.[43]

Partial excusal, however, would continue the instructional process for nonobjecting students. Further, partial excusal would not necessarily advance alternative education by a religious group or denomination. The public school itself could provide the alternative instruction.[44]

Excusal avoids First Amendment Establishment Clause challenges when it is viewed not as an attempt to support a religious practice, but as an attempt to accommodate the religious dissenter.[45] Excusal has been viewed by some as favoritism to religion and, therefore, an establishment of religion. However, by applying the *Lemon* tripartite test of secular purpose, primary effect, and excessive entanglement,[46] excusal overcomes such a constitutional challenge. This test is discussed in detail in chapter 5.

For example, the secular purpose of excusal is to alleviate discriminatory or state-imposed burdens on religious exercise.[47] Such state efforts would be consistent with neutrality even though any such effort, considered in isolation, might appear to aid religion.[48]

A state law may not have the primary effect of advancing or inhibiting religion. Excusal, however, allows a state to avoid altering curriculum, thus advancing religious belief. At the same time, this policy prevents the inhibiting of the free exercise of an individual's religious convictions.

Excusal also avoids excessive entanglement with religion. The objecting student may be excused or assigned an alternative requirement. If a core educational goal is at stake, the school can use testing to determine if the excused student has or is obtaining the necessary skills concerned.[49] Thus, public school officials need never involve themselves in the religious question posed by the objector.

To undercut the legitimacy of excusal, opponents raise the specter of the chaos of children shuffling in and out of classes.[50] They ask how many children will be excused, and how the number will change over time. What impact will excusal have on students who choose to remain? What reallocation of school resources will be necessary if schools are required to monitor children who opt out?[51]

These questions reflect more hypothetical fears than practical appraisals. States already excuse children from some activities that offend their religious beliefs. The most common examples are sex education, gym classes, and health education.[52] The untroubled experience with excusal to date indicates that the excusal remedy should be denied only if actual experience proves disastrous.[53]

In short, excusal provides a legitimate remedy to objections in public schools because it respects the interests of all the parties. Excusal respects parents' rights to direct "the religious and educational upbringing of their children."[54] Excusal also respects the interests of state and local governments and public school officials who must develop curriculum requirements before they are able to predict which courses will be sensitive.[55] Excusal likewise respects the administrative need of a state to operate an efficient educational system.

THE THEORETICAL BASIS FOR EXCUSAL

Not only does excusal provide a legitimate remedy to the tension in the public schools, it may in fact be constitutionally mandated in certain situations. One legal commentator writes: "Under the Free Exercise Clause, the government must show that any policy or action that imposes a substantial burden upon a sincerely held belief which is central to a bona fide religion constitutes that least restrictive means of substantially achieving a compelling end."[56] Even if a governmental action is necessary to achieve a compelling purpose, an individual's belief may be so central that government may be required to pursue a policy of accommodation so as not to coerce individuals to act against their beliefs.[57]

In the case of a public school objection, unless a compelling state interest for the policy or practice in question is found, free exercise of religion requires that those who object on sufficient religious grounds must be exempted.[58] This is especially true if the free exercise right is coupled with another constitutional claim, such as parental rights.[59]

THE LACK OF PRECISE CRITERIA FOR EXCUSAL

Though the theoretical basis exists for requiring excusal of objecting students, the Supreme Court "has not enunciated precise criteria for determining when the free exercise clause requires the implementation of accommodation measures."[60] For example, the Supreme Court has been somewhat inconsistent in the allocation of the burden of proof in free exercise challenges in the public schools.[61] Moreover, academic attempts to clarify this inconsistency lead to further uncertainties in Supreme Court precedent concerning the free exercise test.

Language in two key Supreme Court free exercise cases, *Sherbert v. Verner*[62] and *Wisconsin v. Yoder,*[63] inconsistently allocates a heavy burden of proof on the interests of both sides.

Sherbert concerned an argument that accommodation of a free exercise claim would lead to a threatening amount of spurious claims. Nevertheless, the Supreme Court held that "it would plainly be incumbent upon the [government] to demonstrate that no alternative forms of regulation would combat such abuses without infringing First Amendment rights."[64]

In *Yoder*, the Supreme Court emphatically responded to a free exercise challenge to a state compulsory attendance law:

> The essence of all that has been said and written on the subject is that only those interests of the highest order and those not otherwise served can overbalance legitimate claims to the free exercise of religion.[65]

The language in both quotations above indicates government has a heavy burden of demonstrating the specific necessity of any challenged program or practice, especially if religion or the religious objector is the focus of the program in question.[66]

In contrast, other language in *Yoder* indicates the religious objector should bear the heavy burden of demonstrating that excusal is necessary. The Supreme Court resolved that public school boards or legislatures are better able to determine the necessity of discrete aspects of a school program.[67] The *Yoder* Court noted the difficult task of demonstrating the adequacy of an alternative to the educational program selected by a state.[68] This language allocates a heavy burden of proof on the interests of the religious objector with regard to accommodation.

Attempts have been made to rectify this apparent inconsistency in Supreme Court decisions. In terms of a free exercise claim, one commentator suggests that in the public schools the religious objector would bear the initial burden of showing that: (1) there is a significant burden upon an arguably religious belief, which is both sincerely held and centrally important; (2) any compelling interest can be substantially achieved even with the proposed accommodation; and (3) the proposed accommodation is no more extensive than necessary.[69]

At this point, the burden of proof would then shift to the public school authorities to demonstrate that: (1) no arguably religious belief was substantially burdened; (2) the proposed accommodation would prevent substantial achievement of a school's legitimate compelling interest; or (3) the proposed accommodation remedy would violate the Establishment Clause (for any reason).[70]

This analysis, although helpful, leads to further uncertainties in utilizing the free exercise test—the Supreme Court's apprehension of determining the sincerity or centrality of religious beliefs and the uncertainty as to the precedential nature of the *Sherbert* balancing test.[71]

The free exercise test requires the objector to have made a sincere religious choice rather than a mere personal philosophical choice.[72] However, religious beliefs are constitutionally protected even if they are not "acceptable, logical, consistent or comprehensible to others."[73] Unfortunately, sincerity of religious belief is a vague concept.[74]

The Supreme Court has reemphasized its apprehension of judging the centrality of belief. In *Employment Division, Oregon Department of Human Resources v. Smith*,[75] the Court asked rhetorically: "What principle of law or logic can be brought to bear to contradict a believer's assertion that a particular act is 'central' to his personal faith?"[76] The Court in *Smith* further stated:

It is not within the judicial ken to question the centrality of particular beliefs or practices to a faith, or the validity of particular litigants' interpretation of those creeds.[77]

The Court's apprehension of determining the sincerity or centrality of religious belief creates an uncertainty in the operation of free exercise litigation.

There is also another uncertainty in the application of the free exercise test—the precedential nature of the *Sherbert* balancing test. By allocating the burden of proof between the religious objector and school authorities, a crucial balancing process occurs between the interests of the religious objector and the interests of the state and local governments. This balancing process was first formally applied in the landmark free exercise case *Sherbert v. Verner*.[78]

In *Sherbert*, a woman was denied unemployment benefits solely because she refused to accept employment requiring her to work on Saturday, contrary to her religious beliefs.[79] The Supreme Court noted that if the disqualification were to withstand constitutional challenge, "it must be either because Mrs. Sherbert's disqualification as a beneficiary represents no infringement by the State of her constitutional rights of free exercise, or because any incidental burden on the free exercise of Mrs. Sherbert's religion may be justified by a 'compelling state interest in the regulation of a subject within the State's constitutional power to regulate.'"[80] Utilizing this balancing process, the Supreme Court went on to hold that there was no compelling state interest which justified the substantial infringement of Mrs. Sherbert's right to religious freedom.[81]

The Supreme Court has subsequently applied the *Sherbert* balancing test on at least two other occasions to invalidate state unemployment compensation rules that conditioned the availability of benefits upon an applicant's willingness to work under conditions forbidden by his religion.[82] Moreover, until recently, the balancing process has subsequently been regularly applied in free exercise cases.[83]

The precedential nature of the *Sherbert* balancing test, however, has been increasingly limited by the Supreme Court. The Court noted in *Smith*, "[i]n recent years [the Court has] abstained from applying the *Sherbert* test [outside the unemployment compensation field] at all."[84] However, the Supreme Court in *Smith* stopped short of totally confining *Sherbert* to the unemployment compensation field.[85]

The *Smith* Court did conclude that *Sherbert* was inapplicable to decisions involving "an across-the-board criminal prohibition on a particular form of conduct."[86] The *Smith* case thus leads to even more uncertainty as to the operation of the free exercise test.

In short, the theoretical basis exists for requiring excusal from school curriculum or practices for religiously objecting public school students. Yet the uncertainties as to such things as the allocation of the burden of proof and the operation of the free exercise test makes it difficult to formulate precise criteria to determine when excusal is constitutionally mandated.

COERCION

Two key concepts, coercion and mere exposure, provide a basis for analyzing public school excusal cases. The presence of a coercive effect on the free exercise rights of a student furnishes an impetus for allowing an accommodation. The mere exposure to religiously offensive curriculum or practices supplies a less compelling stimulus for accommodation. However, mere exposure to offensive material or practices should be a sufficient foundation for excusal in public schools.

Accommodation of free exercise rights should occur most readily when the objectionable school curriculum or practice has a coercive effect against the free exercise of religion. The Supreme Court has stated:

> If there is any fixed star in our constitutional constellation, it is that no official, high or petty, can prescribe what shall be orthodox in politics, nationalism, religion, or other matters of opinion, or force citizens to confess by word or act their faith therein.[87]

Therefore, if the religious objector can show a coercive effect of a school's enactment, a stronger impetus for allowing accommodation is created.

In the case of *West Virginia State Board of Education v. Barnette*,[88] the Supreme Court ruled that educational officials could not compel objecting students to violate their religious beliefs by saluting the flag as a regular public school activity. Objecting members of the Jehovah's Witnesses considered the flag an "image" that conflicted with their religious beliefs.[89] The Court held the action of the local authorities went beyond the parameters of their authority in compelling the flag salute and, as a consequence, violated First Amendment principles.[90]

Another example of the impetus created for accommodation by the presence of coercion arose in a challenge to a public school requirement that a conscientious objector participate in the Reserve Officer Training Corps program (R.O.T.C.).[91] A federal appeals court in *Spence v. Bailey*[92] noted the objection to the R.O.T.C. program was based upon "'religious training and belief . . . upon a faith to which all else is subordinate and upon which all else is ultimately dependent.'"[93] The court also pointed out that no other physical education course was offered at the school, leaving R.O.T.C. the only alternative.[94] Nor was any program offered consisting only of those portions of the R.O.T.C. course not objectionable to conscientious objectors.[95]

Interestingly, the *Spence* court noted as well that the R.O.T.C. requirement could have been avoided by attendance at a public technical school. The court, however, rejected this alternative because the school was far removed in distance, and its curriculum did not include the necessary liberal arts courses preparatory to college.[96] As a result, the court in *Spence v. Bailey* upheld the challenge to the R.O.T.C. course requirement, concluding that the conscientious objector was forced to "choose between following his religious beliefs and forfeiting his diploma, on the one hand, and abandoning his religious beliefs and receiving his diploma on the the other hand."[97]

A final example of the compelling effect of coercion on accommodation occurred in a challenge to a pledge of allegiance requirement in a public elementary school.[98] An Illinois statute required an objecting first grader to stand, to put one hand over his heart, and to recite the pledge in "clear and unambiguous prose."[99] The federal district court struck down the state statute, pointing out it was conceivable that the religiously motivated objector could be punished under Illinois law for his failure to comply with the statute.[100]

In contrast, the presence of coercion in a free exercise challenge may not provide sufficient impetus to overcome mandatory vaccination requirements in public schools. Several state courts have apparently upheld mandatory vaccination even when in conflict with parents' religious convictions.[101] However, only in one of these cases did a court conclusively reason that the parent could not "endanger the health of the community by refusing [on religious grounds] to have his daughter vaccinated."[102]

While it has been assumed that states can provide religious exemptions,[103] several decisions may cast doubt on their legality. These cases seem to strike down exemption statutes where the criteria to determine an exemption were considered defective.

For example, in *Avard v. Dupuis*,[104] a federal district court was requested to require the vaccination of a child over his parents' religious objections. The court denied the request on the basis that the compulsory vaccination statute was "vague and standardless and therefore in contravention of the due process clause of the Fourteenth Amendment."[105] The court was disturbed that the statute vested complete discretion in local school boards to determine whether "a child may be excused from immunization for religious reasons."[106]

Likewise, in *Brown v. Stone*,[107] a religious exemption provision in a state immunization requirement was held to violate the Fourteenth Amendment. The court believed the exemption "would discriminate against the great majority of children whose parents have no such religious convictions."[108] In short, the presence of coercion may fail to furnish a compelling impetus for accommodation in a free exercise challenge to a mandatory vaccination requirement in the public schools.

MERE EXPOSURE OBJECTIONS

Mere exposure to religiously offensive public school curricula or practices provides a less compelling stimulus for accommodation. Though the exposure factor has been sufficient to support religious objections, the applicability of this precedent may be limited. One recent federal court decision openly attacked the sufficiency of a mere exposure complaint.[109]

Some precedent exists for religious objection based on mere exposure. The Supreme Court has held that exposing public school children to doctrines offensive to their religion violates free exercise.[110] The Court has held that mere exposure of public school children to religion by reading the Bible, allowing voluntary prayer or even a moment of silence, or posting the Ten Commandments can violate the Establishment Clause.[111]

However, the case for this precedent as a general rationale for excusal is tenuous. For example, the leading case of *Pierce v. Society of Sisters*[112] involved a private school's challenge to a compulsory education statute requiring public education. The Supreme Court in *Pierce* based its holding on the parental right to send a child to a legitimate private institution and on the irreparable injury the private institution would suffer if the statute were enforced.[113] The opinion in *Pierce*, however, did not depend on the existence of a threat of exposure to offensive public school curriculum, requiring accommodation.

The landmark case of *Wisconsin v. Yoder*,[114] however, clearly held that mere exposure to public school curriculum or practices violated free exercise rights. In 1972, members of the Amish religion were convicted of violating Wisconsin's compulsory school attendance law by declining to send their children to public school after they had graduated from the eighth grade. The Amish alleged that high school attendance was contrary to the Amish religion and way of life. They also alleged that they would endanger their own salvation and that of their children by complying with the attendance law.[115] The Supreme Court upheld this mere exposure argument, pointing out that the Amish provided an ideal vocational education for their children in the adolescent years,[116] preparing them for life in the rural Amish community.[117]

However, some courts have hinted that the applicability of *Yoder* may be limited.[118] The Supreme Court cautioned in *Yoder* that its holding may apply to "probably few other religious groups or sects."[119] The fact that the Amish were preparing their children for an existence in an isolated and independent community provided an unusually strong case against mere exposure.

Likewise, utilizing the line of cases cited above (holding that mere exposure to religion in the public schools, such as posting the Ten Commandments and so on, is unconstitutional) is tenuous as support of a policy of excusal. As one commentator has recognized, the voluntary prayer and moment of silence cases can be distinguished on the ground that the children in these cases were not merely exposed to religion but indirectly coerced to join in a religious practice.[120] Such cases seem to have been decided less on the basis of mere exposure to offensive material and more on the issue of an unconstitutional establishment of religion by the schools.

Health or sex education requirements are often opposed by religious objectors on the basis of a mere exposure challenge.[121] However, the Supreme Court in *Yoder* noted that parental rights may be subject to limitation "if it appears that parental decisions will jeopardize the health or safety of the child, or have a potential for significant social burdens."[122]

Nowhere have state interests in the welfare of public schools been more evident than in cases involving local school authority to include sex education as a part of the curriculum. For example, a federal district court rejected a claim by parents that they had an exclusive constitutional right to teach their children about sexual matters in their homes and that such an exclusive right would prohibit the teaching of sex in the schools.[123]

A California appeals court rejected parents' and students' free exercise claims against the implementation of family life and sex education programs.[124] The court pointed out that the parents' pleading lacked specificity as to how the program treated matters of morality, family life, and reproduction in a manner hostile to their theistic religion.[125] Moreover, the court noted the programs were in no way compulsory and, therefore, did not by "'unnecessarily broad means'" contravene the parents' rights.[126]

A case in Connecticut involved the use of public funds to teach a religious philosophy, in a health curriculum, which was contrary to the religious philosophy of the parents involved and which allegedly infringed upon their right to the free exercise of religion by requiring attendance where offensive instruction and information were taught.[127] The court, however, upheld the curriculum requirement, noting that the limits and basis of the parents' claimed privilege to educate their children in this area were not clearly defined in either the allegations or from the evidence.[128]

A final example of a free exercise challenge to a health education requirement involved a group of Plymouth Brethren parents and children who sought exemption from exposure to a New York school curriculum dealing with AIDS prevention. The parents alleged that exposure could destroy the foundation of their children's faith.[129] The state advocated a blanket proposition that there was a compelling interest in educating its youth about AIDS to battle the spread of the disease.[130] The New York Court of Appeals stated:

> In short, while the spread of AIDS heightens and intensifies the public interest in education, it does not overrun other cherished values that may not require sacrifice.[131]

The cherished values[132] the court referred to were the deep religious beliefs asserted by the parents.[133] The court then invalidated the summary judgment granted to the school by the lower court.[134]

A recent federal court decision directly attacked the notion that public school children may be excused from mere exposure to offensive school curriculum or practices on free exercise grounds in *Mozert v. Hawkins County Board of Education*.[135] There seventeen public school children and their parents claimed that required reading of a basic reader series chosen by public school authorities violated their right to free exercise of religion. A federal appeals court held that the school requirement did not create an unconstitutional burden since there was no evidence the students were "required to affirm or deny a belief or engage or refrain from engaging in a practice prohibited or required by their religion."[136] The court noted that "[p]roof that an objecting student was *required* to participate beyond reading and discussing assigned materials, or was disciplined for disputing assigned materials, might well implicate the Free Exercise Clause because the element of compulsion would then be present."[137] In short, the court held that mere exposure was not enough to violate the First Amendment Free Exercise Clause.

RATIONALE FOR MERE EXPOSURE EXCUSAL

Despite the spurning of mere exposure objections, a legitimate theoretical argument may be made to support accommodation in such cases.

First, the public schools inherently compete with parents in the inculcation of values in children. As previously shown, it is impractical to provide balanced attention to all views on all issues. Those views selected may be colored by the manner in which they are taught. The omission of certain views in itself sends a message that such omitted views are not important (at least not in public education).

Second, the impact of exposure on a child's beliefs is difficult or impossible to gauge.[138] An isolated reference to an offensive practice or idea may be unobjectionable. However, repeated references may offend a student, particularly if coupled with disregard for his or her religious beliefs.

Third, a valid argument based on social policy can be made for allowing accommodation of free exercise claims in cases of mere exposure. As one commentator recognizes: "If parents are hindered in their efforts to foster adherence by their children to their views or values, the society risks losing these ideas or values from the marketplace or weakening their 'competitive position.'"[139] Moreover, "unless parents are able to excuse their children from curriculum requirements to which the parents object, the captive audience status of children in the public schools affords governmental officials the opportunity to reduce diversity."[140] Thus, the hindrances to parental instruction and societal development imposed by mere exposure to offensive materials highlight the sufficiency of mere exposure as support for a free exercise challenge in public schools.

GUIDELINES FOR FORMULATING AND IMPLEMENTING EXCUSAL POLICIES

Steps can be taken to encourage smooth accommodation of excusal in the public schools. On the one hand, the Supreme Court has warned that "the First Amendment does not permit the state to require that teaching and learning must be tailored to the principles or prohibitions of any religious sect or dogma."[141] On the other hand, policymakers can and should take prudent steps to respect both the interests of parents in rearing their children and the interest of the state in educating its citizens.

Merely because one cannot formulate precise criteria for determining when excusal is constitutionally mandated does not imply excusal policies cannot be practically formulated and efficiently implemented. Legislatures and school boards have much greater discretion than courts in determining curriculum requirements.[142] Resolution of the conflicting claims between educational stability and rights of religion is often left to state and local administrators[143] who are considered to have expertise with regard to educational needs.[144] An administrative or legislative decision to excuse dissenting students would undoubtedly be given much weight by the courts.[145]

CURRICULUM PREPARATION

Educational policymakers may take steps in the preparation of curriculum to alleviate the tension in the public schools.

First, policymakers must distinguish between essential and nonessential educational ends and means. For example, an elementary school district might have a goal of teaching first graders how to read and discuss simple works of literature. This essential goal should be distinguished from the nonessential means of reading and analyzing one specific book. By making this ends/means distinction, parents who object to the selected reader as religiously offensive can have their children assigned an alternative book.[146] The state can meet its essential educational end while respecting parents' potential objections to a nonessential educational means.

An essential means/nonessential ends distinction can be made. For example, a public school could excuse objecting students from a classroom where religiously offensive activities were taking place for entertainment rather than educational purposes. This principle was recognized in *Davis v. Page*[147] where members of the Apostolic Lutheran faith alleged that the public school refused to allow their children to withdraw from classrooms where audio-visual material violated their children's free exercise rights.[148] The *Davis* court found there was no reasonable alternative to the audio-visual activity without denying the children an effective education. However, the court held that "[w]hen audio-visuals are used to entertain rather than to educate, the vitality of the state's interests diminishes. In this situation, the parents' interests become predominant and the children cannot be required to remain in the classroom."[149] The court, in essence, distinguished between the ends of education and entertainment, upholding an educational means for the former but rejecting the same means for the latter.

Second, policymakers ought to encourage parents to offer feedback on school curricula options so as to ferret out sensitive materials or practices. Utilizing parental feedback, policymakers can intelligently consider whether to make sensitive courses elective. Federal law already sets the standard:

> All instructional material—including teachers' manuals, films, tapes, or other supplementary instructional material—which will be used in connection with any research or experimentation program or project shall be available for inspection by the parents or guardians of the children engaged in such program or project.[150]

For policymakers to tailor the educational program to meet fully religious objections (even if it would be possible) might lead to an unconstitutional establishment of religion.[151] However, for policymakers to gain as much information on parental sentiments before adoption of curriculum requirements will enable educators prudently to lessen unconstitutional infringements on free exercise rights.

Third, policymakers should organize controversial courses, containing materials that may seriously interfere with religious views, into modular units and excuse dissenting students from specific units.[152] This affords less interruption in the overall instructional process and allows for more convenient testing of the excused student.

Fourth, policymakers should avoid coercive influences that might violate students' free exercise rights. This guideline is best illustrated in *Moody v. Cronin*,[153] which involved a free exercise challenge to a requirement that students attend all coeducational physical education classes under penalty of suspension, expulsion, denial of credits for graduation, and other discipline. The federal district court in *Moody* noted the legitimacy of the physical education requirement and determined, absent the financial resources, that the state was not required to provide alternatives.[154] However, the court held the requirement could not be construed in such a way that persons would have to participate in violation of religious teaching or beliefs or be subject to sanctions. The court suggested the school exempt the student from the physical education requirement.[155] Thus, coercive influences on free exercise rights ought to be avoided in order to reduce potential litigation.

PARENTAL OBJECTION GUIDELINES

Educational policymakers can also alleviate some of the tension in public schools by preparing guidelines for parents to follow in objecting to a school practice or curriculum.

First, parents should be encouraged to be specific in their objections to course materials.[156] Specificity allows public school administrators to accommodate objections more easily while protecting the state's educational interest in the requirement. Excusal from an entire course, such as biology, would, public school officials argue, deny excused children very valuable instruction in that general subject.[157] Furthermore, total exemption of a large number of students could foster (in some situations) the notion that state or local governments were tailoring the school curriculum to fit the beliefs of one religious group or denomination.[158]

Second, parents should be encouraged to support their objections by referring to central religious beliefs or deep personal convictions. The rationale for excusal must reflect more than mere dissatisfaction with the curriculum.

One parent's letter to a school board objecting to instruction in the public school illustrates the need for this guideline. The letter included the following statements:

> Our schools are contributing to the Woman's Liberation Movement by making mandatory that the boys take home economics and the girls take shop. . . . The social studies or, if you prefer, geography books which are supplied by the school district are not all American type books. . . . Students are left to make up their own minds rather than to be taught an American point of view.[159]

Such a complaint fails to tie the objections specifically and clearly to a religious faith or dogma.[160] What such objections reflect is that an educational decision is merely distasteful, and these objections will usually fail in court.[161]

Policymakers must be aware that a court may find exemption policies unconstitutional if they give discretionary power to local officials to determine whether a course is religious.[162] However, a parent who provides a deep religious rationale for an objection will avoid having an excusal request rejected for perceived mere distaste with a course or practice.[163] It may be helpful for parents to obtain an endorsement of their request for excusal from an authorized representative of their faith. This practice assists a public school administrator or a court in understanding that an objection rests on a religious tenet.[164]

Third, parents should be encouraged to provide an objective standard by which administrators can determine the extent of the religious objection and the degree of accommodation needed. In making out an excuse, parents should avoid being so "spiritual" or ethereal that it is impossible for a court or policymaker to discern what is offensive to the objector. Contrast the following excerpts from two free exercise objections:

> [Plaintiffs] have introduced evidence that there is worldly music and spiritual music—the former being objectionable. . . . [T]he Davis's pastor testified that only those who have accepted the Spirit of God can distinguish between the worldly and the spiritual.[165]

> The Plaintiffs pointed out that their "convictions about modesty [were] not just rules and regulations that some board member [dreamed] up." . . . The line the Plaintiffs universally followed for "[i]mmodest apparel" was "the knee and halfway up the arm, from the elbow to the shoulder."[166]

The first objection was rejected because "[n]o discernible standards were given by which an objective determination or distinction could be made between the two."[167] The latter objection was upheld because "the Plaintiffs pointed out their objections were based on religious tenets and that there was an objective criteria the court could apply."[168]

Finally, policymakers should encourage parents to take advantage of already available remedies to objections in the public school. For example, a student in the Houston Independent School District sought to enjoin the teaching of evolution as a part of the curriculum and to enjoin the adoption of textbooks which presented the theory of evolution to the exclusion of other theories regarding the origins of people.[169] Although the federal district court refused to order the school to discontinue teaching evolution, the court held the student could take advantage of an excusal provision in the Texas Education Code that was broad enough to encompass the student's objections.[170]

Other free exercise challenges have been rebuffed in the courts because parents failed to pursue existing accommodation remedies. For example, in *Grove v. Mead School District No. 354*,[171] a public school excused a child from a class using a religiously offensive book and assigned the child an alternative book. The student chose to remain in the class. The parents' request to remove the offensive book failed.

In *Hopkins v. Hamden Board of Education*,[172] a court rejected a challenge to a mandatory health education course, noting the parents did not sincerely and seriously pursue their requests to have their children excused in that no showing of adequate cause from attendance was made.

These cases reveal that policymakers can help reduce tension in the public schools by encouraging parents to take advantage of existing school accommodation measures.

ALLEVIATING THE TENSION

The involvement of the public school system in communicating values inevitably leads to conflict with those parents and children who disagree with the selected values. States' interests in universal education may violate parents' rights to direct the religious and educational upbringing of their children.

Excusal policies afford public schools a legitimate remedy to the tension between objections to school curriculum and the interests of state and local governments in the school system. Excusal respects parental rights to direct the upbringing of their children. Excusal also respects the interests of those who must effectively develop curriculum requirements to meet the educational goals of the state and local governments. Excusal as well respects the administrative need of the schools for an efficient educational process.

Although it is difficult to formulate precise criteria for determining when excusal is constitutionally mandated, legislatures and school boards can practically formulate and efficiently implement excusal policies. Educational policymakers must take steps in the preparation of curriculum to encourage accommodation of excusal in the public schools. Also, policymakers should prepare guidelines for parents to follow in objecting to school curriculum or practices. In short, excusal policies, if properly developed, can begin to alleviate much of the tension in the public school system.

15

Release Time in Public Schools

When the state encourages the religious instruction or cooperates with religious authorities by adjusting the schedule of public events to sectarian needs, it follows the best of our traditions.

—Justice William O. Douglas,
Zorach v. Clauson,
343 U.S. 313-14 (1952).

Release time is the practice whereby schools release children during the school day to attend sectarian religious instruction for a short period of time, usually consisting of an hour or less once a week.[1] A local group of churches often sponsors the program, and normally one may choose to attend Protestant, Catholic, or Jewish classes, or no class at all. Those who do not attend usually remain in the classroom where no formal teaching takes place. Those who do attend must first obtain parental permission on a consent form made available by the sponsoring religious group.[2]

Release time has been a part of the public school system in the United States since 1914, when the superintendent of schools in Gary, Indiana, Dr. William Writ, conceived the idea.[3] Previously, no need existed to take children out of the classroom for religious instruction. However, along with the development of modern Establishment Clause analysis[4] and the transformation of America from a rural society to an urban one[5] came the removal of sectarian religion from public schools. It became necessary for children who wanted religious instruction on the spiritual and moral nature of the Bible, as well as on other holy writings, to be educated outside the classrooms. To meet this need, Dr. Writ created release time.

Although the idea spread slowly, each of the contingent states has adopted some form of the release time program at one time or another.[6] In 1959, one writer estimated that some three thousand school districts were

171

involved.[7] Although that number is probably significantly lower today, some regions in America still have active release time programs.

BACKGROUND

Inevitably, opponents have challenged release time in the courtroom. Some believed the 1948 decision of the Supreme Court in *Illinois ex rel. McCollum v. Board of Education*[8] to be the definitive answer to the constitutionality of release time activities. Just one year before, in *Everson v. Board of Education,*[9] the Supreme Court had handed down one of its most far-reaching Establishment Clause decisions. *Everson* applied the First Amendment Religion Clauses to the states by way of the Fourteenth Amendment for the first time.[10] The Supreme Court further proclaimed that the First Amendment did not merely prohibit the establishment of a state church, but also prohibited the use of state funds, no matter how minute, to aid religious groups or sects.[11] *Everson* set the stage for a true test of release time programs.

Vishta McCollum was an atheist whose child attended public school in Champaign, Illinois.[12] When school officials asked her child to participate in the release time program *held on school premises,* Mrs. McCollum sued the school board for breach of her First and Fourteenth Amendment rights.[13] In the light of *Everson,* the Supreme Court agreed that the practice was unconstitutional.[14] Justice Hugo Black, delivering the opinion of the Court, quoted *Everson,* saying:

> Neither a state or a Federal Government can set up a church. Neither can pass laws that aid one religion, aid all religions, or prefer one religion over another. Neither can force or influence a person to go to or to remain away from church against his will or force him to profess a belief or disbelief in any religion. No person can be punished for professing beliefs or disbeliefs, for church attendance or non-attendance. No tax in any amount, large or small, can be levied to support any religious activities or instructions, whatever they may be called, or whatever form they may adopt to teach or practice religion. Neither a state nor the Federal Government can, openly or secretly, participate in the affairs of any religious organizations or groups and vice versa. In the words of Jefferson, the clause against establishment of religion by law was intended to erect "a wall of separation between church and state."[15]

Since the Champaign program used the state's tax-supported school buildings to disseminate religious doctrines and the state's compulsory education laws to provide a forum for religious teaching, the Court struck the practice down to ensure that the wall between church and state "be kept high and impregnable."[16] With this proclamation, the release time issue appeared to be settled. In reality, it was far from settled.

In 1952, less than five years after the Supreme Court decided *McCollum*, it heard the arguments for *Zorach v. Clauson*.[17] The New York City school board permitted schools to release students during the school day to attend religious classes held in religious centers *off school premises*.[18] The board expended no public funds for the program, nor was any religious instruction provided within the bounds of the school.[19] All religious teaching took place *off campus*.[20] In holding that this release time program passed constitutional muster, Justice Douglas wrote:

> We are a religious people whose institutions presuppose a Supreme Being. We guarantee the freedom to worship as one chooses. We make room for as wide a variety of beliefs and creeds as the spiritual needs of man deem necessary. We sponsor an attitude on the part of government that shows no partiality to any one group and that lets each flourish according to the zeal of its adherents and the appeal of its dogma. When the state encourages the religious instruction or cooperates with religious authorities by adjusting the schedule of public events to sectarian needs, it follows the best of our traditions. For it respects the nature of our people and accommodates the public service to their spiritual needs.[21]

Several explanations exist for the different results. First, the Court used *Zorach* to clarify *McCollum*. The Court seemed to frame *McCollum* as a narrow decision, limited to the facts in that case. Justice Douglas found three distinct facts present in Champaign which were not found in New York—the expenditure of public funds, the use of the public school buildings for religious instruction, and the force of the public school system to promote the program.[22] In Champaign, officials sent students to other parts of the school for the religious classes.[23] Since the state provided heat and light, it expended a small amount of money for the program.[24] Also, in Champaign, since the classes were held inside the school building, the state created an appearance of government sponsorship of the content of the classes.[25] Further, in Champaign the state expended a minimal amount of money for administrative costs in keeping attendance records for the religious classes.[26]

New York, on the other hand, did not expend any public funds to support the program.[27] The New York program featured classes held in nearby church buildings, with the result being no appearance of government sponsorship.[28] The Court found that the school system in New York did not use its status to promote the religious classes;[29] the Champaign system did.[30]

A second possibility for the different result is the effect of public pressure and opinion.[31] One commentator has noted that the Supreme Court's decision in *McCollum*, "was greeted with adverse criticism 'almost without parallel in volume and intensity.'"[32] Catholics and evangelical Protestants led the uproar, which by and large drowned out the praises of the less vocal Jewish and liberal Protestant organizations.[33] Many concerned Americans cited Justice Robert Jackson's concurring opinion in which he concluded that the breadth of the majority's opinion could lead to a total ban of anything religious in public schools—a radical proposition in those days.[34] Because of this public opinion, ongoing release time programs were slow to be challenged.[35]

MODERN TESTS

Whatever the reasoning, *Zorach* has been the precedent for release time cases since 1952. Its holding, simply stated, is that release time programs held *off school premises* do not, without anything more, violate the Constitution.[36] The modern Supreme Court, however, has decided a number of cases and developed tests that affect the analysis of *Zorach* and its relationship to release time programs. Of these, perhaps none are more important than the tests found in *Lemon v. Kurtzman*[37] and *Wallace v. Jaffree*.[38] These tests are discussed in greater detail in chapter 5.

Chief Justice Burger delivered the opinion of the Supreme Court in *Lemon*. He codified past decisions into the tripartite *Lemon* test in terms of the Establishment Clause:

> Every analysis in this area must begin with consideration of the cumulative criteria developed by the Court over many years. Three such tests may be gleaned from our cases. First, the statute must have a secular legislative purpose; second, its principal or primary effect must be one that neither advances or inhibits religion; finally, the statute must not foster "an excessive government entanglement with religion."[39]

The Supreme Court has used this test almost exclusively in every Establishment Clause case since 1971. At first glance, the test appears to overrule *Zorach*. However, even with the *Lemon* test, the Court has cited *Zorach* as valid law.[40]

Many lower courts have sought ways to reconcile the test with *Zorach*. One way has been to apply subjective reasoning to the second and third part of the test, while answering that the secular purpose of the statute which permits release time activities is to "accommodate the religious needs of the people."[41]

A second way of reconciling *Lemon* with *Zorach* has been to view the test in the "illuminating" light of *Zorach*. Since the *Zorach* decision is still valid, release time obviously passes each part of the *Lemon* test in one manner or another.[42] Finally, some courts have simply stated that *Zorach* is the exception to the rule, and they do not apply the *Lemon* test at all.[43]

More recently, Justice O'Connor has sought to refine the *Lemon* test with her endorsement test. Writing her concurrence in *Jaffree*, Justice O'Connor stated:

> Direct government action endorsing religion or a particular religious practice is invalid under this approach because it "sends a message to

nonadherents that they are outsiders, not full members of the political community, and an accompanying message to adherents that they are insiders, favored members of the political community." Under this view, *Lemon's* inquiry as to the purpose and the effect of a statute requires courts to examine whether government's purpose is to endorse religion and whether the statute actually conveys a message of endorsement. (citations omitted)[44]

This endorsement test does not appear, on its surface, to overrule release time activities. However, one can easily envision a release time program which appears to endorse religion as opposed merely to accommodating it. The endorsement test would most likely strike down such a program.

THREE QUESTIONS: AN ANALYSIS

As noted in Justice Douglas's opinion in *Zorach*, several elements, if present, raise suspicion as to the constitutionality of the release time program.[45] The questions to be asked are: (1) Has there been an expenditure of public funds on behalf of the program? (2) Is the program taught on school grounds? (3) Has the power of the school system been used to promote the program? By examining various release time court cases, one finds many pertinent subparts to each of these questions.

EXPENDITURE OF PUBLIC FUNDS

In many cases, the expenditure of state funds is the basis for declaring a release time program unconstitutional.

One obvious part of release time programs is the need for parental consent before the child can take part in the program. All parents receive a consent form. They sign and return the card if they desire their child to participate. If these forms are printed by the school with public funds, then constitutional suspicion is raised concerning the entire program. In *McCollum* and *Zorach*, the cards were not printed by the school district; the religious council incurred the cost of printing in both cases.[46]

However, in *Lanner v. Wimmer*[47] a similar problem arose when the school district paid for the cost of attendance slips disseminated to the religious classes. Although the federal court of appeals believed that this was "an admittedly minor matter,"[48] it nonetheless presented the "potential for unconstitutional entanglement of public schools with religious instruction."[49] Further, assumption by the public school of the responsibility of gathering these attendance reports overlooked "less entangling alternatives."[50] Release time personnel should have been responsible for delivering the slips to the school as well as for their printing costs. It should be noted that the *Lanner* court did not declare the entire release time program to be in violation of the First Amendment (only the practice of assuming the cost for the slips). The court of appeals agreed with the lower court's ruling that, even with some unconstitutional features, it need not hold the entire program unconstitutional.[51]

Another area where school districts may become excessively entangled with religious instruction is in the use of public funds to promote the release time classes.[52] Often, the sponsoring religious organization advertises the classes on school bulletin boards and in school newspapers. If the school district participates in the funding of these, even with the copying of flyers, an entanglement problem might arise. Further, instructors in release time programs must be paid with private funds; the school district cannot bear this expense.

Finally, the issue of "credit" raises many questions with regard to the expenditure of public funds on behalf of religious instruction. Although several types of credit are available in public schools, the type that can involve the use of state funds is "credit as it is used to measure the school's eligibility for state financial aid."[53] Daily attendance records determine eligibility for this type of funding. In certain states, a school can receive funding for a pupil only if the pupil attends school a certain amount of time each day.

In *Lanner v. Wimmer*[54] a federal appellate court held that the school's acceptance of funds, based on attendance figures which included release time classes, was not unconstitutional. The Court reasoned that because the funds are used for the support of the school, they "do not in any way support or enhance the released-time classes."[55] Even if the program received a minor secondary benefit, "not all legislative programs that provide indirect or incidental benefit to a religious institution are prohibited by the Constitution."[56]

LOCATION OF THE CLASSES

The *location* of the release time classes also plays an important role in deciding whether or not the program is constitutional. The decisions in *McCollum* and *Zorach* make clear that the religious classes cannot be held on school grounds.[57]

Location is an obvious problem. If the release time program classes are held on school premises, then some public funds would be used to support the program by way of providing heat, light, custodial services, and incidental materials.[58] Also, by allowing the classes to meet on public school premises, the school board is creating the "perception of endorsement."[59]

Some have attempted to circumvent the location issue by leasing public school classrooms to religious groups for nominal rent.[60] This approach only resolves the funding problem; the potential endorsement problem remains. Even with the funding problem resolved, courts have struck down this type of program as unconstitutional.[61] In deciding a school room rental case, a federal district court in *Ford v. Manuel*[62] held that "the Policy [rental agreement] impermissibly advances nonsecular interests in that it creates, for impressionable eight- and nine-year-old children, the appearance of official support for religion."[63]

Release time officials frequently hold classes in transportable trailers or converted, privately-owned school buses. If the buses or trailers are parked on private property, there is no problem with their use. Two cases from Virginia have dealt specifically with this issue.

In *Smith v. Smith*,[64] a federal appeals court upheld a release time program that took place in trailers parked on streets adjacent to the schools. More recently, though, a federal district court in *Doe v. Shenandoah County School Board*[65] enjoined a release time program which utilized private school buses parked on the street in front of the school.[66] The court believed that the "symbolic impact" of the location of the buses, even though they were not on land titled to the school, was harmful in that it created the "appearance of official involvement."[67] The restraining order prohibited the buses from parking "in close proximity" to the school.[68] Even so, the practice of holding classes in transportable classrooms off school grounds is a popular one, especially in rural areas where fewer options are available.

The preferred option is the use of local church buildings located close to the schools, partly because of the reluctance of the courts to invade the domain of religious officials.[69] This was the option used in *Zorach*.[70]

In *Lanner*, the students attended religious classes in a church building which was connected to the school by a sidewalk, was tapped into the school's public address system, and had an architectural style similar to the school.[71] The court held that it had no authority to dictate the worthiness of the architecture of a religious institution's building.[72] Moreover, the court believed that the sidewalk and the public address system, as long as the religious organization paid for their installation and upkeep, did nothing more than keep the church from encroaching on the school's time and resources.[73]

Zoning laws often ensure that most schools are in the same area as churches. Local churches may, therefore, be the most logical places for release time classes to be held.

COERCIVE POWER OF THE PUBLIC SCHOOL SYSTEM

The actions of the school system and its employees in relation to the release time program are vital to determining the validity of such programs. A school system can promote a release time program in violation of the First Amendment in many ways.

One of the more complex ways is the inevitable benefit release time programs receive from compulsory attendance laws. The reasoning is that since children are required to attend school, the state is providing religious groups with a forum to present their message. In *Ford v. Manuel*,[74] a federal district court held that it was unlawful for religious instruction to benefit from compulsory education laws.[75] Also, a federal court of appeals has noted that "it is the Texas compulsory education machinery that draws the students to the school and provides any audience at all for the religious activities."[76] However, it must not be forgotten that New York also had a compulsory attendance law in effect at the time *Zorach* was decided, and the Court did not perceive this as a significant factor.

Further, since the state by law requires children to attend school, it should require schools to accommodate the religious beliefs of students by allowing them to use a small part of the school day for religious instruction. A child should not have to sacrifice his or her right to a public education because of a constitutionally protected religious belief.[77]

Some litigants have challenged release time programs on the grounds that such programs necessarily force children to violate attendance laws.[78] At least one court has taken issue with this reasoning.[79] The compulsory education law of the state of Washington allowed absences for many different reasons, including those reasons which were "sufficient."[80] The Washington Supreme Court allowed absences for attending release time programs for the "sufficient reason" that religion "is essential to the well-being of the community."[81]

Another unconstitutional use of the public school system to promote religious activity may be the involvement of public school teachers. Since teachers receive their salaries from public funds, their involvement in the release time programs may create excessive entanglement between the state and religious instruction.

The difficulty comes in determining when teachers have become unconstitutionally involved. Some courts have ruled that public school teachers may not participate in the dissemination of registration cards for release time classes.[82] Others have hinted that even their availability for discipline in "emergency situations" would be unconstitutional.[83] All would seem to agree that teachers may not endorse the programs to their students or encourage them to participate.

Likewise, difficulty comes in determining the role of the religious instructors. Most courts have held that the instructors may not "recruit" students in the public school.[84] However, some have concluded that availability of such instructors during registration to answer questions regarding the program was not unconstitutional.[85] Generally, courts respect the impressionable nature of elementary school children and seek to keep the school environment free from outside distractions, including visitors.[86] At the minimum, a religious instructor may come onto, or to the edge of, school premises to collect the children for transportation to the program site.

The policy of granting students credit for successfully completing the release time program is another impermissible promotion of the program. As early as 1918, a court held: "[T]o give credit in the public schools for study of historical, biographical, narrative, and literary features of the Bible, pursued under sectarian agents, is to give credit for sectarian teaching and influence, contrary to [the State Constitution of Washington]."[87] More recently, the federal court in *Lanner* decided that giving credit for courses taught at religious institutions, even if they were not "mainly denominational," involved excessive entanglement between the state and the religious organization.[88] The reasoning for this is clear.

First, if the state offers credit for release time programs, it is encouraging students to participate by offering a "reward."[89] Second, if the state offers credit, then it might seek to regulate what is being taught in the religious classes, leading to an Establishment Clause problem.

Finally, the least acceptable means by which a school system might promote release time activities is coercion. Courts have universally held that to coerce a student to accept a particular religious belief is against the fundamental tenets of the Constitution. In fact, the Supreme Court in *Zorach* permitted release time activities in New York because it found no evidence that the school district coerced students to attend: "If in fact coercion were used, if it were established that any one or more teachers were using their office to persuade or force the students to take the religious instruction, a wholly different case would be presented."[90] Even the most subtle forms of coercion are impermissible when dealing with school-age children. As previously noted, many courts deem this class of individuals "impressionable" and in need of special protection.[91]

ACCOMMODATION AND NEUTRALITY

Although *Zorach* upheld the constitutionality of release time programs, public school administrators still need to consider many factors before establishing the program within a school district. The administrator should pursue two goals: accommodation and neutrality. Students should be permitted access to a release time program in order to accommodate their religious beliefs.[92] The *Lanner* court suggested that "there must be some measure of accommodation to avoid the constitutionally impermissible result of totally subordinating either religion clause to the other."[93] Also, as noted above, courts have used accommodation to meet the secular purpose part of the *Lemon* test.[94]

The school should be completely neutral in allowing release time as an option for its students. If the school encourages or discourages religion in any way, the program will fail.[95] Courts have never held that release time contravenes the Establishment Clause. Instead, only the manner in which the program is implemented has been called into question.[96] Because of this, each element of the program must be examined with close scrutiny to determine whether such elements are constitutional.

REGISTRATION

Before a program can be established, the sponsoring religious group must learn which students wish to participate in the classes. Of course, schools should require parental consent before they allow minor children to participate.

Courts have complicated the registration phase of the program by the different rules they have promulgated. For example, in *Shenandoah*, a federal court created a dilemma by prohibiting religious instructors from entering school grounds and also prohibiting public school teachers from passing out registration cards.[97] The most appropriate way to resolve this problem is for the religious organization to ask the school for a mailing list of all the students and their parents.[98] The religious organization could then mail registration cards directly to the students with limited involvement from school officials. The students or parents would then return the cards to the school so that school officials could properly excuse the students.

A second way to register students for release time classes is to place the registration card in the packet of registration materials disseminated by the school.[99] To prevent the appearance of school endorsement, no advertising material should accompany the card. Further, if the school has a registration day on which it requires students to come to the school to sign up for classes, no release time official should be present unless other nonschool personnel are also there. A release time official could set up a booth to answer questions only if other booths are present for other elective courses.[100]

Another, less desirable way to handle registration cards is to distribute them to the students directly in class. This, however, immediately raises the problem for the public school of an appearance of endorsement (no matter who actually passes them out). In addition, if the public school teacher passes out the cards, an expenditure problem is raised since the school uses public funds to pay for the time it takes to handle this task. If the religious instructor distributes them, a coercion problem may be raised. At most, the religious instructor should distribute the cards, give a brief explanation of the program, and arrange to retrieve the cards at a later time. Certainly, neither instructor should offer rewards for completing the cards.

CLASS LOCATION

The location of the program is another important factor to consider in implementing a release time program. As suggested earlier, an ideal place to hold classes is a local church building. This provides an environment that is outside the purview of the state, yet is often conveniently located close to the school.

If no church building is nearby, a second option is to hold the classes in portable trailers. This option provides a private setting within walking distance of the school. However, great care should be taken to avoid parking the trailers on school property. The buses or trailers should be parked on property which is privately owned (with permission of the landowner). Some courts have, however, allowed officials to park the vehicles on public streets near the school.[101]

Other possible options may be available. Recreational centers frequently rent rooms which may be suitable for instruction. Renting school property (although allowed in many areas by statute) may create the impression of endorsement and should be avoided.[102]

CLASS SCHEDULING

Scheduling of the release time program is still another factor for administrators to consider. Release time activities usually last approximately one hour once a week during the school year. However, this is not an important factor in determining whether the program is constitutional.[103]

Some programs have classes which are conducted before the school day begins and after it ends, with successful results.[104] The traditional release time program, however, takes place during the school day. An hour of the school district's time is a reasonable accommodation for release time classes.

LOGISTICS

At the designated hour for the release time classes, the public school teacher should escort the students to an area where the religious instructor assumes responsibility for the children and transports them to the site of the release time program. In most programs, this means walking to a nearby structure. However, courts have made no requirement that the site be within walking distance. One can conceive of a program in which transportation by bus is necessary.

While the class is in session, the students are under the care and responsibility of the release time instructor. This means that the instructor is the authorized disciplinarian for the unruly child. For this reason, the registration card signed by the parent should include a waiver of liability statement (as well as an explanation of the types of discipline that the instructor will use).

Since the state passes compulsory attendance laws, it should be responsible for the discipline of truants. However, the religious instructor should cooperate with the school by taking attendance and reporting the results.

The activities of the students who do not choose to attend the release time program has been a recurrent problem.[105] The problem is that students who remain in the classroom cannot receive formalized instruction without penalizing those who choose to attend the release time program. Conversely, parents of students who do not attend the program complain that their children are being forced into an environment of detention. One court has held that this did not violate a state constitution because teachers assigned special projects to the students who remained in the classroom.[106]

In addition, one can schedule the class time during a nonacademic portion of the day, such as recess or art, which would encroach less on academic time of all students. Whatever method an administrator uses, he or she must seek to balance the needs of both groups of students.

INSTRUCTORS AND TEACHING MATERIALS

To avoid entanglement problems, the sponsoring religious organization should select the instructors for release time programs. Public school employees should not teach the release time programs, even on a part-time basis. Such could create the appearance of endorsement (as well as the possibility of the expenditure of state funds for religious instruction). Aside from this restriction, teacher selection is at the discretion of the sponsoring organization, and no approval is needed from the school administration.[107]

Likewise, the material taught is at the complete discretion of the religious organization. It may be totally sectarian in nature. The material may also include historical information related to biblical theology.

Many release time programs incorporate moral and patriotic lessons into the curriculum. Obviously, the broader the scope of material taught, the more students it will attract.

CONCLUSION

Although the popularity of release time programs may have dwindled throughout the years, they are still as constitutional today as they were when the Supreme Court announced its ruling in *Zorach*.

Modern tests have had little effect on release time. They only serve as a reminder that the program has had a special constitutional niche carved out in more than forty years of court decisions.

Although courts have not called the program itself into question, they have examined its implementation. For this reason, great care should be taken in implementing a program in a local school district. Accommodation and neutrality should be the goals of any school district that permits a release time program.

PART SIX

Holidays and Graduation Prayers

The holding of the Court today plainly does not foreclose teaching about the Holy Scriptures or about the differences between religious sects in classes in literature or history. Indeed, whether or not the Bible is involved, it would be impossible to teach meaningfully many subjects in the social sciences or the humanities without some mention of religion. To what extent, and at what points in the curriculum, religious materials should be cited are matters which the courts ought to entrust very largely to the experienced officials who superintend our Nation's public schools. . . . Any attempt to impose rigid limits upon the mention of God or references to the Bible in the classroom would be fraught with dangers.

—Justice William Brennan,
Abington School District v. Schempp,
374 U.S. 203, 300-01 (1963)
(Brennan, J., concurring).

16

Religious Holiday Observances

Any notion that these symbols pose a real danger of establishment of a state church is far-fetched indeed.

—Chief Justice Warren Burger,
Lynch v. Donnelly,
465 U.S. 668, 686 (1984).

American culture is replete with traditions that are religious in origin.[1] The close relationship between religion and American cultural heritage has been the source of frequent legal conflict. In particular, Christmas observances in public schools[2] and other forums[3] have been the source of much confusion and controversy. Observances include, but are not limited to, classroom discussion and study of a holiday or an assembly attended by more than one class to commemorate or learn about a holiday.

These observances have been legally challenged for violating the First Amendment Establishment Clause. In short, it is claimed that the Constitution proscribes all government (including public schools) recognition of and participation in religious holidays.

It must be remembered that the term "holiday" is derived from "holy day." Thus, what many think of as mere school vacations may originate from traditional religious observances. While constitutional challenges to religious holiday observances in public schools most frequently arise during the Christmas season, numerous religious holidays are recognized and often celebrated in the public calendar. The list of such festivals includes Christmas, Easter, Thanksgiving, Halloween, St. Valentine's Day, St. Patrick's Day, Mardi Gras, and, in some communities, Rosh Hashanah, Yom Kippur, Hanukkah, and Ramadan.[4]

The Christmas holiday will be the focus of this analysis because of its prominence in both the culture at large and many public school programs. The principles discussed, however, readily apply to other religious holidays.

A HISTORICAL PERSPECTIVE

The celebration of Christmas has not always been a prominent festival in Western culture. In the fourth century, Pope Julius I designated a feast day commemorating the Nativity of Jesus Christ.[5]

The widespread observance of Christmas in America did not emerge in its present form until well into the last century. In fact, some early Americans resisted the celebration of Christmas. For example, the Puritan founders of the Massachusetts Bay Colony vigorously opposed all public celebrations of the holiday. To the Puritans, the Christmas feast was a "Popish" practice lacking biblical foundation.[6] A Massachusetts law of 1659 imposed penalties upon "anybody who is found observing, by abstinence from labor, feasting, or any other way, any such days as Christmas day."[7]

By the mid-nineteenth century, Christmas had overcome much of the early Puritan resistance and was an increasingly popular, distinctive holiday. In 1836, for instance, Alabama became the first state to declare Christmas a legal holiday. By the end of the century, the remaining states and territories had followed suit.[8]

Official recognition of the Christmas holiday by the states was also reflected in public school calendars. Toward the end of the nineteenth century and into the twentieth century, states began enacting laws mandating school closure on December 25.[9] Soon it was customary for schools to dismiss their pupils for an extended Christmas vacation.

For nearly a century, public schools have observed the Christmas season. Typically, the holiday is celebrated with school plays, musical programs, montages, and decorations commemorating the birth of Jesus Christ.

However, as early as 1906, disputes arose over the content of such celebrations. In that year, thousands of Jewish students in New York City staged an emotionally charged and highly effective citywide boycott of the public schools to protest mandatory Christmas assemblies.[10]

More recent history is replete with challenges to religious holiday observances in public schools. For example, in Ithaca, New York, a school superintendent issued a policy mandating that all songs mentioning Jesus Christ be banned in music classes and annual Christmas programs.[11] A Minnesota school board barred Christmas trees, nativity scenes, the singing of religious and secular carols, and appearances by Santa Claus on school premises.[12]

Many school administrators have assumed that any acknowledgment of the nation's religious heritage is unconstitutional, and they have stripped the public schools of all remaining vestiges of traditional religious holiday observances. But they misunderstand what the Constitution mandates concerning religion in American public life. The Constitution, and the United States Supreme Court's interpretation of it, afford a certain latitude as to religious expression, activities, and observances.

ACCOMMODATING NEUTRALITY

While it is true that certain state action involving religion transgresses Constitutional guarantees, "not every involvement of religion in public life," Supreme Court Justice William Brennan has acknowledged, "is unconstitutional."[13] Accommodating neutrality (see chapter 5) is a position the Supreme Court has consistently espoused. In essence, it means that government action which is "simply a tolerable acknowledgment of beliefs widely held among the people of this country" is not *per se* an unconstitutional "establishment" of religion.[14] In fact, the Supreme Court has said that the Constitution does not require complete separation of church and state.

> [The Constitution] *affirmatively mandates accommodation,* not mere tolerance, of all religions, and forbids hostility toward any. . . . Anything less would require the "callous indifference" we have said was never intended by the Establishment Clause. . . . Indeed, we have observed, such hostility would bring us into "war with our national tradition as embodied in the First Amendment's guaranty of the free exercise of religion."[15]

The spirit of accommodating neutrality was specifically recognized in the context of Christmas observances in 1984 in *Lynch v. Donnelly.*[16] There the Supreme Court upheld a municipality's custom of erecting a nativity scene surrounded by secular symbols of the season. In *Lynch,* the Court instructed that "taking official note of Christmas, and of our religious heritage" is not necessarily an unconstitutional endorsement of religion.[17] "There is an unbroken history," the Court continued, "of official acknowledgment by all three branches of government of the role of religion in American life from at least 1789."[18]

The Supreme Court favorably reviewed numerous public practices embedded in American history and traditions that recognize religious holidays:

> Our history is replete with official references to the value and invocation of Divine guidance in deliberations and pronouncements of the Founding Fathers and contemporary leaders. Beginning in the early colonial period long before Independence, a day of Thanksgiving was celebrated as a religious holiday to give thanks for the bounties of Nature as gifts from God. President Washington and his successors proclaimed Thanksgiving, with all its religious overtones, a day of national celebration and Congress made it a National Holiday more than a century ago. That holiday has not lost its theme of expressing thanks for Divine aid any more than has Christmas lost its religious significance.
>
> Executive Orders and other official announcements of Presidents and of the Congress have proclaimed both Christmas and Thanksgiving National Holidays in religious terms. And, by Acts of Congress, it has long been the practice that federal employees are released from duties on

these National Holidays, while being paid from the same public revenues that provide the compensation of the Chaplains of the Senate and the House and the military services. Thus, it is clear that Government has long recognized—indeed it has subsidized—holidays with religious significance. . . .

Art galleries supported by public revenues display religious paintings . . . with religious messages, notably the Last Supper, and paintings depicting the Birth of Christ, the Crucifixion, and the Resurrection, among many others with explicit Christian themes and messages. . . .

There are countless other illustrations of the Government's acknowledgment of our religious heritage and governmental sponsorship of graphic manifestations of that heritage. Congress has directed the President to proclaim a National Day of Prayer each year "on which [day] the people of the United States may turn to God in prayer and meditation at churches, in groups, and as individuals." Our Presidents have repeatedly issued such Proclamations. Presidential Proclamations and messages have been issued to commemorate Jewish Heritage Week and the Jewish High Holy Days. . . . Through this accommodation, as Justice Douglas observed, governmental action has "follow[ed] the best of our traditions" and "respect[ed] the religious nature of our people."[19]

Significantly, the Supreme Court opined that "Christmas hymns and carols in public schools" are one of the legitimate "forms of taking official note of Christmas, and of our religious heritage."[20] The Court concluded, "[a]ny notion that these symbols pose a real danger of establishment of a state church is far-fetched indeed."[21]

Lynch v. Donnelly dealt, of course, with the display of a nativity scene by a municipality. A more sensitive question, however, concerns religious observances in public schools.[22]

RELIGIOUS HOLIDAY OBSERVANCES IN THE PUBLIC SCHOOLS

Although the Supreme Court has decided a number of cases concerning religion and the public schools (see chapter 5), the Court has never specifically addressed the constitutionality of religious observances in public schools.

Thus, there is no definitive guidance as to what is or is not permitted. However, the Court's decisions in other controversies pertaining to religion and the public schools probe the limits of constitutionally permissible holiday practices. Carefully analyzed, these opinions, together with lower federal court holdings, suggest guidelines to be followed that will allow any such holiday observances in the public schools.

The leading judicial pronouncement on how public schools may observe religious holidays is *Florey v. Sioux Falls School District 49-5*.[23] In *Florey*, a federal appellate court affirmed a school board policy which permitted the observance of holidays with both a secular and religious basis, provided that the commemorations are conducted in a "prudent and objective manner."[24]

The Supreme Court declined to review this case, allowing the appeals court ruling to stand. Although the *Florey* decision is not binding on federal courts outside its particular circuit, as a decision of the highest federal court to address the holiday issue in public schools, it stands as persuasive precedent. The *Florey* opinion, for example, was the basis of an opinion on the constitutionality of Christmas programs in public schools offered by the attorney general of Arkansas.[25]

The facts of *Florey* are important. In 1977, the school district received a parent's complaint that Christmas programs performed by two kindergarten classes were "replete with religious content."[26] In response, the superintendent of schools "set up a citizen's committee to study the issue of church and state in relationship to school district functions,"[27] and to formulate rules outlining the bounds of what is constitutionally permissible under the First Amendment's Establishment Clause. After deliberations and public hearings, the school board adopted the policy recommended by the committee.

The policy unequivocally stated that "no religious belief or nonbelief should be promoted by the school district or its employees, and none should be disparaged."[28] The express purpose of the policy was the advancement of the "students' knowledge and appreciation of the role that our religious heritage has played in the social, cultural, and historical development of civilization."[29]

In pertinent part, the policy provided that only holidays with both a religious and secular basis may be observed. Music, art, literature, and drama may be included in the curriculum only if presented in a prudent and objective manner and only as a part of the cultural and religious heritage of the holiday. Religious symbols may be used only as a teaching aid or resource and only if they are displayed as a part of the cultural and religious heritage of the holiday and are temporary in nature.[30]

Dissatisfied with the new policy, the original complainant, with the assistance of the American Civil Liberties Union (ACLU), filed a lawsuit in federal district court seeking to invalidate the rules and to enjoin their enforcement. The plaintiff alleged that the policy constituted an "establishment of religion" in violation of the First Amendment. The district court upheld the school board policy, and the federal appeals court affirmed the decision.

THE *LEMON* TEST

The *Florey* court evaluated the school board policy under the tripartite test enunciated in 1971 by the Supreme Court in *Lemon v. Kurtzman*.[31] This test (see chapter 5), developed over many years, must be satisfied in order for a challenged practice to pass constitutional muster.[32]

When evaluating a school's religious holiday observance under the

Lemon test, courts are concerned with more than the mere content (or text) of holiday programs.[33] Courts are also concerned with the degree of government involvement and the *context* in which the program is presented. If teachers and administrators participate in the preparations, if school schedules are rearranged to accommodate holiday observances, and if school resources and facilities are set aside for such programs, government appears to be directly involved. The greater and more intimate the involvement, the more intense the constitutional scrutiny by the courts.

An evaluation of "context" entails a review of the time, place, and atmosphere of the observance.[34] If holiday observances take place in a setting in which pupils expect to study and learn about the holiday rather than in a devotional or worshipful atmosphere (in a passive rather than active sense), then the context may serve what the courts consider a neutralizing function.[35] Constitutional analysis of religious holiday observances pursuant to the *Lemon* tripartite test thus takes into account the elements of content, context, and degree of government involvement in the program.

SECULAR PURPOSE

The first prong of the tripartite test requires that each action, requirement, or rule promulgated by state agencies (such as public schools) have a secular purpose. The appropriate inquiry is not whether there is a secular purpose for the presentation of religious music or symbols in holiday pageants. Rather, the question is whether there is a secular purpose for allowing the holiday observance *as a whole,* of which religious songs and symbols are only a part.[36]

The *Florey* court took particular notice of the language of the policy which asserted that only holidays with both a religious and secular basis were to be observed. The dual nature of such holidays, because it de-emphasizes the religious elements, reduces constitutional problems with the policy.

Moreover, the appeals court in *Florey* noted that the policy served the secular purposes of advancing the students' knowledge of society's cultural and religious heritage, as well as providing students the opportunity to perform publicly a full range of music, drama, and poetry, including that with religious content.[37] The district court had earlier observed that to forbid students from studying or performing music because of its religious content "would give students a truncated view of our culture."[38]

The Supreme Court itself has recognized the mere fact that a practice has a purely religious origin or that it coincides with the beliefs of a religion does not necessarily render the activity unconstitutional. In *McGowan v. Maryland,*[39] for example, the Court upheld Sunday closing laws despite their undeniable religious origin because the "present purpose and effect" of such laws is to provide a uniform day of rest and recreation for all citizens.[40]

The *Florey* policy, unlike the school prayer cases, did not involve pervasively religious exercises.[41] Indeed, holiday activities were not mandated in *Florey*. The policy merely accommodated the inclusion of certain programs in the curriculum in the event that teachers believed such programs would enhance their overall instructional plan. As the federal appeals court observed, "[t]he rules are an attempt to delineate the scope of permissible activity within the district, not to mandate a statewide program of religious inculcation."[42]

The *Florey* rationale is consistent with those cases decided by the Supreme Court wherein certain religious practices in public schools were held unconstitutional. Contrary to popular misconceptions, for example, the school prayer cases did not foreclose all teaching about the Bible or religion (see discussion of these cases in chapter 5). In *Schempp* (the 1963 Bible-reading decision), the Supreme Court counseled that objective teaching about religion is indispensable to a quality education:

> [I]t might well be said that one's education is not complete without a study of comparative religion or the history of religion and its relationship to the advancement of civilization. It certainly may be said that the Bible is worthy of study for its literary and historic qualities. Nothing we have said here indicates that such study of the Bible or of religion, when presented objectively as part of a secular program of education, may not be effected consistently with the First Amendment.[43]

Likewise, the *Florey* court held that Christmas carols, like religious dramas, paintings, and other forms of artistic expression, are undoubtedly worthy of study.[44] This is consistent with the comments in an earlier Supreme Court decision: "Music without sacred music, architecture minus the cathedral, or painting without the Scriptural themes would be eccentric and incomplete, even from a secular point of view."[45]

Indeed, public schools bear an affirmative duty as part of their educational mission to develop curricula that will create an awareness of and appreciation for American religious heritage and traditions.[46] This may include the singing of Christmas carols in the public schools, according to the *Florey* court.

PRINCIPAL OR PRIMARY EFFECT

Under the second prong of the *Lemon* test, in order to pass constitutional muster, the principal or primary effect of the government action in question must be one that neither advances nor inhibits religion.

The ACLU argued in *Florey* that Christmas carols are nothing more than prayers set to music, and holiday programs are so like a worship service that they necessarily have the effect of advancing religion.[47] Although the Supreme Court has acknowledged that the advancement or inhibition of religion is indeed forbidden, the Court has asserted that the "study" of religion need not be expunged from the curriculum "when presented objectively as part of a secular program of education."[48]

To determine whether religion was advanced or inhibited by the school district policy, the *Florey* court "looked to see if a genuine 'secular program of education' is furthered by the rules."[49] The school policy, the court noted, provided that religion is to be neither promoted nor disparaged in the schools. Moreover, the express purpose of the school policy was to teach about the customs and cultural heritage of the United States and other countries. Furthermore, the *Florey* court found that "public performance may be a legitimate part of secular study."[50]

The advancement of these legitimate educational objectives was found to be the "principal effect" of the policy in *Florey*. The school board guidelines allowed the presentation of materials so integrated into American culture and heritage that, although of religious origin, they have acquired a significance no longer confined only to the religious sphere of life.[51] As the court held: "Since all programs and materials authorized by the [school board] rules must deal with the secular or cultural basis or heritage of the holidays and since the material must be presented in a prudent and objective manner and symbols used as a teaching aid, the advancement of a 'secular program of education,' and not of religion, is the primary effect of the rules."[52]

In *Florey*, the plaintiffs sought to establish that since some students would perceive the material as religious in nature despite the acknowledged secular benefits, the challenged policy failed the "primary effect" test. The appeals court, emphasizing the significant modifiers "primary" and "principal," held that a mere showing that some students might perceive a religious effect was insufficient to invalidate the policy. Rather, plaintiffs must demonstrate that the holiday programs could not legitimately be used for other than religious purposes.[53]

While public school administrators should, of course, be sensitive to the religious beliefs or disbeliefs of students and should attempt to avoid conflict, they need not, and should not, as the *Florey* court held, sacrifice the quality of the students' education by censoring all curricular material that is religious in origin.[54] "It would be literally impossible," the court concluded, "to develop a public school curriculum that did not in some way affect the religious or nonreligious sensibilities of some of the students or their parents."[55]

EXCESSIVE ENTANGLEMENT

The entanglement prong of the *Lemon* test addresses the concern that a close association between religion and the educational program will foster an impermissible emphasis upon religious doctrines or continuing governmental involvement in and/or oversight of the challenged activity. There was some doubt whether this inquiry was even applicable in *Florey*, since it normally had been applied in situations involving state aid to parochial schools.[56]

The *Florey* court, adopting the district court finding, held that the entanglement test was not violated. Examining the school board policy as a whole, the appeals court concluded it would be speculation to find that any sect or religious institution would benefit under the policy. Moreover, there was no aid flowing directly from the public school to any religion. Finally, and most importantly, the *Florey* court noted that instead of "entangling the schools in religion, the rules provide the means to ensure that the [school] district steers clear of religious exercises."[57]

THE ENDORSEMENT TEST

In recent years, the Supreme Court and lower federal courts have increasingly utilized another test to determine when government action impinges upon the First Amendment Establishment Clause. This has been denominated the "endorsement test" and was first formulated in *Lynch v. Donnelly*[58] by Justice Sandra Day O'Connor. In *Lynch*, Justice O'Connor proposed the endorsement test (see chapter 5) as an alternative to or refinement of the *Lemon* test.

Although the endorsement test was formulated subsequent to the decision in *Florey*, it would appear to have a bearing on cases concerned with Christmas observances in the public schools. This fact necessitates a discussion of this doctrine. Justice O'Connor's "endorsement test" states that a government action is invalid if it creates the perception that government is endorsing or disapproving a religion.[59] The fundamental concern is whether the challenged governmental activity conveys "a message to nonadherents that they are outsiders, not full members of the political community, and an accompanying message to adherents that they are insiders, favored members of the political community."[60] Therefore, according to the endorsement test, a governmental action or law which does not create a perception of endorsement could be upheld even though it actually has a primary effect of advancing or inhibiting religion.[61] Similarly, a government action or law which creates a perception of endorsement would be unconstitutional even though it neither advances nor inhibits religion.[62] The relevant perception under Justice O'Connor's test is that of an informed, objective observer familiar with the text, legislative history, and the implementation of the governmental policy in question.[63]

Various lower courts have followed Justice O'Connor's endorsement test.[64] Some commentators argue that the Supreme Court "treats the 'no endorsement' test as an occasional supplement to the reigning *Lemon* test, but not as a successor to, or even a definitive refinement of, that test."[65] However, the Supreme Court has turned to the endorsement test to decide some recent Establishment Clause controversies.[66]

Justice Harry Blackmun, writing in a 1989 decision, stated that the endorsement test is merely an articulation of principles already underlying the Supreme Court's Establishment Clause jurisprudence. Blackmun further noted that the term "endorsement" only rephrases Supreme Court holdings prohibiting "favoritism" or "promotion" of religion.[67]

In essence then, the endorsement test does not alter the Supreme Court's position that government accommodation of religion is mandated by the Constitution.[68] In other words, by accommodating religion, the government does not necessarily endorse it.[69] Thus, in situations similar to *Florey*, religious holiday observances should pass the endorsement test.

THE FREE EXERCISE ISSUE

In addition to asserting a violation of the Establishment Clause, the plaintiffs in *Florey* also claimed the school policy violated students' free exercise rights. It was argued that religious holiday observances in the schools offended the religious sensibilities of objecting students, demeaned their religious beliefs, and thereby violated their free exercise rights.

While acknowledging that the state must avoid hostility toward any religious belief and may not coerce a student to participate in any activity contrary to his or her convictions, the *Florey* court noted that public schools are not required to delete all curricular materials that some student or sect claims to be offensive or disparaging to religion. Absent an Establishment Clause violation, the answer is not to deprive the school of a beneficial educational tool. Rather, the appropriate remedy may be to permit offended students to be excused from participation.[70] Thus, finding no Establishment Clause violation and the inclusion of an excusal provision (see chapter 14), the *Florey* court dismissed the free exercise claim.[71]

PRACTICAL GUIDELINES

The following is a summary of guidelines that permit religious holiday observances in the public schools. These guidelines are drawn from numerous court decisions and legal scholarship. These guidelines are offered as assistance to public school administrators in establishing their own policies.

PRESENTATION AND PURPOSES OF RELIGIOUS HOLIDAY OBSERVANCES

Holidays rooted in religious traditions but with diverse secular manifestations may be recognized and observed in public schools through educational materials and assembly programs. Materials should be presented in a manner that serves the academic goal of educating students about the diverse religious heritage of American society and the role of religion in the social, cultural, and historical development of civilization.

Schools should, as the *Florey* court recognized, utilize religious holiday observances to foster among students and parents mutual respect for and understanding of the diverse cultural, ethnic, and religious backgrounds represented in society[72] and to promote a spirit of peace and good will.[73]

Religious holiday ceremonies may also offer students a forum in which to perform publicly the great musical and literary works associated with traditional holidays. These have acquired a significance no longer confined exclusively to the religious sphere of life. Public performance is a legitimate aspect of secular study.[74]

Class discussions or activities related to holiday observances may also advance the legitimate secular purpose of ensuring the rights of students to engage in expressive activity without unreasonable restraint and discrimination based on the content of their speech.[75]

These are a few of the legitimate purposes for religious holiday observances in public schools. A school district's *written* guidelines governing such observances should state expressly their secular purposes in order to avoid subsequent claims that the policy was adopted with the impermissible intent to advance religion.

OBJECTIVE AND PRUDENT ACKNOWLEDGMENT OF RELIGIOUS HOLIDAYS

Religious holidays may be acknowledged in public schools through instructional materials or assembly programs. However, schools may not engage in religious advocacy, rituals, or devotional exercises. While school districts and their employees may educate about religious traditions, they may not promote or disparage any religion. Teachers must assiduously avoid the occasion of religious holidays as an opportunity to proselytize.

Schools have an affirmative duty to teach about religious, cultural, and ethnic observances, but religious topics must be studied in "an unbiased and objective manner without sectarian indoctrination."[76] Therefore, music, literature, drama, and other forms of artistic expression having religious themes or sources may be a part of the curriculum for school-sponsored discussions and assembly programs "if presented in a prudent and objective manner and as a traditional part of the cultural and religious heritage of the particular holiday."[77] To avoid constitutional challenge, holiday musical programs should not be exclusively or predominantly religious in content.

USE OF RELIGIOUS SYMBOLS

The use of religious symbols—such as a cross, nativity scene, menorah, or other symbol—is permitted, provided the symbols are used as instructional tools or resources, displayed on a *temporary* basis,[78] and, exhibited as examples of the cultural and religious heritage attendant to the religious holiday.[79] Holiday symbols arguably drained of all vestiges of their religious source or significance—such as Christmas trees or holly wreaths[80]—and religiously neutral holiday symbols—such as the Easter bunny or snowmen—can be displayed in public schools.[81]

This guideline was affirmed by the *Florey* court, but its validity was cast in doubt by *dictum* in the Supreme Court's decision in *County of Allegheny v. American Civil Liberties Union, Greater Pittsburgh Chapter*.[82] In *Allegheny*, the Court upheld the combined display of religious and secular symbols on the steps of a city hall, but hinted that a similar display in a public school may be inappropriate.[83]

This use of religious symbols in public schools must also be evaluated in the light of *Stone v. Graham*,[84] in which the Supreme Court ruled that the Ten Commandments may not be displayed on public school classroom walls. The Court held that the "purpose for posting the Ten Commandments . . . is plainly religious in nature."[85] The guideline set forth above, in contrast, serves the legitimate secular purpose of providing teachers visual, instructional aids to assist in the study of and "about" religion and religious traditions.[86]

A student may choose to create religious artworks or symbols to commemorate religious holidays, but school officials should not encourage or discourage such creations, nor should they be used by school officials to promote religion. Also, a student may bring such religious symbols to school to exhibit and discuss as part of a "show and tell" program.[87]

VOLUNTARY PARTICIPATION AND EXCUSAL POLICIES

Forcing a pupil to participate in or even attend an activity inimical to his or her religious or nonreligious beliefs raises serious free exercise concerns, even absent an Establishment Clause violation.[88] Any student who does not wish to participate in classroom discussions or school assemblies because of religious beliefs or reasons of conscience must be excused with no loss of standing or punishment.[89]

School administrators must be aware of the often subtle and indirect coercion attendant to excusal policies (see chapter 14). Such policies, as Supreme Court Justice William Brennan has argued, may subject religious minorities to a "cruel dilemma. In consequence, even devout children may well avoid claiming their right and simply continue to participate in exercises distasteful to them because of an understandable reluctance to be stigmatized as atheists or nonconformists simply on the basis of their request [to be excused]."[90] Moreover, under current Establishment Clause jurisprudence, excusing objecting pupils from a specific discussion or activity is not a valid rationale for school sponsorship of religious exercises or worship for nonobjecting students.

Voluntary programs or excusal provisions protect students whose religious principles would be violated if they were forced to participate in religious holiday observances. "In constitutional terms," according to one commentator, "voluntarism largely negates alleged governmental interference with the free exercise of religion. However, the question of voluntary versus mandatory participation is irrelevant where the issue is establishment of religion. The courts have repeatedly stated that if a program violates the Establishment Clause, it cannot be saved by declaring it voluntary" or including an excusal provision.[91]

COMPULSORY ATTENDANCE AND RELIGIOUS HOLIDAYS

As discussed above, all students should have the opportunity to be excused without penalty from participating in discussions or activities related to religious holiday observances.[92] A different question is whether a student may be exempted from compliance with compulsory attendance laws in order to observe a religious holiday.

Many jurisdictions provide statutory exemptions to allow students and their parents to observe religious holidays on days when school is in session. Where there is no statutory exemption, the First Amendment Free Exercise Clause requires, as one federal appellate court has held, a reasonable number of excused absences without penalty (such as refusing to provide make-up assignments or lowering grades) to observe religious holidays.[93]

One state court has held that public school officials may even prohibit the scheduling of extracurricular activities on Friday night, Saturday, and Sunday morning to avoid conflicts with students' religious beliefs.[94] It is improbable, however, that a court would compel a school to reschedule a school-related activity in order for a student to attend.[95] For example, one federal appeals court has held that a school is not required to reschedule commencement exercises in order to avoid a conflict with the Sabbath observed by an Orthodox Jewish student.[96]

EQUAL TREATMENT FOR ALL RELIGIOUS FAITHS

In an effort to achieve balance, many school districts schedule Hanukkah celebrations to coincide with Christmas programs and devote attention to the religious holidays of other faiths during the appropriate season. Although constitutional concerns are heightened when schools observe the holidays of one religious faith only, such concerns are not necessarily resolved by observing the holidays of many religions. If the observance of one religious faith constitutes an impermissible "establishment of religion," the constitutional violation is not ameliorated by promoting other religions through holiday observances.[97]

The educational objective of the school is indeed advanced by expanding students' knowledge of diverse religious heritages, traditions, and customs. However, school officials must not forget that religious holidays, regardless of the religion represented, must be observed in an objective and prudent manner, without sectarian indoctrination.

STUDENT-INITIATED RELIGIOUS EXPRESSION

Restriction or prohibition by public officials of student-initiated, spontaneous self-expression in speech, music, or visual arts is not consistent with constitutional requirements. Indeed, the First Amendment guarantees all citizens, including public school students, freedoms of speech, association, and religious exercise. As the Supreme Court has held, the constitutional rights of students or teachers are not "shed at the schoolhouse gate."[98] In this respect, public school officials have a compelling interest in ensuring that students exercise their fundamental First Amendment rights which, by the way, outweigh any remote Establishment Clause concerns.[99] Thus, students have the right to express themselves even if the content of their speech is religious, and their speech occurs in a public school.[100]

Such expressions of religious belief or nonbelief must be accommodated "so long as the activity does not disrupt or otherwise intrude upon the basic educational functions of the school or require any direction or supervision by [school employees]."[101] Of course, this guideline does not authorize structured religious practices in the schools under the guise of "spontaneous student expression."

Students have the right to distribute in public schools religiously oriented material such as holiday greeting cards or newspapers.[102] While school officials may impose content-neutral time, place, and manner restrictions on such activity to prevent disruption of the educational process, they are enjoined from enforcing blanket bans on such activities.[103]

CONCLUSION

In *Lynch v. Donnelly*,[104] the Supreme Court upheld the constitutionality of a municipality's maintenance of a nativity scene within the context of a larger holiday display including secular symbols of the season. Many in the religious community applauded the Court's decision.

Lynch was later modified in *County of Allegheny v. American Civil Liberties Union, Greater Pittsburgh Chapter*.[105] There the Supreme Court sustained a city's display of a Christmas tree and Hanukkah menorah outside city hall, but forbade another government agency from displaying inside a government building a creche that was not presented in the context of a larger secular holiday exhibit.

Like *Lynch*, many welcomed the *Florey* decision as an affirmation of the role of religion in public life. The holding of *Florey*, however, is somewhat limited. The *Florey* court specifically rejected the notion that the policy permitted activities "religious in nature." Rather, the policy authorized the "study" of religion and religious instruction when presented objectively as part of a secular program of education.[106]

Christmas and other holidays which were religious in their inception have been so assimilated into and secularized by American culture that they can no longer be classified exclusively as "holy days."[107] Consequently, some have argued that performing religious songs and using religious symbols in religious holiday observances in the public school, within the strictures of the *Lemon* test, debase the deeply spiritual significance of these holidays and serve only to secularize and acculturate the songs and symbols.[108]

Those who take religion seriously have reason to be alarmed when courts and public officials proclaim that nativity scenes[109] or Christmas carols[110] or Sabbath days[111] have been drained of all religious significance.[112] Indeed, one commentator has argued that if Christians were to seek to revive the spiritual significance of Christmas as a strictly religious "holy day," they might justifiably attack the secular aspects of Christmas observances in public schools as acts hostile to their religion and thus constitutionally impermissible.[113]

Another critic of holiday observances has argued that the "watering down of a Christmas program in order to 'balance' its religious content with secular content is a secularizing force. Ironically, those teachers who try to promote Christianity by placing some religion into their Christmas programs do not understand the consequences of their actions."[114]

Unquestionably, there is considerable sentiment in society for promoting religious holiday observances, even under the strictures of current Establishment Clause jurisprudence. For many, this is a modest attempt, for example, to keep "Christ in Christmas" and to acknowledge the significant role of religion in the public life of the nation. Yet, in the current legal environment, such efforts may only accelerate the secularization of public life.

17

Graduation Prayers

*To invoke Divine guidance . . . is not . . . an "establishment"
of religion or a step toward establishment; it is simply a tolerable acknowledgment of beliefs widely held among the
people of this country.*

—Chief Justice Warren Burger,
Marsh v. Chambers,
463 U.S. 783, 792 (1983).

The constitutional validity of governmental prayer was a source of
debate in the First Congress[1] and has more recently posed a difficult
question for the United States Supreme Court.[2] The Supreme Court has
decided only two questions with regard to government-initiated prayer.

The first challenge the Supreme Court considered was whether a state
could sanction prayers to be recited by school children.[3] The Court held that
a law requiring a child to recite a state-written prayer in the public schools
was unconstitutional. In line with this decision, the Court (some two
decades later) also invalidated a state law which required the school to provide a moment of silence for meditation or voluntary prayer.[4]

Second, in *Marsh v. Chambers,*[5] the Supreme Court considered
whether a law that provides for a state-paid legislative chaplain violates the
First Amendment Establishment Clause. The Court there held that a prayer
delivered by such a chaplain was a constitutional "acknowledgment of
beliefs widely held among the people of this country."[6] *Marsh* may be distinguished by the fact that it did not take place in a public school and that
there was a long history of legislative prayer (including the founding era).

While the constitutionality of classroom prayer and legislative prayer
has been addressed by the Supreme Court, the Court has not confronted the
issue of whether invocations and benedictions delivered in public high
school graduation ceremonies are constitutional.[7] Such will be discussed in
light of First Amendment guarantees.[8] Because the courts have primarily

focused on the Establishment Clause in assessing the validity of governmental acts which touch religion, discussion will center around the potential for this type of violation.[9] Issues of free speech and free exercise are also implicated and will be addressed accordingly.

AN ATTEMPT AT AN ANSWER:
STEIN V. PLAINWELL COMMUNITY SCHOOLS

The opinion in *Stein v. Plainwell Community Schools*[10] involved two cases. In both cases, the parents of school children sought to enjoin the invocations and benedictions to be delivered at commencement. In both districts, the graduation ceremony was voluntary, and the receipt of a diploma was not contingent on attendance.

In one district, the prayers were delivered by student volunteers chosen from a group of honor students. The content of the prayer was the sole responsibility of the student speaker.[11]

In the other district, the school's service was organized by the students. The students normally decided to include an invocation and benediction in the program and elected a senior class representative who chose the speaker.

The *Stein* court held that the decision in *Marsh* (upholding legislative prayer) was applicable to invocations delivered at high school graduation ceremonies. The federal appeals court saw a similarity in the two types of prayer and engaged in analysis by analogy. The court reasoned that because graduation ceremonies are analogous to the legislative sessions referred to in *Marsh*, the standard applied in *Marsh* would apply to the *Stein* scenario. As Justice O'Connor noted in her concurrence in *Lynch v. Donnelly*,[12] the invocation serves to "solemniz[e] public occasions, express . . . confidence in the future, and encourag[e] what is worthy of appreciation in society."[13] The *Stein* court maintained that it would be inconsistent to sanction invocations for judges and legislators, yet not for students memorializing their passage to adulthood.

In distinguishing between invocations given at graduation and classroom prayer, the court in *Stein* recognized, as did the Supreme Court in *Marsh*, that the opportunity for coercion at a graduation service is not nearly so great as in the classroom. Neither is there great potential for religious indoctrination. The public nature of the ceremony and the presence of parents creates a wholly different atmosphere from that in a classroom. Furthermore, the teacher-student relationship, a determining factor in the "school prayer" cases, is absent. Thus, when the court faced the decision of whether to apply the classroom prayer cases or the ceremonial prayer case, it reasoned that graduation prayers were analogous to *Marsh*.

Even though the *Stein* court held that the *Marsh* standard was applicable, indicating that it would affirm the lower court, the *Stein* court reversed, holding that the prayers at issue were in violation of the *Marsh* standard. In one case, the speaker had invoked the Christian Deity. The court held that using this language was unconstitutional.[14]

Alternatively, the court in *Stein* held that the prayer must be as *neutral* as that used in other governmental forums. The concurring judge explained as well that the prayer cannot be sectarian or denominational[15] and stressed that it must be similar to prayer delivered in state legislatures, in Congress, and in the courts. In sum, the court scrutinized the content of the prayer and determined that its language did not conform to the American civil religion.

Problems with *Stein*

The *Stein* court faced a difficult decision. Obviously, several constitutional tests could have been employed to reach a conclusion.[16] The question centered on which test was most appropriate. The lower court in *Stein* recognized that the practice of including invocations and benedictions in high school commencements falls into the gray area between classroom prayer and legislative prayer. The task for courts in such situations, it was reasoned, is to decide whether the practice is closer to white or black.[17]

The court could have relied solely on the school prayer cases and determined that graduation prayers were unconstitutional. It could have chosen a strict *Marsh* analysis, or it could have analyzed the facts according to the test formulated in *Lemon v. Kurtzman*.[18] The dilemma the court faced is understandable. While a graduation ceremony is certainly not a legislative session, neither is it a classroom setting in which the state is daily making its students recite prayers. Because the Supreme Court has held one practice to be constitutional and the other invalid, the task of determining the validity of graduation prayers can be a difficult one.

While the *Stein* court paid lip service to *Marsh*, the court did not hold true to that standard in its application.[19] In *Stein*, the court expressly considered the content of the prayers and held that they were unconstitutional on that basis. In *Marsh*, however, the Supreme Court specifically absolved the judiciary of the right to assess the content of prayer.[20] The *Marsh* Court countered the assertion that the prayers were of the Judeo-Christian tradition by ruling that the content of the prayer was out of the judiciary's reach. It did recognize that if the speaker's purpose was to proselytize, advance a certain faith, or criticize a belief, a court was justified in finding the prayer unconstitutional. However, absent these elements, a court could not consider the content of prayer.

The judicial scrutiny of content could not even be invoked to exclude references to Jesus Christ.[21] A review of the record in *Marsh* is instructive on this point. The chaplain in *Marsh* conceded in his deposition that he often mentioned Jesus Christ in his prayers.[22] The chaplain testified that his prayers were Christian, but not sectarian,[23] and that he was not attempting to proselytize.[24] The Supreme Court in *Marsh* required nothing more and found no constitutional violation.[25]

In a footnote,[26] the *Marsh* Court referenced the chaplain's testimony where he stated that he had stopped using Jesus Christ's name. The chaplain testified that at some point he had dropped the reference, as a personal privilege, because a friend approached him in confidence and requested that he not mention Jesus Christ.[27] The Supreme Court did not indicate that this was determinative; and the Court did not instruct the chaplain to refrain from invoking Jesus Christ's name in the future.

The reasoning behind the Supreme Court's view in *Marsh* that it should abstain from an inquiry into content is obvious. The line between what is and is not acceptable would be too arbitrary to draw. One court may have evaluated the prayer and found that it was constitutional, while another court might find that the same prayer invokes Christian Deity.[28] As the federal district court in *Weisman v. Lee*[29] stated: "What must follow is gradual judicial development of what is acceptable public prayer."[30] Yet this result was clearly proscribed in *Engel v. Vitale*[31] where the Supreme Court opposed the proposition that the government could "control, support or influence the kinds of prayer the American people can say."[32] Thus, while the school is sponsoring the event, the one giving the prayer is not a state actor and should not be made to conform to a certain creed or dogma.

The *Stein* court's flawed logic was a result of misreading the issue.[33] The dissenting judge recognized that the issue was not *what kind* of prayer was constitutional, but whether *any* prayer was constitutional.[34] The plaintiffs argued that invocations that mention God or a Supreme Being, whether they be Christian, Jewish or any other religion, violate the Constitution. However, the court bypassed that issue and instead decided the case based on content, saying the prayer "employ[ed] the language of Christian theology."[35] Reading between the lines, the *Stein* court obviously concluded that prayer at graduation was constitutional as long as it did not go beyond the American civil religion (presumably the standard followed by Congress and the courts).

The *Stein* court focused on the content of the prayer without determining whether the speaker was attempting to proselytize or criticize a certain faith, thus creating a much stricter standard than that applied in *Marsh*.[36] The court held that the prayer must not go beyond the point of being "civil."[37]

However, in *Lynch v. Donnelly*,[38] the Supreme Court implied that the invocations given during legislative sessions are still religious.[39] The Supreme Court acknowledged that the invocations upheld in *Marsh* identified with a particular religion as the nativity scene did in *Lynch*. Yet the *Stein* court made it clear that if a prayer could be identified with the Christian religion, it would be held unconstitutional.[40]

The prayers used in opening legislative sessions in the nation's capital would seem to violate the *Stein* test. For example, only six days before the, *Marsh* decision was handed down, the United States Senate opened in a prayer that recognized the "Eternal God" as "[o]mnipotent," referenced God as the "Father in Heaven," and closed "in the name of the Prince of Peace."[41] In a prayer delivered six days after *Marsh*, the Senate chaplain quoted Psalm 127:1 and called on "the Lord" four times. The Senate chaplain also closed by invoking the "name of Him whose human perfection lay in obedience to [God]."[42]

Seven years later, the Senate prayers still reveal a preference for Christianity. On January 23, 1990, the prayer offered by the chaplain included a quotation from the book of Joshua in the Bible. The prayer also asked that "God, [the] Lord of history" would "help the Senators to take God seriously and to recover the theological connections and the spiritual commitments of our Founding Fathers, . . . [i]n light of this total bankruptcy of atheism as government policy." The prayer closed in "His name who is truth, justice, and righteousness incarnate."[43] Surely, if the *Stein* court was serious about upholding prayers similar to the prayers given in the nation's legislative sessions,[44] the Plainwell High School prayer would have withstood scrutiny.

Not surprisingly, the aftermath of the *Stein* decision has been confusion. Lower court decisions made after *Stein* have held that prayers in commencement ceremonies violate the Constitution.[45]

The reasoning engaged by either position on the issue of graduation prayers merits study. One can only guess at the result the Supreme Court would reach in such a case. However, when these arguments are carefully considered in light of accommodation and other constitutional principles, graduation prayers should be permitted.

THE SCHOOL PRAYER CASES

The *Stein* court made one point with which most commentators agree;[46] that is, graduation invocations should be distinguished from the prayers held unconstitutional in *Engel*[47] and *Schempp*.[48] The *Stein* court recognized the distinction,[49] but the dissent analyzed the issue more thoroughly. After discussing various landmark Supreme Court cases addressing religion in the public schools,[50] the dissent found that throughout the Supreme Court's opinions there is a common strand. The opinions indicate that the Supreme Court looks to four aspects of the challenged practices to determine if the practices are acceptable.[51]

The first aspect is the regularity with which the state performed the religious act.[52] In both *Engel* and *Schempp*, the prayers were recited every day.[53] The concern here is that when a prayer is repeated daily, the risk of indoctrination becomes greater.

The second aspect is whether the practice occurs in the classroom. In both cases, the setting was of critical importance in determining the constitutionality of the state action. For instance, in *Schempp* the Supreme Court noted that the school asked everyone to stand and recite the prayer in unison.[54] The exercises were part of the curricular activities of the school, and the students were compelled by law to attend. The Supreme Court also noted that the exercises were performed in a public school building under the guidance and participation of a teacher.[55] The concern here is evident. If a teacher stands before a group of young children every day and tells them to pray, the students feel compelled to participate. While the laws involved in both cases included provisions for those who did not want to participate, the Supreme Court reasoned that the day-to-day pressure to conform may force a student unwillingly to concede.[56]

The third concern, and perhaps the most important, was that the state was writing prayers for the people.[57] The Supreme Court was justifiably wary about school-initiated, school-sponsored, school-sanctioned prayers. Justice Hugo Black, no less than three times, explained in *Engel* the danger involved in state-composed prayer. Justice Black noted that the prayer in *Engel* was "composed by governmental officers as part of a governmental program to further religious beliefs."[58] Further, Justice Black noted:

> The First Amendment was added to the Constitution to stand as a guarantee that neither the power nor the prestige of the Federal Government would be used to control, support or influence the kinds of prayer the American People can say. . . . [G]overnment in this country, be it state or federal, is without power to prescribe by law any particular form of prayer which is to be used as an official prayer in carrying on any program of governmentally sponsored religious activity.[59]

The fourth issue of concern was that the practices were directed to young, impressionable students, creating a greater risk of indoctrination. As Justice Sandra Day O'Connor noted in her concurrence to *Wallace v. Jaffree:*[60] "This Court's decisions have recognized a distinction when government-sponsored religious exercises are directed at impressionable children who are required to attend school."[61]

In light of the above guidelines, graduation invocations do not demand the same scrutiny.[62] For example, a graduation invocation is voiced only one time per year, and a substantially different audience attends each time. Invocations are remote, isolated, and abbreviated acts[63] which pose no threat of indoctrination.[64]

The setting of a graduation service stands in stark contrast to the classroom where mandatory prayers are recited. The invocation is not recited or said in a classroom as part of a curricular activity,[65] but is said after school hours. It is part of a ceremony occurring after the students have completed the prerequisites for graduate status.[66] Thus, the prayer is usually given before graduates and other adults (unlike the classroom setting of *Engel*). Furthermore, the graduation service is as much a community event as a school event. Therefore, this is not a situation where the state has mandated that a prayer be incorporated into the students' daily routine.

The coercion found in classroom prayer is absent at graduation.[67] The students are not required to attend the ceremony,[68] nor is the receipt of a diploma contingent on attendance.[69] The students are adults at this point. Thus, there is less susceptibility to peer pressure. The teacher-student relationship is not implicated because the prayer is normally given by an outside person.

The graduation prayer is certainly not one officially sanctioned by the state. Until the speaker delivers the invocation, no one else knows what will be said.[70] The state is not composing a prayer to be recited by its students, but is merely allowing a *private* individual to pray before a public event. There would be more danger of government-written prayers if the speaker were required to tailor the prayer a certain way rather than let the speaker pray to God as he or she sees fit.[71] The Supreme Court's concern that a public official (on the public payroll) is performing religious activities is not implicated in a graduation case.[72]

Finally, the audience attending a graduation ceremony is comprised, not of young students in their formative years, but of students entering adulthood.[73] The remainder of the audience is made up of friends and parents who, if they brought young children, are present to dispel any myths to which their children might be exposed. In fact, the dissenting judge in *Stein* asserted that "[h]ere there is, at most, a kind of acknowledgment of religion in a brief part of an annual commencement ceremony, which takes place outside of any classroom setting, and is not directed towards influencing young children at a formative period."[74]

The argument that a high school senior is too impressionable to be exposed to an invocation at graduation appears unfounded. At eighteen years of age, these students have the right to vote for their political leaders. The men are required to register so that they might be called on to defend the country. The women have the right in many states to make a decision to get an abortion without parental consent. It seems untenable then to say that these graduates, who are legally presumed to have the mental ability and maturity to make such important decisions, would be adversely affected by listening to a brief prayer (often less than sixty seconds).

Clearly, there can be little logic in contending that a brief prayer, spoken once a year, composed by a private individual, and delivered to adult men and women can be compared with a prayer written by the government, led by school officials, and recited on a daily basis to young students.

THE *MARSH* ANALYSIS

The *Stein* court attempted to apply a *Marsh* analysis to graduation prayers. However, as noted above, the court did not invoke a pure *Marsh* analysis, but modified it to include an inquiry into content.

The first barrier to the *Marsh* criterion is language in two Supreme Court opinions implying that the reasoning in *Marsh* cannot be utilized in a public school case. Justice O'Connor, for example, reasoned in *Wallace v. Jaffree*[75] that a historical analysis, like the one invoked in *Marsh*, cannot be used in a case involving prayer in the public school because at the time of the framing of the Constitution there were few public schools. Also, Justice William Brennan, in a footnote to *Edwards v. Aguillard*,[76] noted that *Marsh* was not "useful in determining the proper roles of church and state in public schools, since free public education was virtually nonexistent at the time the Constitution was adopted."[77]

While it is an oversimplification to assert that public schools did not exist in the eighteenth century,[78] the practice was not widespread. Yet, assuming arguendo that no public schools existed, the *Marsh* analysis is not rendered inappropriate. Justice O'Connor's and Justice Brennan's statements were made in the context of "religion in the classroom" cases. As has been previously discussed, religion in the classroom poses an entirely different question than the brief acknowledgment of religion at graduation. Therefore, while the Justices' statements are certainly true in the context of the facts they were addressing, the same cannot be imputed to a graduation service. The framers' thoughts in terms of a historical analysis on the extent to which religion should be a part of the classroom is not in question in a graduation case. Thus, the language quoted above does not automatically render the *Marsh* standard inapplicable. This becomes clear through closer analysis of the decision in *Marsh*.

In *Marsh v. Chambers*, the United States Supreme Court held that a law that established a state-paid legislative chaplain who gave invocations at the beginning of each day did not violate the Constitution. The Court did not use the traditional *Lemon* test[79] (discussed above) as determinative of its decision but instead used a historical approach. The Court stated that opening "sessions of legislative and other deliberative public bodies with prayer is deeply embedded in the history and tradition of this country."[80]

The Supreme Court recognized that the tradition of opening sessions with prayer delivered by a paid chaplain originated in the First Continental Congress.[81] The Court placed special emphasis on the fact that Congress voted in favor of the appointment of a chaplain only three days before it agreed on the final wording of the Bill of Rights.[82]

The Supreme Court noted that a historical pattern alone does not render a practice constitutional. However, the action taken by the framers was more than just a historical pattern. The action proved not only the constitutional intent of the original framers, but also proved that they did not find this *specific* act in violation of the First Amendment.

The Supreme Court reasoned that the prayers posed no more threat for an establishment of religion than did other accommodations approved by the Court, such as providing buses for parochial school children, grants to religious colleges to erect educational buildings, or tax exemptions to religious entities.[83]

In discussing history, the Court explained that the framers of the Constitution did not view opening prayers as proselytizing activities or as an endorsement of a particular religion. Instead, they viewed invocations as conduct which simply "harmonize[d] with the tenets of some or all religions."[84] The Court also noted that those who heard the prayers were adults who were "presumably not readily susceptible to 'religious indoctrination.'"[85]

The Supreme Court summed up its holding:

In light of the unambiguous and unbroken history of more than two hundred years, there can be no doubt that the practice of opening legislative sessions with prayer has become part of the fabric of our society. To invoke Divine guidance . . . is not . . . an "establishment" of religion or a step toward establishment; it is simply a tolerable acknowledgment of beliefs widely held among the people of this country. As Justice Douglas observed, "[w]e are a religious people whose institutions presuppose a Supreme Being."[86]

Thus, the Supreme Court not only looked at the history of the practice, but also considered the basis upon which history had determined that the practice was constitutional.

APPLYING *MARSH* TO GRADUATION INVOCATIONS

There are basically two ways one could interpret *Marsh*. The narrow view is that the *Marsh* decision rested solely on the fact that the First Congress voted for a legislative chaplain simultaneous with the writing of the First Amendment. Under such a strict approach, graduation prayers would not withstand a *Marsh* inquiry.[87]

A second way to interpret *Marsh* is to view it as a decision that rested not only on the specific history of the practice, but also on the reasons the practice had been approved.[88] In taking this approach, one could draw an analogy between legislative prayers and other ceremonial recognitions of religion in American society. Graduation prayers could be assessed using history and reason[89] to determine if they would pose any more of a threat to Establishment Clause concerns than the chaplains posed in *Marsh*. Because history has been used by the Supreme Court in assessing the constitutionality of a practice,[90] a historical look at graduation is then in order.

THE HISTORY OF THE CEREMONY

The first graduation services began in Oxford, England, as early as the twelfth century.[91] In America, the tradition began at Harvard in 1642. The program "consisted of a prayer by the president of the institution and addresses by members of the graduating class."[92] Commencement exercises in public high schools were not started until 1842. The high schools primarily copied the university format and thus included prayer.[93]

Graduation ceremonies in America have strong religious roots. Harvard University was basically founded for religious purposes, which meant that the graduation services emphasized religious matters.[94] When public schools began to copy the university ceremonies, many of the religious traditions were included.

While graduation services are not now religious, vestiges of religion remain in the ceremonies. For example, the procession is an offshoot of the clerical processions that occur in the church.[95] Furthermore, as one author has suggested, the churches have worked on creating dignified and impressive ceremonies for years. Therefore, if there is a question as to the proper procedure, the pattern of the church should be followed.[96]

Unquestionably, the traditional graduation service today includes prayer. Indeed, a commencement program today consists of "an invocation, a commencement address, the awarding of earned degrees, the awarding of honorary degrees, and the benediction."[97] *A Guide to Academic Protocol* recognizes that prayer is a traditional element in the commencement program. In instructing the inexperienced in how to plan a commencement, it advises school officials to begin with the national anthem, followed by an invocation. It is further suggested that a benediction be delivered at the close of the ceremony prior to the recessional.[98]

While the tradition of graduation prayers predates the founding of America, there seems to be no evidence that the framers saw such acts as harmful. One can only guess what the framers may have thought, but a review of Thomas Jefferson's University of Virginia records might be enlightening.

Jefferson saw no inconsistency between the doctrine of religious liberty and the practice of prayer at a public school graduation service. One of the earliest "Order of Exercises" for the University of Virginia is dated June 26, 1850. The program lists the order of events, which was to begin with prayer.[99]

Furthermore, at the Founder's Day Celebration the university holds every year to honor Thomas Jefferson (who authored the *Virginia Bill for Religious Freedom*), the program begins with an invocation.[100] Certainly, this evidence is not contemporaneous with the drafting of the First Amendment and consequently does not demand the deference given to contemporaneous acts. However, the fact that the record shows that early in its history the University of Virginia delivered prayer in its graduation service may indicate that such a practice was not offensive to Jefferson himself.

THE *LEMON* TEST

An important question in a *Marsh* analysis is to determine whether the practice in question would threaten to establish a religion. Graduation prayers, as discussed above, are analogous to legislative prayers, which have withstood an Establishment Clause challenge. Moreover, graduation invocations are certainly as innocuous as the government involvement in religion that has been upheld in other cases.[101] It must be remembered that the graduation service, like the prayer in *Marsh*, is directed primarily to adults who are not as susceptible to indoctrination or peer pressure as children. Furthermore, as the Supreme Court noted in *Marsh*, opening a ceremony in prayer does not serve to proselytize or endorse religion. Unlike classroom prayer, the graduation invocation bears a striking resemblance to the acknowledgments of religion contained in our legislative and judicial ceremonies.

If the Supreme Court considered this question today, it could decide it in relation to the issues in *Marsh*. As Justice Kennedy has explained:

> *Marsh* stands for the proposition, not that specific practices common in 1791 are an exception to the otherwise broad sweep of the Establishment Clause, but rather that the meaning of the Clause is to be determined by reference to historical practices and understandings. Whatever test we choose to apply must permit not only legitimate practices two centuries old but also any other practice with no greater potential for an establishment of religion. . . . A test for implementing the protections of the Establishment Clause that, if applied with consistency, would invalidate long-standing traditions cannot be a proper reading of the Clause."[102]

However, the predominant test used by the Supreme Court in assessing the validity of an Establishment Clause claim is found in *Lemon v. Kurtzman*.[103] (*Lemon* is discussed in chapter 5.) The *Lemon* test consists of three parts.

The first prong of *Lemon* requires government officials to act with a secular purpose. The second proscribes laws which have the primary effect of advancing or inhibiting religion; and the third proscribes laws which create an excessive entanglement between the government and religion.[104] While this test has been used in almost every Supreme Court decision implicating the First Amendment Establishment Clause,[105] the Court has not bound itself to the test.[106]

The *Lemon* test has been the subject of criticism both on and off the Supreme Court.[107] Accordingly, Justice O'Connor has made an attempt to clarify the test.[108] She argues that the purpose prong of the test "ask[s] whether government's actual purpose is to endorse or disapprove of religion."[109] Similarly, she asserts that the effects prong asks whether, irrespective of government's actual purpose, the practice under review conveys "a message of endorsement or disapproval."[110] Justice O'Connor was concerned that endorsement "sends a message to non-adherents that they are outsiders, not full members of the political community, and an accompanying message to adherents that they are insiders, favored members of the political community."[111]

The extent to which the Supreme Court has adopted Justice O'Connor's test is unclear. In *County of Allegheny v. American Civil Liberties Union, Greater Pittsburgh Chapter*,[112] it appeared as if the Court had adopted the endorsement test.[113] Yet, the Supreme Court's decision in *Mergens v. Board of Education of the Westside Community Schools*[114] seems to demonstrate that while the endorsement test clarifies *Lemon*, *Lemon* remains the basic standard by which to judge an Establishment Clause claim.[115] However, it does seem clear that in certain instances the Supreme Court is applying what may be termed the "*Lemon*/endorsement test."[116]

Prayer and Secular Purpose

Does the secular purpose requirement mean that a law or government action must be motivated solely by a secular purpose? Or does it mean that a law or government action can be motivated by a religious purpose as long as a legitimate secular purpose is present? The Court has upheld the latter.[117] If a law could be invalidated because it coincided with someone's religious beliefs, even a law proscribing murder would be invalidated.[118] Thus, if the Supreme Court has found that the legislature or policymaking body had a legitimate secular purpose, the law or policy will pass constitutional scrutiny.

Furthermore, the Supreme Court has stressed that deference must be given to the legislature.[119] As Justice O'Connor notes: "Even if the text and official history of a statute express no secular purpose, the statute should be held to have an improper purpose only if it is beyond purview that endorsement of religion or a religious belief was and is the law's reason for existence."[120] Likewise, the Supreme Court has emphasized that it would only invalidate government action when the activity was "motivated wholly by religious considerations . . . [e]ven when the benefit to religion was substantial."[121]

Another clarification the Supreme Court has made concerning the secular purpose prong is that the purpose must be viewed in context. The Court has held that focusing on the religious component where there is no evidence that its inclusion was a "purposeful surreptitious effort to express some kind of subtle governmental advocacy of a particular message" constitutes plain error.[122] As such, to "[f]ocus exclusively on the religious component of any activity would inevitably lead to its invalidation under the Establishment Clause."[123] Harvard law professor Laurence Tribe agrees: "The definition of 'secular' here must be a generous one [or] virtually nothing that government does would be acceptable; laws against murder, for example, would be forbidden because they overlapped the fifth commandment of the Mosaic Decalogue."[124]

Everyone, however, knows that prayer is a religious activity. In fact, prayer has been termed a "quintessential religious act" by one federal court of appeals.[125] The point is, as the court noted in *Stein*,[126] the invocation has a dual purpose.[127] For the minister the prayer may be religious, but for various members of the audience the prayer will simply be a formal way to open and close a public ceremony. In their eyes, the prayer is not a quintessential religious act. Furthermore, as noted above, it is incorrect to focus solely on the prayer. The prayer must be seen in the context of the whole service much as the creche was seen in the context of the entire display in those cases decided by the Supreme Court.[128]

When seen in context, the invocations pass the first prong of the *Lemon* test. The purpose of the graduation service is "wholly secular."[129] The primary reason to hold a graduation service is ceremonial, to honor the graduates with the awarding of diplomas. All other activities are peripheral.[130] An invocation and benediction take up a small part of the entire evening. And while even a *de minimis* infringement of the rights of an individual must not be tolerated,[131] the brevity of the prayer may be taken into consideration in assessing the purpose of the program.[132] Considering the overall program, one can hardly assert that the school has a solely religious purpose in allowing such brief prayers.

Important here is that the *Lemon* analysis demands an inquiry into the purpose of the *governing body*, not the individual actors.[133] The school officials hold graduation for the purpose of presenting diplomas to students who have fulfilled the requirements. Surely, one cannot seriously argue that the school's purpose in awarding diplomas is to lure the students in so that they can hear a brief prayer (often less than a minute) and be influenced to adopt the values or beliefs of the one praying. When one looks at the purpose of the school officials, it becomes clear that a secular purpose exists for the ceremony.

Even if one contends that the analysis centers solely on the prayer, there is still a secular purpose. There are three legitimate secular purposes for including invocations and benedictions in graduation ceremonies. First, and probably most important, is the recognition of the tradition implicit in the practice. Invocations at graduation are just as much a tradition as wearing caps and gowns or as the processional and recessional. These prayers are simply the standard way to open a ceremonial graduation service. By allowing them, the school is merely preserving a long-standing tradition.[134]

Second, the school's purpose may be to allow its students to plan or participate in the service.[135] When this is the practice, the students may decide to include the prayer. If they do not want to begin the service with an invocation, they can insert something else. However, when the students choose to use an invocation, the school should not overrule their decision, but encourage their leadership and organizational skills.

The third secular purpose recognizes the reasoning underlying the tradition. A prayer is, and has long been, an acceptable way to open a ceremonial service. A prayer serves the purpose of setting a formal tone,[136] creating a note of dignity and decorum,[137] drawing the audience's attention,[138] honoring a student,[139] reducing tension,[140] and impressing on the audience that the event to follow demands their attention and their contemplation.[141]

In conclusion, without evidence to the contrary, it cannot be seriously contended that the purpose of the school in including an invocation and benediction is to endorse religion. This practice merely acknowledges American religious and historical roots.[142]

Primary Effect

There are basically two ways to determine whether a practice has the primary effect of advancing or inhibiting religion. The first determines whether the practice has the effect of substantially benefiting religion.[143] The second, most often engaged, determines whether the practice has the primary effect of endorsing a religion.[144]

The first inquiry can be answered easily. The Supreme Court has made it clear that *incidental* benefits accruing to religion do not invalidate a religious practice.[145] The Establishment Clause is not violated simply because an act "happens to coincide or harmonize with the tenets of some or all religions."[146] "To say that a prayer benefits or advances religion because it is inherently religious and not secular is question-begging and unsatisfying."[147]

The second approach demands a more in-depth analysis. The Supreme Court's concern with government endorsement of religion is that the nonadherent might feel less than a full member of the political community. When government creates a "symbolic union"[148] between the government and religion, the potential for endorsement exists.

As with the secular purpose prong, one can focus exclusively on the prayer or, in contrast, look at the prayer in the context of the ceremony as a whole. When viewed in context, the invocation and benediction pose no threat that the government is endorsing religion. The nature of the ceremony and the purpose of the commencement diminish any potential effect of such endorsement.

Several factors are involved—essentially the same factors used to distinguish graduation cases from the cases addressing religion in the schools. The fact that the practice is performed once a year, to a different audience, made up of primarily adults who voluntarily attend, is not a part of the school's day-to-day curricular activities, is performed in the context of a ceremonial public event, is merely an acknowledgment of religious heritage and tradition, and has the purpose of solemnizing the event and creating an air of dignity serve to refute the contention that there is an effect of endorsement. The prayers are merely too incidental and remote to be said to create a "symbolic union" between religion and the state.[149]

As a consequence, the graduates will, as the *Stein* court recognized, most likely view the prayers as merely a "commonplace ritual" that they will "observe at many private and public ceremonies that they attend in the remainder of their adult lives."[150] To some graduates the prayer may have a religious purpose, but to others it may just be a ritual employed in public events.

Many American governmental practices include religious elements. For instance, the President of the United States is sworn in on the Bible. The House of Representatives chamber has "In God We Trust" inscribed on the wall. The Supreme Court opens its sessions with a cry to God to "save this honorable Court." A United States citizen sees the word *God* on each coin he or she carries.[151] Nonreligious people in a graduation audience will most likely ignore the prayer just as they ignore all the other religious references in American public life. In some sense, American citizens have come to expect that in public ceremonies religion might play a small part. If an "objective observer acquainted with the . . . history"[152] of graduation viewed a ceremony, he or she should not feel like a nonadherent, lacking the status of a full member of the political community.[153]

Excessive Entanglement

The entanglement prong of the *Lemon* test is usually not implicated in a graduation case. Thus, some courts do not even address it.[154] However, in some instances an entanglement analysis is appropriate.[155]

To be excessively entangled with religion, the government can be administratively entangled or entangled in political divisiveness.[156] Yet the limited administrative involvement in graduation invocations and benedictions will almost never result in entanglement.[157] None of the traditional factors of entanglement are involved. The school district does not pay the speaker; the graduation takes place in a public, not a private, school; the prayer occurs only once a year so it does not require continuous surveillance; the law proscribes analyzing content.[158]

While perhaps some divisiveness may be created, the Supreme Court has held that factor not to be determinative.[159] Further, the Court has indicated unwillingness to apply the divisiveness inquiry to cases other than those involving subsidies to religious organizations.[160]

THE FREE EXERCISE CLAUSE

The Free Exercise Clause has been employed by both sides on this issue. Those who contest the practice contend that when they are forced to listen to a prayer, their right to freely exercise their religion has been violated. The person advocating the prayer argues that by proscribing prayer at an important event in his life, his free exercise rights are violated.

The Free Exercise Clause protects an individual from government compulsion to adhere to certain beliefs or practices.[161] It also prohibits government from conditioning a substantial governmental benefit on an act which would interfere with someone's religious convictions. For in so doing, the government would be pressuring a person to modify his or her behavior to receive that benefit.[162]

The initial inquiry is whether a high school graduate is being coerced into performing an act against his or her beliefs.[163] The standard of proof here is difficult to meet. For while some coercion may exist, very few could prove that they had renounced their beliefs or adopted new ones because they attended a graduation ceremony.[164] As one constitutional authority recognizes: "Research has not revealed that listening to the invocation is contrary to anyone's religious or conscientious beliefs."[165] If such a remote acknowledgment of religion violated free exercise, the motto "In God We Trust" would seem to violate it as well.

The fact that graduation ceremonies are voluntary lessens the element of coercion.[166] One federal court has stated:

> While there are indirect pressures to attend, there are no substantial demands to partake. No audience recitation is involved and a student may think what he will concerning what is going on. The Court recognizes that some may be offended by what is said, but is not convinced that

the Constitution protects individuals from this type of offense. It cannot see how what is likely to be said in any way will inhibit the plaintiffs in the practice and pursuit of their religious beliefs.[167]

The government does not have to cater to the extremely sensitive individual.[168] In *Epperson v. Arkansas,*[169] the Supreme Court explained that the state has no legitimate interest in protecting any or all religions from views distasteful to them.[170]

A second aspect of the free exercise inquiry is that of denial of a significant governmental benefit in order to avoid violating religious beliefs. Courts addressing this issue have, however, held that attending graduation is not a significant benefit conferred by the state.[171] The expectation the student has in attending graduation is that of receiving the diploma. In most every school, the diploma may be obtained at a place other than the graduation, and while graduation services are important, the forfeiting of them does not rise to a deprivation of a constitutional right.[172]

Simply stated, prayer at graduation compels no one to worship. The person has the right to stay seated, not bow his head, not take off his cap, or not attend. The state is, therefore, not violating his or her right to exercise freely his or her religion.[173]

THE FREE SPEECH CLAUSE

At least one judge has recognized a potential free speech claim. In a concurring opinion, the judge viewed the act of enjoining the invocation as a prior restraint[174] in stating that "[n]o court can enjoin speech on the basis of an unsupported assertion that it may offend the sensibilities of some prospective listener."[175] The concurring opinion also asserts that courts cannot assume that the speaker will not take into account the ceremonial setting and diversity of the audience and fashion the speech accordingly. There is no reason to conclude that the speaker "would not fashion an appropriate message which neither requires any individual to participate in an affirmation which might run counter to his personal belief nor places the state's imprimatur on any sectarian declaration."[176]

The only court which has analyzed the issue on a free speech basis was *Lundberg v. West Monona Community School District.*[177] There the plaintiffs were seeking an injunction to force a public school board to reinstate an invocation. The school officials were personally in favor of the practice, but had been persuaded into banning the invocation by persons advising them of its possible unconstitutionality.[178]

In assessing the free speech claim, a federal district court engaged the forum analysis and determined that the high school graduation ceremony is a nonpublic forum.[179] The court held that it was proper to ban prayer in a nonpublic forum as long as the ban was against all prayer and not limited to that prayer which would offend the school board. When all prayer was excluded on a reasonable basis, the *Lundberg* court held that the board was acting within the bounds of the Constitution.[180]

The court analogized the subject matter to that in *Hazelwood School District v. Kuhlmeier.*[181] In *Hazelwood*, the Supreme Court ruled that a public school has a right to ban certain subjects it deems inappropriate for students. The students in that case were being exposed to school newspaper articles that discussed birth control, pregnancy, and other sexually related subjects. The *Lundberg* court saw its decision as analogous to *Hazelwood* because, the "[s]chool [b]oard deemed religion inappropriate."[182]

GUIDELINES

In setting guidelines to avoid a determination of unconstitutionality, one must recognize that there is disagreement among the courts as to what constitutes an unconstitutional act. However, some safeguards will lessen the chances of unconstitutionality.

The logical beginning point is the administrative function. A school can adopt a policy of allowing the student body to plan the graduation service. When the students choose to include an invocation and benediction in the ceremony, it takes the school out of the planning and organizing phase, thus reducing the risk of endorsement.[183]

The school should not be involved in authorizing the content of the prayer.[184] However, if the students choose to include an invocation and benediction, the school may want to advise the speaker to keep the prayer brief and nonevangelical.[185] Additionally, the school should not pay the minister.[186]

The graduation speaker offering the prayer should not be a state employee.[187] If a minister is preferred over another person, an effort should be made to have ministers from different religions participate.[188] Also, school officials should refrain from mentioning the speaker's religious affiliation or church.[189] The school should not put this information in the program distributed at the ceremony.[190] Further, the school should grant access to any speaker who expresses a desire to pray.[191]

There should be a voluntary attendance policy for the ceremony, including an easy method for students to receive their diplomas if they choose not to attend. Also, to reduce the appearance of coercion, the school should allow everyone to stay seated during the prayer.[192]

OPTIONS

The issue of invocations and benedictions has been a difficult question for the courts. Consequently, many different approaches have been taken and new tests have been developed. Thus, a court has many options.

First, it could follow *Stein* and permit prayer that does not involve Christian language. Second, it could follow the *Marsh* analysis and allow all prayer regardless of content as long as the speaker was not proselytizing. Or finally, a court could invoke the *Lemon*/endorsement test and view the prayer in the context of the graduation. However, a strict separationist court could apply this test and determine that the practice violates the Constitution. Because there is so much uncertainty in this area, a school should implement some of the suggested procedures that could better withstand constitutional scrutiny.

PART SEVEN

The Marketplace of Ideas

It is the purpose of the First Amendment to preserve an uninhibited marketplace of ideas in which truth will ultimately prevail, rather than to countenance monopolization of that market, whether it be by the government itself or a private licensee.

—Justice Byron White,
*Red Lion Broadcasting Company v.
Federal Communications Commission*
395 U.S. 367, 390 (1969).

18

The Open Society

Our peculiar security is in possession of a written Constitution. Let us not make it a blank paper by construction.

—Thomas Jefferson

The liberties of expression, association, religion, the freedom of a public forum, and the right to the equal protection of the laws are in a sense all components of the right of citizens to open communication. What is the value of these communication rights?

It might be argued that to deny religious expression in the public school does not completely destroy the right of religious communication. Rather, it merely restricts the time and place of the communication. Further, it might be argued that only one subject matter is eliminated, leaving communication perfectly open on all other subjects.

Similar arguments were made to the United States Supreme Court in the case of *Thomas v. Collins.*[1] There a labor union officer was held in contempt of a court order prohibiting him from soliciting union members without first registering with the state. The state unsuccessfully contended that it was a small thing to ask him to register. The Supreme Court held that "[t]he restraint is not small when it is considered what was restrained,"[2] and emphasized that "it is the character of the right, not of the limitation"[3] that is placed upon the scales of justice.

With respect to the argument that religious expression by students, teachers, and others can be had at another time and place, the Supreme Court proclaimed in *Schneider v. State*[4] that "one is not to have the exercise of this liberty of expression in appropriate places abridged on the plea that it may be exercised in some other place."[5] Likewise, in the case of *Healy v. James*[6] the Supreme Court reiterated the importance of student associational freedoms:

[T]he [student] group's possible ability to exist outside the campus community does not ameliorate significantly the disabilities imposed by [the
failure to recognize the group as an official campus organization]. We are
not free to disregard the practical realities.[7]

The practical realities are that if students are, for example, to communicate with other students on any subject, they must do it where students
come together — *at school.*

At the secondary school and university level, the rights presently held
by teachers and students are substantial. The teacher's constitutional right
to academic freedom and the student's right to hear both provide a constitutional base from which a nonstudent may gain access to the campus.
Moreover, the Supreme Court's affirmation of the Equal Access Act provides clear guidelines for equal treatment of student religious organizations.

Educational officials, therefore, do not have a compelling state interest
in denying equal treatment to religion or religious topics and practices on
the public school campus. To the contrary, as the United States Supreme
Court has held, the state must accommodate religion and religious freedom
in such instances.

The classroom has been said to be the marketplace of ideas. As long as
material is relevant to the subject matter being taught and is presented
objectively, it is suggested that school authorities should preserve the marketplace concept and maintain the freedoms essential to a proper administration of the education system.

We live in a nation today where young men and women are exposed
to a great amount of data and as a result are maturing at a much earlier age.
The time has passed when it can be validly argued that the young must be
shielded. Instead, they must be provided with an adequate educational base
from which to confront a world that abounds with devastating crises.

One effective way of providing such an educational base is by allowing freedom of religious expression. In this way, not only can the educational objective be attained, but also precious and ancient liberties can be
preserved.

NOTES

PREFACE

1. *See, e.g., Widmar v. Vincent,* 454 U.S. 263 (1981); *Mergens v. Board of Education of the Westside Community Schools,* 110 S. Ct. 2356 (1990).
2. Laurence Tribe, *American Constitutional Law,* 2d ed. (Mineola, NY: Foundation Press, 1988), p. viii.

CHAPTER ONE: *Public Education and Value Equanimity*

1. On the subject of the "manipulation of consciousness" in education, law professors Stephen Arons and Charles Lawrence argue that teaching is never value-neutral, and that the choice of values to be transmitted by the schools lies with the political majorities or interest groups that control particular school systems. Stephen Arons and Charles Lawrence, *The Manipulation of Consciousness: A First Amendment Critique of Schooling,* 15 Harv. CR. – C. L. L. Rev. 309, 316-317 (1980).
2. *Webster's New Collegiate Dictionary* (Springfield, Mass: G. & C. Merriam Co., 1975), pp. 583, 586.
3. *Pierce v. Society of Sisters,* 268 U.S. 510, 535 (1925).
4. *West Virginia Board of Education v. Barnette,* 319 U.S. 624, 642 (1943).
5. *Brown v. Board of Education,* 347 U.S. 483, 493 (1954).
6. *Ambach v. Norwick,* 441 U.S. 68, 77 (1979).
7. *Board of Education, Island Trees Union Free School District v. Pico,* 457 U.S. 853, 864 (1982).
8. *Id.*
9. *Id.* at 876 (Blackmun, J., concurring), 889 (Burger, J., dissenting), 896 (Powell, J., dissenting), and 909 (Rehnquist, J., dissenting).
10. These three philosophies are outlined in Kohlberg and Mayer, *Development as the Aim of Education,* 42 Harv. Educ. Rev. 449, 451-455 (1972). This "three-theory" analysis is also applied to the Supreme Court's rulings on First Amendment rights in public schools. *See* Note, *Education and the Court: The Supreme Court's Educational Ideology,* 40 Vand. L. Rev. 939, 942-949 (1987).
11. Kohlberg and Mayer, *supra* note 10, at 451.
12. *Id.* at 455.
13. A. S. Neill, *Summerhill* (New York: Hart Publishing Co., 1960), p. 297. Neill's strong romanticist educational philosophy should be distinguished from the

romanticism behind the more mainstream Montessori "directed play" system. Neill dismissed the Montessori system as "an artificial way of making the child learn by doing." *Id.* at 25.

14. G. H. Mead, *Movements of Thought in the Nineteenth Century* (Chicago: University of Chicago Press, 1936), p. 61.

15. Mead, Charles W. Morris (ed.), *Mind, Self, and Society from the Standpoint of a Social Behaviorist* (Chicago: University of Chicago Press, 1934/1962), p. 61.

16. "Behaviorism" may be considered a psychological theory that views man as an animal who behaves in response to external stimuli, rather than as a rational being who acts according to innate, uniquely "mental" processes. Because it considers observed behavior the only valid psychological datum, behaviorism rejects as obsolete all concepts of mind and consciousness. One prominent behaviorist is B. F. Skinner; his theory's implications for educational philosophy are considered in chapter 2.

17. Kohlberg and Mayer, *supra* note 10, at 452-453.

18. *Id.* at 454.

19. A major federal case dealing with spiritually objectionable curricula is *Mozert v. Hawkins County Board of Education*, 827 F.2d 1058 (6th Cir. 1987), *cert. denied*, 56 U.S.L.W. 3569 (U.S. Feb. 22, 1988). The court rejected born-again Christian parents' claim that a school board's use of reading texts that the parents believed promoted secular humanism violated their children's free exercise of religion. Citing a recent Supreme Court ruling, the judges stressed public schools' purpose of teaching values "essential to a democratic society" (*id.* at 1068) and responsibility to "inculcate the habits and manners of civility . . . as indispensable to the practice of self-government" (*id.* at 1071 [Kennedy, C. J., concurring]). See *Bethel School District No. 403 v. Fraser*, 106 S. Ct. 3159, 3164 (1986).

20. Kohlberg and Mayer, *supra* note 10, at 454.

21. *Id.*

22. John Dewey, "Individuality and Experience," in *John Dewey on Education: Selected Writings* (Reginald D. Archambault ed. 1964), pp. 153, 156. This essay first appeared in *Journal of the Barnes Foundation* (1926).

23. John Dewey, *Individualism, Old and New* (New York: Capricorn Books, 1962), pp. 74-75.

24. John Dewey, *The Public and Its Problems* (New York: Henry Holt and Co., 1927), p. 195.

25. Dewey, "My Pedagogic Creed," in *John Dewey on Education: Selected Writings, supra* note 22, at 428. This essay was first published as a pamphlet by E. L. Kellogg and Co. in 1897.

26. *Id.*

27. Dewey's philosophical pragmatism is evident in his comparison of "law" of social life" to "laws of engineering": "If you want certain results, certain means must be found and employed." John Dewey, *The Public and Its Problems* (New York: Henry Holt and Co., 1927), p. 197. He proposed that "views generated in view of special situations" will no longer be "frozen into absolute standards and masquerade as eternal truths." *Id.*, p. 203.

28. Dewey, "My Pedagogic Creed," *supra* note 25, at 433.

29. See Mass. Const. pt. II, ch. IV, sec. I, art. I (1780); Mich. Const. art. XI, sec. 1 (1909); Miss. Const. art. VI, sec. 16 (1817) and art. VII, sec. 14 (1832); N. C. Const. art. IX, sec. 1 (1868, 1876); Ohio Const. art. VII, sec. 3 (1802) and art. I, sec. VII, Bill of Rights (1851). For a compendium of these provisions, see Samuel Windsor Brown, *The Secularization of American Education* (New York: Russell & Russell, 1912, 1967), pp. 98-99.

30. *See* Brown, *supra* note 29, chapter XII.
31. *See generally* Richard D. Mosier, *Making the American Mind: Social and Moral Ideas in the McGuffey Readers* (New York: King's Crown Press, 1947), p. 168.
32. *McGuffey's Newly Revised Rhetorical Guide* (Cincinnati: Winthrop B. Smith and Co., 1853), p. 347.
33. *See* Mosier, *supra* note 31, chapter 3.
34. *See* Idaho Const. art. IX, sec. 1 (1890); Minn. Const. art. VIII, sec. 1 (1857); Miss. Const. art. VIII, sec. 1 (1868); S. D. Const. art. VIII, sec. 1 (1889); Tenn. Const. art. XI, sec. 1 (1834). For a compendium of these provisions, *see* Brown, *supra* note 29, at 100-102.
35. Horace Mann, Joy Elmer Morgan (ed.), *Horace Mann: His Ideas and Ideals* (Washington, D.C.: National Home Library Foundation, 1936), pp. 118-119.
36. *Id.* at 143.
37. *Abington School District v. Schempp,* 374 U.S. 203, 238-239 (1963) (Brennan, J., concurring).
38. Schwarz, *No Imposition of Religion: The Establishment Clause Value,* 77 Yale L.J. 692, 701 (1968). In his book *Compelling Belief: The Culture of American Schooling* (New York: McGraw Hill, 1983), Stephen Arons sees a similar dilemma following from his conviction that value neutrality in education is impossible. One reviewer remarks that if this conviction is correct, Arons correctly concludes that "government control of compulsory education and the First Amendment's prohibition against established ideology are irreconcilable." Charles R. Lawrence, *Education for Self-Government: Reassessing the Role of the Public School in a Democracy,* 82 Mich. L. Rev. 810, 816 (1984).
39. *See Edwards v. Aguillard,* 482 U.S. 578 (1987).
40. Moskowitz, *The Making of the Moral Child: Legal Implications of Values Education,* 6 Pepperdine L. Rev. 105, 136, quoting *Manone v. Haden,* 329 Pa. 213, 233, 197 A. 344, 352 (1938).
41. For an elaboration of this progressivist critique of romanticism, see Kohlberg and Mayer, *supra* note 10, at 469-472.
42. *See* Welch, *The State as a Purveyor of Morality,* 56 Geo. Wash. L. Rev. 540, 551 (1988).
43. In cases in which the Supreme Court has accommodated minority viewpoints within public schools in opposition to efforts to impose conformity, the Court has in fact relied on the First Amendment's Free Speech or Free Exercise of religion clauses instead of the Fourteenth Amendment's provision that a state shall not deprive any person of "the equal protection of the laws." While striking down a state law requiring that all public school students salute the flag, the Court remarked that legislation that collides with the Fourteenth Amendment is much more definitely unconstitutional if it also collides with the First Amendment. *Barnette,* 319 U.S. at 639.
44. *See* Gottlieb, *In the Name of Patriotism: The Constitutionality of "Bending" History in Public Secondary Schools,* 62 N.Y.U. L. Rev. 497, 537 (1987).
45. *See Schempp,* 374 U.S. at 222.
46. Arons and Lawrence, *supra* note 1, at 319.
47. John Stuart Mill, "On Liberty," in *On Liberty and Considerations on Representative government* (R. B. McCallum ed. 1947), p. 95.
48. While's Mill's individualism resembles the educational romanticist's, his views on children conflict with more extreme forms of romanticism. Mill wrote that children "must be protected against their own actions," and that society has "absolute power" over its members "during all the early portion of their existence" in order to "try whether it could make them capable of rational conduct in life." *Id.* at 9, 73.

49. *Id.* at 52.
50. For example, in the *Mozert* case (*supra* note 19), one judge conceded that plaintiffs' exercise of religion was indeed burdened by the school board's use of allegedly offensive reading texts, and that accommodation of their religion would not be an establishment of religion; but he concluded that when it comes to setting curricula, local school boards are "entitled to say, 'my way or the highway.'" 827 F.2d at 1074 (Boggs, C.J., concurring).
51. One major ruling since *Mozert* concerning alleged promotion of "secular humanism" in public school curricula indicates judicial acceptance of "public" value inculcation not only as the norm, but also as a positive good. The district court held that textbooks that omitted reference to religion in American history impermissibly promoted a religion of secular humanism. The federal circuit court of appeals reversed, reasoning that though the books instilled values consistent with secular humanism, such values were the "fundamental values" whose inculcation is a "major objective of public education." *Smith v. Board of Commissioners of Mobile County,* 827 F.2d 684, 692 (11th Cir. 1987).
52. 310 U.S. 586 (1940), *rev'd* 319 U.S. 624 (1943).
53. 319 U.S. 624 (1943).
54. *Gobitis,* 310 U.S. at 600. A rather nonindividualist bias motivated Justice Frankfurter's reasoning here; he asserted that "[t]he preciousness of the family relation, the authority and independence which give dignity to parenthood, indeed the enjoyment of all freedom" presuppose the "ordered society" summarized by the flag that the local school board required all students and teachers to salute. *Id.*
55. *Schempp,* 374 U.S. at 241-242 (Brennan, J., concurring).
56. As quoted in William Shirer, *The Rise and Fall of the Third Reich* (New York: Simon and Schuster, 1980), p. 249.
57. The Supreme Court has said, for example, that a primary objective of public education is the "inculca[tion of] fundamental values necessary to the maintenance of a democratic political system." *Bethel School District No. 403 v. Fraser,* 478 U.S. 675, 681 (1986); citing *Ambach,* 441 U.S. at 76-77.
58. Arons and Lawrence, *supra* note 1, at 316.
59. Gottlieb, *supra* note 44, at 536. This difficulty of separating facts from values need not lead to the conclusion some have drawn that the "marketplace of ideas" concept must be entirely abandoned as being based upon false assumptions concerning objective truth and rationality. See Stanley Ingber, *The Marketplace of Ideas: A Legitimizing Myth,* 1984 Duke L. J. 29, 90; Robert Paul Wolff, *The Poverty of Liberalism* (Boston: Beacon Press, 1968), pp. 15-17. Like John Milton, those suffering religious persecution should still be able to confess "who ever knew Truth put to the worse, in a free and open encounter?" Milton, *Areopagitica* (Cambridge: Cambridge University Press, 1918), p. 58.
60. Welch, *supra* note 42, at 549.
61. Ingber, *Religion or Ideology?: A Needed Clarification of the Religion Clauses,* 41 Stan. L. Rev. 233, 238 (1989).
62. Arons and Lawrence, *supra* note 1, at 317.
63. Note, *Teaching Inequality: The Problem of Public School Tracking,* 102 Harv. L. Rev. 1318, 1332 (1989). The Supreme Court observed that racial segregation "generates a feeling of inferiority as to [students'] status in the community that may affect their hearts and minds in a way unlikely ever to be undone." *Brown v. Board of Education,* 347 U.S. 483, 494 (1954).
64. Arons and Lawrence, *supra* note 1, at 317.
65. Kohlberg and Mayer, *supra* note 10, at 475-476.
66. 421 U.S. 349 (1975).

67. *Id.* at 371-372.
68. Arons and Lawrence, *supra* note 1, at 317 (footnote omitted).
69. On this point, *see* Ingber, *The Marketplace of Ideas: A Legitimizing Myth, supra* note 61, at 30 and footnote 144; Stephen Arons, *Compelling Belief: The Culture of American Schooling* (New York: McGraw-Hill, 1983), pp. 85-185.
70. *See* Sherry, Book Review, *Republican Citizenship in a Democratic Society*, 66 Tex. L. Rev. 1229, 1232 (1988). This review is of Amy Gutmann's *Democratic Education* (Princeton: Princeton University Press, 1987).
71. Sherry, *supra* note 70, at 1231.
72. *Id.* at 1232.
73. James Coleman, *The Adolescent Society* (New York: Free Press of Glencoe, 1961), p. 3 (emphasis in original).
74. Dewey, *The School and Society,* quoted in Robert H. Bremner (ed.), *Children and Youth in America: A Documentary History, Volume II* (Cambridge, Mass.: Harvard University Press, 1971), p. 1119.
75. *See* Merrill Harmin, Howard Kirschenbaum, and Sidney Simon, *Clarifying Values Through Subject Matter* (Minneapolis: Winston Press, 1974).
76. Note, *Delconte v. State: Some Thoughts on Home Education,* 64 N.C. L. Rev. 1302, 1323 (1986). The author argues that the possibilities of state indoctrination through such subjects makes the preservation of a home-schooling alternative "imperative." *Id.* at 1324.
77. Harry C. Bredemeir and Rubard M. Stephenson, *The Analysis of Social Systems* (New York: Holt, Rinehart, and Winston, 1962), p. 119.

CHAPTER TWO: *Rights and Human Dignity*

1. Edward J. Bloustein, *Privacy as an Aspect of Human Dignity: An Answer to Dean Prosser,* 39 N.Y.U. L. Rev. 962, 963 (1964).
2. *See, e.g.,* Samuel Dash, Richard F. Schwartz, and Robert E. Knowlton, *The Eavesdroppers* (New York: Da Capo Press, 1971); Vance Oakley Packard, *The Naked Society* (New York: D. McKay Co., 1964); Edith J. Lapidus, *Eavesdropping on Trial* (Rochelle Park, N.J.: Hayden Book Co., 1974).
3. Bloustein, *supra* note 1, at 962. The view of privacy as an independent value received its classic statement in Warren and Brandeis, *The Right of Privacy,* 4 Harv. L. Rev. 193 (1890). The view of privacy as a composite of interests is attributed to Prosser, *Privacy,* 48 Calif. L. Rev. 383 (1960).
4. C. S. Lewis, *The Abolition of Man* (New York: Macmillan, 1947), pp. 34, 43.
5. *Id.* at 46, 47.
6. This consensus was embodied in the medieval individualism (which John Dewey rejected) that prevailed when the Church existed to secure the salvation of individual souls. *See* chapter 1.
7. Alberto Moravia, *Man as an End: A Defense of Humanism,* B. Wall, trans. (Westport, Conn.: Greenwood Press, 1976), p. 30.
8. *Id.* at 31.
9. For a definition of "behaviorism," *see* chapter 1.
10. B. F. Skinner, *Beyond Freedom and Dignity* (New York: Knopf, 1972), p. 198.
11. *Id.* at 200-201.
12. Declaration of Independence, *reprinted in* Organic Laws of the United States, U.S. Code at xxxi (1976).
13. Gaillard Hunt, ed., *The Writings of James Madison, Vol. 5, 1787-1790* (New York: G. P. Putnam's Sons, 1904).
14. *Id.* at 132.

15. James Kent, *Commentaries on American Law*, Vol. 2 (Boston: Little, Brown, 1858), pp. 35-36 (emphasis in original).

16. Roland H. Bainton, *The Travail of Religious Liberty* (Hamden, Conn.: Shoestring Press, 1971), p. 260.

17. *Id.* at 259.

18. U. S. Const. amend. I. When ratified, the First Amendment, as well as the entire Bill of Rights, applied only to the federal government. However, the First Amendment was made applicable to the states through the Fourteenth Amendment and the process of "selective incorporation" of Bill of Rights provisions as binding on the states. *See, e.g., Cantwell v. Connecticut,* 310 U.S. 296, 303 (1940); *Everson v. Board of Education,* 330 U.S. 1 (1947).

19. Arons and Lawrence, *The Manipulation of Consciousness: A First Amendment Critique of Schooling,* 15 Harv. C.R. – C.L. L. Rev. 309, 311-312 (1980).

20. *Id.* at 312. *See also Gillette v. United States,* 401 U.S. 437, 469 (1971) (Douglas, J., dissenting).

21. Concerning the dangers of values inculcation as imposed upon a captive public school audience, see Stephen Arons, *Compelling Belief: The Culture of American Schooling* (New York: McGraw-Hill, 1983).

22. Supreme Court Justice Sandra Day O'Connor's test for determining whether the First Amendment's Establishment Clause has been violated may support judicial recognition of the communicative effect of such denial of rights. According to this test, governmental disapproval of religion in violation of the Establishment Clause occurs when a message is sent to religious nonadherents "that they are insiders, favored members of the political community," and to religious adherents "that they are outsiders, not full members of the political community." *Lynch v. Donnelly,* 465 U.S. 668, 688 (1984) (O'Connor, J., concurring).

23. Courts sometimes stress primary and secondary school students' supposed immaturity as grounds for prohibiting religious expression or any sort of "religious" instruction in public schools. In concurring with the Supreme Court's ruling striking down a state law requiring balanced treatment of evolution and creationism in science courses, one justice remarked that "the difference in maturity between college-age and secondary students" may affect constitutional analysis of any integration of religious studies into public school curricula. *Edwards v. Aguillard,* 482 U.S. 578, 608 (1987) (Powell, J., concurring). Students' possible perception of school "endorsement" of religion has been cited as grounds for striking down a public high school's policy allowing student religious groups to meet during noninstructional hours. *Clark v. Dallas Independent School District,* 671 F. Supp. 1119, 1123 (N.D. Tex. 1987), *modified,* 701 F. Supp. 594 (N.D. Tex. 1988), *dismissed,* 880 F.2d 411 (5th Cir. 1989). Students' "impressionability" has been cited as grounds for prohibiting a fifth grade public school teacher from silently reading his Bible during classroom hours. *Roberts v. Madigan,* 702 F. Supp. 1505, 1516 (D. Colo. 1989). However, the Supreme Court questioned the maturity factor in *Mergens v. Board of Education of the Westside Community Schools,* 110 S. Ct. 2356, (1990). The implications of differing views of "student capacity" (i.e., impressionability or maturity) are discussed in chapter 7.

24. Ruti Teitel, *When Separate Is Equal: Why Organized Religious Exercises, Unlike Chess, Do Not Belong in the Public Schools,* 81 Nw. U. L. Rev. 174, 182 (1986). This rationale was behind the *Clark* ruling cited above. The district court reasoned that while "[t]he Establishment Clause does not exist in a position of perpetual supremacy," the questions raised concerning the Free Exercise and Establishment Clauses "must, in the context presented here, be resolved in favor

of the Establishment Clause." *Clark v. Dallas Independent School District,* 671 F. Supp. at 1124.

25. This mentality is evident in Teitel's assertion that the Equal Access Act (20 U.S.C. Secs. 4071-4074) "mandates government *sponsorship* of prayer in public schools." Teitel, *supra* note 24, p. 175 (emphasis added). In fact, the Equal Access Act simply allows student religious groups to meet during noninstructional hours within public high schools that have created a limited open forum for student speech.

26. This rationale was rejected in *Mergens v. Board of Education of the Westside Community Schools,* 110 S. Ct., 2356 (1990).

27. As discussed further in chapter 4, the concern for scrupulous avoidance of "establishments" of religion within the public realm is based upon an ignorance or misinterpretation of the history behind the First Amendment's Religion Clauses.

28. Arons and Lawrence, *supra* note 19, at 312 (emphasis in original).

29. *Id.*

30. *Id.*

31. Joe Wittmer and Robert D. Myrick, *Facilitative Teaching: Theory and Practice,* 2nd ed. (Minneapolis: Educational Media Corp., 1980), p. 167.

32. *Id.*

33. *Id.* at 168.

34. *See id.* at 103-27.

35. *Id.* at 121.

36. *Id.* at 115.

37. *Id.* at 171.

38. *Id.* This particular exercise may at least be a roundabout way of evading the Supreme Court's ban on the posting of the Ten Commandments within public school classrooms. *See generally Stone v. Graham,* 449 U.S. 39 (1980).

39. Wittmer and Myrick, *supra* note 31, at 181.

40. Kathleen M. Gow, *Yes, Virginia, There Is Right and Wrong!* (Toronto: John Wiley and Sons Canada Ltd., 1980), p. 38.

41. 20 U.S.C. Sec. 1232h(a) (West 1990).

42. 20 U.S.C. Sec. 1232h(b) (West 1990).

43. B. F. Skinner, *About Behaviorism* (New York: Knopf, 1974), p. 184.

44. *Beyond Freedom and Dignity, supra* note 10, at 128.

45. *Id.* at 128.

46. Lawrence Kohlberg, Charles Levine, Alexandra Hewer, *Moral Stages: A Current Formulation and a Response to Critics* (Basel: S. Karger, 1983), p. 71.

47. It is argued that behaviorist ideologies of education are not opposed to the cultural transmission philosophy *per se,* but in fact *systematize* the cultural transmission philosophy's focus on cultural standards by considering solely "the relation between behavior and the environment" (*Beyond Freedom and Dignity, supra* note 10, at 15), neglecting the internal states of mind that romanticist educational philosophers consider intrinsically valuable. *See* Lawrence Kohlberg and Rochelle Mayer, *Development as the Aim of Education,* 42 Harv. Educ. Rev. 449, 460-61 (1972). Skinner has claimed that "[a]bstract thinking is the product of a particular kind of environment, not of a cognitive faculty." *Beyond Freedom and Dignity, supra* note 10, at 189.

48. The emphasis of modern values education on social usefulness over absolute standards of truth and morality accords with the philosophical pragmatism of John Dewey, the foremost progressivist educational philosopher. *See* chapter 1.

49. Skinner writes, "Perhaps we cannot design a successful culture as a whole, but we can design better practices in piecemeal fashion." *Beyond Freedom and Dignity, supra* note 10, at 156.
50. *Id.* at 154.
51. *Illinois ex rel. McCollum v. Board of Education,* 333 U.S. 203, 235 (1948) (Jackson, J., concurring). *See also Mozert v. Hawkins County Board of Education,* 827 F.2d 1058, 1073 (6th Cir. 1987), *cert. denied,* 56 U.S.L.W. 3569 (U.S. Feb. 22, 1988). (Kennedy, C. J., concurring).
52. *See e.g., Engel v. Vitale,* 370 U.S. 421 (1962); *Abington School District v. Schempp,* 374 U.S. 203 (1963).
53. *Shelton v. Tucker,* 364 U.S. 479, 487 (1960).
54. Note, *Freedom and Publication: The Need for New Standards,* 50 Notre Dame L. Rev. 530, 531 (1975).
55. *Tinker v. Des Moines Independent Community School District,* 393 U.S. 503, 511 (1969).
56. *Id.*
57. *In re Gault,* 387 U.S. 1 (1967).
58. *See generally* Comment, *Students' Constitutional Rights in Public Secondary Education,* 14 Washburn L. J.106 (1975).
59. 393 U.S. 503 (1969).
60. *Tinker's* continued vitality is evident in several subsequent Supreme Court rulings. In *Goss v. Lopez,* 419 U.S. 565 (1975), the Fourteenth Amendment's Due Process Clause protection was held applicable to students faced with temporary suspension from school. In *New Jersey v. T.L.O.,* 469 U.S. 325 (1985), the Court ruled that school officials are not only subject to First Amendment controls (per *Tinker*), but also to Fourth Amendment controls, such that they cannot force students to submit to unreasonable searches. *But cf. Wood v. Strickland,* 402 U.S. 308 (1975), in which the Court held that although school officials are not immune from damage liability in Sec. 1983 *civil rights* actions, compensatory awards will be appropriate only where the officials acted with an impermissible motivation such as would render unreasonable any "good faith" characterization. *See also Ingraham v. Wright,* 430 U.S. 651 (1977), holding that *Tinker* leaves school officials with authority to control students' conduct through corporal punishment.
61. *Engel v. Vitale,* 370 U.S. 421 (1962).
62. *Abington School District v. Schempp,* 374 U.S. 203 (1963).

CHAPTER THREE: *Avoiding Religious Apartheid*

1. *Brandon v. Board of Education of the Guilderland Central School District,* 635 F.2d 971, 973 (2d Cir. 1980), *cert. denied,* 454 U.S. 1123 (1981).
2. *Id.*
3. The Equal Access Act (20 U.S.C. Secs. 4071-4074), enacted by Congress in 1984, *allows* faculty supervision of public high school student religious and political group meetings which the school must permit if it has created a limited open forum for student speech. While the Act states that school officials may not promote, lead, or participate in any such meeting, it permits "[t]he assignment of a teacher, administrator, or other school employee to the meeting for custodial purposes." 20 U.S.C. Sec. 4072(2). The Supreme Court has found this provision of the Act, as well as the Act in general, constitutional. *See Mergens v. Board of Education of the Westside Community Schools,* 110 S. Ct. 2356 (1990).
4. *Brandon,* 635 F. 2d at 973.

5. *Id.* The First Amendment provides: "Congress shall make no law respecting an establishment of religion, or prohibiting the free exercise thereof; or abridging the freedom of speech, or of the press; or the right of the people peaceably to assemble, and to petition the Government for a redress of grievances." U. S. Const. amend. I.
6. 487 F. Supp. 1219 (N.D. N.Y.), *aff'd*, 635 F.2d 971 (2d Cir.), *cert. denied*, 454 U.S. 1123 (1980).
7. *Brandon*, 635 F.2d at 978-80.
8. *Id.* at 978.
9. For example, federal courts have held that First Amendment Establishment Clause concerns "outweighed" the free speech rights of public high school students to meet as a student-initiated prayer club during the school's regularly scheduled activity period, *Bender v. Williamsport Area School District*, 563 F. Supp. 697 (M.D. Penn. 1983), *rev'd*, 741 F.2d 538 (3d Cir. 1984), *vacated*, 475 U.S. 503, *reh'g denied*, 476 U.S. 1132 (1986); that a school policy permitting religious meetings and Bible distribution on public elementary school premises during school hours made possible an "intrusion of the church into the precincts of the state" that would probably not occur if the same activities took place on a university campus or public square, *Bell v. Little Axe Independent School District No. 70*, 766 F.2d 1391, 1407 (10th Cir. 1985); that a school district's plan to provide a federally funded remedial education program in public school for female Hasidic Jews, whose sect required separation of the sexes in schooling, was probably invalid because its primary effect was to advance religion, *Parents' Association of P.S. 16 v. Quinones*, 803 F.2d 1235 (2d Cir. 1986); that the Equal Access Act (see *supra* note 3) would "require an unconstitutional result" if applied to a claim brought by students who met for prayer on public school property," because their conflict with a school district policy had to be "resolved in favor of the Establishment Clause," *Clark v. Dallas Independent School District*, 671 F. Supp. 1119 (N.D. Tex. 1987), *modified*, 701 F. Supp. 594 (N.D. Tex. 1988), *appeal dismissed*, 880 F. 2d 411 (5th Cir. 1989); that public elementary school officials could require removal of religious books from a classroom library and require a teacher to keep his Bible out of sight and refrain from reading it during class hours, *Roberts v. Madigan*, 702 F. Supp. 1505 (D. Colo. 1989); that allowing public high school students to use a classroom before the school day for a religious meeting "would impermissibly advance" religion, *Garnett v. Renton School District No. 403*, 874 F.2d 608, 611 (9th Cir. 1989), *appeal filed*, 110 S. Ct. 362 (1989); and that school officials could ban prayer at a public high school graduation, even if it constituted a public forum, because of the state's interest in "preventing the violation of the Establishment Clause," *Lundberg v. West Monona Community School District*, 731 F. Supp. 331, 347 (N.D. Iowa 1989). Several of these rulings, specifically *Bender, Clark*, and *Garnett*, may have been effectively overturned by the Supreme Court's decision in *Mergens, supra* note 3. In *Bender* and *Clark*, the courts conceded the schools in question had created a "limited open forum" for student speech; the *Clark* court referred specifically to the Equal Access Act's definition of such a forum (671 F. Supp. at 1124). While the *Garnett* court denied that the school had created a "limited public forum" even though it allowed "co-curricular activities" on campus (874 F.2d 609, 612), the Supreme Court has placed a broad construction upon the term "noncurriculum related student group" within the meaning of the Act, in light of "Congress' intent to provide a low threshold for triggering the Act's requirements." *Mergens*, 110 S. Ct. at 2364. The Equal Access Act is discussed further in chapter 11.

10. See, e.g., Ares, Religious Meetings in the Public High School: Freedom of Speech or Establishment of Religion?, 20 University of California-Davis L. Rev. 313 (1987); Teitel, When Separate Is Equal: Why Organized Religious Exercises, Unlike Chess, Do Not Belong in the Public Schools, 81 Nw. U. L. Rev. 174 (1987); Teitel, The Unconstitutionality of Equal Access Policies and Legislation Allowing Organized Student-Initiated Religious Activities in the Public Schools: A Proposal for a Unitary First Amendment Forum Analysis, 12 Hastings Const. L. Q. 529 (1985); Note, The Right of Public High School Students to Conduct a Prayer Group on Public School Premises During Student Activity Period, 10 T. Marshall L. J. 449 (1985).

11. See Whitehead, Avoiding Religious Apartheid: Affording Equal Treatment for Student-Initiated Religious Expression in Public Schools, 16 Pepperdine L. J. 229 (1989).

12. Ares, supra note 10, at 336-37.

13. See, e.g., Piele and Pitt, The Use·of School Facilities by Student Groups for Religious Activities, 13 Journal of Law and Education 197 (1984); Stone, The Equal Access Controversy: The Religion Clauses and the Meaning of "Neutrality," 81 Nw. U. L. Rev. 168 (1986); Strossen, A Framework for Evaluating Equal Access Claims by Religious Groups: Is There a Window for Free Speech in the Wall Separating Church and State?, 71 Cornell L. Rev. 143 (1985); Note, Religious Liberty in the Public High School: Bible Study Clubs, 17 J. Marshall L. Rev. 933 (1984); Note, The Constitutional Dimensions of Student-Initiated Religious Activity in Public High Schools, 92 Yale L. J. 499 (1983) [hereinafter Student-Initiated Activity]; Note, The Constitutionality of Student-Initiated Religious Meetings on Public School Grounds, 50 U. Cinn. L. Rev. 740 (1981).

14. See, e.g., Edwards v. Aguillard, 482 U.S. 578 (1987), (involving state-mandated "balanced treatment" of evolution and creation in public school curricula); Wallace v. Jaffree, 472 U.S. 38 (1985) (involving state law authorizing a one-minute period of silence "of meditation or voluntary prayer"); Stone v. Graham, 449 U.S. 39 (1980), reh'g denied, 449 U.S. 1104 (1981) (involving state-mandated posting of the Ten Commandments in public classrooms); Abington School District v. Schempp, 374 U.S. 203 (1963) (involving state-mandated Bible reading and recitation of the Lord's Prayer in public schools); Engel v. Vitale, 370 U.S. 421 (1972) (involving the state's composition of an official prayer to be read in public schools); McCollum v. Board of Education, 333 U.S. 203 (1948) (involving use of public school facilities for students' religious education under school district's "released time" program.

15. See generally Whitehead, supra note 11.

16. Black, The Bill of Rights, 35 N.Y.U. L. Rev. 865, 867 (1960).

17. 370 U.S. 421 (1962).

18. Id. at 425, 429-30.

19. 374 U.S. 203 (1963).

20. Id. at 241.

21. Walz v. Tax Commission, 397 U.S. 664, 693 (1970) (Brennan, J., concurring).

22. See Wieman v. Updegraff, 344 U.S. 183 (1952); Sweezy v. New Hampshire, 354 U.S. 234 (1957).

23. See Tinker v. Des Moines Independent Community School District, 393 U.S. 503 (1969).

24. It appears that just such an attitude may account for many public school textbooks' handling of religion's importance in American history and contemporary American life. See Paul C. Vitz, Religion and Traditional Values

in Public School Textbooks: An Empirical Study (Washington, D.C.: National Institute of Education, 1985).

25. *Schempp*, 374 U.S. at 225, 300 (Brennan, J., concurring). This dictum has been appealed to as a reason to permit public school observance of religious holidays with both a "religious" and "secular" basis. *Florey v. Sioux Falls School District 49-5*, 619 F.2d 1311, 1315-16 (8th Cir.), *cert. denied*, 449 U.S. 987 (1980).

26. *Zorach v. Clauson*, 343 U.S. 306, 313-14 (1952). The Court held that a city education law permitting public schools to release students for religious instruction *off* of school premises did not violate the Establishment Clause, but rather was the sort of governmental action that "respects the religious nature of our people and accommodates the public service to their spiritual needs." *Id.* at 314.

27. *See Widmar v. Vincent*, 454 U.S. 263, 276 (1981) where the Court remarked that the state's interest in achieving church-state separation by forbidding a student religious group to meet on a state university campus is regulated by the Free Speech Clause as well as the Free Exercise Clause.

CHAPTER FOUR: *The Historical Logic*

1. *Everson v. Board of Education*, 330 U.S. 1, 33 (1947) (Rutledge, J., dissenting).

2. *Walz v. Tax Commission*, 397 U.S. 664, 671 (1970). *See also Lynch v. Donnelly*, 465 U.S. 668, 673-78 (1984), and *Marsh v. Chambers*, 463 U.S. 783, 786-92 (1983), reviewing the history of governmental deference to America's religious heritage.

3. *Walz*, 397 U.S. at 671. *See also Lynch*, 465 U.S. at 678, where the Court concludes that the history it had just reviewed "may help explain why the Court consistently has declined to take a rigid, absolutist view of the Establishment Clause."

4. Leo Pfeffer, an attorney who has represented parties or filed briefs in many church-state cases before the Supreme Court, is often considered a leading advocate of a strict separation between church and state. For an autobiographical sketch of Pfeffer and bibliography of his work, *see* James Wood, ed., *Religion and State: Essays in Honor of Leo Pfeffer* (Waco, TX: Baylor University Press, 1985).

5. *See e.g., Engel v. Vitale*, 370 U.S. 421, 436 (1962) (a state-sponsored public school prayer is an establishment of religion even though it "does not amount to a total establishment of one religion to the exclusion of all others"); *Abington School District v. Schempp*, 374 U.S. 203, 233 (1963) (Brennan, J., concurring) (the prohibition of "an official church" is not "the full extent of the prohibitions against official involvements in religion"); *Mueller v. Allen*, 463 U.S. 388, 400 (1983) (the Establishment Clause "extends beyond prohibitions of a state church or payment of state funds to one or more churches"). However, not all justices have followed this trend in Establishment Clause jurisprudence. *See, e.g., Wallace v. Jaffree*, 472 U.S. 38, 98-9 (1985) (Rehnquist, J., dissenting) (the Establishment Clause inclusion was motivated by a fear of "a national church," not by concern "about whether the Government might aid all religions evenhandedly").

6. Justice Joseph Story, a leading Unitarian of his time who served on the Supreme Court from 1811 to 1845, wrote:

> Probably at the time of the adoption of the Constitution, and of the amend-
> ment to it now under consideration, the general, if not the universal, sen-
> timent in America was that Christianity ought to receive encouragement

from the state so far as was not incompatible with the private rights of conscience and freedom of worship.

2 J. Story, *Commentaries on the Constitution of the United States*, 2d ed. (Boston: Little, Brown, 1891) pp. 593-95. *See also* Thomas Cooley, *The General Principles of Constitutional Law in the United States of America* (Boston: Little, Brown and Co., 1898), p. 224.

7. *See Wallace*, 472 U.S. at 80 (O'Connor, J., concurring). Although she concurred in the Court's prohibition of a "moment of silence" for prayer in public schools partly because "free public education was virtually nonexistent in the late eighteenth century," Justice O'Connor noted that the Court had "properly looked to history" in upholding legislative prayer, tax exemptions for churches, and Sunday closing laws.

8. *Schempp*, 374 U.S. at 237-41 (Brennan, J., concurring).

9. *Id.* at 255 (Brennan, J., concurring).

10. *Id.* at 294 (Brennan, J., concurring), *quoted in Lemon v. Kurtzman*, 403 U.S. 602, 642 (1971) (Brennan, J., concurring).

11. *Id.* at 295 (Brennan, J., concurring). Justice Brennan attempted to distinguish this stance from one of "official hostility toward religion." *Id.*

12. The notion of a "high and impregnable" wall separating church and state originates in *Everson v. Board of Education*, 330 U.S. 1, 18 (1947).

13. *See Webster's New Collegiate Dictionary* (Springfield, Mass.: G. and C. Merriam, 1975), pp. 1227-1228.

14. *See, e.g., Bender v. Williamsport Area School District*, 475 U.S. 534, 553-55 (1986) (Burger, C. J., dissenting); *School District of Grand Rapids v. Ball*, 473 U.S. 373, 382 (1985); *Lynch*, 465 U.S. at 714 (Brennan, J., dissenting); *Marsh*, 463 U.S. at 802-03 (Brennan, J., dissenting); *Thomas v. Review Board*, 450 U.S. 707, 717 (1981); *McDaniel v. Paty*, 435 U.S. 618, 629, 636 (1978); *Maher v. Roe*, 432 U.S. 464, 475 n.8 (1977); *Roemer v. Board of Public Works*, 426 U.S. 736, 747 (1976) (plurality opinion); *Meek v. Pittenger*, 421 U.S. 349, 372 (1975); *Committee for Public Education & Religious Liberty v. Nyquist*, 413 U.S. 756, 792-93 (1973); *Wisconsin v. Yoder*, 406 U.S. 205, 220 (1972); *Gillette v. United States*, 401 U.S. 437, 449, 469 (1971); *Welsh v. United States*, 398 U.S. 333, 372 (1970) (White, J., dissenting); *Epperson v. Arkansas*, 393 U.S. 97, 103-04, 109 (1968); *Board of Education v. Allen*, 392 U.S. 236, 242, 249 (1968); *Sherbert v. Verner*, 374 U.S. 398, 409, 422-23 (1963); *Schempp*, 374 U.S. at 215-22, 226 (1963); *Engel*, 370 U.S. at 443 (1962) (Douglas, J., concurring); *McGowan v. Maryland*, 366 U.S. 420, 564 (1961) (Douglas, J., dissenting); *Everson*, 330 U.S. at 18 (1947).

15. *Lynch*, 465 U.S. at 673.

16. *See, e.g., Wallace*, 472 U.S. at 91-114 (Rehnquist, J., dissenting); *Marsh*, 463 U.S. at 786-92; *Walz*, 397 U.S. at 719-27 (Douglas, J., dissenting); *McGowan*, 366 U.S. at 434-36. *See also Everson*, 330 U.S. at 8-16; *cf. Reynolds v. United States*, 98 U.S. 145, 162-64 (1878) (analyzing the Free Exercise Clause's historical meaning).

17. Dumas Malone, *Jefferson the Virginian* (Boston: Little, Brown, 1948), p. 262.

18. This bill is considered "one of the most important sources of this nation's founding principles outside the Constitution." Sanford Kessler, *Locke's Influence on Jefferson's "Bill for Establishing Religious Freedom,"* 25 Journal of Church and State 231 (1983).

19. Daniel L. Dreisbach, *Real Threat and Mere Shadow: Religious Liberty and the First Amendment* (Westchester, Ill.: Crossway Books, 1987), p. 120 (footnotes omitted).

20. These were: "A Bill for Saving the Property of the Church Heretofore by Law Established," "A Bill for Appointing Days of Public Fasting and Thanksgiving," and "A Bill Annulling Marriages Prohibited by the Levitical Law." For a discussion of these bills, *see id.* at 120-22.
21. Ordinance of 1787, art. 3 (1787), reprinted in *Documents Illustrative of the Formation of the Union of American States* (Washington, D.C.: Government Printing Office, 1927), p. 52 (emphasis supplied).
22. For a compendium of these provisions, *see* Samuel Windsor Brown, *The Secularization of American Education* (New York: Russell & Russell, 1912, 1967), pp. 98-9.
23. Northwest Ordinance, ch. 8, 1 Stat. 50-1 (1845).
24. *See generally* Terry Eastland, "In Defense of Religious America," *Commentary* (June 1981).
25. *Id.* at 40.
26. Henry Steele Commager (Preface), *McGuffey's Fifth Eclectic Reader,* as cited in John Whitehead, *The Freedom of Religious Expression in Public Universities and High Schools,* 2d ed. (Westchester, Ill.: Crossway Books, 1986), p. 14.
27. Richard D. Mosier, *Making the American Mind: Social and Moral Ideas in the McGuffey Readers* (New York: King's Crown Press, 1947), p. 17.
28. *See* Robert Cord, *Separation of Church and State: Historical Fact and Current Fiction* (New York: Lambeth Press, 1982), p. 23.
29. *Id.*
30. *Marsh v. Chambers,* 463 U.S. at 787-88.
31. *See* Cord, *supra* note 28, at 27-9.
32. *Id.* at 28.
33. *See id.* at 29-36.
34. *Id.* at 27.
35. *Everson,* 330 U.S. at 13.
36. "A Bill for Saving the Property of the Church Heretofore by Law Established." *See* Dreisbach, *supra* note 19, at 120.
37. *See* Mark DeWolfe Howe, *The Garden and the Wilderness: Religion and Government in American Constitutional History* (Chicago: University of Chicago Press, 1965), p. 10.
38. *Id.* at 11.
39. *Reynolds v. United States,* 98 U.S. 145, 164 (1878).
40. *Id.*
41. Chester James Antieau, Arthur T. Downey, and Edward C. Roberts, *Freedom from Federal Establishment: Formation and History of the First Amendment Religion Clauses* (Milwaukee: Bruce, 1964), pp. 207-09.
42. *See Reynolds,* 98 U.S. at 163.
43. Dreisbach, *supra* note 19, at 115-16, 119.
44. *See Engel,* 370 U.S. at 428-29; *Everson,* 330 U.S. at 11-13, 33-42.
45. *See* James Madison, *Letters and Other Writings of James Madison, Fourth President of the United States,* 4 Vols. (New York: R. Worthington, 1884), Vol. 1, pp. 62-9; Philip S. Foner, ed., *Basic Writings of Thomas Jefferson* (New York: Willey Book Co., 1944), pp. 48-9.
46. *Letters and Other Writings of James Madison,* Vol. 1, *supra* note 45, at 165.
47. *Foner, supra* note 45, at 48.
48. *Engel,* 370 U.S. at 427-28.
49. *Id.* at 429.
50. As quoted in Adrienne Koch and William Peden, eds., *The Life and Selected Writings of Thomas Jefferson* (New York: Random House, 1944), p. 332.
51. *Id.* (emphasis supplied).

52. As quoted in Koch and Peden, *supra* note 50, at 341.
53. The adoption of the Fourteenth Amendment eventually resulted in the First Amendment Establishment Clause's applicability to the states. However, the Fourteenth Amendment's adoption makes evidence of the framers' intent no less relevant. For example, in *Marsh v. Chambers*, 463 U.S. 783, 790-91 (1983), the Supreme Court said:

> In applying the First Amendment to the states through the Fourteenth Amendment, *Cantwell v. Connecticut*, 310 U.S. 296, 303 (1940), it would be incongruous to interpret that Clause as imposing more stringent First Amendment limits on the states than the draftsmen imposed on the Federal Government.

54. *See* Act of March 3, 1803, ch. 20, 2 Stat. 155-56 (1845); Act of April 26, 1802, ch. 30, 2 Stat. 236-37 (1845); and Act of March 19, 1804, ch. 26, 2 Stat. 271-72 (1845).
55. A Treaty Between the United States of America and the Kaskaskian Tribe of Indians, 7 Stat. 78-9 (1846).
56. *Id.*
57. *Lynch*, 465 U.S. at 678 (citation omitted), *quoting* Joseph Story, *Commentaries on the Constitution of the United States*, Vol. 3 (Boston: Hilliard, Gray, and Co., 1833), p. 728.
58. Thomas M. Cooley, *The General Principles of Constitutional Law in the United States of America* (Boston: Little, Brown, and Co., 1898), pp. 205-06.
59. *Id.* at 225, 266. Cooley attributed prosecution of blasphemy, which has now been generally abandoned, to the need to "take notice that the prevailing religion of the country is Christian." *Id.* at 226. As America becomes more religiously diverse, this kind of governmental practice would seemingly be untenable as a form of "affirmative accommodation" of religion.
60. Dreisbach, *supra* note 19, at 123 (footnotes omitted).
61. *Everson*, 330 U.S. at 18.
62. 330 U.S. 1 (1947).
63. *See id.* at 15-16.
64. *Lynch*, 465 U.S. at 673.
65. Jefferson's desire to accommodate public university students' religious beliefs and practices influenced his entire ideal of the university curriculum. He wrote:

> The want of instruction in the various creeds of religious faith existing among our citizens presents . . . a chasm in general instruction of the useful sciences. . . . *A remedy, however, has been suggested of promising aspect, which, while it excludes the public authorities from the domain of religious freedom, will give to the sectarian schools of divinity the full benefit of the public provisions made for instruction in the other branches of science.* . . . It has, therefore, been in contemplation, and suggested by some pious individuals, who perceive the advantages of associating other studies with those of religion, *to establish their religious schools on the confines of the University,* so as to give to their students ready and convenient access and attendance on the scientific lectures of the University; and to maintain, by that means, those destined for religious professions on as high a standing of science, and of personal weight and respectability, as may be obtained by others from the benefits of the University. Such establishments would offer the further and great advantage of *enabling the students of the University to attend religious exercise[s] with the professor of their particular sect, whether in rooms of the building still to be erected,*

and destined to that purpose under impartial regulations, as proposed in the same report of the commissioners, *or in the lecturing room of such professor.* . . . Such an arrangement would *complete the circle* of the useful sciences embraced by this institution, and would fill the chasm now existing, on principles which would leave inviolate the constitutional freedom of religion. *The Writings of Thomas Jefferson,* Mem. Ed., Albert Ellery Bergh, ed. (Washington, D.C., issued under the auspices of The Thomas Jefferson Memorial Association of the U. S., 1907), p. 36(emphasis supplied).

66. Saul K. Padover, ed., *The Complete Jefferson* (New York: Duell, Sloan & Pearce, Inc., 1943), p. 1111.
67. *See* J. O. Wilson, *Public Schools of Washington,* Vol. 1, Records of the Columbia Historical Society (1987), p. 4.
68. *Id.* at 5.
69. *Id.* at 6.
70. James Madison was a member of the Board of Visitors that approved the report Jefferson made as rector, providing an indication of Madison's views on the constitutionality of voluntary religious worship and education in public schools. "Regulations Adopted by the Board of Visitors of the University of Virginia, October 4, 1824, Jefferson, Madison, Breckenridge, Cocke, Loyally and Cabell Being Present," as cited in Padover, *supra* note 66, at 1110.
71. Foner, *supra* note 45, at 48.
72. "An Act for Establishing Elementary Schools" (1817), in *The Writings of Thomas Jefferson,* Vol. 17 (Albert Ellery Bergh ed. 1907) p. 425.
73. Letter to Peter Carr, September 7, 1814, in *The Writings of Thomas Jefferson,* Vol. 19 (Andrew A. Lipscomb ed. 1905) p. 213.
74. *Id.* at 214.
75. "An Act for Establishing Elementary Schools," *supra* note 72, at 424.
76. *Id.* at 423, n.5. By its recognition of parents' rights *not* to educate their children, this Act foreshadows the Supreme Court's ruling that Amish children whose parents consider high school attendance contrary to their religion must not be forced to attend school until age sixteen. *See Wisconsin v. Yoder,* 406 U.S. 205 (1972).
77. 1 *Annals of Congress* (Gales and Seaton, eds., 1834), p. 454.
78. *See Wisconsin v. Yoder,* 406 U.S. 205 (1972). There the Supreme Court stated: "A way of life that is odd or even erratic but interferes with no rights or interests of others is not to be condemned because it is different." *Id.* at 224.
79. Dreisbach, *supra* note 19, at 162 (footnote omitted).

CHAPTER FIVE: *Affirmative Accommodation*

1. U. S. Const. Amend. 1.
2. In the Supreme Court's seminal modern ruling on church-state relations, Justice Hugo Black wrote for the Court:

> The "establishment of religion" clause of the First Amendment means at least this: Neither a state nor the Federal Government can set up a church. Neither can pass laws which aid one religion, aid all religions, or prefer one religion over another.

Everson v. Board of Education, 330 U.S. 1, 15 (1947). Justice Black's declaration that the state may not even pass laws that "aid all religions" is problematic. In the process of providing religion constitutionally required accommodation, it is inevitable that some laws have the effect of "aiding all religions." The Supreme Court has since admitted this. *Lynch v. Donnelly*, 465 U.S. 668, 673 (1984).

3. *See Zorach v. Clauson*, 343 U.S. 306, 314, 315 (1952); *McCollum v. Board of Education*, 333 U.S. 203, 211 (1948).

4. *See Sherbert v. Verner*, 374 U.S. 398 (1963) (state unemployment compensation statute found to be an unconstitutional burden on free exercise of religion as applied to private employee who was denied compensation because she refused for religious reasons to work on Saturday); *Wisconsin v. Yoder*, 406 U.S. 205 (1972) (state law requiring school attendance until age sixteen violated free exercise rights of Amish parents whose religion opposed their children's attendance at high school). It appeared that these two rulings meant that the Supreme Court had established the free exercise of religion as a "supreme" interest, so that free exercise claims would be upheld without reference to any other First Amendment interest. Pfeffer, *The Supremacy of Free Exercise*, 61 Geo. L. J. 1115, 1139-1140 (1973). However, it now appears that the Supreme Court will strike down neutral, generally applicable laws that burden religiously motivated action only if such action implicates the Free Exercise Clause "in conjunction with other constitutional protections." *Employment Division, Department of Human Resources of State of Oregon v. Smith*, 110 S. Ct. 1595, 1601 (1990).

5. *See, e.g., Engel v. Vitale*, 370 U.S. 421 (1962) (school district's mandated recitation of state-composed prayer in public schools struck down as an establishment of religion); *Abington School District v. Schempp*, 374 U.S. 203 (1963) (state-mandated Bible reading and recitation of the Lord's prayer struck down as an establishment of religion).

6. *See Tilton v. Richardson*, 403 U.S. 672, 677 (1971).

7. Some commentators claim that there is a "natural antagonism" between the Establishment and Free Exercise Clauses. *See* J. Nowack, R. Rotunda, and J. Young, *Handbook on Constitutional Law* (St. Paul, Minn.: West Publishing Co., 1983), p. 849. This tension is *artificial* because it is "unnatural," not inherent in the clauses themselves, but rather based on mistaken constructions of the clauses. Note, *Reconceptualizing Establishment Clause Cases as Free Exercise Class Actions*, 98 Yale L. J. 1739, 1741-1742 (1989) (authored by Scott J. Ward). *See also* Laurence Tribe, *American Constitutional Law*, 2d ed. (Mineola, N.Y.): The Foundation Press, 1988), pp. 1158-1169; *Wallace v. Jaffree*, 472 U.S. 38, 82 (1985) (O'Connor, J., concurring); *Sherbert v. Verner*, 374 U.S. 398, 414 (1963) (Stewart, J., concurring).

8. Note, *Permissible Accommodations of Religion: Reconsidering the New York "Get" Statute*, 96 Yale L. J. 1147, 1151 (1987) (footnotes omitted). *Compare* Kahan, *Jewish Divorce and Secular Courts: The Promise of Avitzur*, 73 Geo. L. J. 193, 205 (1984); Warmflash, *The New York Approach to Enforcing Religious Marriage Contracts: From Avitzur to the "Get" Statute*, 50 Brooklyn L. J. 229, 240-241 (1984). *Cf.* Comment, *Damned if You Do, Damned if You Don't: Religious Shunning and the Free Exercise Clause*, 137 U. Pa. L. Rev. 271 (1988).

9. *See* Note, *Bowen v. Kendrick: Establishing a New Relationship Between Church and State*, 38 Am. U. L. Rev. 953, 954 (1989); Note, *The Myth of Religious Neutrality by Separation in Education*, 71 Va. L. Rev. 127, 133 (1985); Giannella, *Religious Liberty, Nonestablishment, and Doctrinal Development: Part I. The Religious Liberty Guarantee*, 80 Harv. L. Rev. 1381, 1389 (1967), and *Part II. The Nonestablishment Principle*, 81 Harv. L. Rev. 513, 514-15 (1968).

10. Gianella, *Part II. The Nonestablishment Principle*, *supra* note 9, at 523 n. 27.

11. *See, e.g., Everson v. Board of Education,* 330 U.S. 1 (1947), where the Supreme Court upheld a state law authorizing reimbursement to parents of funds spent for transporting their children on buses to both public and parochial schools. The Court has held that religious institutions must be allowed certain public benefits, such as police and fire protection, or "the state and religion would be aliens to each other — hostile, suspicious, and even unfriendly." *Zorach v. Clauson,* 343 U.S. 306, 312 (1952). *See also Walz v. Tax Commission,* 397 U.S. 664, 671, 676 (1970).

12. The state unemployment compensation statute at issue in *Sherbert v. Verner,* 374 U.S. 398 (1963) is an example of general welfare legislation that may impinge upon exercise of religion by individuals.

13. Justice Brennan observed that nineteenth-century immigration "exposed the public schools to religious diversities and conflicts unknown to the homogeneous academics of the eighteenth century." *Abington School District v. Schempp,* 374 U.S. 203, 272 (1963) (Brennan, J., concurring).

14. 397 U.S. 664 (1970).

15. *Id.* at 669. In making this concession, the Court appealed to its abandonment of the "absolutely straight course" in Establishment Clause jurisprudence expressed in *Sherbert. Sherbert v. Verner,* 374 U.S. at 422.

16. Appealing to history, the Court stressed that for the First Amendment's framers, "the 'establishment' of a religion connoted sponsorship, financial support, and active involvement of the sovereign in religious activity." *Walz,* 397 U.S. at 668. This appears to be a narrower construction of "establishment" than that implied in the *Everson* Court's declaration that government may not even pass laws that "aid all religions." *Everson,* 330 U.S. at 15. Further departure from the *Everson* construction of "establishment of religion" is evident in the Court's declaration that "[a] law is not unconstitutional simply because it *allows* churches to advance religion, which is their very purpose." *Corporation of Presiding Bishop v. Amos,* 483 U.S. 327, 337 (1987) (emphasis in original).

17. *Walz,* 397 U.S. at 669.

18. *See* Note, *The Free Exercise Boundaries of Permissible Accommodation Under the Establishment Clause,* 99 Yale L. J. 1127, 1146 (1990); Note, *Developments in the Law — Religion and the State: II. The Complex Interaction Between Religion and Government,* 100 Harv. L. Rev. 1606, 1638 (1987); Paulsen, *Religion, Equality, and the Constitution: An Equal Protection Approach to Establishment Clause Adjudication,* 61 Notre Dame L. Rev. 311, 313 (1986); Note, *Reinterpreting the Religion Clauses: Constitutional Construction and Conceptions of the Self,* 97 Harv. L. Rev. 1468, 1470-71 (1984); Comment, *A Non-Conflict Approach to the First Amendment Religion Clauses,* 131 U. Pa. L. Rev. 1175, 1177 (1983); Choper, *The Religion Clauses of the First Amendment: Reconciling the Conflict,* 41 U. Pitt. L. Rev. 673, 700 (1980); Moore, *The Supreme Court and the Relationship Between the "Establishment" and "Free Exercise" Clauses,* 42 Tex. L. Rev. 142, 194, 197-98 (1963).

19. *See Texas Monthly v. Bullock,* 109 S. Ct. 890, 912 (1989) (Scalia, J., dissenting); *Sherbert,* 374 U.S. at 414 (Stewart, J., concurring); *Schempp,* 374 U.S. at 305-07 (Goldberg, J., concurring).

20. *See, e.g., Witters v. Washington Commission for the Blind,* 474 U.S. 481 (1986) (benefits to blind individuals at religiously-affiliated universities); *Mueller v. Allen,* 463 U.S. 388 (1983) (tuition benefits for students attending sectarian schools); *Tilton v. Richardson,* 403 U.S. 672 (1971) (construction grants to sectarian colleges and universities); *Board of Education v. Allen,* 392 U.S. 236 (1968) (lending state-approved secular textbooks to all secondary school students); *Thomas v. Review Board,* 450 U.S. 707 (1981) (unemployment

benefits to employee who terminated employment because of religious objection to work involved); *Sherbert v. Verner*, 374 U.S. 398 (1963) (unemployment benefits to employee who refused employment because of conflict with religious beliefs).

21. *See* Kurland, *The Supreme Court, Compulsory Education, and the First Amendment's Religion Clauses*, 75 W. Va. L. Rev. 213, 237 (1973). *See generally* Comment, *Constitutional Law — Religious Exercises in Public Schools*, 20 Ark. L. Rev. 320, 325 (1967).

22. Laurence Tribe, *American Constitutional Law* (Mineola, N.Y.: The Foundation Press, 1978), pp. 827-28. For a critique of this theory, *see* Note, *Defining "Religion" in the First Amendment: A Functional Approach*, 74 Cornell L. Rev. 532, 535 *passim* (1989).

23. Note, *Toward a Constitutional Definition of Religion*, 91 Harv. L. Rev. 1056, 1089 (1978). This author concludes that a "bifurcated definition of religion" (which corresponds to Tribe's proposed definition) "fairly accommodates the individual's liberty of belief within the confines of the affirmative secular state." *Id.*

24. *See* Note, *Secular Humanism in Public School Textbooks: Thou Shalt Have No Other God (Except Thyself)*, 63 Notre Dame L. J. 358, 376-79 (1988) where the argument is that textbooks that "promote as truth faith statements on matters of *ultimate concern* . . . will give government the appearance of endorsing religion." (emphasis added) *Id.* at 377. This commentator, therefore, criticizes the ruling in *Mozert v. Hawkins County Board of Education*, 827 F.2d 1058 (6th Cir. 1987), *cert. denied*, 56 U.S.L.W. 3569 (U.S. Feb. 22, 1988) in which the court not only denied plaintiff parents' claim that their children's textbooks promoted "secular humanism" and were thus religiously objectionable, but also upheld the board of education's elimination of an "alternative reading program" that had been arranged for their children. *Id.* The "ultimate concern" standard for defining religion has been criticized as "incapable of yielding sound results across a spectrum of religion cases" and likely to "make assessment of sincerity especially difficult." Greenawalt, *Religion as a Concept in Constitutional Law*, 72 Calif. L. Rev.753, 811 (1984).

25. Tribe, *American Constitutional Law*, 2d ed., *supra* note 22, at 1186-88.

26. *Id.* at 1169.

27. Concerning the framers' "familiarity with exemptions on account of religious scruple," *see* McConnell, *The Origins and Historical Understanding of Free Exercise of Religion*, 103 Harv. L. Rev. 1409, 1511-13 (1990).

28. *See, e.g., Jaffree v. Wallace*, 705 F.2d 1526, 1531 (11th Cir. 1983), *aff'd*, 472 U.S. 38 (1985).

29. *See, e.g.* Merel, *The Protection of Individual Choice in Religion: A Consistent Understanding of Religion Under the First Amendment*, 45 U. Chi. L. Rev. 805, 806 (1978).

30. Paulsen, *supra* note 18, at 313 (footnote omitted) (emphasis in original). Another commentator states similarly that the Free Exercise Clause protects "the individual's choice of his identity," and the Establishment Clause protects "the pluralistic structure of the background social institutions necessary to make that choice both possible and meaningful." Note, *Developments in the Law — Religion and the State: II. The Complex Interaction Between Religion and Government, supra* note 18, at 1638.

31. Comment, *A Non-Conflict Approach to the First Amendment Religion Clauses, supra* note 18, at 1178.

32. *Id.* at 1178-179 (footnote omitted) (emphasis supplied).

33. Note, *The Free Exercise Boundaries of Permissible Accommodation Under the Establishment Clause, supra* note 18, at 1146.
34. *The Compact Edition of the Oxford English Dictionary,* Vol. 1 (London: Oxford University Press, 1979), p. 59.
35. Note, *The Constitutionality of the 1972 Amendment to Title VII's Exemption for Religious Organizations,* 73 Mich. L. Rev. 538, 551 (1975).
36. Laycock, *Equal Access and Moments of Silence: The Equal Status of Religious Speech by Private Speakers,* 81 Nw. U. L. Rev. 1, 3 (1986).
37. *Id.* (footnote omitted) (emphasis supplied).
38. 465 U.S. 668 (1984).
39. *Id.* at 673 (citations omitted) (emphasis supplied).
40. *Id.* at 681. Chief Justice Warren Burger, writing for the Court, observed that it would be "a stilted overreaction contrary to our history" to forbid the use of the creche "at the very time people are taking note of the season with Christmas hymns and carols in *public schools* and other public places." *Id.* at 686 (emphasis added). Cf. *Allegheny County v. American Civil Liberties Union, Greater Pittsburgh Chapter,* 109 S. Ct. 3086, 3103-04 (1989), where the Court, distinguishing *Lynch* on the facts, held the municipal creche display at issue unconstitutional because "nothing in the context of the display detracts from the creche's religious message."
41. 472 U.S. 38 (1985). *See also Walter v. West Virginia,* 610 F. Supp. 1169 (S.D. W. Va. 1985).
42. *Id.* at 43. *See also Edwards v. Aguillard,* 482 U.S. 578 (1987), in which a statute was invalidated that required the teaching of creation-science whenever the theory of evolution was taught. The Court, however, found that the statute's primary effect was to advance a religious doctrine.
43. *Zorach v. Clauson,* 343 U.S. 306, 314 (1952).
44. *See, e.g., Zorach v. Clauson,* 343 U.S. 306, 313-14 (1952); *Engel v. Vitale,* 370 U.S. 421, 433-34 (1962); *Abington School District v. Schempp,* 374 U.S. 203, 212-13 (1963); *Walz v. Tax Commission,* 397 U.S. 664, 669 (1970); *Roemer v. Board of Public Works,* 426 U.S. 736 (1976).
45. *Walz,* 397 U.S. at 669.
46. *Roemer v. Board of Public Works,* 426 U.S. 736, 745-46 (1976) (emphasis supplied).
47. *Everson,* 330 U.S. at 15.
48. *See, e.g., Lanner v. Wimmer,* 662 F.2d 1349 (10th Cir. 1981). The court reasoned that because there is no "impregnable wall of separation" within "the milieu of public education, there must be some measure of accommodation." *Id.* at 1352.
49. Note, *Permissible Accommodations of Religion, supra* note 8, at 1152 (emphasis supplied).
50. *Id.*
51. The *Everson* Court observed that "parents might be reluctant to permit their children to attend schools which the state had cut off from such general government services as ordinary police and fire protection, connections for sewage disposal, public highways and sidewalks." *Everson,* 330 U.S. at 17-8. The Court did not explicitly distinguish *these* burdens on parents from any burden that could follow from denial of the state subsidies for school buses at issue in this case, but such a distinction may have been implied.
52. *Braunfeld v. Brown,* 366 U.S. 599, 606-07 (1961). State certification requirements for parochial school teachers, though they increase the cost of religious education, may be an example of an "indirect" burden on free exercise

(per *Braunfeld*) that may be upheld. *See* Note, *Permissible Accommodations of Religion, supra,* note 8, at 1153.
53. Tribe, *American Constitutional Law,* 2d ed., *supra* note 22, at 1169.
54. 330 U.S. 1 (1947).
55. *Id.* at 18.
56. *See, e.g.,* Note, *Permissible Accommodations of Religion, supra* note 8, and Tribe, *supra* note 22; Adams and Emmerich, *A Heritage of Religious Liberty,* 137 U. Pa. L. Rev. 1559, 1654 (1989); Note, *Developments in the Law — Religion and the State; II. The Complex Interaction Between Religion and Government, supra* note 18, at 1728; McConnell, *Accommodation of Religion,* 1985 Sup. Ct. Rev. 1 (1985). *See also* Whitehead, *Accommodation and Equal Treatment of Religion: Federal Funding of Religiously-Affiliated Child Care Facilities,* 26 Harv. J. on Legis. 573 (1989).
57. Note, *Permissible Accommodations of Religion, supra* note 8, at 1152.
58. 403 U.S. 602 (1971), *reh'g denied,* 404 U.S. 876 (1971).
59. *Id.* at 612-13 (emphasis supplied).
60. *Roemer,* 426 U.S. at 747 (emphasis supplied).
61. *See generally Marsh v. Chambers,* 463 U.S. 783 (1983); *Lynch v. Donnelly,* 104 S. Ct. 1355 (1984). *See also* the discussion of the *Lemon* test in *Mueller v. Allen,* 463 U.S. 388, 394 *passim* (1983).
62. McConnell, 26 Sup. Ct. Rev., *supra* note 27, at 1-2.
63. 465 U.S. 668 (1984).
64. The "endorsement" test, however, is at least as problematic as the *Lemon* test:

> Far from eliminating the inconsistencies and defects that have plagued establishment analysis, the "no endorsement" test would introduce further ambiguities and analytical deficiencies into the doctrine. Moreover, the theoretical justifications offered for the test are unpersuasive.

Smith, *Symbols, Perceptions, and Doctrinal Illusions: Establishment Neutrality and the "No Endorsement" Test,* 86 Mich. L. Rev. 266, 267 (1987).
65. *Id.* at 688-92 (O'Connor, J., concurring).
66. *Id.* at 688.
67. *Id.* at 691-92.
68. *Id.*
69. *See Wallace v. Jaffree,* 472 U.S. 38, 76 (1985) (O'Connor, J., concurring).
70. Smith, *supra* note 70, at 267.
71. *See, e.g., American Civil Liberties Union v. City of Birmingham,* 791 F.2d 1561, 1563 (6th Cir.), *cert. denied,* 107 S. Ct. 421 (1986); *Bollenbach v. Board of Education,* 659 F. Supp. 1450, 1465 (S.D.N.Y. 1987).
72. Smith, *supra* note 70, at 267.
73. *See, e.g., Texas Monthly v. Bullock,* 109 S. Ct. 890, (1989); *County of Allegheny v. American Civil Liberties Union,* 109 S. Ct. 3086 (1989).
74. 109 S. Ct. 3086 (1989).
75. *Id.* at 3103.
76. *Id.* at 3115.
77. *Id.* at 3100.
78. *Id.* at 3101.
79. *See Lynch v. Donnelly,* 465 U.S. 668, 693 (1984) (O'Connor, J., concurring).
80. For a review of the increased legal recognition of students' rights, *see* Hafen, *Developing Student Expression Through Institutional Authority: Public Schools as Mediating Structures,* 48 Ohio St. L. J. 663; 677-93 (1987).
81. *See, e.g., Engel v. Vitale,* 370 U.S. 421 (1962); *Abington School District v. Schempp,* 374 U.S. 203 (1963); *Wallace v. Jaffree,* 472 U.S. 38 (1985).

82. One commentator insists that "the idea that the secular orientation of the public school curriculum is itself a religion or anti-religion is, in practice, a paradox the Establishment Clause can't afford to accept." Note, *Developments in the Law — Religion and the State: II. The Complex Interaction Between Religion and Government, supra* note 18, at 1673-74.

83. Schwarz, *No Imposition of Religion: The Establishment Clause Value,* 77 Yale L. J. 692, 701 (1968).

84. John Dewey, "My Pedagogic Creed," in *John Dewey on Education: Selected Writings* (Reginald D. Archambault ed. 1964), p. 431.

85. *Id.* at 439. The Supreme Court has cited with approval Dewey's perception of public schools as an "assimilative force." *See Ambach v. Norwick,* 441 U.S. 68, 77 (1979).

86. Alfred North Whitehead, *The Aims of Education and Other Essays* (New York: Macmillan, 1959), p. 23.

87. *See* Diamond, *The First Amendment and Public Schools: The Case Against Judicial Intervention,* 59 Tex. L. Rev. 477, 498 (1981).

88. *See Smith v. Board of School Commissioners of Mobile County,* 827 F.2d 684, 692 (11th Cir. 1987). The Supreme Court had earlier stressed public schools' role in inculcating values deemed necessary for democracy. *See, e.g., Ambach v. Norwick,* 441 U.S. 68, 76-7 (1979); *Bethel School District No. 403 v. Fraser,* 478 U.S. 675, 681 (1986).

89. 333 U.S. 203 (1947).

90. *Id.* at 216-17 (Frankfurter, J., concurring).

91. 347 U.S. 483 (1954).

92. *Id.* at 493.

93. John Dewey, *A Common Faith* (New Haven, Conn.: Yale University Press, 1934), p. 84.

94. *Id.*

95. *Id.* at 86, 87. The *Humanist Manifesto I,* which Dewey and thirty-three other prominent humanists signed, may articulate the "religious faith" Dewey advocated. *See* 6 *New Humanist* (May-June 1933).

96. 333 U.S. 203, 231 (1948).

97. 330 U.S. 1, 23-4 (1947) (Jackson, J., concurring).

98. *Id.* at 24.

99. *See Clark v. Dallas Independent School District,* 671 F. Supp. 1119, 1122 (N.D. Tex. 1987), *modified,* 701 F. Supp. 594 (N.D. Tex. 1988), *dismissed,* 880 F.2d 411 (5th Cir. 1989).

100. *Lynch,* 465 U.S. at 684. Citing this proposition from *Lynch,* one federal court observed that because *any* accommodation of religious free exercise is politically divisive, "[i]f political divisiveness were the test for entanglement, no governmental accommodation of religion would survive establishment scrutiny." *May v. Cooperman,* 780 F.2d 240, 247 (3d Cir. 1985).

101. 333 U.S. 203 (1948).

102. 370 U.S. 431 (1962).

103. 374 U.S. 203 (1963).

104. 449 U.S. 39, *reh'g denied,* 449 U.S. 1104 (1981).

105. 105 S. Ct. 2479 (1985). *See also May v. Cooperman,* 780 F.2d 240 (3d Cir. 1985).

106. 482 U.S. 578 (1986).

107. The lower federal courts have followed suit. *See, e.g., Garnett v. Renton School District No. 403,* 874 F.2d 608 *appeal filed,* 110 D. Ct 362 (1989) (high school's denial of a student religious group's request to meet in a classroom violated neither the Equal Access Act nor the Constitution); *Stein v. Plainwell*

Community Schools, 822 F.2d 1406 (6th Cir. 1987) (benediction at high school graduation employing Christian theology and prayer found unconstitutional); *May v. Evansville-Vanderburgh School Corporation*, 787 F.2d 1105 (7th Cir. 1986) (religious meetings held by teachers on public school property unconstitutional); *Bell v. Little Axe Independent School District*, 766 F.2d 1391 (10th Cir. 1985) (group meetings at elementary school unconstitutional); *May v. Cooperman*, 780 F.2d 240 (3d Cir. 1985) (state statute providing for one minute of silence at beginning of school day unconstitutional); *Nartowicz v. Clayton County School District*, 736 F.2d 646 (11th Cir. 1984) (school's practice of permitting student religious groups to meet on school property and churches to announce events over school public address system unconstitutional); *Walter v. West Virginia Board of Education*, 610 F. Supp. 1169 (D.C. W. Va. 1985) (amendment to state constitution for brief time of personal and private contemplation, meditation, or prayer in public schools unconstitutional); *Crockett v. Sorenson*, 568 F. Supp. 1422 (W.D. Va. 1983) (public school's Bible program unconstitutional); *Duffy v. Las Cruces Public Schools*, 557 F. Supp. 1013 (D.N. Mex. 1983) (statute allowing moment of silence in public schools unconstitutional); *Karen B. v. Treen*, 653 F.2d 897 (5th Cir. 1981), *aff'd*, 455 U.S. 913 (1982) (statute authorizing students or teachers to initiate prayer at start of school day unconstitutional); *Lubbock Civil Liberties Union v. Lubbock Independent School District*, 669 F.2d 1038 (5th Cir. 1982), *cert. denied*, 103 S. Ct. 800 (1983) (school board policy of permitting students to use school facilities outside regular school hours for religious purposes unconstitutional); *Hall v. Board of School Commissioners of Conecuh County*, 656 F.2d 999 (5th Cir. 1981) (conducting morning devotional reading over school's public address system and a Bible literature course in a manner that promoted religion unconstitutional); *Collins v. Chandler Unified School District*, 644 F.2d 759 (1981), *cert. denied*, 454 U.S. 863 (1981) (student council members' recitation of prayers and Bible verses at school assemblies unconstitutional); *Brandon v. Board of Education of Guilderland Central School District*, 635 F.2d 971 (2d Cir. 1980), *cert. denied*, 454 U.S. 1123 (1981), *reh'g denied*, 455 U.S. 983 (1982) (school's refusal to allow students to meet on school facilities for prayer meetings before or after school unconstitutional); *Malnak v. Yogi*, 592 F.2d 197 (3d Cir. 1979) (teaching course called Science of Creative Intelligence-Transcendental Meditation unconstitutional); *Meltzer v. Board of Public Instruction of Orange County*, 548 F.2d 559 (5th Cir. 1977), *modified cert. denied*, 439 U.S. 1089 (1978) (distribution of Gideon Bibles, Bible readings in school facilities, and a state statute requiring teachers to "inculcate by precept and example . . . every Christian virtue" unconstitutional); *Despain v. DeKalb County Community School District*, 384 F.2d 836 (7th Cir. 1967), *cert. denied*, 390 U.S. 906 (1968) (prayer recited by class prior to morning snack unconstitutional); *Stein v. Oshinsky*, 348 F.2d 999 (2d Cir. 1965) *cert. denied*, 382 U.S. 957 (1965) (school officials could constitutionally prevent students from having an opportunity for prayer in the classroom); *Clark v. Dallas Independent School District*, 671 F. Supp. 1119 (N.D. Tex. 1987), *modified*, 701 F. Supp. 594 (N.D. Tex. 1988), *dismissed*, 880 F.2d 411 (5th Cir. 1989) (student religious meetings on school property unconstitutional); *Ford v. Manuel*, 629 F. Supp. 771 (N.D. Ohio 1985) (student religious group's meetings after school hours unconstitutional); *Graham v. Central Community District*, 608 F. Supp. 531 (D. Iowa 1985) (religious invocations and benedictions at high school graduation unconstitutional); *Goodwin v. Cross Country School District No. 7*, 394 F. Supp. 417 (E.D. Ark. 1973) (student council members' reading of

Bible verses and the Lord's prayer over school intercom and distribution of Gideon Bibles unconstitutional).

State courts have issued similar rulings. *See, e.g., Perumal v. Saddleback Valley Unified School District,* 243 Cal. Rptr. 545 (Cal. App. 1988) (religious literature distribution on school property prohibited); *Johnson v. Huntington Beach Union High School District,* 68 Cal. App. 3d 1, 137 Cal Rptr. 43 (1977) (student religious clubs on school premises unconstitutional).

But *see Mergens v. Board of Education of the Westside Community Schools,* 867 F.2d 1076 (8th Cir. 1989), *aff'd,* 110 S. Ct. 2356 (1990) (denial of student's right to operate Christian club violated Equal Access Act); *Florey v. Sioux Falls School District,* 619 F.2d 1311 (8th Cir. 1980), *cert. denied,* 449 U.S. 987 (1980) (rules permitting public school Christmas observances with religious elements constitutional); *Reed v. Van Hoven,* 237 F. Supp. 48 (W.D. Mich. 1965) (student-initiated voluntary prayer before start of school day constitutional); *American Civil Liberties Union v. Albert Gallatin Area School District,* 307 F. Supp. 637 (W.D. Pa. 1969) (daily Bible readings and recitation of the Lord's Prayer unconstitutional when directed by school authorities).

108. As quoted in Comment, *Constitutional Law — Religious Exercises and the Public Schools,* 20 Ark. L. Rev. 320, 325-26, n.44 (1967).

109. *Schempp,* 374 U.S. at 225.

110. *Id.* at 300 (Brennan J., concurring) (emphasis supplied).

111. *Id.* at 306 (Goldberg, J., concurring).

112. Tushnet, *The Constitution of Religion,* 18 Conn. L. Rev. 701, 723 (1986).

113. *Schempp,* 374 U.S. at 306 (Goldberg, J., concurring).

114. *Zorach v. Clauson,* 343 U.S. 306, 312-13 (1952). *See also Marsh v. Chambers,* 463 U.S. 783, 792 (1983) (allowing prayer in state legislatures is simply a tolerable acknowledgment of beliefs widely held among this nation's people); *Wallace v. Jaffree,* 472 U.S. 38, 89-90 (1985) (Burger, J., dissenting) ("the religious observances of others should be tolerated and, where possible, accommodated").

115. *See Roemer v. Board of Public Works,* 426 U.S. 736, 745-46 (1976).

116. *Zorach,* 343 U.S. at 314.

117. *Marsh,* 463 U.S. at 792.

118. *Walz,* 397 U.S. at 673, *citing Sherbert v. Verner,* 374 U.S. 398, 423 (1963) (Harlan, J., dissenting); *Braunfeld v. Brown,* 366 U.S. 599, 608 (1961).

119. *Walz,* 397 U.S. at 669.

120. *Zorach,* 343 U.S. at 313-14.

121. 374 U.S. at 225 (quoting *Zorach,* 343 U.S. at 314). *See Crockett v. Sorenson,* 568 F. Supp. 1422, 1425-426 (W.D. Va. 1983); *Jaffree v. Board of School Commissioners of Mobile County,* 554 F. Supp. 1104, 1108 (S.D. Ala. 1983).

122. 367 U.S. 488 (1961).

123. *Id.* at 495, n.11.

124. *See, e.g., Smith v. Board of School Commissioners of Mobile County,* 827 F.2d 684 (11th Cir. 1987), in which parents of school children challenged, unsuccessfully, the mandatory use of textbooks that, taken as a whole, implied that moral values are not derived from God or any transcendent source.

125. *See* Comment, *Humanistic Values in the Public School Curriculum: Problems in Defining an Appropriate "Wall of Separation,"* 61 Nw. U. L. Rev. 795, 807 (1966).

126. *See, e.g., Smith v. Ricci,* 446 A.2d 501, 507 (N.J. 1982), *dismissed,* 459 U.S. 962 (1982) (regulation requiring local school board to develop and implement a "family life education program" found "barren of any requirement that a point of view, be it secular or religious, must be stressed to the exclusion of others");

Citizens for Parental Rights v. San Mateo Board of Education, 124 Cal. Rptr. 68, 88 (1975), *dismissed,* 425 U.S. 908 (1976), *reh'g denied,* 425 U.S. 1000 (1976) (there is no basis for the argument that the family life and sex education program in effect establishes a "religion of secularism" in the schools).

127. *Citizens for Parental Rights,* 124 Cal. Rptr. at 87.
128. *Zorach,* 343 U.S. at 313-14.

CHAPTER SIX: *Public Forum Issues*

1. *Police Department of the City of Chicago v. Mosley,* 408 U.S. 92 (1972).
2. *Texas v. Johnson,* 109 S. Ct. 2533 (1989).
3. *Tinker v. Des Moines Independent Community School District,* 393 U.S. 503 (1969).
4. *See, e.g.,* Farber & Nowak, *The Misleading Nature of Public Forum Analysis: Content and Context in First Amendment Adjudication,* 70 Va. L. Rev. 1219 (1984). "Public forum analysis might well be called the 'geographical' approach to First Amendment law, because results often hinge almost entirely on the speaker's location." *Id.* at 1220. *See also* Note, *Public Forum Analysis After Perry Education Association v. Perry Local Educators' Association — A Conceptual Approach to Claims of First Amendment Access to Publicly Owned Property,* 54 Fordham L. Rev. 545 (1986).
5. "Nothing in the Constitution requires the Government freely to grant access to all who wish to exercise their right to free speech on every type of government property...." *Cornelius v. NAACP Legal Defense & Education Fund,* 473 U.S. 788, 799-800 (1985).
6. *Perry Education Association v. Perry Local Educators' Association,* 460 U.S. 37, 49 (1983).
7. Other commentators have identified additional classifications. *See,* for example, Leedes, *Pigeon Holes in the Public Forum,* 20 U. Rich. L. Rev. 499 (1986).
8. Murphy, *Access to Public School Facilities and Students by Outsiders,* 16 School Law Bulletin 9, 10 (Winter 1985).
9. *Perry,* 460 U.S. at 43.
10. *Schneider v. New Jersey,* 308 U.S. 147, 163 (1939).
11. *Hague v. C.I.O.,* 307 U.S. 496, 515 (1939).
12. *Amalgamated Food Employees Union Local 590 v. Logan Valley Plaza, Inc.,* 391 U.S. 308, 315 (1968).
13. *Perry,* 460 U.S. at 45.
14. *Id.* at 44.
15. *Mosley, supra* note 1.
16. *Perry,* 460 U.S. at 45.
17. *See generally Grayned v. City of Rockford,* 408 U.S. 104 (1972).
18. *Perry,* 460 U.S. at 44.
19. *See Southeastern Promotions, Ltd. v. Conrad,* 420 U.S. 546 (1975).
20. *Concerned Women for America v. Lafayette County and Oxford Public Library,* 699 F. Supp. 95 (N.D. Miss. 1988), *aff'd* 883 F.2d 32 (5th Cir. 1989). *See also Brown v. Louisiana,* 383 U.S. 131 (1966).
21. *See Stewart v. D.C. Armory Board,* 863 F.2d 1013 (D.C. Cir. 1988).
22. *See Widmar v. Vincent,* 454 U.S. 263 (1981).
23. *Hazelwood School District v. Kuhlmeier,* 108 S. Ct. 562, 568 (1988), *quoting Cornelius v. NAACP Legal Defense and Educational Fund, Inc.,* 473 U.S. 788, 802 (1985).
24. *Cornelius,* 473 U.S. at 802.
25. *Perry,* 460 U.S. at 46.

26. *Id.* at 45.
27. *Id.*
28. *Id.* at 44.
29. *Id.* at 46.
30. See *Student Government Association v. Board of Trustees of the University of Massachusetts,* 868 F.2d 473, 480 (1st Cir. 1989).
31. *Perry,* 460 U.S. at 46.
32. 454 U.S. 263 (1981).
33. *Perry,* 460 U.S. at 46.
34. See, e.g., *Jones v. North Carolina Prisoners' Union,* 433 U.S. 119 (1977) (prisons); *Greer v. Spock,* 424 U.S. 828 (1976) (military base); *Lehman v. City of Shaker Heights,* 418 U.S. 298 (1974) (plurality opinion) (buses).
35. *Perry,* 460 U.S. at 46 (quoting *United States Postal Service v. Council of Greenburgh Civic Associations,* 453 U.S. 114, 129 [1981]).
36. *United States Postal Service v. Council of Greenburgh Civic Association,* 453 U.S. 114, 129-130 (1981), quoting *Greer v. Spock,* 424 U.S. 828, 836 (1976), in turn quoting *Adderley v. Florida,* 385 U.S. 39, 47 (1966).
37. *Perry,* 460 U.S. at 46 (emphasis supplied).
38. *Id.* at 49.
39. *Id.* at 48.
40. *Greer v. Spock,* 424 U.S. 828 (1976).
41. *Perry,* 460 U.S. at 46 (emphasis supplied).
42. *Id.* at 49. It is unclear from an analytical point of view whether the term "limited public forum" is synonymous with the term "forum by designation." Justice Blackmun has suggested the terms are interchangeable. *Cornelius,* 473 U.S. at 813 (Blackmun, J., dissenting). It has been suggested by others that there is a subtle analytical difference between the two concepts. It could be argued that a designated public forum is a forum intentionally opened to free speech activities, and once opened to the public at large, the government is bound by the same standards that apply in a traditional public forum. A limited public forum, on the other hand, is more specifically carved out of the nonpublic forum for expressive activity of a particular subject matter or nature, narrowly tailored to conform to the purposes to which the property is dedicated. One eminent commentator has also indicated there may be subtle analytical distinctions between the two:

> The distinction between such a limited public forum and a designated forum under category (2), which is limited to certain purposes, is by no means clear. A limited public forum must permit access by "other entities of similar character" to those for whom access has been permitted. What constitutes such a "similar character" may depend, of course, upon subjective characterizations and may well be the subject of judicial manipulation. Although there may be subject-matter, or "status" exclusion, there may not be exclusion based simply upon the point-of-view of the putative speaker.

M. Nimmer, *Nimmer on Freedom of Speech,* Section 4.09[D] n. 168 (1984 student ed.).
43. *Id.* at 46.
44. Leedes, *Pigeon Holes in the Public Forum,* 20 U. Rich. L. Rev. 449, 522 (1986).
45. See *Miller v. California,* 413 U.S. 15, 23 (1973) (citations omitted). ("This much has been categorically settled by the Court, that obscene material is unprotected by the First Amendment.")
46. *Brandenburg v. Ohio,* 395 U.S. 444, 447 (1969).

47. *See Gertz v. Robert Welsh, Inc.*, 418 U.S. 323 (1947); *New York Times Co. v. Sullivan*, 376 U.S. 254 (1964).
48. *See Central Hudson Gas & Electric Corporation v. Public Service Commission*, 447 U.S. 254 (1980).
49. *See New York v. Ferber*, 458 U.S. 747 (1982). (Child pornography need not be technically obscene before the state may prohibit or restrict it.)
50. *See, e.g., Central Hudson*, 447 U.S. 254; *Miller*, 413 U.S. 15; *Brandenburg*, 395 U.S. 444; *New York Times Co.*, 376 U.S. 254.
51. *See Laycock, Equal Access and Moments of Silence: The Equal Status of Religious Speech by Private Speakers*, 81 Nw. U. L. Rev. 1, 46-47 (1986).

CHAPTER SEVEN: *Student Capacity*

1. Laurence Tribe, *American Constitutional Law* (Mineola, N.Y.: Foundation Press, 1978), p. 825.
2. *See Strossen, A Framework for Evaluating Equal Access Claims by Student Religious Groups: Is There a Window for Free Speech in the Wall Separating Church and State?*, 71 Cornell L. Rev. 143, 147 (1985).
3. *Id. See also Keyishian v. Board of Regents*, 385 U.S. 589, 603 (1967); *Board of Education, Island Trees Union Free School District v. Pico*, 457 U.S. 853, 864 (1982) (plurality opinion). Concerning the tension public schools may face as they try to fulfill both goals, *see* Mitchell, *Secularism in Public Education: The Constitutional Issues*, 67 B.U. L. Rev.603, 699-706 (1987).
4. The marketplace of ideas concept may also be traced back to the Supreme Court's ruling striking down a state statute requiring all school children to salute the American flag. The Court said that the schools' training of young people for citizenship is sufficient reason "not to strangle the free mind at its source and teach youth to discount important principles as mere platitudes." *West Virginia Board of Education v. Barnette*, 319 U.S. 624, 637 (1942).
5. *See Wieman v. Updegraff*, 344 U.S. 183 (1952).
6. *Id.* at 195 (Frankfurter, J., concurring) (emphasis supplied).
7. *Sweezy v. New Hampshire*, 354 U.S. 234, 250 (1957).
8. 385 U.S. 589 (1967). The Court had in its previous term struck down a loyalty oath applied to a public elementary or secondary school teacher. *See Elfbrandt v. Russell*, 384 U.S. ll (1966).
9. *Shelton v. Tucker*, 364 U.S. 479, 487 (1960). This ruling struck down a state law requiring all public school or college teachers to file an annual affidavit listing all organizations to which they belonged or regularly contributed.
10. *Keyishian*, 385 U.S. at 603.
11. John Milton wrote:

    And though all the winds of doctrine were let loose to play upon the earth, so Truth be in the field, we do injuriously by licensing and prohibiting to misdoubt her strength. Let her and Falsehood grapple; who ever knew Truth put to the worse, in a free and open encounter?

    See Areopagitica (Cambridge: Cambridge University Press, 1918), p. 58.
12. 393 U.S. 503 (1969).
13. *Id.* at 512.
14. *Id.* at 511.
15. *See, e.g., Pratt v. Independent School District No. 831, Forest Lake*, 670 F.2d 771, 776 (8th Cir. 1982) (film may not be removed from public high school curriculum to suppress an ideological viewpoint).

16. *See, e.g., Scheck v. Baileyville School Committee,* 530 F. Supp. 679, 687 (D. Maine 1982) (injunction against banning of book from school library granted because "[p]ublic schools are major marketplaces of ideas"); *Right to Read Defense Committee v. School Committee of Chelsea,* 454 F. Supp. 703, 710 (D. Mass. 1978) (because "a school should be a readily accessible warehouse of ideas," injunction granted to return student anthology to high school library); *Minarchini v. Strongsville City School District,* 541 F.2d 577, 583 (6th Cir. 1976) (school library "a mighty source in the free marketplace of ideas," "a forum for silent speech"). *But see Zykan v. Warsaw Community School Corporation,* 631 F.2d 1300, 1304 (7th Cir. 1980) (high school students' lack of intellectual skills cited as justifying removal of books from school library).

17. *See, e.g., Riseman v. School Commission of Quincy,* 439 F.2d 148, 149 (1st Cir. 1971) (student's distribution of political literature not a "material disruption" of class work according to *Tinker*). *But see Eisner v. Stamford Board of Education,* 440 F.2d 803, 807 (2d Cir. 1971) (marketplace of ideas concept limited where the state has authority to prohibit students' distribution of political literature that will interfere with school discipline).

18. *See, e.g., Russo v. Central School District No. 1,* 400 F.2d 623, 633 (2d Cir. 1972), *cert. denied,* 411 U.S. 932 (1973) (because tenth graders "readily perceive the existence of conflicts in the world around them," teacher was fired for refusing to pledge allegiance to the flag); *James v. Board of Education of Central District No.1,* 461 F.2d 566, 573 (2d Cir.), *cert. denied,* 409 U.S. 1042 (1972), *reh'g denied,* 410 U.S. 947 (1973) (because free marketplace of ideas assumptions do apply to school-age children, high school teacher was improperly fired for wearing black arm band to protest Vietnam War). *But see Burns v. Rovaldi,* 477 F. Supp. 270, 276 (D. Conn. 1979) (because a fifth grade schoolroom is not "a public forum traditionally devoted to speech and assembly," firing of teacher for exposing students to communist ideas was not based on activities protected by the First Amendment). *Id.*

19. *See, e.g., Wilson v. Chancellor,* 418 F. Supp. 1358, 1368 (D. Or. 1976) (because "today's high school students are surprisingly sophisticated, intelligent, and discerning," order banning all political speakers from public high school was unreasonable). *Compare Bender v. Williamsport Area School District,* 741 F.2d 538, 564 (3rd Cir. 1984) (Adams, C. J., dissenting) (high school students' ability to participate in a marketplace of ideas limits public school officials' authority "to control the student body's exposure to views not endorsed by the school board." *Id.*

20. Strossen, *supra* note 2, at 147.

21. *See Bethel School District v. Fraser,* 478 U.S. 675, 683 (1986) (because public high school student's sexually suggestive school assembly speech "could well be seriously damaging to its less mature audience," the First Amendment did not prevent the school district from disciplining the student).

22. *See Federal Communications Commission v. Pacifica Foundation,* 438 U.S. 726, 749 (1977) ("offensive expression may be withheld from the young without restricting the expression at its source"); *Ginsberg v. New York,* 390 U.S. 629, 638 (1968) (the definition of obscenity may be "adjusted" for minors). *Cf. Prince v. Massachusetts,* 321 U.S. 158, 170 (1944) ("the power of the state to control the conduct of children reaches beyond the scope of its authority over adults").

23. *Tinker,* 430 U.S. at 507. *Compare New Jersey v. T.L.O.,* 469 U.S. 325, 336 (1985) (because of compulsory education laws, schools do not act merely with authority delegated by parents, but are subject to Fourth Amendment search and seizure requirements while ensuring school discipline).

24. *Ingraham v. Wright,* 430 U.S. 651, 682 (1977) (*Tinker* does not require that the Eighth Amendment's cruel and unusual punishment prohibition apply to disciplinary corporal punishment in public schools).

25. *See, e.g., Arnold v. Board of Education of Escambia County,* 880 F.2d 305, 314 (11th Cir. 1989) (because "[t]he law's concept of a family presumes that parents possess what a child lacks in maturity, . . . [p]arental consultation is particularly desirable regarding the abortion decision"); *Schaill by Kross v. Tippecanoe County School Corporation,* 864 F.2d 1309, 1324 (7th Cir. 1988) (drug testing of high school athletes reasonable because "an environment conducive to learning must be maintained"); *Brands v. Sheldon Community School,* 671 F. Supp. 627, 634 (N.D. Iowa 1987) (suspension of high school athlete from team due to sexual conduct with sixteen-year-old fellow student reflects "legitimate school board concerns" according to *Tinker*); *Horton v. Goose Creek Independent School District,* 690 F.2d 470, 480 (1st Cir. 1982), *cert. denied,* 463 U.S. 1207 (1983) (school district's contraband detection program reasonable because students are "too young to be considered capable of mature restraint in their use of illegal substances or dangerous instrumentalities").

26. *See, e.g., Trachtman v. Anker,* 563 F.2d 512, 519 (2d Cir. 1977), *cert. denied,* 435 U.S. 925 (1978) (high school's prohibition of sex questionnaire among students was a reasonable measure to protect students "compelled by law to attend school" from "emotional disturbance").

27. 393 U.S. at 509.

28. *McCollum v. Board of Education,* 333 U.S. 203, 227 (1948) (Frankfurter, J., concurring).

29. *See* Strossen, *supra* note 2, at 147.

30. *School District of Grand Rapids v. Ball,* 473 U.S. 373, 390 (1985).

31. *See, e.g., Roberts v. Madigan,* 702 F. Supp. 1505, 1516 (D. Colo. 1989) (prohibition of fifth-grade teacher's Bible reading in classroom justified by appeal to "the potential effect of his actions on impressionable fifth grade students"); *Clark v. Dallas Independent School District,* 671 F. Supp. 1119, 1123 (N.D. Tex. 1987), *modified,* 701 F. Supp. 594 (N.D. Tex. 1988), *rev'd and remanded,* 880 F.2d 411 (5th Cir. 1989) (school district's policy allowing student religious groups to conduct programs before or after school struck down because it "carries with it an implicit approval by school officials of these programs"); *Bender v. Williamsport Area School District,* 563 F. Supp. 697 (M.D. Penn. 1983), *rev'd,* 741 F. 2d 538 (3d. Cir. 1984), *vacated,* 475 U.S. 503, *reh'g denied,* 476 U.S. 1132 (1986) (student religious group was rightly denied equal access to public high school because "elementary and secondary schools, unlike universities, are not the academic battleground").

32. 110 S. Ct. 2356 (1990).

33. *See, e.g., Campus Crusade for Christ v. Centennial School District,* 1990 U.S. App. LEXIS 10048, p. 43 (3rd Cir. 1990) (student religious group's use of public high school auditorium outside of school hours for evangelistic program upheld because the high school's "fear of a mistaken inference of endorsement is largely self-imposed, because the school itself has control over any impressions it gives its students"). This ruling follows the Supreme Court's reasoning in *Mergens.* There the Court stated that "secondary school students are mature enough and are likely to understand that a school does not endorse or support student speech that it merely permits on a nondiscriminatory basis." 110 S. Ct. at 2372.

34. *See* Laurence Tribe, *American Constitutional Law,* 2d ed. (Mineola, N.Y.: Foundation Press, 1988), pp. 1177-79.

35. *Id.* at 1177.

36. *See, e.g.,* Teitel, *When Separate Is Equal: Why Organized Religious Exercises, Unlike Chess, Do Not Belong in the Public Schools,* 81 Nw. U. L. Rev. 174, 183-84 (1986).

37. *See* 110 S. Ct. at 2366-68.

38. Laycock, *Equal Access and Moments of Silence: The Equal Status of Religious Speech by Private Speakers,* 81 Nw. U. L. Rev. l, 51-52 (1986).

39. 110 S. Ct. at 2381. (Marshall, J., concurring) (emphasis supplied).

40. 454 U.S. 263 (198).

41. *See id.* at 274, where this proposition is implied by the Court's observation that an open forum at a public university "'would no more commit the University ... to religious goals' than it is 'now committed to the goals of the Students for a Democratic Society, the Young Socialist Alliance,' or any other group eligible to use its facilities" (*quoting* the ruling below in *Chess v. Widmar,* 635 F.2d 1310, 1317 [8th Cir. 1980]). The *Widmar* Court thus affirmed both that religious speech should not be distinguished from political speech, and that (as applied later to public high school students in Justice Marshall's *Mergens* concurrence) school officials' actions are dispositive in evaluating student capacity.

42. *See, e.g., Bell v. Little Axe Independent School District No. 70,* 766 F. 2d 1391 (10th Cir. 1985). *Bender v. Williamsport Area School District,* 741 F.2d 538, 548 (3rd Cir. 1984), *aff'd,* 475 U.S. 534 (1986), *reh'g denied,* 476 U.S. 1132 (1986). One federal court had also claimed that high school and college students differ in ability "to screen fact from propaganda" with respect to student newspapers. *Schwartz v. Schuker,* 298 F. Supp. 238, 242 (E.D. New York 1969).

43. *Bender v. Williamsport Area School District,* 563 F. Supp. 697 (M.D. Penn. 1983), *rev'd,* 741 F. 2d 538 (3d Cir. 1984), *vacated,* 475 U.S. 534 (1986), *reh'g denied,* 476 U.S. 1132 (1986).

44. *Id.* at 556 (Powell, J., dissenting).

45. 110 S. Ct. at 2372.

46. Neil Postman, *The Disappearance of Childhood* (New York: Delacorte Press, 1982), pp. 74-75. For Postman's general discussion of the mass media's effect on childhood, *see id.,* pp. 67-74.

47. *Id.* at 75.

48. *See generally* David Elkind, *The Hurried Child: Growing Up Too Fast Too Soon* (Reading, Mass.: Addison-Wesley Publishing Co., 1981).

49. *See* John David Burkholder, *Religious Rights of Teachers in Public Education,* 18 Journal of Law & Education 335, 350 (1989).

50. Joyce Wolfgang Williams and Marjorie Stith, *Middle Childhood: Behavior and Development* (New York: Macmillan Publishing Co., 1974), p. 341.

51. *Id.*

52. *Id.* at 358-59. The authors cite three papers by David Elkind: *The Child's Conception of His Religious Denomination, I: The Jewish Child,* 99 Journal of Genetic Psychology 209 (1961); *The Child's Conception of His Religious Denomination, II: The Catholic Child,* 101 Journal of Genetic Psychology 185 (1962); *The Child's Conception of His Religious Denomination, III: The Protestant Child,* 103 Journal of Genetic Psychology 291 (1963).

53. David Moshman, *Children, Education, and the First Amendment: A Psycholegal Analysis* (Lincoln, Nebr.: University of Nebraska Press, 1989), p. 75. Moreover, during its consideration of the Equal Access Act, the Senate Judiciary Committee examined the evidence and specifically concluded that "students below the college age can understand that an equal access policy is one of State neutrality toward religion, not of State favoritism or sponsorship." 130 Cong. Rec. S8357 (daily ed. June 27, 1984) (statement of Senator Durenberger). Another senator

said the Act's cosponsors seek "to make clear that the same rule of law [as applies to colleges] applies to students in our public secondary schools." 130 Cong. Rec. S8356 (daily ed. June 27, 1984) (statement of Senator Bumpers).

54. Moshman, *supra* note 53, at 33.

55. Note, *The Constitutional Dimensions of Student-Initiated Religious Activity in Public High Schools*, 92 Yale L. J. 449, 507-09 (1983).

56. *Id.* at 509.

57. Strossen, *supra* note 2, at 148-49.

58. Hafen, *Hazelwood School District and the Role of First Amendment Institutions*, 1988 Duke L. J. 685, 700 (1988). Hafen quotes A. S. Neill's statement: "If left to himself without adult suggestion of any kind, [the child] will develop as far as he is capable of developing." *Id.* See A. S. Neill, *Summerhill: A Radical Approach to Child Rearing* (New York: Hart Publishing Co., 1960), p. 4.

59. *See, e.g., Ambach v. Norwick*, 441 U.S. 68, 77 (1979) (while upholding statute forbidding any noncitizen's certification as a public school teacher, the Court argues that social science has confirmed "perceptions of public schools as inculcating fundamental values"); *Minersville School District v. Gobitis*, 310 U.S. 586, 591 (1940), *rev'd*, 319 U.S. 624 (1943) (in upholding compulsory flag salute in state's schools, the Court called "the promotion of national cohesion" an "interest inferior to none in the hierarchy of legal values"); *Bell v. U-32 Board of Education*, 630 F. Supp. 939, 944 (D. Vt. 1986) (school asserts school board's "responsibility to transmit societal values" in support of school board's prohibition of play containing mature themes but little profanity); *Zykan v. Warsaw Community School Corporation*, 631 F.2d 1300, 1305 (7th Cir. 1980) (while upholding school board's removal of books from library and curriculum, court stresses "need for intellectual and moral guidance from a body capable of transmitting the mores of the community"). *See also* Levin, *Educating Youth for Citizenship: The Conflict Between Authority and Individual Rights in the Public School*, 95 Yale L. J. 1647 (1986).

60. *See, e.g., Ambach v. Norwick*, 441 U.S. 68, 77, 78 (1979) (while upholding statute forbidding any noncitizen's certification as a public school teacher, the Court cites Dewey's emphasis on public school's role as an assimilative force and stresses teachers' role in "shaping student's experience to achieve educational goals").

61. Jean-Jacques Rousseau, *Emile, or On Education*, trans. A. Bloom (New York: Basic Books, Inc., 1979), p. 90.

62. For a presentation of guidelines for public schools to follow as they inculcate such values by instructing on political or moral matters, *see* van Geel, *The Search for Constitutional Limits on Government's Authority to Inculcate Youth*, 62 Tex. L. Rev. 197, n. 289 (1983).

63. *See, e.g., Scheck v. Baileyville School Committee*, 530 F. Supp. 679, 686 (D. Maine 1982) (in granting injunction to restore banned book to public high school library, the court argued, in favor of the "right to receive information," that "[t]he public school remains a most important public resource in the training and development of youth for citizenship and individual fulfillment"). *Compare Hazelwood School District v. Kuhlmeier*, 108 S. Ct. 562, 580 (1988) (Brennan, J., dissenting) (in dissenting from the Supreme Court's upholding of a public high school's censorship of materials deemed inappropriate for students from a curriculum-related student newspaper, Justice Brennan concludes: "The young men and women of Hazelwood East expected a civics lesson, but not the one the Court teaches them today"). *Id.*

CHAPTER EIGHT: *The Rights of Students*

1. *See* discussion of students' rights in chapters 1-3.
2. *See, e.g., In Re Gault,* 387 U.S. 1 (1967).
3. 319 U.S. 624 (1943).
4. The resolution required all teachers and students "to participate in the salute honoring the Nation represented by the Flag; provided, however, that refusal to salute the Flag be regarded as an Act of insubordination, and shall be dealt with accordingly." *Id.* at 626.
5. *Id.* at 642.
6. *Id.* at 637.
7. *Id.* at 642.
8. 393 U.S. 503 (1969).
9. *Id.* at 506.
10. *Id.* at 511.
11. *Id.* at 508.
12. *Id.* at 507.
13. *Id.* at 511.
14. *Id.*
15. *Id.*
16. *Id.*
17. *Id.*
18. *Id.* at 509.
19. *Id.* at 508 (emphasis supplied).
20. *Id.* at 512. (quoting *Keyishian v. Board of Regents,* 385 U.S. 589, 603 [1967]).
21. *Id.* at 511.
22. *Id.* at 513.
23. *Id.* at 511 (quoting *Burnside v. Byars,* 363 F.2d 744, 749 [5th Cir. 1966]).
24. *Bolger v. Youngs Drug Products Corporation,* 463 U.S. 60, 84 (1983) (Stevens, J., concurring).
25. Toms and Whitehead, *The Religious Student in Public Education: Resolving a Constitutional Dilemma,* 27 Emory L. J. 3, 32 (1978) (emphasis in original).
26. *Zorach v. Clauson,* 343 U.S. 306, 315 (1952).
27. *Walz v. Tax Commission of New York,* 397 U.S. 664, 669 (1970).
28. *Zorach,* 343 U.S. at 315.
29. *Rivera v. East Otero School District,* 721 F. Supp. 1189, 1195 (D. Colo. 1989).
30. *Tinker,* 393 U.S. at 508.
31. *NAACP v. Button,* 371 U.S. 415, 433 (1963). *See generally* Schauer, *Fear, Risk and the First Amendment: Unraveling the "Chilling Effect,"* 58 B.U. L. Rev. 685 (1978).
32. *Abington School District v. Schempp,* 374 U.S. 203, 225 (1963) (quoting *Zorach v. Clauson,* 343 U.S. 306, 314 [1952]).
33. As noted by Professor Kauper:

> If the protection afforded in the name of religious freedom against a state-prescribed nontheistic orthodoxy is that a person cannot be compelled to participate, whereas the protection afforded in the name of the Establishment Clause is that a person may demand that any exercise promoting theistic belief be completely eliminated, the result is that the freedom protected by the Establishment Clause is regarded as having a higher value than the freedom protected by the Free Exercise Clause.

Kauper, *Prayer, Public Schools and the Supreme Court,* 61 Mich. L. Rev. 1031, 1063 (1963).

34. The Supreme Court has recognized the need for a balance of interests in the First Amendment. For example, in *Mueller v. Allen*, 463 U.S. 388 (1983), the Court noted: "As *Widmar* and our other decisions indicate, a program . . . that *neutrally provides state assistance to a broad spectrum of citizens* [i.e., religious and nonreligious] is not readily subject to challenge under the Establishment Clause." *Id.* at 398-99 (emphasis supplied); *see also Widmar v. Vincent*, 454 U.S. 263 (1981); *Bowen v. Kendrick*, 108 S. Ct. 2562 (1988); *Corporation of Presiding Bishop v. Amos*, 483 U.S. 327 (1987).

35. 454 U.S. 263 (1981).

36. *Id.* at 264-65.

37. *Id.* at 266-67.

38. *Id.* at 284-85 (White, J., dissenting). Justice White cited the school prayer and Bible reading cases as support for his argument. *Id.* at 285. *See Engel v. Vitale*, 370 U.S. 421 (1962) and *Abington School District v. Schempp*, 374 U.S. 203 (1963).

39. *Widmar v. Vincent*, 454 U.S. at 269-70 n.6.

40. *Id.*

41. *Id.* at 270 n.6; *see Heffron v. International Society for Krishna Consciousness, Inc.*, 452 U.S. 640 (1981).

42. 20 U.S.C. Sec. 4071(a) and (b) (emphasis supplied).

43. 110 S. Ct. 2356 (1990).

44. *Mergens v. Board of Education of the Westside Community Schools*, 110 S. Ct. 2356 (1990).

45. *Id.*

46. 20 U.S.C. Sec. 4071-4074.

47. *Mergens*, 110 S. Ct. 2356.

48. *Id.* at 2372.

49. Senate Report No. 98-357, p. 8 (1984).

50. The Supreme Court has held:

> [T]he protection they [the framers] sought was not solely for persons in intellectual pursuits. It extends to more than abstract discussion, unrelated to action. The First Amendment is a charter for government, not for an institution of learning. "Free trade in ideas" means free trade and the *opportunity to persuade* to action, not merely to describe facts.

> *Thomas v. Collins*, 323 U.S. 516, 537 (1945) (emphasis added).

51. *Id.*

52. *Cary v. Board of Education of Adams-Arapahoe*, 427 F. Supp. 945, 949 (D. Colo. 1977), *aff'd*, 598 F.2d 535 (10th Cir. 1979).

53. *Id.*

54. *Shanley v. Northeast Independent School District*, 462 F.2d 960, 972 (5th Cir. 1972).

55. *Id.*

56. *Tinker*, 393 U.S. at 511.

57. *Id.*

58. *Id.*

59. *City of Madison Joint School District No. 8 v. Wisconsin Employment Relations Commission*, 429 U.S. 167, 175 n.8 (1976); *Perry Education Association v. Perry Local Education Association*, 460 U.S. 37, 46 (1983); *Grayned v. City of Rockford*, 408 U.S. 104, 120 (1972).

60. *Keyishian v. Board of Regents*, 385 U.S. 589, 603 (1967).

61. *Board of Education, Island Trees Union Free School District No. 26 v. Pico*, 457 U.S. 853, 880 (1982).

62. Murphy, *The Prior Restraint Doctrine in the Supreme Court: A Reevaluation*, 51 Notre Dame Law. 898, 898-99 (1976).
63. *Tinker*, 393 U.S. at 514.
64. *See, e.g., Bystrom v. Fridley High School, Independent School District No. 14*, 822 F.2d 747, 755 (1987).
65. 509 F.2d 652 (1st Cir. 1974). *See also Gay Student Services v. Texas A & M University*, 737 F.2d 1317 (5th Cir. 1984), *cert. denied*, 471 U.S. 1001 (1985); *Gay and Lesbian Students Association v. Gohn*, 850 F.2d 361 (8th Cir. 1988).
66. *Gay Students Organization of the University of New Hampshire v. Bonner*, 509 F. 2d at 660 (quoting *NAACP v. Alabama*, 357 U.S. 449, 460 [1958] [emphasis supplied]). *See also Menora v. Illinois High School Association*, 683 F.2d 1030 (7th Cir. 1982). *But cf. American Future Systems, Inc. v. State University of New York College at Cortland*, 565 F. Supp. 754 (N.D. N.Y. 1983), where distinction is made concerning commercial speech.
67. *NAACP v. Alabama*, 357 U.S. 449, 460 (1958).
68. 408 U.S. 169 (1972).
69. *See Gay Student Services v. Texas A & M University*, 737 F.2d 1317 (5th Cir. 1984), *cert. denied*, 471 U.S. 1001 (1985), where the university refused to recognize officially homosexual student groups. The court stated that "the denial of recognition to a student group wishing to express its own views on the same or similar subjects is clearly the sort of viewpoint-based discrimination forbidden by *Perry* in any type of public forum." *Id.* at 1333.
70. *Healy*, 408 U.S. at 181.
71. *See Scoville v. Board of Education of Joliet Township High School District 204*, 425 F.2d 10, 13, n. 5 (7th Cir.), *cert. denied*, 400 U.S. 826 (1970), where a court of appeals noted: "The fact that [the other case] involved a university is of no importance, since the relevant principles and rules apply generally to both high schools and universities." *See also Bender v. Williamsport Area School District*, 563 F. Supp. 697 (M.D. Penn. 1983), *rev'd*, 741 F. 2d 538 (3d Cir. 1984), *vacated*, 475 U.S. 503, *reh'g denied*, 467 U.S. 1132 (1986).
72. 110 S. Ct. at 2371.
73. 393 U.S. at 512.
74. *See Frasca v. Andrews*, 463 F. Supp. 1043, 1050 (E.D. N.Y. 1979).
75. *See e.g., Shanley v. Northeast Independent School District, Bexar County, Texas*, 462 F.2d 960 (5th Cir. 1972).
76. *Quarterman v. Byrd*, 453 F.2d 54, 58 (4th Cir. 1971). *See also Baughman v. Freienmuth*, 478 F.2d 1345 (4th Cir. 1973).
77. *Id. Cf. Kania v. Fordham*, 702 F.2d 475 (4th Cir. 1983).
78. 721 F. Supp. 1189 (D. Colo. 1989).
79. *Id.* at 1191.
80. *Id.*
81. *Id.*
82. *Id.*
83. *Id.* at 1192-93.
84. *Id.* at 1195.
85. 110 S. Ct. at 2372 (emphasis in original).
86. 721 F. Supp. at 1195.
87. *See Board of Education, Island Trees Union Free School District No. 26 v. Pico*, 457 U.S. 853, 867 (1982).
88. *Id.* at 867.
89. *Id.* at 868.
90. *Id.*

91. See *Loewen v. Turnipseed*, 488 F. Supp. 1138, 1153 (N.D. Miss. 1980) (citing *Meyer v. Nebraska*, 262 U.S. 390 [1923]).
92. 457 U.S. 853 (1982).
93. *Id.* at 871.
94. *Id.* at 877-78.
95. *Id* . at 871.
96. *Id.* at 871-72.
97. *Id.* at 861-62.
98. 702 F. Supp. 1505 (D. Colo. 1989).
99. *Id.* at 1513.
100. *Pico*, 457 U.S. at 869.
101. 670 F.2d 771 (8th Cir. 1982).
102. *Id.* at 776.
103. *Id.* at 779.
104. *Id.* at 777.
105. 827 F.2d 1058 (6th Cir. 1987), *cert. denied*, 484 U.S. 1066 (1988).
106. *Id.* at 1061.
107. *Id.* at 1066.
108. *Id.* at 1070.
109. 465 F.2d 797 (6th Cir. 1972).
110. 484 F. Supp. 270 (C.D. Ill. 1979).
111. See generally *Tinker*, 393 U.S. 503 (1969).
112. 108 S. Ct. 562 (1988).
113. *Id.* at 571.
114. *Id.* at 569.
115. *Id.*
116. *Id.* at 568.
117. *Id.* at 569.
118. *Id.* at 570.
119. *Id.*
120. *Id.*
121. *Id.* at 569.
122. *Id.* at 569 n.2.
123. *Id.*
124. See *Rivera v. East Otero School District*, 721 F. Supp. 1189, 1195 (D. Colo. 1989).
125. *Tinker*, 393 U.S. at 512-13.
126. See *Police Department of Chicago v. Mosley*, 408 U.S. 92, 95 (1972).
127. *Cornelius v. NAACP Legal Defense & Education Fund, Inc.*, 473 U.S. 788, 806 (1985).
128. *Mosley*, 408 U.S. at 96.
129. See *Widmar*, 454 U.S. at 269.
130. See generally *Terminiello v. Chicago*, 337 U.S. 1 (1949).
131. *Id.*
132. *Bethel School District v. Fraser*, 478 U.S. 675, 681 (1986) (emphasis supplied).
133. See *Hazelwood*, 108 S. Ct. at 569-70.
134. *Near v. Minnesota ex. rel. Olson County Attorney*, 283 U.S. 697, 713 (1931); *Patterson v. Colorado*, 205 U.S. 454, 462 (1907). A more recent explanation of the prohibition against prior restraints appears in *Southeastern Promotions, Ltd. v. Conrad*, 420 U.S. 546, 559 (1975). Writing for the majority, Justice Blackmun stated:

[A] free society prefers to punish the few who abuse rights of speech *after* they break the law than to throttle them and all others beforehand. It is always difficult to know in advance what an individual will say, and the line between legitimate and illegitimate speech is often so finely drawn that the risks of freewheeling censorship are formidable.

Id.

135. *Id.*
136. *Hazelwood,* 108 S. Ct. at 569.
137. *Id.* at 570.
138. *Id.*
139. *Id.*
140. *See* Shiffrin, *Government Speech,* 27 UCLA L. Rev. 565, 649-51 (1980).
141. *Id.*
142. *See* Dent, *Religious Children, Secular Schools,* 61 S. Cal. L. Rev. 863, 908 (1988).
143. *Bolger v. Youngs Drug Products Corporation,* 463 U.S. 60, 84 (1983) (Stevens, J., concurring).
144. *Id.*
145. 478 U.S. 675 (1986).
146. *Id.* at 677-78.
147. *Hazelwood,* 108 S. Ct. at 571.
148. *Burnside v. Byars,* 363 F.2d 744, 748 (5th Cir. 1966).
149. *Hazelwood,* 108 S. Ct. at 571.
150. *Epperson v. Arkansas,* 393 U.S. 97, 104 (1968).
151. 110 S. Ct. at 2372.
152. *Id.* at 2372-73.

CHAPTER NINE: *The Rights of Faculty*

1. *Police Department of Chicago v. Mosley,* 408 U.S. 92, 95 (1972).
2. *Red Lion Broadcasting Company v. Federal Communications Commission,* 395 U.S. 367, 390 (1969).
3. *Poe v. Ullman,* 367 U.S. 497, 514 (1961) (Douglas, J., dissenting) (emphasis supplied).
4. *Shelton v. Tucker,* 364 U.S. 479, 487 (1960). *See also Kingsley International Picture Corporation v. Regents of University of State of New York,* 360 U.S. 684, 688 (1959), where the Supreme Court stated that the "First Amendment's basic guarantee is of freedom to advocate ideas."
5. *Sweezy v. New Hampshire,* 354 U.S. 234, 250 (1957).
6. *Keyishian v. Board of Regents,* 385 U.S. 589, 603 (1967).
7. *Edwards v. Aguillard,* 482 U.S. 578, 586 n. 6 (1987).
8. Burkholder, *Religious Rights of Teachers in Public Education,* 18 Journal of Law and Education 335, 345 (1989). *See also* Note, *Religious Rights of Public School Teachers,* 23 UCLA L. Rev. 763, 769 (1976) (quoting Hoffman, *A Note on Academic Freedom,* 44 Phi Delta Kappa 185 [1963]).
9. *Keyishian v. Board of Regents,* 385 U.S. 589, 603 (1967).
10. *See, e.g., Kingsville Independent School District v. Cooper,* 611 F.2d 1109 (5th Cir. 1980); *Dean v. Timpson Independent School District,* 486 F. Supp. 302 (E.D. Tex. 1979); *Parducci v. Rutland,* 316 F. Supp. 352 (M.D. Ala. 1970).
11. *Cary v. Board of Education,* 427 F. Supp. 945 (D. Colo. 1977), *aff'd,* 598 F.2d 535, 543 (10th Cir. 1979).
12. *Parducci v. Rutland,* 316 F. Supp. 352, 355 (M.D. Ala. 1970).

13. Freeman, *The Supreme Court and First Amendment Rights of Students in the Public School Classroom: A Proposed Model of Analysis,* 12 Hastings Const. L. Q. 1, 20 (1984).
14. *Kingsville Independent School District v. Cooper,* 611 F.2d 1109, 1113 (5th Cir. 1980).
15. *See generally Ferguson v. Thomas,* 430 F.2d 852 (5th Cir. 1970).
16. *Parducci ,* 316 F. Supp. at 357.
17. *Keyishian,* 385 U.S. at 603.
18. *Keefe v. Geanakos,* 418 F.2d 359, 362 n. 9 (1st Cir. 1969), *citing Wieman v. Updegraff,* 344 U.S. 183, 194, 195 (1952); *Mailloux v. Kiley,* 448 F.2d 1242, 1243 (1st Cir. 1971).
19. *Keyishian,* 385 U.S. at 604.
20. 393 U.S. 503 (1969).
21. 393 U.S. at 513.
22. *Tinker,* 393 U.S. at 506. *See also Connecticut State Federation of Teachers v. Board of Education Members,* 538 F.2d 471, 478 (2d Cir. 1976).
23. *See Texas State Teachers Association v. Garland Independent School District,* 777 F.2d 1046, 1053 (5th Cir. 1985) (teachers' communications may be suppressed only when they materially or substantially interfere with the activities or discipline of the school). *But see Fowler v. Board of Education of Lincoln County, Kentucky,* 819 F.2d 657, *cert. denied,* 108 S. Ct. 502 (1987) (teacher's conduct in showing film containing violence and nudity in high school was not protected expressive or communicative conduct).
24. 461 F.2d 566 (2d Cir. 1972), *cert. denied,* 409 U.S. 1042 (1972), *reh'g denied,* 410 U.S. 947 (1973).
25. *Id.* at 571.
26. *See* the discussion of *Tinker* in chapter 8.
27. *James v. Board of Education,* 461 F.2d 566, 573 (2d Cir. 1972), *cert. denied,* 409 U.S. 1042 (1972), *reh'g denied,* 410 U.S. 987 (1973).
28. *See generally Bender v. Williamsport Area School District,* 563 F. Supp. 697 (M.D. Penn. 1983), *rev'd,* 741 F.2d 538 (3rd Cir. 1984), *vacated,* 475 U.S. 503 (1986), *reh'g denied,* 476 U.S. 1132 (1986); *see also Widmar v. Vincent,* 454 U.S. 263 (1981).
29. *James,* 461 F. 2d at 574.
30. *Id.* at 575.
31. *Id.* at 575.
32. *Shelton v. Tucker,* 364 U.S. 479, 487 (1960), quoted in *Keyishian v. Board of Regents,* 385 U.S. 589 (1967); *Tinker v. Des Moines Independent Community School District,* 393 U.S. 503, 512 (1969).
33. 393 U.S. at 511; *see also Burnside v. Byars,* 363 F.2d 744, 749 (5th Cir. 1966).
34. *Giboney v. Empire Storage and Ice Company,* 336 U.S. 490, 501-02 (1949); *Cox v. Louisiana,* 379 U.S. 559, 564 (1965), *reh'g denied,* 380 U.S. 926 (1965).
35. *Cooper v. Eugene School District No. 4J,* 301 Or. 358, 723 P.2d 298 (1986), *appeal dismissed,* 107 S. Ct. 1597 (1987); *Zellers v. Huff,* 55 N.M. 501, 236 P.2d 949 (1951); *Commonwealth v. Herr,* 78 A. 68 (Pa. 1910); *O'Connor v. Hendrick,* 77 N.E. 612 (N.Y. 1906).
36. *Hysong v. School District of Gallitzin Borough,* 164 Pa. 629, 657, 30 A. 482, 484 (1884).
37. *Hysong,* 164 Pa. at 656, 30 A. at 483; *Rawlings v. Butler,* 290 S.W.2d 801, 804 (Ky. 1956).
38. *Cooper,* 301 Or. at 358, 723 P.2d at 298; *Zellers,* 55 N.M. at 501, 236 P.2d at 949; *Commonwealth,* 78 A. at 68; *O'Connor,* 77 N.E. at 612.
39. *Cooper,* 301 Or. at 381, 723 P.2d at 313.

40. See Adams v. Campbell County School District, 511 F.2d 1242 (10th Cir. 1975); Cary v. Board of Education of the Adams-Arapahoe School District 28-J, 427 F. Supp. 945 (D. Colo. 1977), aff'd, 598 F.2d 535 (10th Cir. 1979).
41. See Palmer v. Board of Education of the City of Chicago, 603 F.2d 1271 (7th Cir. 1979), cert. denied, 444 U.S. 1026 (1980) (upheld dismissal of kindergarten teacher who refused to teach patriotic topics).
42. Board of Education, Island Trees Union Free School District v. Pico, 457 U.S. 853, 869 (1982).
43. Peterson, The Law and Public School Operation, 2d ed. (New York: Harper & Row, 1978), pp. 321-34; Reutter, The Law of Public Education (Mineola, NY: Foundation Press, 1970), pp. 107-14, 116-25.
44. Epperson v. Arkansas, 393 U.S. 97, 107 (1968) (emphasis supplied).
45. Wieman v. Updegraff, 344 U.S. 183, 196 (1952).
46. Epperson v.Arkansas, 393 U.S. 97, 115-16 (1968) (Stewart, J., concurring).
47. But see Solmitz v. Maine School Administrative District No. 59, 495 A.2d 812 (Me. 1985), where the school board cancelled a teacher-initiated school-wide "Tolerance Day" at which a homosexual was to speak. The court stated that "[h]owever broad the protections of academic freedom may be, they do not permit a teacher to insist upon a given curriculum for the whole school where he teaches." Id. at 817.
48. See generally Albaum v. Carey, 283 F. Supp. 3 (E.D. N.Y. 1968) (the state may not deny tenure or job benefits because of the teacher's exercise of free speech). See also Dombrowski v. Pfister, 380 U.S. 479 (1965) (conversations about teacher organizations cannot be prohibited; a teacher has the freedom to associate by bringing others with her to her contract negotiations).
49. Hunter, Curriculum, Pedagogy, and the Constitutional Rights of Teachers in Secondary Schools, 25 Wm. & Mary L. Rev. 1, 70 (1983).
50. Id. See, e.g., Sherbert v. Verner, 374 U.S. 398 (1963).
51. Id.
52. Abington School District v. Schempp, 374 U.S. 203, 225 (1963). Even the Ten Commandments could be an appropriate subject of study in a secular educational program.
53. 374 U.S. 203 (1963).
54. Id. at 225.
55. See generally Kohlberg and Mayer, Development as the Aim of Education, 42 Harv. Educ. Rev. 449 (1972) for a discussion of educational philosophy.
56. City of Madison Joint School District No. 8 v. Wisconsin Employment Relations Commission, 429 U.S. 167, 175 n. 8 (1976); Perry Education Association v. Perry Local Educators' Association, 460 U.S. 37, 46 (1983); Grayned v. City of Rockford, 408 U.S. 104, 120 (1972).
57. These three principles are taken from: Abington School District v. Schempp, 374 U.S. 203 (1963); Florey v. Sioux Falls School District 49-5, 464 F. Supp. 911 (D. S.D. 1979), aff'd, 619 F.2d 1311 (8th Cir.), cert. denied, 449 U.S. 987 (1980); Parducci v. Rutland, 316 F. Supp. 352 (M.D. Ala. 1970); Zykan v. Warsaw Community School Corporation, 631 F.2d 1300 (7th Cir. 1980).
58. See LaRocca v. Board of Education of Rye City School District, 406 N.Y.S.2d 348 (App. Div. 1978), appeal dismissed, 386 N.E.2d 266 (N.Y. 1978) (teacher dismissed for recruiting students to join her religious organization and using classroom to promote tenets of religious faith); Dale v. Board of Education, Lemon Independent School District 322-2, 316 N.W.2d 108 (S.D. 1982) (biology teacher denied contract renewal for devoting excessive instructional time to biblical theory of creation in violation of school board's guidelines).
59. See Malnak v. Yogi, 592 F.2d 197 (3rd Cir. 1979).

60. *Zorach v. Clauson,* 343 U.S. 306, 314 (1952); *Abington School District v. Schempp,* 374 U.S. 203, 305 (1963) (Goldberg, J., concurring); *Larson v. Valente,* 456 U.S. 28, 44-45 (1982).
61. *See Crockett v. Sorenson,* 568 F. Supp. 1422, 1431 (W.D. Va. 1983).
62. 418 F. Supp. 1358 (D. Or. 1976).
63. *Id.* at 1361-62.
64. *Id.* at 1363.
65. *Id.* at 1366, 1367.
66. *Id.* at 1363.
67. *Id.*
68. *Id.* at 1363, 1367.
69. *Id.* at 1364.
70. *Id.*
71. *See generally Amalgamated Food Employees Union Local 590 v. Logan Valley Plaza, Inc.,* 391 U.S. 308 (1968).
72. *See Texas State Teachers Association v. Garland Independent School District,* 777 F.2d 1046 (5th Cir. 1985), *aff'd,* 107 S. Ct. 41 (1986); *May v. Evansville-Vanderburgh School Corporation,* 787 F.2d 1105, 1108 (7th Cir. 1986).
73. 614 F. Supp. 355 (D.C. Mich. 1985).
74. *Id.* at 358.
75. *Id.* at 360.
76. 461 F.2d 566 (2d Cir. 1972).
77. *Id.* at 568.
78. 443 F.2d 422 (10th Cir. 1971), *dismissed,* 333 F. Supp. 107 (D. Wyo. 1971).
79. *Id.* at 433.
80. 558 F. Supp. 449 (E.D. Penn. 1983).
81. *Id.* at 457.
82. *See generally Shelton v. Tucker,* 364 U.S. 479 (1960); *Pickering v. Board of Education,* 391 U.S. 563 (1968); *Fisher v. Snyder,* 346 F. Supp. 396 (D. Neb. 1972), *aff'd,* 476 F.2d 375 (8th Cir. 1973); *Alabama Education Association v. Wallace,* 362 F. Supp. 682 (M.D. Ala. 1973); *Bertot v. School District No. 1, Albany County, Wyoming,* 522 F.2d 1171 (10th Cir. 1975); *Smith v. Price,* 446 F. Supp. 838 (M.D. Ga. 1977).
83. 777 F.2d 1046 (5th Cir. 1985), *aff'd,* 107 S. Ct. 41 (1986).
84. *See Texas Teachers,* 777 F.2d at 1053.
85. *Id.*
86. *May v. Evansville-Vanderburgh School Corporation,* 787 F.2d 1105, 1107, 1116 (7th Cir. 1986).
87. The principle of equality of treatment by the government regarding rights of religious freedom, speech, and association is demonstrated in a number of cases. *See Police Department v. Mosley,* 408 U.S. 92 (1972); *McDaniel v. Paty,* 435 U.S. 618 (1978); *Widmar v. Vincent,* 454 U.S. 263 (1981).
88. *See Pickering v. Board of Education,* 391 U.S. 563 (1968); *Mt. Healthy City Board of Education v. Doyle,* 429 U.S. 274 (1977).
89. *See James,* 461 F.2d 566 (2d Cir. 1972), *cert. denied,* 409 U.S. 1042 (1972), *reh'g denied,* 410 U.S. 947 (1973); *Alabama Education Association,* 362 F. Supp. 682 (M.D. Ala. 1973); *Smith,* 446 F. Supp. 838 (M.D. Ga. 1977).
90. *See Thompson v. Southwest School District,* 483 F. Supp. 1170, 1176-77 (W.D. Miss. 1980).
91. *Id.* at 1182-83.
92. *See generally Pickering v. Board of Education,* 391 U.S. 563 (1968).
93. *See generally Connick v. Myers,* 461 U.S. 138 (1983). *See also Martin v. Parrish,* 805 F.2d 583 (5th Cir. 1983) (college professor's use of profane language in

classroom solely to curse students was not protected expression on a matter of public concern).

94. *Cox v. Dardanelle Public School District,* 790 F.2d 668, 672 (8th Cir. 1986).
95. *See generally Wichert v. Walter,* 606 F. Supp. 1516 (D. N.J. 1985).
96. *See generally McGill v. Board of Education of Pekin Elementary School District No. 108,* 602 F.2d 774 (7th Cir. 1979).
97. *See Cromley v. Board of Education of Lockport Township High School District,* 699 F. Supp. 1283 (N.D. Ill. 1988); *Hammer v. Brown,* 831 F.2d 1398 (8th Cir. 1987); *Lusk v. Estes,* 361 F. Supp. 653 (N.D. Tex. 1973); *Fishman v. Clancy,* 763 F.2d 485 (1st Cir. 1985).
98. *See generally Renfroe v. Kirkpatrick,* 722 F.2d 714 (11th Cir.), *cert. denied,* 469 U.S. 823 (1984); *Reichart v. Draud,* 511 F. Supp. 679 (E.D. Ky. 1981).
99. *See generally Anderson v. Evans,* 660 F.2d 153 (6th Cir. 1981); *Austin v. Mehlville R-9 School District,* 654 S.W.2d 884 (Mo. 1978); *Pietruni v. Board of Education of Brick Township,* 319 A.2d 262 (N.J. Super. 1974).
100. *See generally Derrickson v. Board of Education of the City of St. Louis,* 738 F.2d 351 (8th Cir. 1984); *Cook v. Ashmore,* 579 F. Supp. 78 (N.D. Ga. 1984); *Ferrara v. Mills,* 781 F.2d 1508 (11th Cir. 1986); *Day v. South Park Independent School District,* 768 F.2d 696 (5th Cir. 1985), *cert. denied,* 106 S. Ct. 883 (1986).
101. *See generally Pickering v. Board of Education,* 391 U.S. 563 (1968).
102. *See McPherson v. Rankin,* 107 S. Ct. 2891, 2898 (1987) (citing *Connick v. Myers,* 461 U.S. 138, 150 [1983]).
103. *Id.* at 2900.
104. *See Cox v. Dardanelle Public School District,* 790 F.2d 668, 674 (8th Cir. 1986) (quoting *Pickering v. Board of Education,* 391 U.S. 563, 570 n. 3 (1968)).

CHAPTER TEN: *The Rights of Nonstudents*

1. *Perry Education Association v. Perry Local Educators' Association,* 460 U.S. 37, 45 (1983).
2. *Cornelius v. NAACP Legal Defense and Education Fund,* 473 U.S. 788, 802 (1985) (quoting *Perry Education Association,* 460 U.S. at 45).
3. *Perry Education Association,* 460 U.S. at 45.
4. *Id.; United States Postal Service v. Council of Greenburgh Civic Associations,* 453 U.S. 114, 132 (1981); *Consolidated Edison Company v. Public Service Commission,* 447 U.S. 530, 535-36 (1980).
5. 460 U.S. at 45.
6. *Id.* at 45 n. 7.
7. *Id.* at 45 ("in a public forum the government may impose reasonable restrictions on time, place, or manner of protected speech, provided the restrictions 'are justified without reference to the content of the content of the regulated speech, that they are narrowly tailored to serve a significant governmental interest, and that they leave open ample alternative channels for communication of the information.'") *Ward v. Rock Against Racism,* 109 S. Ct. 2746, 2753 (1989); *Clark v. Community for Creative Non-Violence,* 468 U.S. 288, 293 (1984).
8. *Perry Education Association,* 460 U.S. at 46; *United States Postal Service,* 453 U.S. at 131, n.7.
9. *Hazelwood School District v. Kuhlmeier,* 484 U.S. 260, 267 (1988) (quoting *Hague v. CIO,* 307 U.S. 496, 515 (1939).
10. *Country Hills Christian Church v. Unified School District 512,* 560 F. Supp 1207 (D. Kan. 1983) (citing *Tinker v. Des Moines Independent Community School District,* 393 U.S. 503 (1969).

11. *Country Hills Christian Church*, at 1214-15.
12. *Hazelwood*, 484 U.S. at 267; *Cornelius*, 473 U.S. at 802.
13. 484 U.S. at 267.
14. *Hazelwood*, 484 U.S. at 267 (quoting *Perry Education Association*, 460 U.S. at 46, n.7).
15. *Cornelius v. NAACP Legal Defense and Education Fund*, 473 U.S. 788, 800 (1985).
16. *Perry Education Association*, 460 U.S. at 46.
17. *Police Department of Chicago*, 408 U.S. at 101.
18. *Members of the City Council of the City of Los Angeles v. Taxpayers for Vincent*, 466 U.S. 789, 804 (1984)
19. *Bolger v. Youngs Drug Products Corporation*, 463 U.S. 60, 65 (1983); *Police Department of Chicago*, 408 U.S. at 95 (1972).
20. *See Widmar v. Vincent*, 454 U.S. 263, 269-270 (1981).
21. 454 U.S. 263 (1981).
22. *Id.* at 270, 271.
23. *Id.* at 271.
24. *Id.* at 273.
25. In recent years, this principle has been litigated in the area of military recruiting. *See Clergy and Laity Concerned v. Chicago Board of Education*, 586 F. Supp. 1408 (N.D. Ill. 1984) (school board denied anti-war activists access to its schools while allowing military recruiters access); *Searcey v. Crim*, 681 F. Supp. 821 (N.D. Ga. 1988) (school board denied use of bulletin boards to peace group while opening them to military recruiters); *San Diego Committee v. Governing Board*, 790 F.2d 1471 (9th Cir. 1986) (school board denied peace group permission to advertise in school newspapers while allowing military recruiters to advertise).
26. 354 F. Supp. 592 (D. N.H. 1973), *vacated*, 502 F.2d 1159 (2d Cir. 1973).
27. *Id.* at 601. *See also Garvin v. Rosenau*, 455 F.2 233 (6th Cir. 1972); *Wilson v. Chancellor*, 418 F. Supp. 1348 (D. Or. 1976); *Lawrence University Bicentennial Commission v. City of Appleton*, 409 F. Supp. 1319 (E.D. Wis. 1976); *Vail v. Board Education*, 354 F. Supp. 592 (D.N.H. 1973), *vacated*, 502 F.2d 1159 (1st Cir. 1973); *ACLU v. Radford College*, 315 F. Supp. 893 (W.D. Va. 1970); *Molpus v. Fortune*, 311 F. Supp. 240 (N.D. Miss. 1970), *aff'd*, 432 F.2d 916 (1970); *Smith v. University of Tennessee* 300 F. Supp. 777 (E.D. Tenn. 1969); *Brooks v. Auburn University*, 296 F. Supp. 188 (M.D. Ala.), *aff'd*, 412 F.2d 1171 (1969); *Snyder v. Board of Education*, 286 F. Supp. 927 (N.D. Ill. 1968).
28. *City of Madison Joint School District No. 8 v. Wisconsin Employment Relations Commission*, 429 U.S. 167 (1976).
29. *Cornelius*, 473 U.S. at 811; *M.N.C. Hinesville v. Department of Defense*, 791 F.2d 1466, 1475 (11th Cir. 1986); *see also San Diego Committee Against Registration and the Draft v. Governing Board of Grossmont Union High School District*, 790 F.2d 1471, 1581 (9th Cir. 1986) (by allowing military to place ads in school paper but not allowing ads by those opposed to military service, school officials engaged in viewpoint discrimination).
30. *See Searcey v. Crim*, 681 F. Supp. 821 (N.D. Ga. 1988); *Searcey v. Harris*, 888 F.2d 1314 (11th Cir. 1989)
31. *See generally Searcey v. Crim* and *Searcey v. Harris*, *supra* note 30.
32. 681 F. Supp. 821 (N.D. Ga. 1988).
33. *Id.* at 831.
34. *Id.* at 828.
35. 888 F.2d 1314 (11th Cir. 1989).
36. *Id.* at 1317.

37. *Id.* at 1326.
38. *Id.*
39. *Student Coalition for Peace v. Lower Merion School District Board of School Directors,* 776 F.2d 431, 434-36 (3d Cir. 1985).
40. *Piarowski v. Illinois Community College,* 759 F.2d 625, 629 (7th Cir. 1985), *cert. denied,* 474 U.S. 1007 (1985).
41. 787 F.2d 1105 (7th Cir. 1986).
42. *Id.* at 1113.
43. *Searcey v. Harris,* 888 F.2d 1314, 1324 (11th Cir. 1989); *see generally Cornelius v. NAACP Legal Defense & Education Fund,* 473 U.S. 788 (1984).
44. *See Cornelius,* 473 U.S. at 800; *Perry Education Association,* 460 U.S. at 46.
45. 737 F.2d 1317 (5th Cir. 1984)
46. *Id.* at 1319.
47. *Id.* at 1322.
48. *Id.* at 1223 n.10.
49. *Id.* at 1333 (emphasis supplied).
50. 424 U.S. 828 (1976).
51. *Id.* at 838 n.10.
52. *Id.* at 838-39.
53. *Id.*
54. 408 U.S. 169 (1972).
55. *Id.* at 180 (citing *Shelton v. Tucker,* 364 U.S. 479, 487 [1960]).
56. 684 F. Supp. 1072, 1076.
57. 659 F. Supp. 1239 (W.D. Tex. 1987); *See also Auburn Alliance for Peace and Justice v. Martin,* 684 F. Supp. 1072 (M.D. Ala.), *aff'd,* 853 F.2d 931 (11th Cir. 1988) (university policy of allowing indiscriminate use of Open Air Forum between 11:00 a.m. and 2:00 p.m. reasonable time, place, and manner restriction).
58. 659 F. Supp. at 1239.
59. *Id.* at 1246.
60. *See Brandenburg v. Ohio,* 395 U.S. 444, 447 (1969).
61. *Tinker v. Des Moines Independent Community School Dist.,* 393 U.S. 503, 508 (1969).
62. *See Healy v. James,* 408 U.S. 169, 184 (1972) ("[w]hile a college has a legitimate interest in preventing disruption on the campus, which, under circumstances requiring the safeguarding of that interest, may justify such restraint, a 'heavy burden' rests on the college to demonstrate the appropriateness of that action.") *Id.*
63. 603 F. Supp 963 (N.D. Miss. W.D. 1969), *aff'd,* 446 F.2d 1366 (5th Cir. 1971).
64. *Id.* at 975-76.
65. *Id.* at 974.

CHAPTER ELEVEN: *The Equal Access Act*

1. S. Rep. No. 357, 98th Cong., 2nd Sess. 3 (1984).
2. *Equal Access: A First Amendment Question,* Hearings on S.815 and S.1059 Before the Senate Committee on the Judiciary, 98th Cong., 1st Sess. 2 (1983).
3. Cong. Rec. S6651 (June 6, 1984).
4. *Id.* (June 27, 1984), sec. 8331.
5. *Id.* Sec. 8337.
6. Since its enactment, the courts have construed the Equal Access Act in a number of cases. *See, e.g., Amidei v. Spring Branch Independent School District,* No. H-84-4673 (S.D. Tex. May 9, 1985); *Student Coalition for Peace v. Lower Merion*

School District Board of School Directors, 776 F.2d 431 (3d Cir. 1985); *Salinas v. School District of Kansas City, Missouri*, 751 F.2d 288 (8th Cir. 1984); *Bell v. Little Axe Independent School District No. 70*, 766 F.2d 1391 (10th Cir. 1985).

7. 475 U.S. 534 (1986).
8. *Equal Access: First Amendment Question*, Hearing Before the Senate Committee on the Judiciary, 98th Cong., 2nd Sess. (April 28, 1983), p. 45.
9. *Id.* at 82.
10. *Id.* at 37.
11. *Id.* at 56-57.
12. *Id.* at 38.
13. S. Hrgs., *supra* note 8, at 142.
14. S. Rep. No. 357, 98th Cong., 2nd Sess. ll (1984).
15. *Equal Access: First Amendment Question*, Hearing Before the Senate Committee on the Judiciary, 98th Cong., 2nd Sess. (April 28, 1983), p. 66.
16. *See Action by Attorney General*, S.1059, sec. 4(a)(1).
17. 110 S. Ct. 2356 (1990).
18. *Id.* at 2370.
19. 454 U.S. 263 (1981).
20. *See Tinker v. Des Moines Independent School District*, 393 U.S. 503 (1969).
21. *See* discussion of *Tinker* in chapter 8.
22. 110 S. Ct. 2356 (1990).
23. *Id.* at 2366 (emphasis supplied).
24. *Id.*
25. *Id.* at 2367.
26. *Id.*
27. *Id.*
28. *Id.* at 2366.
29. *Id.*
30. *Id.* at 2366-67.
31. *Id.* at 2369.
32. *Id.* at 2362.
33. *Id.* at 2369.
34. 20 U.S.C. sec. 4071(c).
35. *Mergens*, 110 S. Ct. at 2373.
36. 20 U.S.C. sec. 4072 (2) (emphasis supplied).
37. *Id.*
38. 393 U.S. 503 (1969).
39. *Id.* at 513.
40. *Mergens*, 110 S. Ct. at 2367.
41. 110 S. Ct. 2356 (1990).
42. 403 U.S. 602, *reh'g denied*, 404 U.S. 876 (1971).
43. *Id.* at 612-13 (citations omitted) (quoting *Walz v. Tax Commission*, 397 U.S. 664, 674 [1970]). The test no doubt had its origin in *Abington School District v. Schempp*, 374 U.S. 203 (1963), wherein Justice Clark explained:

> The test may be stated as follows: What are the purpose and primary effect of the enactment? If either is the advancement or inhibition of religion, then the enactment exceeds the scope of legislative power as circumscribed by the Constitution. That is to say that to withstand the strictures of the Establishment Clause, there must be a secular legislative purpose and a primary effect that neither advances nor inhibits religion.

Id. at 222. The tripartite test, however, has been brought into question in some recent cases. *See generally Lynch v. Donnelly,* 465 U.S. 668 (1984); *Marsh v. Chambers,* 463 U.S. 783 (1983). *See also* the discussion of the *Lemon* test in *Mueller v. Allen,* 463 U.S. 388 (1983).

44. *Mergens,* 110 S. Ct. at 2371.
45. *Id.*
46. Laycock, *Equal Access and Moments of Silence: The Equal Status of Religious Speech by Private Speakers,* 81 Nw. U. L. Rev. l, 12 (1986).
47. *Mergens,* 110 S. Ct. at 2372.
48. *Id.*
49. *Id.*
50. *Corporation of Presiding Bishop v. Amos,* 107 S. Ct. 2862, 2868-69 (1987) (quoting *Walz v. Tax Commission,* 397 U.S. 664, 668 [1970]).
51. *Mergens,* 110 S. Ct. at 2373.
52. *Id.*
53. *Id.*
54. For example, authorities for the San Diegnito Union High School District in Encinitas, California, deliberated whether to allow chapters of the Fellowship of Christian Athletes to be formed as extra-curricular high school clubs or whether to permit only curriculum-related clubs. *See Blade-Citizen Encinitas Edition,* October 31, 1990, at A-1.
55. *See,* Arval A. Morris, "The Equal Access Act After *Mergens,*" 61 Educ. L. Rep.. 1139. (Oct. 11, 1990).

CHAPTER TWELVE: *Use of Public School Facilities by Churches and Religious Organizations*

1. *See, e.g., Resnick v. East Brunswick Township Board of Education,* 77 N.J. 88, 101, 389 A.2d 944, 950 (1978) (brief review of this tradition in New Jersey).
2. *See* Murphy, *Access to Public School Facilities and Students by Outsiders,* 16 School Law Bulletin 9 (Winter 1985).
3. *See, e.g., Bender v. Williamsport Area School District,* 563 F. Supp. 697, 715 (M.D. Pa. 1983), *rev'd,* 741 F.2d 538 (3d Cir. 1984), *vacated,* 475 U.S. 534 (1986) (Supreme Court vacated appeals court ruling which, in effect, reinstated district court opinion upholding right of student-initiated prayer club to meet in school facilities during regularly scheduled activity period for student organizations); *Bell v. Little Axe Independent School District No. 70,* 766 F.2d 1391 (10th Cir. 1985) (group meetings at public elementary school unconstitutional); *Nartowicz v. Clayton County School District,* 736 F.2d 646 (11th Cir. 1984) (school district's practice of permitting student religious groups to meet on school property and religious organizations to make announcements over school public address system unconstitutional); *Lubbock Civil Liberties Union v. Lubbock Independent School District,* 669 F.2d 1038 (5th Cir.), *reh'g denied,* 680 F.2d 424 (5th Cir. 1982), *cert. denied,* 459 U.S. 1155 (1983) (school district policy permitting students to meet voluntarily at school either before or after regular school hours for religious discussions violated Establishment Clause); *Brandon v. Board of Education of Guilderland Central School District,* 635 F.2d 971 (2d Cir. 1980), *cert. denied,* 454 U.S. 1123 (1981) (public school board's refusal to allow voluntary, student-initiated religious club to meet on school premises before classes did not violate students' rights to free exercise, speech, association, or equal protection); *Hunt v. Board of Education of County of Kanawha,* 321 F. Supp. 1263 (S.D. W.Va. 1971) (school board's refusal to allow students to meet voluntarily on school premises for purpose of engaging

in group prayer did not violate students' rights of free speech, exercise, and assembly); *Trietley v. Board of Education of City of Buffalo*, 65 A.D.2d 1, 409 N.Y.S.2d 912 (1978) (proposed voluntary Bible study club meetings in public high schools before or after classes would violate Establishment Clause); *Johnson v. Huntington Beach Union High School District*, 68 Cal. App. 3d 1, 137 Cal. Rptr. 43, *cert. denied*, 434 U.S. 877 (1977) (permitting voluntary student Bible study club to meet on public high school campus during school day, even though nonreligious clubs were allowed to meet, held unconstitutional). *See also* cases arising after passage of the Equal Access Act, 20 U.S.C. §§ 4071-74 (1984), *Mergens v. Board of Education of Westside Community Schools*, 1109 S. Ct. 2356 (1990) (pursuant to the Equal Access Act, a student-initiated Bible study club can meet on school premises if other noncurriculum-related student groups may meet); *Garnett v. Renton School District No. 403*, 874 F.2d 608 (9th Cir.), *appeal filed*, 110 S.Ct. 362 (1989) (public high school that allows student groups to use its facilities for curriculum-related clubs, but expressly declines to create "limited open forum," is not required by Equal Access Act or First Amendment to permit student religious club to use school facilities); *Clark v. Dallas Independent School District*, 671 F. Supp. 1119 (N.D. Texas 1987), *modified*, 701 F. Supp. 594 (1988), *rev'd and remanded*, 880 F.2d 411 (5th Cir. 1989). *See also Ford v. Manual*, 629 F. Supp. 771 (N.D. Ohio 1985) (school district's policies and practice s in renting elementary school building to weekday religious education council immediately before and after school hours unconstitutionally advances religion because to impressionable children it creates appearance of official support for religion).

4. *See, e.g., Engel v. Vitale*, 370 U.S. 421 (1962); *Abington School District v. Schempp*, 374 U.S. 203 (1963); *Wallace v. Jaffree*, 472 U.S. 38 (1985).

5. *See, e.g., McCollum v. Board of Education*, 333 U.S. 203 (1948); *Epperson v. Arkansas*, 393 U.S. 97 (1968); *Stone v. Graham*, 449 U.S. 39 (1980); *Edwards v. Aguillard*, 482 U.S. 578 (1987).

6. *See Gregoire v. Centennial School District*, 674 F. Supp. 172, 176 (E.D. Pa. 1987), *aff'd*, 853 F.2d 918 (1988).

7. *See Brandon*, 635 F.2d at 978-79.

8. *Murphy, supra* note 2, at 10.

9. Other commentators have identified additional classifications. *See, e.g.*, Leedes, *Pigeon Holes in the Public Forum*, 20 U. Rich. L. Rev. 499 (1986); James Knicely, *Discrimination in the Public Forum Generally* (Charlottesville, VA: The Rutherford Institute, 1989).

10. *See Cornelius v. NAACP Legal Defense and Education Fund, Inc.*, 473 U.S. 708, 802 (1985).

11. *Id.*

12. *Id.*

13. Laycock, *Equal Access and Moments of Silence: The Equal Status of Religious Speech by Private Speakers*, 81 Nw. U. L. Rev. 1, 46, (1986).

14. *See Southeastern Promotions, Ltd. v. Conrad*, 420 U.S. 546 (1975).

15. *See Concerned Women for America v. Lafayette County and Oxford Public Library*, 699 F. Supp. 95 (N.D. Miss. 1988), *aff'd*, 883 F.2d 32 (5th Cir. 1989). *See also Brown v. Louisiana*, 383 U.S. 131 (1966).

16. *See Stewart v. D.C. Armory Board*, 863 F.2d 1013 (D.C. Cir. 1988).

17. 454 U.S. 263 (1981).

18. *Id.*

19. *See Perry Education Association v. Perry Local Educators' Association*, 460 U.S. 37, 45 (1983).

20. 408 U.S. 104 (1972).

21. *Id.* at 117-18.
22. *United States Postal Service v. Council of Greenburgh Civic Associations, Greenburgh,* 453 U.S. 114, 129-30 (1981), *quoting Greer v. Spock,* 424 U.S. 828, 836 (1976).
23. *See Perry,* 460 U.S. at 46-47; *Cornelius v. NAACP Legal Defense and Educational Fund, Inc.,* 473 U.S. 788, 802-03 (1985); *Widmar,* 454 U.S. at 267. *See also Hazelwood School District v. Kuhlmeier,* 108 S. Ct. 562, 569-70 (1988).
24. *See Widmar,* 454 U.S. at 268; *Gregoire,* 674 F. Supp. at 176-77; *Country Hills Christian Church v. Unified School District No. 512,* 560 F. Supp. 1207, 1215 (D. Kan. 1983).
25. *Deeper Life Christian Fellowship, Inc. v. Board of Education of the City of New York,* 852 F.2d 676, 680 (2d Cir. 1988) (citations omitted).
26. *Country Hills Christian Church v. Unified School District No. 512,* 560 F. Supp. 1207, 1215 (D. Kan. 1983).
27. *Tinker v. Des Moines Independent School District,* 393 U.S. 503, 506 (1969).
28. *Widmar,* 454 U.S. at 267-68 n.5.
29. *Country Hills,* 560 F. Supp. at 1215.
30. *See* M. Nimmer, *Nimmer on Freedom of Speech* § 4.09[D] n. 168 (New York: Matthew Bender, 1984).
31. Murphy, *supra* note 2, at 13.
32. *Gregoire,* 674 F. Supp. at 177. A question arising under the public forum analysis concerns whether a school board which has intentionally created a "limited" public forum may exclude "religious" speech as a class from the forum. The law in this area is far from settled, and thus there are few clear lines. It has been argued that if a school board creates a "limited" public forum, it may reserve use of its facilities for "certain speakers or for discussion of certain topics." In *Gregoire v. Centennial School District,* 674 F. Supp. 172 (3d Cir. 1990), the school board contended that it properly restricted access to the Christian Youth Organization, since the board intended to create a "closed" forum, with access properly restricted to those groups whose purpose is consistent with the educational function and mission of the school. The court disagreed, finding that since the school had previously opened its evening programs to religious discussion, the board had indeed created a "limited open forum" from which the youth group could not be excluded. Additionally, in response to a cross appeal by the Christian group, the court expanded the scope of the district court's permanent injunction, holding that the First Amendment's protection of religious *discussion* also extended to safeguard religious *worship.* Finally, the court found no compelling interest to support the board's flat ban on the distribution of religious literature, which might be necessary and appropriate to objective discussion of religious subject matter. *Deeper Life Christian Fellowship v. Board of Education of the City of New York,* 852 F.2d 676, 680 (2d Cir. 1988), *quoting Calash v. City of Bridgeport,* 788 F.2d 80, 84 (2d Cir. 1986) (for-profit businesses can be excluded from a municipal auditorium characterized as a nonpublic forum available for use only by charitable and nonprofit organizations). *See also Perry,* 460 U.S. at 46 n.7 ("A public forum may be created for a limited purpose such as use . . . for the discussion of certain subjects, *e.g., City of Madison Joint School District v. Wisconsin Public Employment Relations Commission* [429 U.S. 167 (1976)] [school board business]"). One court has suggested, by implication, that a school board could, pursuant to state law, specifically and narrowly define the terms of the limited forum in such a way as to deny use of its facilities by groups which specifically address religious subjects. *See Deeper Life Christian Fellowship,* 852

F.2d at 679. (The Court of Appeals in *Deeper Life,* it seems, confused the legal issues by relying on a nonpublic forum case, *Calash,* to support the proposition that certain topics could be excluded from the limited public forum.) Exclusion based upon subject matter or the speaker's identity need only be reasonable and viewpoint-neutral to pass constitutional muster. *See Board of Airport Commissioners v. Jews for Jesus, Inc.,* 482 U.S. 69 (1987). Distinctions made in determining which groups may use school facilities must be reasonable in the light of the purpose served by the forum and applied in like manner to similarly situated groups. Objective criteria must be followed when determining if a group qualifies to use school facilities under a policy a school board has adopted to govern use of the forum. Practically speaking, however, it may be impossible to draft a policy that would pass constitutional muster since it would likely be vague or too broad or would constitute a prior restraint. If one religious or "religious-like" group is given access to the forum, other religious groups may not be excluded. Clearly, the *practice* of a school board is as important as any *policy* the board may rely on. School board practice is probative of the board's intent in creating the forum. *See Deeper Life Christian Fellowship,* 852 F.2d at 680. In determining whether the government intended to create a limited public forum and whether certain subject matter may be excluded from the forum, courts are increasingly focusing on the nature of the property and its "compatibility" with the expressive activity sought to be conducted there. *Cornelius,* 473 U.S. at 802. *See also Gannett Satellite Information Network v. Metro Transportation Authority,* 745 F.2d 767, 773 (2d Cir. 1984). If a school routinely permits diverse community groups to use its facilities during nonschool hours, it is difficult to see how use of the facilities by a *religious* group on the same terms and conditions as other groups is incompatible—merely because of the religious subject matters addressed by the group—with the nature and purpose of the school facilities. *Concerned Women for America v. LaFayette County and Oxford Public Library,* 699 F. Supp. 95 (N.D. Miss. 1988), *aff'd,* 883 F.2d 32 (5th Cir. 1989), suggests that absent a policy specifically excluding religious or political groups from using public library facilities, the library cannot deny such groups use of its facilities even though the library has "*never before* granted access to *religious* or political groups *similar* to [the plaintiff organization]." *Id.* at 34 (emphasis supplied). The court affirmed the decision of the district court granting preliminary injunction after concluding that the district court had properly found that "the library, by opening up in the past to groups 'hav[ing] little to do with the library's educational and artistic mission,' had created, perhaps 'unwittingly,' a public forum from which it could not now restrict access based upon the content of a group's meeting." *Id.* at 34. But *see Deeper Life Christian Fellowship,* 852 F.2d at 679 ("Under the limited public forum analysis, property remains a nonpublic forum as to all unspecified uses. . . ."). *Concerned Women for America* perhaps reflects Justice Brennan's often-quoted observation that content-based discrimination is not rendered "any less odious" because it distinguishes "among entire classes of ideas, rather than among points of view within a particular class." *Lehman v. City of Shaker Heights,* 418 U.S. 298, 316 (1974) (Brennan, J., dissenting). Too many ideas, it could be argued, are excluded from the public forum when a fully protected category of speech—such as religious speech—is removed from the forum. *See Widmar v. Vincent,* 454 U.S. 263 (1981). Most courts are reluctant to endorse broad or total exclusion of protected categories of speech from the public forum. *See* Leedes, *supra* note 9, at 508. Also, the Supreme Court's decision in affirming the Equal Access Act and subsequent cases should define this area more clearly.

See discussion of *Mergens v. Board of Education of the Westside Community Schools*, 110 S. Ct. 2356 (1990) in chapter 11.

33. Murphy, *supra* note 2, at 13-14 (footnote omitted).
34. *See generally* Annotation, *Schools—Use for Religious Purposes*, 79 A.L.R.2d 1148-1176.
35. *See e.g., Edwards v. Aguillard*, 482 U.S. 578, 583-84 (1987).
36. *See, e.g., Ford v. Manual*, 629 F. Supp. 771 (N.D. Ohio 1985); *May v. Evansville-Vanderburgh School Corp.*, 787 F.2d 1105 (7th Cir. 1986).
37. 454 U.S. 263 (1981).
38. 110 S. Ct. 2356 (1990).
39. *See Country Hills*, 560 F. Supp. 1207; *Wallace v. Washoe County School District*, 701 F. Supp. 187, 189-90 (D. Nev. 1988); *Gregoire*, 674 F. Supp. 172 (3d Cir. 1990). *See also CWA v. Lafayette County*, 699 F. Supp. 95 (N.D. Miss. 1988), *aff'd*, 883 F.2d 32 (5th Cir. 1989) (public library cannot exclude religious speech from public forum). But *see Deeper Life*, 852 F.2d at 679 (*Widmar* not necessarily controlling in public elementary school context).
40. 98 Stat. 1302, 20 U.S.C. sec. 4071-4074.
41. *Mergens*, 110 S. Ct. at 2371.
42. 454 U.S. at 271 (citations omitted).
43. *Id.* at 272 n.11.
44. 463 U.S. 388 (1983).
45. *Id.* at 398-99. *See also Corporation of Presiding Bishop v. Amos*, 107 S. Ct. 2862 (1987); *Bowen v. Kendrick*, 108 S. Ct. 2562 (1988).
46. 560 F. Supp. 1207 (D. Kan. 1983)
47. *Id.* at 1215.
48. *Id.*
49. 674 F. Supp. 172 (E.D. Pa. 1987).
50. *Id.* at 177.
51. *Id.*, citing *Widmar*, 454 U.S. at 267-68.
52. *See, e.g., Lawrence University Bicentennial Commission v. City of Appleton, Wisconsin*, 409 F. Supp. 1319 (E.D. Wis. 1976) (public forum created by school board policy "to encourage use of public school buildings by the people in the community"); *National Socialist White People's Party v. Ringers*, 473 F.2d 1010 (4th Cir. 1973) (en banc) (public forum created by policy of renting to any community organization in "good standing"); *Knights of the Ku Klux Klan v. East Baton Rouge Parish School Board*, 578 F.2d 1122 (5th Cir. 1978) (public forum created by long-standing policy of allowing nonstudent community groups to use school facilities), 643 F.2d 1034 (1981), *vacated*, 102 S. Ct. 626 (1981), *on remand*, 679 F.2d 64 (5th Cir. 1982).
53. 454 U.S. at 269, *citing Heffron v. International Society for Krishna Consciousness, Inc.*, 452 U.S. 640 (1981); *Niemotko v. Maryland*, 340 U.S. 268 (1951); *Saia v. New York*, 334 U.S. 558 (1948). The Court's listing in *Widmar* was only a sampling of the cases it could have cited. Other Supreme Court cases holding that religious speech is entitled to full protection under the Free Speech Clause include *Poulous v. New Hampshire*, 345 U.S. 395 (1953); *Kunz v New York*, 340 U.S. 290 (1951); *Marsh v. Alabama*, 326 U.S. 501 (1946); *Martin v. City of Struthers*, 319 U.S. 141 (1943); *Largent v. Texas*, 318 U.S. 418 (1943); *Cantwell v. Connecticut*, 310 U.S. 296 (1940); *Lovell v. City of Griffin*, 303 U.S. 444 (1938).
54. 454 U.S. at 269-70 n.6 (emphasis in the original).
55. 454 U.S. at 268, *quoting Madison Joint School District v. Wisconsin Employment Relations Commission*, 429 U.S. 167, 1175 n.8 (1976).
56. *Widmar*, 454 U.S. at 271.

57. 403 U.S. 602, 612-13, *reh'g denied*, 404 U.S. 876 (1971). The test requires: "First, the statute [or government policy or practice] must have a secular legislative purpose; second, its principal or primary effect must be one that neither advances nor inhibits religion; finally, the statute must not foster 'an excessive government entanglement with religion.'" *Id.*

58. See *Resnick v. East Brunswick Township Board of Education,* 77 N.J. 88, 109, 389 A.2d 944, 954 (1978).

59. *Widmar,* 454 U.S. at 271-72 n.10.

60. See, *e.g., National Socialist White People's Party v. Ringers,* 473 F.2d 1010 (4th Cir. 1973) (en banc) (use of high school auditorium by Nazi group did not imply government endorsement of the message); *Knights of the Ku Klux Klan v. East Baton Rouge Parish School Board,* 578 F.2d 1122 (5th Cir. 1978), *vacated,* 102 S. Ct. 626 (1981), *on remand,* 679 F.2d 64 (5th Cir. 1982) (same issue). See also *O'Hair v. Andrus,* 613 F.2d 931, 936 (D.C. Cir. 1979) (Pope's Mass on public property did not violate Establishment Clause or result in government endorsement of his message); *Christian Science Reading Room v. City and County of San Francisco,* 784 F.2d 1010, 1014-15 (9th Cir. 1986) ("If the [municipal] Airport endorsed the tenets of Christian Science by renting space to the Reading Room, then it could as easily be argued that it is endorsing the business and labor practices of domestic airlines, the politics and policies of the foreign governments that own airlines, the consumption of alcohol and sourdough bread, and the reading of *Penthouse* magazine. Clearly, it does none of these."). *Id.*

61. See *Widmar,* 454 U.S. at 271-72 n.10; *Wallace,* 701 F. Supp. at 190.

62. *Mergens,* 110 S. Ct. at 2372.

63. *Id.*

64. *Id.* at 2372-73.

65. Laurence Tribe, *American Constitutional Law,* 2d ed. (Mineola, N.Y.: Foundation Press, 1988), p. 1175.

66. 454 U.S. at 273-74.

67. *Id.* at 274. The implication is that if religious groups or religious speech comes to dominate the forum, there may be a violation of the "primary effect" prong of the *Lemon* test. See *Gregoire,* 674 F. Supp. at 178 ("in the absence of any evidence that religious speakers will dominate defendant's open speech forum, it cannot be said that advancement of religion would be the forum's 'primary effect.'").

68. *Id.*

69. See *Mueller v. Allen,* 463 U.S. 388, 398-99 (1983) ("As *Widmar* and our other decisions indicate, a program . . . that neutrally provides state assistance to a broad spectrum of citizens is not readily subject to challenge under the Establishment Clause.").

70. 560 F. Supp. at 1218 (emphasis supplied).

71. See, *e.g., O'Hair v. Andrus,* 613 F.2d 931 (D.C. Cir. 1979) (allowing the Pope to hold Mass on the Capitol Mall, which is open to other groups, only incidentally benefits religion); *Berkshire Cablevision of Rhode Island v. Burke,* 571 F. Supp. 976 (D. R.I. 1983) (upholding state rule requiring cable operators to provide equal access to all religious and parochial institutions); *McCreary v. Stone,* 739 F.2d 716 (2d Cir. 1984), *aff'd by an equally divided court,* 471 U.S. 83 (1985) (erection of nativity scene by private group in public forum did not violate primary effect prong of *Lemon* test).

72. Tribe, *supra* note 65, at 1175 (emphasis in the original).

73. *Lynch v. Donnelly,* 465 U.S. 668, 673 (1984).

74. See, *e.g., Engel v. Vitale,* 307 U.S. 421 (1962).

75. See *Zorach v. Clauson*, 343 U.S. 306, 313-14 (1952).
76. Groups which use school facilities at less than commercial rental rates arguably receive a financial benefit since they avoid making expenditures for other comparable facilities at commercial rental rates or for purchasing their own building.
77. See *Resnick*, 77 N.J. at 120, 389 A.2d at 960 (1978); *Southside Estates Baptist Church v. Board of Trustees*, 115 So.2d 697, 699 (Fla. 1959); *O'Hara v. School Board of Sarasota County*, 432 So.2d 1356 (Fla. App.2 Dist. 1983).
78. *Resnick*, 77 N.J. at 120, 389 A.2d at 960.
79. *Southside Estates*, 115 So.2d at 699.
80. See defendants' argument in *Country Hills*, 560 F. Supp. at 1216.
81. See *Wallace*, 701 F. Supp. at 191 (compelling argument, but no evidence in record to support it); *Country Hills*, 560 F. Supp. at 1216 (same).
82. In *Widmar*, 454 U.S. at 274 n.14, the Court noted:

> University students are, of course, young adults. They are less impressionable than younger students and should be able to appreciate that the University's policy is one of neutrality toward religion. . . . In light of the large number of groups meeting on campus, however, we doubt students could draw any reasonable inference of University support from the mere fact of a campus meeting place.

83. 110 S. Ct. at 2372.
84. 110 S. Ct. at 2372-73.
85. In *Mergens*, Justice O'Connor also noted that since the Act limits participation by school officials at student religious meetings, and that such meetings are held during noninstructional time, the Act avoids the problems that students will emulate teachers as role models and of mandatory attendance problems. *Id.* at 2372.
86. See Tribe, *supra* note 65, at 1175 ("The building is, in a sense, surplus land.").
87. See *Widmar*, 454 U.S. at 269.
88. Professor Douglas Laycock has made the following observation:

> The proposition that government cannot censor speech, and therefore that it does not endorse everything it fails to censor, is not complicated. High school students can understand the proposition if it is explained to them. That is all they need to understand to avoid a mistaken inference of endorsement. . . . The proposition that government does not endorse everything it fails to censor is fundamental to our system of government.

Laycock, *Equal Access and Moments of Silence: The Equal Status of Religious Speech by Private Speakers*, 81 Nw. U. L. Rev. 1, 15 (1986) (footnotes omitted).
89. 110 S. Ct. at 2372.
90. See *Deeper Life*, 852 F.2d at 681. This concern was also addressed in *Ford v. Manuel*, 629 F. Supp. 771 (N.D. Ohio 1985). Not finding a public forum present, the court went on to address the question of whether religious use of school facilities during off-hours would violate the Establishment Clause:

> The constitutional significance of WRE program also is different from that of the use of school facilities by church groups on Saturday afternoons and weekday evenings. *See* Stipulations, Exhibit G, wherein it is stated that the Worldwide Church of God uses public elementary school facilities every Saturday [morning and Tuesday evening for religious services and Bible study respectively]. The message of state support for religion is weak or nonexistent as it relates to the Worldwide Church's use of public school

facilities. Presumably no school children would be present at the time of these meetings, unless brought by members of their family to attend the service. School personnel would not be present. Compulsory school attendance laws obviously are not implicated.

Ford, 629 F. Supp. at 778. The court concluded that school facilities may not be rented for release time religious classes *immediately* before or after school.
91. *Country Hills,* 560 F. Supp. at 1219.
92. *Walz v. Tax Commission,* 397 U.S. 664, 675 (1970).
93. *Resnick,* 77 N.J. at 116, 389 A.2d at 958.
94. Although school officials in *Mergens* argued that excessive entanglement between religion and government would result because a faculty sponsor would be required to be at the meetings, the Supreme Court noted that the Equal Access Act does not allow faculty monitors to participate in any religious meetings, and nonschool persons may not direct, control, or regularly attend activities of student groups. 110 S. Ct. at 2373. Therefore, as the Court stated: "Indeed, as the Court noted in *Widmar,* a denial of equal access to religious speech might well create greater entanglement problems in the forms of invasive monitoring to prevent religious speech at meetings at which such speech might occur." *Id.*
95. *Widmar,* 454 U.S. at 272 n. 11.
96. *See Wallace,* 701 F. Supp. at 190.
97. *Widmar,* 454 U.S. at 272 n. 11, *quoting O'Hair v. Andrus,* 613 F.2d at 936.
98. 560 F. Supp. at 1218.
99. 77 N.J. 88, 389 A.2d 944 (1978).
100. Other courts have viewed this as a problem arising under the "primary effect" prong. *See Wallace,* 701 F. Supp. at 190-92 (converting a portion of a high school building into a church on a permanent basis would support the inference to be drawn by the public that the school district supports the church and that the state has placed its imprimatur on a particular religion).
101. 115 So. 2d 697 (Fla. 1959).
102. *Id.* at 700.
103. *Resnick,* 77 N.J. at 117-18, 389 A.2d at 958-59.
104. *Id.*
105. *See also Pratt v. Arizona Board of Regents,* 110 Ariz. 466, 520 P.2d 514 (1974), in which the Arizona Supreme Court held that leasing the football stadium at Arizona State University for an occasional religious service, and for a fair rental value, is not an appropriation of public property for religious purposes which would violate the Arizona constitution. In that case, Billy Graham sought use of Sun Devil Stadium at Arizona State University for a one week period at a rental value of $39,995. That use was challenged by the plaintiff, a resident taxpayer of Maricopa County, Arizona, as violative of Article 2, § 12 of the Arizona constitution. Although the Arizona Supreme Court found such a use not violative of the Arizona constitution, the court warned:

> [T]he twin keys to the use of this stadium for the purpose stated are fair rental value and the occasional nature of the use. The lease to a religious group, on a permanent basis, of property on the University campus, for example, would be an entirely different matter; because of the permanency of the arrangement, the prestige of the State would be placed behind a particular religion or religion generally. Also, the lease of campus facilities for occasional use, but not for fair rental value, would violate the provision of our Constitution as being an appropriation or application of State property for religious purposes.

110 Ariz. at 469, 520 P.2d at 517.

106. Article VI of the United States Constitution provides as follows:

> This Constitution, and all the Laws of the United States which shall be made in pursuance thereof; and all treaties made, or which shall be made, under the authority of the United States, shall be the supreme law of the land; and the Judges in every State shall be bound thereby, any Thing in the Constitution or Laws of any State to the contrary notwithstanding.

U.S. Const., Art. VI.
107. *Widmar*, 454 U.S. at 276.
108. 435 U.S. 618 (1978).
109. *Country Hills*, 560 F. Supp. at 1218.
110. *See Resnick*, 77 N.J. at 111, 389 A.2d at 955.
111. *See Southside Estates*, 115 So.2d at 700.
112. *See Resnick*, 77 N.J. at 111, 389 A.2d at 955.

CHAPTER THIRTEEN: *The Rights of Parents*

1. Lawrence Cremin, *American Education: The Colonial Experience, 1607-1783* (New York: Harper and Row, 1970), p. 124.
2. Arthur Calhoun, *A Social History of the American Family from Colonial Times to the Present* (New York: Arno Press, 1973), Vol. 1, p. 110.
3. Cremin, *supra* note 1, at 133.
4. *See* E. Beshoner, *Home Education in America: Parental Rights Reasserted*, 49 Mo. L. Rev. 191, 191-192 (1981).
5. *Records of the Governor and Company of Massachusetts Bay in New England, 1647,* Vol. 2, p. 203. *See also* Henry Steele Commager, ed., *Documents of American History* (New York: Appleton-Century-Crofts, Inc., 1949), p. 29.
6. *Records of the Governor, supra* note 5, at 203.
7. Ellwood Cubberly, *The History of Education* (New York: Houghton Mifflin Co., 1920), pp. 365, 366. Beshoner, *supra* note 4, at 191, 192.
8. Cremin, *supra* note 3, at 129. *Also see* William T. Davis, *History of the Town of Plymouth* (Philadelphia: J. W. Lewis & Co., 1885), p. 52.
9. Willystine Goodsell, *A History of the Family as a Social and Educational Institution* (New York: Macmillan, 1915), p. 353; Cremin, *supra* note 1, at 479-85.
10. Calhoun, *supra* note 2, at Vol. 2, pp. 54, 138; Cremin, *supra* note 1, at 479-85.
11. Lawrence Cremin, *The American Common School* (New York: Columbia University, 1951), pp. 87, 88.
12. *Id.* at 88.
13. John C. Fitzpatrick, ed., *The Writings of George Washington* (Washington, D.C.: United States Government Printing Office, 1933), Vol. 3, p. 130.
14. Saul K. Padover, *Jefferson* (New York: Harcourt Brace, 1942), p. 369.
15. *Wisconsin v. Yoder*, 406 U.S. 205, 232 (1972).
16. *Rulison v. Post*, 79 Ill. 567, 573 (1875).
17. *The Trustees of Schools v. The People ex rel. Martin Van Allen*, 87 Ill. 303, 309 (1877).
18. *Id.*
19. *Pierce v. Society of Sisters*, 268 U.S. 510, 518 (1925).
20. *See, e.g., School District No. 18, Garvin County v. Thompson*, 24 Okl. 1 (1909).
21. *Meyer v. Nebraska*, 262 U.S. 390, 400 (1923).
22. *Pierce*, 268 U.S. 510.
23. *Id.* at 535.
24. *Wisconsin v. Yoder*, 406 U.S. 205 (1972).

25. R. Mawdsley, *Parental Rights and Public Education,* 59 Educ. L. Rep. 271-73 (May, 1990).
26. *E.g., see Turner v. Board of Education, North Chicago Community High School District,* 54 Ill. 2d 68, 294 N.E. 2d 264 (1973).
27. *See Smith v. Ricci,* 89 N.J. 514, 446 A.2d 501 (1982); *Buford v. Southeast Dubois County School Corp.,* 472 F.2d 890 (7th Cir. 1973).
28. *See Zweifel v. Joint Dist. No. 1, Belleville,* 76 Wis. 2d 648, 251 N.W.2d 822 (1977); *Pratt v. Independent School Dist. No. 831, Forest Lake,* 670 F.2d 771 (8th Cir. 1982).
29. *See O'Neal v. School District No. 15,* 451 P.2d 791 (Wyo. 1969); *School District of City of Pittsburgh v. Zebra,* 15 Pa. Commonwealth 203, 325 A.2d 330, 333 (1974); *Rosenberg v. Board of Education of City of New York,* 196 Misc. 542, 92 N.Y.S.2d, 344 (S. Ct. 1949).
30. *Smith v. Ricci,* 89 N.J. 514, 446 A.2d 501 (1982); *Buford v. Southeast Dubois County School Corporation,* 472 F.2d 890 (7th Cir. 1973).
31. *See generally Aubrey v. School District of Philadelphia,* 63 Pa. Commonwealth 330, 437 A.2d 1306 (1981); *Williams v. Board of Education of County of Kanawha,* 388 F. Supp. 93, 96 (S.D. W. Va. 1975), *aff'd* 530 F.2d 972 (4th Cir. 1975).
32. *Pratt,* 670 F.2d at 779; *Minarcini v. Strongville City School District,* 541 F.2d 577 (6th Cir. 1976).
33. *See New Jersey v. T.L.O.,* 469 U.S. 325 (1985).
34. *Id.* at 744 n.9.
35. John C. Fitzpatrick, *George Washington Himself* (Indianapolis: Bobbs-Merrill, 1933), p. 19. *See especially* William H. Wilbur, *The Making of George Washington,* 2d ed. (Daytona Beach: Patriotic Education, Inc., 1973).
36. Cremin, *American Education: The Colonial Experience, 1607-1783, supra* note 1, at 483.
37. Robert Douthat Meade, *Patrick Henry: Patriot in the Making* (Philadelphia: J. B. Lippincott, 1957), p. 5.
38. Ian Elliott, ed., *James Madison 1751-1836* (New York: Oceana, 1969), p. 1.
39. John Bigelow, *The Life of Benjamin Franklin, Written by Himself* (Philadelphia: J. B. Lippincott, 1916), Vol. 1, p. 99.
40. 268 U.S. 510 (1929).
41. *Id.* at 534-35.
42. *Id.* at 534.
43. *Id.* at 534.
44. *Id.* at 535.
45. 262 U.S. 390 (1923).
46. *Id.* at 399.
47. 273 U.S. 284 (1927).
48. 406 U.S. 205 (1972).
49. *Id.* at 235-36.
50. *Id.* at 216.
51. *Id.* at 215. The Supreme Court has, however, altered Free Exercise jurisprudence. *See generally Employment Division, Oregon Department of Human Resources v. Smith,* 110 S. Ct. 1595 (1990).
52. *State v. Shaver,* 294 N.W.2d 883 (N.D. 1980); *Scoma v. Chicago Board of Education,* 391 F. Supp. 452 (N.D. Ill. 1974).
53. *See Home Education Reporter* (Charlottesville, VA: The Rutherford Institute, 1990).
54. *Id.*
55. *Id.*

56. Bainham, *Children, Parents and the State,* pp. 46-61 (1988).
57. Yodof, *Library Book Selection and the Public School: The Quest of the Archimedean Point,* 59 Ind. L.J. 527 (1984).
58. Note, *State Indoctrination and the Protection of Non-State Voices in the Schools: Justifying a Prohibition of School Library Censorship,* 35 Stan. L. Rev. 497, 523-33 (1982).
59. *West Virginia State Board of Education v. Barnette,* 319 U.S. 624 (1943).
60. *School District v. Schempp,* 374 U.S. 203, 241-42 (1963); *Brown v. Board of Education,* 347 U.S. 483, 493 (1954); *Illinois ex rel. McCollum v. Board of Education,* 333 U.S. 203, 236 (1948) (Jackson, J., concurring); *see also* Arons & Lawrence, *The Manipulation of Consciousness: A First Amendment Critique of Schooling,* 15 Harv. C.R.-C.L. L. Rev. 309, 309-20 (1980); Note, *The Myth of Religious Neutrality by Separation in Education,* 71 Va. L. Rev. 127, 160 (1985).
61. *Yoder,* 406 U.S. at 214, 234.
62. *Id.* at 214; *see also Epperson v. Arkansas,* 393 U.S. 97, 104 (1968).
63. *United States v. Lee,* 455 U.S. 252, 258 (1982); *Thomas v. Review Board,* 450 U.S. 707 (1981); *Sherbert v. Verner,* 374 U.S. 398, 406-07 (1963).
64. *Yoder,* 406 U.S. at 215.
65. *Id.* at 218; *Sherbert,* 374 U.S. at 403.
66. *Sherbert,* 374 U.S. 398 at 402-03.
67. *Harris v. McRae,* 448 U.S. 297, 319-20 (1980); *Epperson v. Arkansas,* 393 U.S. 97, 102 (1967); *McGowan v. Maryland,* 366 U.S. 420, 442 (1961); *Joseph Burstyn, Inc. v. Wilson,* 343 U.S. 495, 505 (1952).
68. *Yoder,* 406 at 214; *Tinker v. Des Moines Independent Community School District,* 393 U.S. 503, 507 (1969); *Epperson,* 393 U.S. at 107.
69. *Wisconsin v. Yoder,* 406 U.S. 205 (1972).
70. *See McCollum v. Board of Education,* 333 U.S. 203 (1948).
71. *See* Hirschoff, *Parents and the Public School Curriculum: Is There a Right to Have One's Child Excused from Objectionable Instruction?,* 50 S. Ca. L. Rev. 871 (1977).
72. *Id.*
73. *See Williams v. Board of Education,* 388 F. Supp. 93 (S.D. W. Va. 1975), *aff'd,* 530 F.2d 972 (4th Cir. 1975); *Davis v. Page,* 385 F. Supp. 395 (D. N.H. 1974); *Cornwall v. State Board of Education,* 314 F. Supp. 340 (D. Md. 1969), *aff'd* 428 F.2d 471 (4th Cir. 1970) (*per curiam*).
74. J. Piaget, *Six Psychological Studies* 151 (1968).
75. *Mozert v. Hawkins County Board of Education,* 827 F.2d 1058, 1075 (6th Cir. 1987), *cert. denied,* 56 U.S.L.W. 3569 (U.S. Feb. 22, 1988) (Boggs, concurring).
76. Hirschoff, *supra* note 42, at 886. *See generally Hardwick v. Board of School Trustees,* 54 Cal. App. 696, 205 P. 49 (1921); *State ex rel. Kelley v. Ferguson,* 95 Neb. 63, 144 N.W. 1039 (1914); *School Board District No. 18 v. Thompson,* 24 Okla. 1, 103 P. 578 (1909); *State ex rel. Sheibley v. School District No.1,* 31 Neb. 552, 48 N.W. 393 (1891); *Trustees of Schools v. People,* 87 Ill. 303 (1877); *Rulison v. Post,* 79 Ill. 567 (1875); *Morrow v. Wood,* 35 Wis. 59 (1874).
77. Hirschoff, *supra* note 42, at 866.
78. *Id.*
79. *Mozert,* 827 F.2d 1058.
80. *Id.* at 1061.
81. *Id.* at 1060.
82. *Id.* at 1066.
83. *Id.*
84. *Id.* at 1061.

85. *Id.* at 1060.
86. *Id.* at 1061-70.
87. *Id.*
88. 484 F. Supp. 270 (C.D. Ill. 1979).
89. *Id.* at 274.
90. *Id.* at 276-77.
91. *Id.* at 277.
92. *Id.*
93. *See Citizens for Parental Rights v. San Mateo County Board of Education,* 51 Cal. App. 3d 1, 124 Cal. Rptr. 68 (1975), *appeal dismissed,* 425 U.S. 908, *reh'g denied,* 425 U.S. 1000 (1976).
94. *Medeiros v. Kiyosaki,* 52 Haw. 436, 478 P.2d 314 (1970).
95. *Hopkins v. Hamden Board of Education,* 29 Conn. Supp. 397, 289 A.2d 914 (1971), *aff'd,* 165 Conn. 793, 305 A.2d 536 (1973); *Cornwell v. State Board of Education,* 314 F. Supp. 340 (D. Md. 1969), *aff'd,* 428 F.2d 471 (4th Cir 1970) (per curiam).

CHAPTER FOURTEEN: *Excusal: Alleviating the Tension*

1. *See Mozert v. Hawkins County Board of Education,* 827F.2d 1058 (6th Cir. 1987), *cert denied,* 56 U.S.L.W. 3569 (U.S. Feb. 22, 1988).
2. *Id.* at 1070.
3. *See Wallace v. Jaffree,* 472 U.S. 38, 60 n. 51 (1985); *Mailoux v. Kiley,* 323 F. Supp. 1387, 1392 (D. Mass.), *aff'd,* 448 F.2d 1242 (1st Cir. 1971); Mark Yudof, *When Government Speaks: Politics, Law, and Government Expression in America* (Berkeley: University of California Press, 1983), p. 213.
4. *Wallace,* 472 U.S. at 60 n.51.
5. Strossen, *"Secular Humanism" and "Scientific Creationism": Proposed Standards for Reviewing Curricular Decisions Affecting Students' Religious Freedom,* 47 Ohio St. L. J. 333, 369 (1986).
6. Yudof, *supra* note 3, at 892.
7. *Board of Education, Island Trees Union Free School District v. Pico,* 457 U.S. 853, 865 (1982).
8. Hirschoff, *Parents and the Public School Curriculum: Is There a Right to Have One's Child Excused from Objectionable Instruction?,* 50 S. Cal. L. Rev. 871, 907 (1977).
9. Dent, *Religious Children, Secular Schools,* 61 S. Cal. L. Rev. 863, 908 (1988).
10. *Wisconsin v. Yoder,* 406 U.S. 205, 213-14 (1972).
11. *See Commonwealth v. Bey,* 70 A.2d 693, 695, 166 Pa. Super. 136 (1950).
12. *Pierce v. Society of Sisters,* 268 U.S. 510, 535 (1925).
13. *Id.*
14. *See generally Brown v. Board of Education,* 347 U.S. 483 (1954); *see also Yoder,* 406 U.S. at 213 (1972).
15. Dent, *supra* note 9, at 905.
16. *Yoder,* 406 U.S. at 213.
17. *Bethel School District No. 403 v. Fraser,* 478 U.S. 675, 681(1986).
18. *Ambach v. Norwick,* 441 U.S. 68, 76 (1979).
19. *See Roman v. Appleby,* 558 F. Supp. 449, 456 (E.D. Pa. 1983).
20. 406 U.S. at 233-34.
21. *See, e.g., Citizens for Parental Rights v. San Mateo County Board of Education,* 51 Cal. App. 3d l, 124 Cal. Rptr. 68 (1975); *appeal dismissed,* 425 U.S. 908, *U.S. reh'g denied,* 425 U.S. 1000 (1976). *Valent v. New Jersey State Board of Education,* 274 A.2d 832, 144 N.J. Super. 63 (1971), *dismissed on other*

grounds, 288 A.2d 52, 118 N.J. Super. 416 (1972); *Hopkins v. Hamden Board of Education,* 29 Conn. Supp. 397, 289 A.2d 914 (1971), *aff'd,* 165 Conn. 793, 305 A.2d 536 (1973).

22. *See, e.g., Ware v. Valley Stream High School District,* 551 N.Y.S.2d 167, 550 N.E.2d 420 (Ct. App. 1989).
23. *Id.*
24. *Epperson v. Arkansas,* 393 U.S. 97, 106 (1968).
25. Dent, *supra* note 9, at 905.
26. *Id.* at 922.
27. Arons and Lawrence, *The Manipulation of Consciousness: A First Amendment Critique of Schooling,* 15 Harv. C.R.-C.L. L. Rev. 309, 324 (1980).
28. *Murdock v. Pennsylvania,* 319 U.S. 105, 111 (1943). However, the Supreme Court appeared to back away from this position recently in *Bowen v. Roy,* 476 U.S. 693 (1986) (required native American Indians to supply a social security number for their daughter despite religious objection). In *Bowen,* the Court pointed out that it was the religious objectors who sought benefits from the government and not vice versa. Therefore, the Court held, "in no sense does [the requirement] affirmatively compel appellees, by threat of sanctions to refrain from religiously motivated conduct or to engage in conduct that they find objectionable for religious reasons." *Id.* at 703. The Court, however, went on to distinguish the application of its reasoning from situations at elementary and secondary schools which involve compelled attendance of young children. *Id.* at 705. The Court noted that "this distinction warrants a difference in constitutional results." *Id.*
29. Dent, *supra* note 9, at 922.
30. *E.g., Spence v. Bailey,* 465 F.2d 797 (6th Cir. 1972).
31. Hirschoff, *supra* note 8, at 916.
32. *See* Dent, *supra* note 9, at 923.
33. *Id.*
34. Hirshcoff, *supra* note 8, at 906.
35. *Id.*
36. *Id.* at 907.
37. *See* Lines, *Excusal from Public School Curriculum Requirements,* 5 Educ. L. Rep. 691 (1982).
38. *See Zorach v. Clauson,* 343 U.S. 306 (1952).
39. *See, e.g., Grove v. Mead School District No. 354,* 753 F.2d 1528, 1533 (9th Cir.), *cert. denied,* 474 U.S. 826 (1985) (school excused child from class using religiously offensive book and assigned child an alternative book).
40. Dent, *supra* note 9, at 925-26.
41. Lines, *supra* note 37, at 691.
42. *See Zorach v. Clauson,* 343 U.S. 306 (1952).
43. *See* Laycock, *Equal Access and Moments of Silence: The Equal Status of Religious Speech by Private Speakers,* 81 Nw. U. L. Rev. l, 33 (1986).
44. *See, e.g., Grove v. Mead School District No. 354,* 753 F.2d 1528 (9th Cir.), *cert. denied,* 474 U.S. 826 (1985).
45. Lines, *supra* note 37, at 695.
46. *See Lemon v. Kurtzman,* 403 U.S. 602, 612-13 (1971).
47. *Cf.* Laycock, *supra* note 43, at 21.
48. *Id.*
49. Dent, *supra* note 9, at 925.
50. *Id.* at 924-27.
51. *See* Lupu, *Where Rights Begin: The Problem of Burdens on the Free Exercise of Religion,* 102 Harv. L. Rev. 933, 951 (1989).

52. Dent, *supra* note 9, at 924-27.
53. *Id.* at 925.
54. *Wisconsin v. Yoder*, 406 U.S. at 213, 214 (1972).
55. Lines, *supra* note 37, at 691.
56. Strossen, *supra* note 5, at 385-86.
57. *Id.* at 386.
58. *See* Recent Developments, *The Constitutionality Under the Religion Clauses of the First Amendment of Compulsory Sex Education in Public Schools*, 68 Mich. L. Rev. 1050, 1061 (1970).
59. *See Employment Division, Oregon Department of Human Resources v. Smith*, 110 S. Ct. 1595, 1601 (1990).
60. Strossen, *supra* note 5, at 386 n. 264.
61. *Id.* at 389.
62. 374 U.S. 398 (1963).
63. 406 U.S. 205 (1972).
64. 374 U.S. at 407.
65. 406 U.S. at 215.
66. Strossen, *supra* note 5, at 839. Free exercise jurisprudence has been affected by *Employment Division, Oregon Department of Human Resources v. Smith*, 110 S. Ct. 1595 (1990). In this case, the Supreme Court held that criminal laws of general availability, if challenged on pure free exercise grounds, do not have to meet the compelling state interest test.
67. 406 U.S. at 235.
68. *Id.*
69. Strossen, *supra* note 5, at 390.
70. *Id.* at 392.
71. *See Sherbert v. Verner*, 374 U.S. 398 (1963).
72. *See Thomas v. Review Board*, 450 U.S. 707, 713-15 (1981).
73. *Id.* at 714.
74. Dent, *supra* note 9, at 900.
75. 110 S. Ct. 1595 (1990).
76. *Id.* at 1604.
77. *Id.* at 1604 (quoting from *Hernandez v. Commissioner*, 109 S. Ct. 2136, 2149 [1989]).
78. 374 U.S. 398 (1963).
79. *Id.* at 399.
80. *Id.* at 403.
81. *Id.* at 406-409.
82. *Thomas v. Review Board*, 450 U.S. 707 (1981); *Hobbie v. Unemployment Appeals Commission of Florida*, 480 U.S. 136 (1987).
83. *See* Laurence Tribe, *American Constitutional Law*, 2d ed. (Mineola, N.Y.: Foundation Press, 1988), pp. 1251-75.
84. 110 S. Ct. at 1602.
85. *Id.* at 1603.
86. *Id.*
87. *West Virginia State Board of Education v. Barnette*, 319 U.S. 624, 642 (1943).
88. *Id.*
89. *Id.* at 629.
90. *Id.* at 642.
91. *See Spence v. Bailey*, 465 F.2d 797 (6th Cir. 1972).
92. *Id.*
93. *Id.* at 800.
94. *Id.* at 798.

95. *Id.*
96. *Id.*
97. *Id.* at 800.
98. *See Sherman v. Community Consolidated School District 21 of Wheeling Township*, 714 F. Supp. 932 (N.D. Ill. 1989).
99. *Id.* at 936-37.
100. *Id.* at 937.
101. *See* Dent, *supra* note 9, at 54, citing *McCartney v. Austin*, 293 N.Y.S.2d 188 (Sup. Ct., Broome County, Special Term 1968), *aff'd*, 298 N.Y.S.2d 26 (N.Y. App. Div. 1969); *Board of Education of Mountain Lakes v. Maas*, 152 A.2d 394 (N.J. Super. 1959), *aff'd*, 158 A.2d 330 (N.J.), *cert. denied*, 363 U.S. 843 (1960); *Mosier v. Barren County Board of Health*, 215 S.W.2d 967 (Ky. App. 1948).
102. *Mosier*, 215 S.W.2d at 969.
103. *See, e.g.*, Ala. code sec. 16-30-1 et seq.; Colo. Rev. Stat. sec. 25-4-901 et seq.; D.C. Code Ann. sec. 31-501 et seq.
104. 376 F. Supp. 479 (D. N.H. 1974).
105. *Id.* at 481.
106. *Id.*
107. 378 So. 2d 218 (Miss. 1979), *cert. denied*, 449 U.S. 39 (1980).
108. *Id.* at 223.
109. *See Mozert v. Hawkins County Board of Education*, 827 F.2d 1058 (6th Cir. 1987), *cert. denied*, 56 U.S.L.W. 3569 (U.S. Feb. 22, 1988).
110. *See* Dent, *supra* note 9, at 889, citing *Pierce v. Society of Sisters*, 268 U.S. 510 (1925); *Wisconsin v. Yoder*, 406 U.S. 205 (1972).
111. *See generally Wallace v. Jaffree*, 472 U.S. 38 (1985) (moment of meditation or voluntary prayer); *Stone v. Graham*, 449 U.S. 39 (1980) (posting of the Ten Commandments in classrooms); *Abington School District v. Schempp*, 374 U.S. 203 (1963) (reading of Bible); and, *Engel v. Vitale*, 370 U.S. 421 (1962) (voluntary prayer).
112. 269 U.S. 510 (1925).
113. *Id.* at 532.
114. 406 U.S. 205 (1972).
115. *Id.* at 209.
116. *Id.* at 224.
117. *Id.*
118. *See, e.g.*, *Ware v. Valley Stream High School District*, 551 N.Y.S. 2d 167, 174 (Ct. App. 1989).
119. 406 U.S. at 235.
120. Dent, *supra* note 9, at 888.
121. *See e.g.*, *Cornwell v. State Board of Education*, 314 F. Supp. 340 (D. Md. 1969), *aff'd*, 428 F.2d 471 (4th Cir. 1970) *(per curiam)*; *Moody v. Cronin*, 484 F. Supp. 270 (C.D. Ill. 1979); *Citizens for Parental Rights v. San Mateo County Board of Education*, 51 Cal. App. 3d 1, 124 Cal. Rptr. 68 (1975), *appeal dismissed*, 425 U.S. 908, *U.S. reh'g denied*, 425 U.S. 1000 (1976); *Davis v. Page*, 395 F. Supp. 395 (D. N.H. 1974); *Valent*, 274 A.2d 832 144 N.J. Dupee. 63 (1971), *dismissed on other grounds*, 288 A.2d 52, 118 N.J. Super. 416 (1972). *Hopkins v. Hamden Board of Education*, 29 Conn. Supp. 397, 289 A.2d 914 (1971), *aff'd*, 165 Conn. 793, 305 A.2d 536 (1973). *Mitchell v. McCall*, 273 Ala. 625, 143 So.2d 629 (1962).
122. 406 U.S. at 233-34.
123. *Cornwell v. State Board of Education*, 314 F. Supp. 340, 342 (D. Md. 1969).
124. *Citizens for Parental Rights v. San Mateo County Board of Education*, *supra* note 121.

125. *Id.* at 22.
126. *Id.* at 31.
127. *Hopkins v. Hamden Board of Education, supra* note 121.
128. *Id.* at 920-21.
129. *Ware*, 551 N.Y.S. 2d at 177.
130. *Id.* at 176.
131. *Id.* at 177.
132. *Id.*
133. *Id.*
134. *Id.* at 178.
135. 827 F.2d 1058 (6th Cir. 1987).
136. *Id.* at 1070.
137. *Id.* at 1064 (emphasis in original).
138. Dent, *supra* note 9, at 892.
139. Hirschoff, *supra* note 8, at 908-09.
140. *Id.* at 909.
141. *See Epperson v. Arkansas*, 393 U.S. 97, 106 (1968).
142. Lines, *supra* note 37, at 695.
143. Rice, *Conscientious Objection to Public Education: The Grievance and the Remedies*, 1978 B.Y.U. L. Rev. 847, 866.
144. Hirschoff, *supra* note 8, at 945-46.
145. Lines, *supra* note 37, at 695.
146. *See, e.g., Grove v. Mead School District No. 354*, 753 F.2d 1528 (9th Cir.), *cert. denied*, 474 U.S. 826 (1985).
147. 385 F. Supp. 395 (D. N.H. 1974).
148. *Id.* at 397.
149. *Id.*
150. *See* 34 C.F.R. sec. 98.3 (1990).
151. *See, e.g., Epperson v. Arkansas*, 393 U.S. 97 (1968).
152. Lines, *supra* note 37, at 698.
153. 484 F. Supp. 270 (C.D. Ill. 1979).
154. *Id.* at 277.
155. *Id.*
156. *See generally Citizens for Parental Rights v. San Mateo County Board of Education*, 51 Cal. App. 3d 1, 22 (1975) (The court noted that the pleading lacked specificity as to how the health education program treated matters of morality, family life, and reproduction in a manner that was hostile to the parents' theistic religion); *Hopkins v. Hamden Board of Education*, 289 A.2d 914, 920-21 (Conn. C.P. 1971) (The court noted the record disclosed open and express objection to "sex education," as such, but indicated approval of education in adjusting to the menstrual period and of certain other sex-related instruction appearing in the printed curriculum).
157. Lines, *supra* note 37, at 697.
158. *Cf. Epperson v. Arkansas*, 393 U.S. 97 (1968).
159. *See Davis v. Page*, 395 F. Supp. at 403 (D. N.H. 1974).
160. *See also McCartney v. Austin*, 293 N.Y.S.2d 188 (N.Y. App. Div. 1968) *aff'd*, 298 N.Y.S. 2d 26 (N.Y. App. Div. 1969) where the court overruled an objection to a child's vaccination. The court noted that the parent's faith was Roman Catholicism—a faith which does not have any proscriptions against inoculation.
161. *See, e.g., Quimette v. Babbie*, 405 F. Supp. 525 (D. Vt. 1975).
162. *Cantwell v. Connecticut*, 310 U.S. 296, 305 (1940).
163. *See Quimette*, 405 F. Supp. 525 (D. Vt. 1975).

164. *See, e.g., Wisconsin v. Yoder*, 406 U.S. 205 (1972), where the Amish used an expert witness to inform the court that the Old Order Amish religion pervaded the entire Amish way of life; *see also Abington School District v. Schempp*, 374 U.S. 203 (1963) (expert testified that portions of the New Testament were offensive to Jewish tradition); N.Y. Education Law sec. 3204[5] (McKinney 1990) (requires verified petition by an authorized religious representative for excusal from health and hygiene study). However, such a requirement is not constitutionally required. *See generally Frazee v. Illinois Department of Employment Security*, 109 S. Ct. 1514 (1989).

165. *Davis*, 395 F. Supp. at 405.
166. *Moody*, 484 F. Supp. at 274-75.
167. *Davis*, 395 F. Supp. at 405.
168. *Moody*, 484 F. Supp. at 275.
169. *See Wright v. Houston Independent School District*, 366 F. Supp. 1208 (S.D. Tex. 1972).
170. *Id.* at 1211-12.
171. 753 F.2d 1528 (9th Cir.), *cert. denied*, 474 U.S. 826 (1985).
172. 289 A.2d 914 (Conn. C.P. 1971).

CHAPTER FIFTEEN: *Release Time in Public Schools*

1. Comment, *The Released Time Program in Public Schools*, 10 Baylor L. Rev. 292, 296 (1950) (hereinafter referred to as "The Released Time").
2. *Id.*
3. *See Illinois ex rel. McCollum v. Board of Education*, 333 U.S. 203, 224 (1948).
4. *See Lanner v. Wimmer* 463 F. Supp. 867 (D. Utah 1978), *aff'd in part and rev'd in part*, 662 F.2d 1349, 1352 (10th Cir. 1981).
5. *The Released Time, supra* note 1, at 296.
6. *Id.* at 297.
7. *Id.*
8. 333 U.S. 203 (1948).
9. 330 U.S. 1 (1946).
10. *Id.*
11. *Id.* at 15-16.
12. *The Released Time, supra* note 1, at 299.
13. *McCollum*, 333 U.S. at 205.
14. *Id.* at 212.
15. *Id.* at 210-11 (quoting *Everson*, 330 U.S. at 15-16).
16. *McCollum*, 333 U.S. at 212.
17. 343 U.S. 306 (1952).
18. *Id.* at 308.
19. *Id.* at 309.
20. *Id.* at 308.
21. *Id.* at 313.
22. *Id.* at 315.
23. *McCollum*, 333 U.S. at 205.
24. *Id.* at 234.
25. *McCollum*, 333 U.S. at 205.
26. *Id.* at 209.
27. *Zorach*, 343 U.S. at 308-09.
28. *Id.* at 308.
29. *Id.* at 311.
30. *McCollum*, 333 U.S. at 212.

31. Note, *The "Released Time" Cases Revisited*, 83 Yale L. J. 1202, 1228 (1974).
32. *Id.* at 1222.
33. *Id.* at 1222-23.
34. *McCollum*, 333 U.S. at 235.
35. St. Louis and Portland were the only two cities to have their programs enjoined because of the *McCollum* decision. New York's program was in the process of being challenged. Note, *The "Released Time" Cases Revisited*, *supra* note 31, at 1223.
36. *See Lanner*, 662 F.2d at 1357. *Cf. Perry v. School District*, 344 P.2d 1036, 1040 (1959).
37. 403 U.S. 602 (1971).
38. 472 U.S. 38 (1985). Justice O'Connor's delineation of the endorsement test was a refinement of earlier discussions of the test in a prior case. *See generally Lynch v. Donnelly* 465 U.S. 668 (1984).
39. *Lemon*, 403 U.S. at 612-13 (citations omitted).
40. *See, e.g., Meek v. Pittenger*, 421 U.S. 349, 359 (1975).
41. *See, e.g., Lanner*, 662 F.2d at 1357.
42. *See, e.g., Smith v. Smith*, 523 F.2d 121, 124 (4th Cir. 1975), *cert. denied*, 423 U.S. 1073 (1976).
43. *Id.* at 124.
44. *Wallace*, 472 U.S. at 69 (citations omitted).
45. *Zorach*, 343 U.S. at 315.
46. *McCollum*, 333 U.S. at 208; *Zorach*, 343 U.S. at 309.
47. *Lanner*, 662 F.2d at 1358.
48. *Id.*
49. *Id.*
50. *Id.* at 1359.
51. *Lanner v. Wimmer*, 463 F.Supp 867, 883 (D. Utah 1978), *aff'd in part and rev'd in part*, 662 F.2d 1349 (10th Cir. 1981).
52. *See generally McCollum*, *supra* note 3 and *Zorach*, *supra* note 17.
53. *Lanner*, 662 F.2d at 1362.
54. *Id.* at 1363.
55. *Id.*
56. *Meek*, 421 U.S. at 359.
57. *See Lanner*, 662 F.2d at 1354.
58. *McCollum*, 333 U.S. at 234.
59. *See Ford v. Manuel*, 629 F. Supp. 771, 774 (N.D. Ohio 1985).
60. *Id.* at 772.
61. *Id.* at 779.
62. 629 F. Supp. 771 (N.D. Ohio 1985).
63. *Id.* at 777.
64. 523 F. 2d, 121, 122 (4th Cir. 1975), *cert denied*, 423 U.S. 1073 (1976).
65. No. 90-0128-H (W.D. Va. 1990).
66. The placement of the school buses was not the only basis for the decision to grant a temporary restraining order to the plaintiff. The court also cited coercion and perception problems based on the facts.
67. *Id.*
68. *Id.*
69. *See, e.g., Lanner*, 662 F.2d at 1359.
70. 343 U.S. at 308.
71. *Id.*
72. *Id.*
73. *Id.* at 1359.

74. 629 F. Supp. 771 (N.D. Ohio 1985).
75. *Id.* at 778.
76. *Lubbock Civil Liberties Union v. Lubbock Independent School District,* 669 F.2d 1038, 1046 (5th Cir. 1982), *reh'g denied,* 680 F.2d 424 (5th Cir. 1982), *cert. denied,* 459 U.S. 1155 (1983).
77. *See Lanner,* 662 F.2d at 1353.
78. *See Perry v. School District,* 344 P.2d 1036, 1043 (1959).
79. *Id.* at 1036.
80. *Id.* at 1043.
81. *Id.*
82. *Shenandoah, supra* note 65.
83. *Ford,* 629 F. Supp. at 774.
84. *See, e.g., Shenandoah, supra* note 65.
85. *See, e.g., Lanner,* 662 F.2d at 1355.
86. *See, e.g., Ford,* 629 F. Supp. at 774. *See also Shenandoah, supra* note 65.
87. *State ex rel. Dearle v. Frazier,* 173 P. 35, (1918).
88. *Lanner,* 662 F.2d at 1361.
89. The *Lanner* court, however, rejected this analysis when it upheld the granting of credit to meet elective credit requirements. 662 F.2d at 1361.
90. *Zorach,* 343 U.S. at 311. Note that the admission of evidence to support a coercion claim was denied on a technicality. *Zorach,* 343 U.S. 311 n. 7.
91. *Ford,* 629 F. Supp. at 777.
92. *Zorach,* 343 U.S. at 315.
93. *Lanner,* 662 F.2d at 1352.
94. *Id.* at 1357.
95. *McCollum,* 333 U.S. at 210-211 (quoting *Everson,* 330 U.S. at 15-16).
96. *See Perry,* 344 P.2d at 1040.
97. *Shenandoah, supra* note 65.
98. This method was upheld in *Smith, supra* note 65.
99. This method was upheld in *Lanner, supra* note 51.
100. *Id.*
101. *Smith,* 523 F.2d at 122.
102. *See generally Ford,* 629 F. Supp. at 771.
103. *See Lanner,* 662 F.2d at 1359.
104. *See Ford,* 629 F. Supp. at 772.
105. *See generally* Boston, *Time Out for Religion,* 43 Church and State 128 (1990).
106. *See Perry,* 344 P.2d at 1043.
107. The facts in *McCollum* indicate that the superintendent approved of and supervised the religious instructors. *McCollum,* 333 U.S. at 208.

CHAPTER SIXTEEN: *Religious Holiday Observances*

1. *See, e.g.,* A. James Reichley, *Religion in American Public Life* (Washington, D.C.: The Brookings Institution, 1985).
2. *See, e.g., Florey v. Sioux Falls School District 49-5,* 464 F. Supp. 911 (D. S.D. 1979), *aff'd,* 619 F.2d 1311 (8th Cir.), *cert. denied,* 449 U.S. 987 (1980); *R.J.J. v. Shineman,* 658 S.W.2d 910 (Mo. App. 1983); *Muka v. Sturgis,* 53 A.D.2d 716, 383 N.Y.S.2d 933 (1976); *Committee Against Religious Encroachment in Schools v. Board of Education,* Civil No. 1841-72 (D. N.J. November 20, 1972); *Chamberlin v. Dade County Board of Public Instruction,* 17 Fla. Supp. 183 (Cir. Ct. 1961), *aff'd,* 143 So. 2d 21 (Fla. 1962), *vacated and remanded,* 374 U.S. 487, *judgment reinstated,* 160 So. 2d 97 (Fla.), *rev'd,* 377 U.S. 402 (1964).

3. *See, e.g., Society of Separationists v. Clements*, 677 F. Supp. 509 (W.D. Tex. 1988); *American Civil Liberties Union v. City of St. Charles*, 794 F.2d 265 (7th Cir.), *cert. denied*, 479 U.S. 961 (1986); *Allen v. Morton*, 495 F.2d 65 (D.C. Cir. 1973). *See also Curran v. Lee*, 484 F.2d 1348 (2d Cir. 1973) (challenge to city-sponsored St. Patrick's Day Parade).
4. *See* C. Lewis, ed., *A Calendar of Religious Holidays and Ethnic Festivals, September 1988 to August 1990* (National Conference of Christians and Jews).
5. Albert J. Menendez, *The December Dilemma: Christmas in American Public Life* (Silver Spring, MD: Americans United for Separation of Church and State, 1988), p.7. *See generally* W. Dawson, *Christmas: Its Origin and Associations* (London: Elliot Stock, 1902); P. Snyder, *December 25th* (New York: Dodd, Mead & Co., 1985).
6. *See Lynch v. Donnelly*, 465 U.S. 668, 720-21 (1984) (Brennan, J., dissenting).
7. *See generally* W. Dawson, *Christmas: Its Origin and Association* (London: Elliot Stock, 1902).
8. *Id.* at 723; Menendez, *supra* note 5, at 10.
9. Menendez, *supra* note 5, at 49. *See generally* James H. Barnett, *The American Christmas: A Study in National Culture* (New York: Macmillan, 1954).
10. Bloom, *A Successful Jewish Boycott of the New York City Public Schools—Christmas 1906*, 70 American Jewish History 180-88 (December 1980).
11. *See* Note, *Religious-Holiday Observances in the Public Schools*, 48 N.Y.U. L. Rev. 1116, 1144 n. 174 (1973); *see also Muka v. Sturgis*, 53 A.D.2d 716, 383 N.Y.S.2d 933 (1976).
12. *See* Menendez, *supra* note 5, at 64.
13. *Abington School District v. Schempp*, 374 U.S. 203, 232 (1963) (Brennan, J., concurring).
14. *Marsh v. Chambers*, 463 U.S. 783, 792 (1983).
15. *Lynch*, 465 U.S. at 673 (emphasis supplied, citations omitted). *See also Zorach v. Clauson*, 343 U.S. 306, 313-14 (1952), where the Court stated:

> We are a religious people whose institutions presuppose a Supreme Being. We guarantee the freedom to worship as one chooses. We make room for as wide a variety of beliefs and creeds as the spiritual needs of man deem necessary. . . . When the state encourages religious instruction or cooper- ates with religious authorities by adjusting the schedule of public events to sectarian needs, it follows the best of our traditions. For it then respects the religious nature of our people and accommodates the public service to their spiritual needs. To hold that it may not, would be to find in the Constitution a requirement that the government show a callous indiffer- ence to religious groups. That would be preferring those who believe in no religion over those who do believe.

16. 465 U.S. 668 (1984).
17. *Id.* at 686.
18. *Id.* at 674.
19. *Id.* at 675-78 (citations omitted).
20. *Id.* at 686.
21. *Id.*
22. *Cf. Edwards v. Aguillard*, 482 U.S. 578, 583-84 (1987) (Establishment Clause must be applied with special sensitivity in the public school context).
23. 464 F. Supp. 911 (D. S.D. 1979), *aff'd*, 619 F.2d 1311 (8th Cir.), *cert. denied*, 449 U.S. 987 (1980).
24. 619 F.2d at 1319.
25. *See* Arkansas O.A.G. 88-115 (1988).

26. 464 F. Supp. 911, 912 (D. S.D. 1979).
27. *Id.* at 913.
28. *Florey*, 619 F.2d at 1319.
29. *Id.*
30. *Id.* at 1319-20.
31. 403 U.S. 602, *reh'g denied*, 404 U.S. 876 (1971). The Court stated: "First, the statute [or government practice] must have a secular legislative purpose; second, its principal or primary effect must be one that neither advances nor inhibits religion; finally, the statute must not foster 'an excessive government entanglement with religion.'" *Id.* at 612-13.
32. *Id.* at 612-13. The tripartite test, however, has been brought into question in some recent cases. *See, e.g., Marsh v. Chambers*, 463 U.S. 783 (1983); *Lynch v. Donnelly*, 465 U.S. 668 (1984). *See also* discussion of the *Lemon* test in *Mueller v. Allen*, 463 U.S. 388 (1983); Comment, *The Constitutionality of Christmas Programs in Public Schools—Should the United States Supreme Court Modify Its Interpretation of the Establishment Clause?*, 11 S. Ill. U. L. J. 1233, 1238-47 (1987).
33. *See Malnak v. Yogi*, 592 F.2d 197, 202 n.7 (3d Cir. 1979).
34. Note, *Religious-Holiday Observances in the Public Schools*, 48 N.Y.U. L. Rev. at 1138.
35. Laurence Tribe, *American Constitutional Law*, 2d ed. (Mineola, N.Y.: Foundation Press, 1988), p. 1294.
36. *See Society of Separationists v. Clements*, 677 F. Supp. at 511.
37. *Florey*, 619 F.2d at 1314.
38. *Florey*, 464 F. Supp. at 916.
39. *McGowan v. Maryland*, 366 U.S. 420 (1961).
40. *Id.* at 445.
41. *See* Casenote, *Christmas Carols in School Assemblies May Be Constitutional*, 31 Mercer L. Rev. 627, 633 (1980).
42. *Florey*, 619 F.2d at 1315.
43. *Schempp*, 374 U.S. at 225. *See also id.* at 300-01 (Brennan, J., concurring):

> The holding of the Court today plainly does not foreclose teaching *about* the Holy Scriptures or about the differences between religious sects in classes in literature or history. Indeed, whether or not the Bible is involved, it would be impossible to teach meaningfully many subjects in the social sciences or the humanities without some mention of religion. To what extent, and at what points in the curriculum, religious materials should be cited are matters which the courts ought to entrust very largely to the experienced officials who superintend our Nation's public schools. . . . Any attempt to impose rigid limits upon the mention of God or references to the Bible in the classroom would be fraught with dangers.

   See also Edwards v. Aguillard, 482 U.S. 578, 606-08 (1987) (Powell, J., concurring); *Grove v. Mead School District*, 753 F.2d 1528 (9th Cir.), *cert. denied*, 474 U.S. 826 (1985).
44. *Florey*, 619 F.2d at 1316-17 n.5.
45. *See McCollum v. Board of Education*, 333 U.S. 203, 236 (1948) (Jackson, J., concurring). *See also Crockett v. Sorenson*, 568 F. Supp. 1422, 1427-29 (W.D. Va. 1983).
46. *See* Casenote, *New Guidance from the Eighth Circuit on the Scope of Permissible Religious Accommodation in Public Schools?*, 49 University of Missouri at Kansas City Law Review 219, 230-31 (1981); Woodruff, *Religious*

Holidays and the Public Schools, 16 Religion and Public Education 123, 124 (Winter 1989).

47. Pevar, *Public Schools Must Stop Having Christmas Assemblies*, 24 St. Louis U. L. J. 327, 347 (1980). Stephen L. Pevar was the American Civil Liberties Union attorney who represented the plaintiffs in *Florey*.
48. See *Schempp*, 374 U.S. at 225.
49. *Florey*, 619 F.2d at 1316.
50. *Id.*
51. *Id.*
52. *Id.* at 1317.
53. *Id. See also* Smith and Hayes, *A Christmas Carol Revisited: Humbug in the Sioux Falls Schools*, 24 St. Louis U. L. J. 359, 369-72 (1980).
54. *Id.*
55. *Id.*
56. *Id.* at 1318.
57. *Id.*
58. 465 U.S. 668 (1984).
59. *Lynch*, 465 U.S. at 688-92 (O'Connor, J., concurring).
60. *Id.* at 688.
61. *Id.* at 691-92.
62. *Id.*
63. See *Wallace v. Jaffree*, 472 U.S. 38, 76 (1985) (O'Connor, J., concurring).
64. *See, e.g.*, *American Civil Liberties Union v. City of Birmingham*, 791 F.2d 1561, 1563 (6th Cir.), *cert. denied*, 107 S. Ct. 421 (1986).
65. *See, e.g.*, Smith, *Symbols, Perceptions, and Doctrinal Illusions: Establishment Neutrality and the "No Endorsement Test,"* 86 Mich. L. Rev. 266, 275 (1987). Smith also notes:

   > Far from eliminating the inconsistencies and defects that have plagued establishment analysis, the "no endorsement" test would introduce further ambiguities and analytical deficiencies into the doctrine. Moreover, the theoretical justifications offered for the test are unpersuasive.

   Id. at 267.
66. *See, e.g.*, *Texas Monthly v. Bullock*, 109 S. Ct. 890 (1989); *County of Allegheny v. American Civil Liberties Union, Greater Pittsburgh Chapter*, 109 S. Ct. 3086, 3100-05 (1989).
67. *County of Allegheny v. American Civil Liberties Union, Greater Pittsburgh Chapter*, 109 S. Ct. at 3100-01.
68. See *id.* at 3105 n.51 ("Government efforts to accommodate religion are permissible when they remove burdens on the free exercise of religion."); *id.* at 3121 (O'Connor, J., concurring in part) ("government can *accommodate* religion by lifting government-imposed burdens on religion"). But see *id.* at 3111 (the concept of "accommodation" does not permit government-sponsored display of creche).
69. For an analysis of Justice O'Connor's endorsement test as applied to religious holiday observances in public schools, *see* Comment, *The Constitutionality of Christmas Programs in Public Schools—Should the United States Supreme Court Modify Its Interpretation of the Establishment Clause?* 11 S. Ill. U. L. J. 1233, 1252-55 (1987).
70. *See* Smith and Hayes, *A Christmas Carol Revisited: Humbug in the Sioux Falls Schools*, 24 St. Louis U. L. J. at 373-74.
71. *Florey*, 619 F.2d at 1318-19.
72. *Id.* at 1319.

73. *Id.* at 1326 (McMillian, C.J., dissenting).
74. *Id.* at 1316.
75. *See Widmar v. Vincent,* 454 U.S. 263 (1981). *See generally* Whitehead, *Avoiding Religious Apartheid: Affording Equal Treatment for Student-Initiated Religious Expression in Public Schools,* 16 Pepperdine L. Rev. 229 (1989); Note, *Religious Expression in the Public School Forum: The High School Student's Right to Free Speech,* 72 Geo. L. J. 135 (1983); Note, *The Constitutional Dimensions of Student-Initiated Religious Activity in Public High Schools,* 92 Yale L. J. 499 (1983).
76. *Florey,* 619 F.2d at 1319.
77. *Id.*
78. Note, *The Establishment Clause and Its Application in the Public Schools,* 59 Neb. L. Rev. 1143, 1164 (1980).
79. *Florey,* 619 F.2d at 1319-20.
80. *See City of St. Charles,* 794 F.2d at 271.
81. *See County of Allegheny v. American Civil Liberties Union, Greater Pittsburgh Chapter,* 109 S. Ct. 3086 (1989) (secular holiday symbols or symbols substantially divested of religious meaning do not raise Establishment Clause concerns since they do not convey a message of endorsement of religion).
82. 109 S. Ct. 3086 (1989).
83. *Id.* at 3115 n.69.
84. 449 U.S. 39 (1980).
85. *Id.* at 41.
86. *Cf.* Opinions of the Justices, 108 N.H. 97, 228 A.2d 161 (1967) (in pre-*Graham* opinion, plaques in public schools bearing motto "In God We Trust" held to be permissible); *Lawrence v. Buchmueller,* 40 Misc. 2d 300, 243 N.Y.S.2d 87 (Sup. Ct. Westchester County 1963) (court held that erection of creche on school premises during portion of school Christmas recess at no expense to school district did not violate Establishment Clause); *Baer v. Kolmorgan,* 14 Misc. 2d 1015, 181 N.Y.S.2d 230 (Sup. Ct. Westchester County 1958) (court upheld erection of privately sponsored and supported nativity scene on public school lawn when school not in session). However, it must be noted that some of these decisions occurred before some Supreme Court decisions finding certain religious practices unconstitutional in the public schools. *See, e.g., Engel v. Vitale,* 370 U.S. 421 (1962); *Abington School District v. Schempp,* 374 U.S. 203 (1963).
87. *See* M. Braveman, *The December Dilemma* (American Jewish Committee, 1986), p. 6
88. *See Florey,* 619 F.2d at 1318-19. *See also Wisconsin v. Yoder,* 406 U.S. 205 (1972); *West Virginia State Board of Education v. Barnette,* 319 U.S. 624 (1943).
89. Note, *Religious-Holiday Observances in the Public Schools,* 48 N.Y.U. L. Rev. at 1144. *See also Crockett v. Sorenson,* 568 F. Supp. 1422, 1431 (W.D. Va. 1983).
90. *Schempp,* 374 U.S. at 288-90 (Brennan, J., concurring). *See also Ring v. Board of Education,* 245 Ill. 334, 351, 92 N.E. 251, 256 (1910).
91. Note, *Religious-Holiday Observances in the Public Schools,* 48 N.Y.U. L. Rev. at 1141. *See also Schempp,* 374 U.S. at 224-25.
92. *See generally Wisconsin v. Yoder,* 406 U.S. 205 (1972); *West Virginia State Board of Education v. Barnette,* 319 U.S. 624 (1943).
93. *See Church of God v. Amarillo Independent School District,* 511 F. Supp. 613 (N.D. Tex. 1981), *aff'd,* 670 F.2d 46 (5th Cir. 1982).
94. *See Student Members of the Playcrafters v. Board of Education,* 177 N.J. Super. 66, 424 A.2d 1192, *aff'd,* 88 N.J. 74, 438 A.2d 543 (1981).

95. Mark Stern, *Religion and the Public Schools: A Summary of the Law* (American Jewish Congress, September 1989), pp. 17-18.
96. *Smith v. North Babylon Union Free School District*, 844 F.2d 90 (2d Cir. 1988) (graduation exercise on Saturday did not violate Orthodox Jewish student's free exercise rights, as long as attendance at graduation was not a prerequisite to student's receipt of high school diploma).
97. Note, *Religious-Holiday Observances in the Public Schools*, 48 N.Y.U. L. Rev., at 1126.
98. *Tinker v. Des Moines Independent School District*, 393 U.S. 503, 506 (1969). *See generally* Smith, *Constitutional Rights of Students, Their Families, and Teachers in the Public Schools*, 10 Campbell L. Rev. 353 (1988).
99. *Widmar v. Vincent*, 454 U.S. 263, 276 (1981); *see also Mergens v. Board of Education of the Westside Community Schools*, 110 S. Ct. 2356 (1990).
100. *See Florey*, 619 F.2d at 1320. *But see Guidry v. Calcasieu Parish School Board*, No. 87-2122-LC (W.D. La. filed Feb. 22, 1989).
101. Note, *Religious-Holiday Observances in the Public Schools*, 48 N.Y.U. L. Rev., at 1142.
102. *See Thompson v. Waynesboro Area School District*, 673 F. Supp. 1379 (M.D. Pa. 1987), *aff'd by an equally divided court*, Case No. 88-5235 (3d Cir., May 1989); *Rivera v. East Otero School District*, 721 F. Supp. 1189 (D. Colo. 1989).
103. *See Vail v. Board of Education*, 354 F. Supp. 592 (D. N.H. 1973).
104. 465 U.S. 668 (1984).
105. 109 S. Ct. 3086 (1989).
106. A Missouri Court of Appeals in *R.J.J. v. Shineman* (1983), similarly upheld a Christmas program including religious carols conducted in a local church, concluding the pageant was "secular and without religious impact, objective or interplay." 658 S.W.2d 910, 912 (Mo. App. 1983).
107. Smith and Hayes, *A Christmas Carol Revisited: Humbug in the Sioux Falls Schools*, 24 St. Louis U. L. J., at 370-71.
108. *See* Brief of Amicus Curiae William P. Thompson, Stated Clerk of the General Assembly of the United Presbyterian Church in the United States of America, at 4, *Florey v. Sioux Falls School District 49-5*, No. 79-1277 (8th Cir., filed April 22, 1980).
109. *Lynch*, 465 U.S. 668. (1st Cir. 1984).
110. *Florey*, 619 F.2d 1311. (8th Cir. 1980).
111. *McGowan*, 366 U.S. 420. (Md App. Ct. 1961).
112. *See* Laycock, *Toward a General Theory of the Religion Clauses: The Case of Church Labor Relations and the Right to Church Autonomy*, 81 Colum. L. Rev. 1373, 1384 (1981).
113. Note, *Religious-Holiday Observances in the Public Schools*, 48 N.Y.U. L. Rev., at 1140. *See also Zorach v. Clauson*, 343 U.S. 306, 314 (1952).
114. Pevar, *Public Schools Must Stop Having Christmas Assemblies*, 24 St. Louis U. L. J., at 354-55.

CHAPTER SEVENTEEN: *Graduation Prayers*

1. *See Marsh v. Chambers*, 463 U.S. 783, 791-92 (1983).
2. *See Marsh v. Chambers*, 463 U.S. 783 (1983) (chaplain's prayers before legislative session held constitutional); *Abington School District v. Schempp*, 374 U.S. 203 (1963) (state-mandated prayer and Bible reading in public school unconstitutional); *Engel v. Vitale*, 370 U.S. 421 (1962) (state-mandated prayer in public school unconstitutional).
3. *See Engel*, 370 U.S. at 424-25 (1962); *Schempp*, 374 U.S. 203 (1963).

4. *See Wallace v. Jaffree*, 472 U.S. 38 (1985).
5. 463 U.S. 783 (1983).
6. *Id.* at 792.
7. Another issue left untouched by the Supreme Court is the constitutionality of baccalaureate services. *See Chamberlin v. Dade County Board of Public Instruction*, 17 Fla. Supp. 183 (Cir. Ct. 1961), *aff'd*, 143 So. 2d 21 (Fla. 1962), *vacated and remanded*, 374 U.S. 487, *judgment reinstated*, 160 So. 2d 97 (Fla.), *rev'd*, 377 U.S. 402 (1964). The nature of a baccalaureate service is markedly different from that of a graduation ceremony. Baccalaureate Sunday is a tradition which takes place the Sunday before graduation. M. Gunn, *A Guide to Academic Protocol* 74 (1969). The service is predominantly religious. A processional hymn, an invocation, choral hymns, Bible reading, an address by a minister, a benediction, and a recessional hymn are traditional elements of a baccalaureate service. Choper, *Religion in the Public Schools: A Proposed Constitutional Standard*, 47 Minn. L. Rev. 329, 407-08 (1963). Because the service is primarily religious in nature, the analysis used in determining its constitutionality is different from that used when examining prayers delivered at graduation, which is a secular ceremony. This area is beyond the scope of our discussion. For articles and cases which address the constitutionality of a baccalaureate service, *see Goodwin v. Cross County School District No. 7*, 394 F. Supp. 417 (E.D. Ark. 1973); *Miller v. Cooper*, 56 N.M. 355, 244 P.2d 520 (1952); 3 Op. Att'y Gen. 82-002 (Wyo. 1982); Diliberto, *Federal and State Constitutionality of Baccalaureate Services in the Public Schools*, 15 Ohio N.U. L. Rev. 527 (1988); DuPuy, *Religion, Graduation, and the First Amendment: A Threat or A Shadow?* 35 Drake L. Rev. 323, 324-28 (1985-86) [hereinafter DuPuy].
8. The First Amendment reads: "Congress shall make no law respecting an establishment of religion or prohibiting the free exercise thereof; or abridging the freedom of speech, or of the press, or the right of the people peaceably to assemble, and to petition the Government for a redress of grievances" U.S. Const. amend. I.
9. The graduation service is a school-sponsored event. Even if the students have the responsibility of organizing the ceremony, the school is the final authority as to what will be included and what will be excluded. The service is normally held on school grounds in school facilities, and school employees participate in their official capacity. *See Lundberg v. West Monona Community School District*, 731 F. Supp. 331, 337 (N.D. Iowa 1989).
10. 822 F.2d 1406 (6th Cir. 1987).
11. *Stein v. Plainwell Community Schools*, 610 F. Supp. 43, 45 (W.D. Mich. 1985), *rev'd*, 822 F.2d 1406 (6th Cir. 1987). The students were told to keep the prayers brief. They were required to practice before the speech teacher, but the court noted that the school did not monitor the content. *Id.*
12. 465 U.S. 668 (1984).
13. *Stein*, 822 F.2d at 1409 (quoting *Lynch*, 465 U.S. at 692-93) (O'Connor, J., concurring).
14. The court was very concerned about the use of Jesus Christ's name in the invocation. *Id.* at 1410. *See also* Judge Milburn's reference to footnote 2 of the majority opinion. *Id.*
15. *Id.* at 1410 (Milburn, J., concurring).
16. *See* Comment, *Stein v. Plainwell Community Schools: The Constitutionality of Prayer in Public High School Commencement Exercises*, 22 Ga. L. Rev. 469, 491-93 (1988) [hereinafter Georgia].

17. *Stein v. Plainwell Community Schools*, 610 F. Supp. 43, 46 (W.D. Mich. 1985), *rev'd*, 822 F.2d 1406 (6th Cir. 1987).
18. 403 U.S. 602, *reh'g denied*, 404 U.S. 876 (1971). In *Lemon*, the Supreme Court held: "First, the statute must have a secular legislative purpose; second, its principal or primary effect must be one that neither advances nor inhibits religion; finally, the statute must not foster 'an excessive government entanglement with religion.'" 403 U.S. at 612-13 (citations omitted).
19. *See* Note, *Invocations and Benedictions—Is the Supreme Court "Graduating" to a Marsh Analysis?*, 65 U. Det. L. Rev. 769, (1988) [hereinafter Detroit]. The author notes that the court did not "carry *Marsh* to its logical conclusion." *Id.* at 795.
20. *Marsh v. Chambers*, 463 U.S. 783, 794-95 (1983).
21. *See Berlin v. Okaloosa County School District*, No. PCA 87-30450-RV (N.D. Fla. March 1, 1988) (WESTLAW 85937) [hereinafter *Berlin*].
22. *Marsh v. Chambers*, 463 U.S. 783 app. at 77 (1983) [hereinafter Joint Appendix]. *See also* Brief for Respondent at 3, *Marsh v. Chambers*, 463 U.S. 783 (1983) (No. 82-23), where respondent stated that one-half of Reverend Palmer's prayers mentioned Jesus Christ. It is clear from Dr. Palmer's deposition that opposing counsel was trying to prove that his prayers were Christian. The Court recognized the dilemma that a judicial body would face if it engaged in such line drawing.
23. *Id.* at 76. Nonsectarian as defined by Dr. Palmer meant that it "does not promote the furtherance of any specific group, cult or division of the Judeo-Christian faith." *Id.* at 77.
24. Joint Appendix, *supra* note 22, at 61.
25. This fact raises an interesting point. Some courts have defined sectarian as anything that could be attributed to Christianity. *See Stein*, 822 F.2d at 1410 (where the Court holds that the prayers "employ the language of Christian theology." *Id.*). However, the *Marsh* Court obviously disagreed. The chaplain clearly admitted that his prayers could be characterized as Christian, yet the Court held them to be valid. Furthermore, Dr. Palmer's definition of sectarian included Christian sects. He said that to call a major religion a "sect" would "be a gross injustice to millions of people around the world." For instance, the Islam religion cannot be called a sect, nor could the Jewish faith or the Christian faith. Joint Appendix, *supra* note 22, at 77.
26. *Marsh*, 463 U.S. at 793 n.14.
27. Joint Appendix, *supra* note 22, at 78.
28. *See* Note, *An Establishment Clause Analysis of Graduation Ceremony Invocations: Stein v. Plainwell Community Schools*, 21 Conn. L. Rev. 133, 158 (1988) [hereinafter Connecticut].
29. 728 F. Supp. 68 (D.R.I. 1990).
30. *Id.* at 74.
31. 370 U.S. 421 (1962).
32. *Id.* at 429.
33. 822 F.2d at 1411-12.
34. *Id.* at 1411.
35. *Id.* at 1410.
36. *See* Comment, *Ceremonial Invocations at Public High School Events and the Establishment Clause*, 16 Fla. St. U. L. Rev. 1001, 1014 (1989) [hereinafter Florida].
37. *Stein*, 822 F.2d at 1409.
38. 465 U.S. 668 (1984).
39. *Id.* at 685-86. *See also Berlin v. Okaloosa*, No. PCA-87-30450-RV (N.D. Fla. March l, 1988) (WESTLAW 85937) at 40 n.9 (referencing *Stein*, 822 F.2d at 1410).

40. 822 F.2d at 1410.
41. Senate, 98th Cong., 1st Sess. (1983). "Prince of Peace" is clearly a reference to Jesus Christ.
42. Senate, 98th Cong., 1st Sess. (1983).
43. Senate, 101st Cong., 2d Sess. (1990). Again, this is clearly a reference to Jesus Christ.
44. *Stein*, 822 F.2d at 1410.
45. See *Weisman v. Lee*, 728 F. Supp. 68 (D.R.I. 1990); *Lundberg v. West Monona Community School District*, 731 F. Supp. 331 (N.D. Iowa 1989); *Bennett v. Livermore Unified School District*, 193 Cal. App. 3d 1012, 238 Cal. Rptr. 819 (1987). See also *Graham v. Central Community School District*, 608 F. Supp. 531 (S.D. Iowa 1985); *Kay v. David Douglas School District*, 79 Or. App. 384, 719 P.2d 875 (1986), *rev'd on other grounds*, 303 Or. 574, 738 P.2d 1389 (1987), *cert. denied*, 484 U.S. 1032 (1988). See also *Jager v. Douglas County School District*, 862 F.2d 824 (11th Cir. 1989), *cert. denied*, 109 S. Ct. 2431 (1989) (invocation at high school football games unconstitutional); *Collins v. Chandler Unified School District*, 644 F.2d 756 (9th Cir 1981), *cert. denied*, 454 U.S. 863 (1981) (invocation at student council assemblies unconstitutional); *Doe v. Aldine Independent School District*, 563 F. Supp. 883 (S.D. Tex. 1982) (singing of school prayer at extracurricular activities unconstitutional).
46. See Connecticut, *supra* note 28, at 155-57; Georgia, *supra* note 16, at 491; Comment, *Invoking the Presence of God at Public High School Graduation Ceremonies: Graham v. Central Community School District*, 71 Iowa L. Rev. 1247, 1256 n.90 (1986) [hereinafter Iowa]. But see *Jager*, 822 F.2d at 831; *Weisman*, 728 F. Supp. at 74. The *Jager* court relied on *Doe*, 563 F. Supp. 883 (S.D. Tex. 1982), in determining that extracurricular activities are in some way compulsory because students want to attend. Using this reasoning, the court held that the school prayer cases were implicated. The flaw in this logic is twofold. First, one has to assume that although voluntary, the graduation service by its nature is compulsory. Second, in *Engel* and *Schempp* the Supreme Court considered many factors in holding that the prayers were unconstitutional. Compulsory attendance was just one. Further, the Supreme Court in *Schempp* distinguishes the facts in *Schempp* from *Zorach v. Clauson*, 343 U.S. 306 (1952), by noting that the only factor present in the program upheld in *Zorach* was compulsory attendance. This makes for an argument that the Supreme Court requires more than one factor, compulsory attendance, to invalidate a practice. *Abington School District v. Schempp*, 374 U.S. 203, 223 (1963).
47. *Engel v. Vitale*, 370 U.S. 423 (1962).
48. *Abington School District v. Schempp*, 374 U.S. 203 (1963). *Engel* and *Schempp* are the cases most applicable because they proscribe prayer in school. Other school cases, *Wallace v. Jaffree*, 472 U.S. 38 (1985), and *Stone v. Graham*, 449 U.S. 39 (1980), seem to indicate that all religious references should be kept out of the school and thus could be applied to invalidate graduation prayers as well. However, *Wallace* and *Stone* do not stand for such a proposition. In both *Wallace* and *Stone*, the Supreme Court determined that the state's only purpose was to advance religion, consequently the Court had no choice but to invalidate the practice. See *Stein*, 822 F.2d at 1413-14. The Supreme Court did not hold that all religious references must be banned from the school. In fact, in *Engel* the Court expressly noted that school children would be allowed to recite historical documents referencing a Supreme Being or sing an anthem that acknowledged God. Justice Black also noted that there was nothing inconsistent with the Constitution if the students were exposed to the many "manifestations in our public life of belief in God. Such patriotic or ceremonial occasions bear no true

resemblance to the unquestioned religious exercise that the State . . . has sponsored in this instance." *Engel,* 370 U.S. at 435 n.21.

49. 822 F.2d at 1409.
50. Judge Wellford in his dissent discussed *McCollum v. Board of Education,* 333 U.S. 203 (1948); *Zorach v. Clauson,* 343 U.S. 306 (1952); *Abington School District v. Schempp,* 374 U.S. 203 (1963); *Engel v. Vitale,* 370 U.S. 421 (1962); *Stone v. Graham,* 449 U.S. 39 (1980); *Grand Rapids School District v. Ball,* 473 U.S. 373 (1985).
51. *Stein,* 822 F.2d at 1414-15.
52. Other courts have recognized that a day-to-day religious routine is one of the factors with which the Court was concerned in *Engel* and *Schempp. Wood v. Mt. Lebanon Township School District,* 342 F. Supp. 1293, 1294 (W.D. Pa. 1972); *Weist v. Mt. Lebanon School District,* 320 A.2d 362 (Pa. 1974), *cert. denied,* 419 U.S. 967 (1974).
53. *Engel,* 370 U.S. at 424; *Schempp,* 374 U.S. at 205, 211.
54. 374 U.S. at 207.
55. *Id.* In *Engel,* the teacher either led or participated in the prayers, and the prayers were recited in the classroom. *Engel,* 370 U.S. at 422. In *Schempp,* Justice Brennan noted that the reason the Court had invalidated the law in *McCollum v. Board of Education,* 333 U.S. 203 (1943) (but upheld the law in *Zorach v. Clauson,* 343 U.S. 306 [1952]) was that in *McCollum* the program "placed the religious instructor in the public school classroom in precisely the position of authority held by the regular teachers of secular subjects, while the *Zorach* program did not." *Schempp,* 374 U.S. at 262. Thus, an important distinction in the two programs was that in one the teaching occurred in the classroom, and in the other it occurred outside the classroom.
56. *Engel,* 370 U.S. at 430.
57. See *Bogen v. Doty,* 598 F.2d 1110, 1113 (8th Cir. 1979).
58. *Engel,* 370 U.S. at 425.
59. *Id.* at 430.
60. 472 U.S. 38 (1985).
61. *Id.* at 81 (O'Connor, J., concurring).
62. There are concededly some similarities between the two scenarios. Usually graduation ceremonies are held on school property; they are conducted by school authorities and attended by students who are, most likely, dressed in school robes. See *Berlin v. Okaloosa County School District,* 16 No. PCA 87-30450-RV (N.D. Fla. March 1, 1988) (WESTLAW 85937).
63. *Weist v. Mt. Lebanon School District,* 320 A.2d 362, 370 (Pa. 1974), *cert. denied,* 419 U.S. 967 (1974) (Pomeroy, J., concurring).
64. "Calculated indoctrination does not exist in an annual practice that lasts only for a few minutes." Connecticut, *supra* note 28, at 149. See also *Jager v. Douglas County School District,* 862 F.2d 824, 837 (11th Cir. 1989), *cert. denied,* 109 S. Ct. 2431 (1989) (Peck, J., concurring).
65. *Weist,* 320 A.2d at 369.
66. *Wood v. Mt. Lebanon Township School District,* 342 F. Supp. 1293, 1294 (W.D. Pa. 1972).
67. See Connecticut, *supra* note 28, at 155-56.
68. While the voluntary nature of the ceremony is not determinative under *Engel,* 370 U.S. 421, 431 (1962), it is nonetheless a factor to take into consideration in assessing the overall atmosphere of the ceremony.
69. *Weist,* 320 A.2d at 369.
70. See *Wood v. Mt. Lebanon Township School District,* 342 F. Supp. 1293, 1294 (W.D. Pa. 1972).

71. The federal district court in *Stein* pointed to the fact that the school did not review the content of the prayers or participate in them. *Stein v. Plainwell Community Schools*, 610 F. Supp. 43, 45 (W.D. Mich. 1985), *rev'd*, 822 F.2d 1406 (6th Cir. 1987). In that way, the school avoided the accusation that the state officially composed the prayer.

72. *Id.* at 1295.

73. As Justice O'Connor has noted, ceremonial acknowledgments of religion such as Presidential Proclamations are different from school prayer because they are "directed primarily at adults who presumably are not readily susceptible to unwilling religious indoctrination." *Wallace v. Jaffree*, 472 U.S. 38, 81 (1985) (O'Connor, J., concurring).

74. *Stein v. Plainwell Community Schools*, 822 F.2d 1406, 1415 (6th Cir. 1987) (Wellborn, J., dissenting).

75. 472 U.S. 38, 80 (1985) (O'Connor, J., concurring).

76. 107 S.Ct. 2573 (1987).

77. *Id.* at 2576 n.4.

78. *See* DuPuy, *supra* note 7, at 356-64.

79. *See Lemon v. Kurtzman*, 403 U.S. 602, 612-13 (1971), *reh'g denied*, 404 U.S. 876 (1971).

80. *Marsh*, 463 U.S. at 786.

81. *Id.* at 787.

82. *Id.* at 788.

83. *See id.* at 791.

84. *Id.* at 792 (quoting *McGowan v. Maryland*, 366 U.S. 420, 442 [1961]).

85. *Id.*

86. *Id.* at 792 (quoting *Zorach v. Clauson*, 343 U.S. 306, 313 [1952]).

87. *See* Georgia, *supra* note 16, at 492-93. One author suggested that even under such a strict reading of *Marsh*, graduation prayers should stand. DuPuy, *supra*, at 356-64. This view is premised first on the fact that the *Marsh* Court did not limit its decision to legislative prayers, but would hold the same for any case where it could be shown that the intent of the framers, as seen by their practice, was that a specific act was constitutional. A historical analysis of graduation invocations indicates that they date as far back as the founding of the country. The commonly held view that public education was nonexistent is not wholly accurate. In fact, history illustrates that such framers as Thomas Jefferson were not adverse to using the Bible as a primary text in the public schools. One commentator concludes that the framers must have known of the practice of invocations at graduation and must not have seen a problem with it. *Id.* This argument would be useful if the *Marsh* test rested solely on the general history of the practice, but under a strict application this view does little to show that the framers considered the issue and held that it was constitutional. It would be inaccurate to argue that because the framers knew of the role religion played in the few public schools of the time, they must have believed that graduation prayers were constitutional. To assert that the framers' acquiescence to religion in the schools is tantamount to a legislative enactment made contemporaneous with the writing of the First Amendment is also questionable. There appears to be no evidence that the framers discussed the issue while drafting the First Amendment. *See id.* They could not have because public high school graduations did not begin until 1842. Thus, a reliance on a specific indication that the framers saw graduation prayers as constitutional, while they probably would, is misplaced.

88. *See* Detroit, *supra* note 19, at 973-76. This is the interpretation applied in *Stein*.

89. *See Wallace v. Jaffree*, 472 U.S. 38, 81 (1985) (O'Connor, J., concurring) ("When the intent of the Framers is unclear, I believe we must employ both history and reason in our analysis."). *Id.*

90. *See Lynch v. Donnelly*, 465 U.S. 668, 674, 677 (1984); and *Walz v. Tax Commission*, 397 U.S. 664, 678, 681 (1970). In *Walz* the Court quoted the familiar statement by Justice Holmes that "if a thing has been practiced for two hundred years by common consent, it will need a strong case for the [f]ourteenth [a]mendment to affect it." *Walz* at 678 (quoting *Jackson v. Rosenbaum Co.*, 260 U.S. 22, 31 [1922]).

91. *See* Fink, *Evaluation of Commencement Practices in American Public Secondary Schools* (1940).

92. *Id.* at 24.

93. *Id.* at 20.

94. H. McKown, *Commencement Activities* (1931).

95. Kevin Sheard, *Academic Heraldry in America* (Marquette, Mich.: Northern Michigan University Press, 1962).

96. *Id* at 69.

97. *Id.* at 71.

98. *See generally* Mary Gunn, *A Guide to Academic Protocol* (New York: Columbia University Press, 1969).

99. *See* University of Virginia Library, Archives, Charlottesville, Va.

100. *See* University of Virginia Founder's Day Program, April 13, 1907, University of Virginia Library, Archives, Charlottesville, Va.

101. *See Everson v. Board of Education*, 330 U.S. 1 (1947); *Tilton v. Richardson*, 403 U.S. 672 (1971); and, *Walz v. Tax Commission*, 397 U.S. 664 (1970).

102. *Allegheny County v. American Civil Liberties Union, Greater Pittsburgh Chapter*, 109 S. Ct. 3086, 3142 (1989) (Kennedy, J., dissenting).

103. 403 U.S. 602, *reh'g denied*, 404 U.S. 876 (1971).

104. *Id.* at 612-13.

105. The Court declined to apply the test in *Marsh v. Chambers*, 463 U.S. 781 (1983).

106. The Court in *Lemon* stated that the wall of separation is not an impregnable wall but a "blurred, indistinct, and variable barrier depending on all the circumstances of a particular relationship." *Lemon*, 403 U.S. at 614. The Court has also recognized that "we can only dimly perceive the lines of demarcation in this extraordinarily sensitive area of constitutional law." *Id.* at 612. The Court has thus disclaimed any adherence to a single test or criterion when reviewing an Establishment Clause issue. *See Lynch v. Donnelly*, 465 U.S. 668, 679 (1984).

107. *See Allegheny County v. American Civil Liberties Union, Greater Pittsburgh Chapter*, 109 S. Ct. 3086, 3134 (1989) (Kennedy, J. dissenting); *Wallace v. Jaffree*, 472 U.S. 38, 110 (1985) (Rehnquist, J., dissenting).

108. *See Lynch v. Donnelly*, 465 U.S. 668, 687 (1984) (O'Connor, J., concurring).

109. *Id.* at 690.

110. *Id.*

111. *Id.* at 688.

112. 109 S. Ct. 3086 (1989).

113. *Id.* at 3140-41 n.6 (Kennedy, J., concurring).

114. 110 S. Ct. 2356, 2367 (1990).

115. In *Mergens*, the Court incorporated the endorsement test into the *Lemon* test. *See Id.*

116. *See generally Mergens v. Board of Education of the Westside Community Schools*, 110 S. Ct. 2356 (1990).

117. *See Lynch*, 465 U.S. at 681 n.6.

118. *See McGowan v. Maryland*, 366 U.S. 420, 442 (1961).

119. *See Wallace v. Jaffree*, 472 U.S. 38, 72 (1985) (O'Connor, J., concurring).
120. *Id.* at 75 (quoting *Epperson v. Arkansas*, 393 U.S. 97, 108 [1968]). O'Connor reemphasizes this point in *Mergens* where she cites *Edwards v. Aguillard*, 482 U.S. 578, 586 (1987) and *Mueller v. Allen*, 463 U.S. 388, 394-95 (1983), for the proposition that the Court is reluctant to impute wrong motives to a lawmaking body when a secular purpose could be discerned from the wording of the law. *Mergens*, 110 S. Ct. at 2363.
121. *Lynch v. Donnelly*, 465 U.S. 668, 680 (1984).
122. *Id.* at 680. *See also Wallace v. Jaffree*, 472 U.S. 38, 56 (1985); and *Florey v. Sioux Falls School District 49-5*, 464 F. Supp. 911 (D.S.D. 1979), *aff'd*, 619 F.2d 1311, 1314 (8th Cir. 1980), *cert. denied*, 449 U.S. 987 (1980).
123. *Lynch*, 465 U.S. at 680.
124. Laurence Tribe, *American Constitutional Law* (Mineola, N.Y.: Foundation Press, 1978), p. 835.
125. *Karen B. v. Treen*, 653 F.2d 897, 901 (5th Cir. 1981), *aff'd mem.*, 455 U.S. 913 (1982). Several courts have held that an invocation cannot possibly have a secular purpose because it is inherently religious. *See Jager v. Douglas County School District*, 862 F.2d 824 (11th Cir. 1989), *cert. denied*, 109 S. Ct. 2431 (1989); *Graham v. Central Community School District*, 608 F. Supp. 531 (S.D. Tex. 1985); *Lundberg v. West Monona Community School District*, 731 F. Supp. 331 (N.D. Iowa 1989); *Doe v. Aldine Independent School District*, 563 F. Supp. 883 (S.D. Tex. 1982); *Bennett v. Livermore Unified School District*, 193 Cal. App. 3d 1012, 238 Cal. Rptr. 819 (1987).
126. 610 F. Supp. 43 (W.D. Mich. 1985).
127. *See also Kay v. David Douglas School District*, 79 Or. App. 384, 719 P.2d 875, 883 n.1 (1986), *rev'd on other grounds*, 303 Or. 574, 738 P.2d 1389 (1987) *cert. denied*, 484 U.S. 1032 (1988). (Rossman, J., dissenting); *Lincoln v. Page*, 241 A.2d 799, 800-01 (N.H. 1968); Iowa, *supra* note 46, at 1258.
128. *See Lynch v. Donnelly*, 465 U.S. 668 (1984); *Allegheny County v. American Civil Liberties Union, Greater Pittsburgh Chapter*, 109 S. Ct. 3086 (1989).
129. *Sands v. Morongo Unified School District*, 262 Cal. Rptr. 452, 489 (1989), *pet. for review granted*, 264 Cal. Rptr. 683, 782 P.2d 1139 (1989).
130. *Grossberg v. Deusebio*, 380 F. Supp. 285, 289 (E.D. Va. 1974).
131. *See Schempp*, 374 U.S. at 225.
132. *See Lincoln v. Page*, 241 A.2d 799, 800 (N.H. 1968).
133. A prayer case is a unique situation because, if the purpose of the speaker can be imputed to the government, then it is valid to look at his purpose. But when the speaker is not a government agent and in fact has been chosen by nongovernment agents, students, it is difficult to impute his or her purpose to the school officials.
134. *See Stein*, 610 F. Supp. at 48; Connecticut, *supra* note 28, at 160.
135. *See Stein*, 610 F. Supp. at 48.
136. *See Stein*, 610 F. Supp. 43; *Sands v. Morongo Unified School District*, 262 Cal. Rptr. 452, 459, *pet. for review granted*, 264 Cal. Rptr. 683, 782 P.2d 1139 (1989); *Bogen v. Doty*, 598 F.2d 1110, 1113-14 (8th Cir. 1979); Connecticut, *supra* note 28, at 159-60.
137. *See Sands*, 264 Cal. Rptr. 452 at 459.
138. *Id.*
139. Connecticut, *supra* note 28, at 159-60.
140. *See Berlin v. Okaloosa County School District*, No. PCA-87-30450-RV (N.D. Fla. March 1, 1988) (WESTLAW 85937) at 25.
141. One of the arguments against allowing graduation prayers is that a religious act cannot be employed to reach a secular end. *Jager v. Douglas County School*

District, 862 F.2d 824 (11th Cir. 1989); *Doe v. Aldine Independent School District*, 563 F. Supp. 883 (S.D. Tex. 1982). However, in *Jager* and *Doe* the court relies on Supreme Court "prayer in classroom" cases. As noted earlier, the facts and circumstances of the classroom cases are totally distinguishable from a short invocation. Furthermore, if that proposition were true, the Supreme Court in *Engel* would have been incorrect in asserting that the Bible can be used in a secular curricular setting. Justice O'Connor also counters the proposition. She recognized that "legislative prayers . . . and the printing of 'In God We Trust' on our coins," undeniably religious activities, serve the *secular purpose* of "solemnizing public occasions, expressing confidence in the future and encouraging the recognition of what is worthy of appreciation in society." *Allegheny County v. American Civil Liberties Union, Greater Pittsburgh Chapter*, 109 S. Ct. 3086 (1989) (O'Connor, J., concurring) (citations omitted) (emphasis added). Evidently, Justice O'Connor does not believe that invocations must be invalidated because they employ religious means to reach a secular end. *See also Berlin, supra* note 21, at 27.

142. *See Allegheny County*, 109 S. Ct. at 3118 ("such government acknowledgments of religion are not understood as conveying an endorsement of particular religious beliefs"). *Id.*

143. *See School District v. Ball*, 473 U.S. 373, 393-95 (1985); *Lynch*, 465 U.S. at 682 (1984); *Grossberg v. Deusebio*, 380 F. Supp. 285 (E.D. Va. 1974).

144. *Allegheny County*, 109 S. Ct. at 3101; *Mergens*, at 2366.

145. *Mergens*, 110 S. Ct. at 2366; *Lynch*, 465 U.S. at 683; *Sands*, 262 Cal. Rptr. at 460.

146. *See McGowan v. Maryland*, 366 U.S. 420, 442 (1961).

147. DuPuy, *supra* note 7, at 350.

148. *See generally Weisman v. Lee*, 728 F. Supp. 68 (D.R.I. 1990).

149. *See Berlin, supra* note 21, at 35.

150. *Stein*, 610 F. Supp. at 49. *See also Wood*, 342 F. Supp. at 1295; *Grossberg*, 380 F. Supp. at 285.

151. *Allegheny County*, 109 S. Ct. at 3143 (1989) (Kennedy, J., dissenting).

152. *See Wallace v. Jaffree*, 472 U.S. 38, 66 (1985).

153. *See Brandon v. Board of Education*, 635 F.2d 971, 979 (2d Cir. 1980), *cert. denied* 454 U.S. 1123 (1981) (statement that when a clergy briefly appears at a high school graduation ceremony, no image of official state approval is created).

154. *See Lundberg v. West Monona Community School District*, 731 F. Supp. 331 (N.D. Iowa 1989); *Weisman v. Lee*, 728 F. Supp. 68 (D.R.I. 1990).

155. *See Nartowicz v. Clayton School District*, 736 F.2d 646 (11th Cir. 1984); *Collins v. Chandler Unified School District*, 644 F.2d 756 (9th Cir. 1981), *cert. denied*, 454 U.S. 863 (1981); *Doe v. Aldine Independent School District*, 563 F. Supp. 883 (S.D. Tex. 1982); Florida, *supra* note 36, at 1028-30.

156. *Lemon*, 403 U.S. at 615.

157. Connecticut, *supra* note 28, at 163; Iowa, *supra* note 46, at 1268.

158. *Sands v. Morongo Unified School District*, 262 Cal. Rptr. 452, 461, *pet. for review granted*, 264 Cal. Rptr. 683, 782 P.2d 1139 (1989).

159. *Lynch v. Donnelly*, 465 U.S. 668, 684 (1984).

160. *Id.* citing *Mueller v. Allen*, 463 U.S. 388, 403-04 n.11 (1983).

161. *Smith v. Board of Education*, 844 F.2d 90, 92 (2d Cir. 1988).

162. *Id.* at 93.

163. *Abington School District v. Schempp*, 374 U.S. 203, 222-23 (1963).

164. *Berlin v. Okaloosa County School District*, No. PCA-87-30450-RV (N.D. Fla. March 1, 1988) (WESTLAW 85937) at 33.

165. Choper, *supra* note 7, at 408. One court also notes:

Some consciences are very tender and very highly developed, so much so that the possessor regards as being wrong many things that the law regards as harmless. Some refrain from playing cards for amusement, some from dancing, some from attending places of amusement and some from all these things because they consider it wrong to participate in or countenance them. The law regards none of these things as being essentially wrong in itself. At the same time, it recognizes the right of anyone to stay away from them where the promptings of conscience indicate that it would be wrong to attend.

Conway v. District Board of Joint School District, 162 Wis. 482, 156 N.W. 477 (1916).

166. See Wood v. Mt. Lebanon Township School District, 342 F. Supp. 1293, 1295 (W.D. Pa. 1972); Weist v. Mt. Lebanon School District, 320 A.2d 262, 365 (Pa. 1974), cert. denied, 419 U.S. 967 (1974).

167. Grossberg v. Deusebio, 380 F. Supp. 285, 290 (S.D. Iowa 1974).

168. DuPuy, supra note 7, at 346.

169. 393 U.S. 97 (1968).

170. Id. at 103-04. Also see Crowley v. Smithsonian Institution, 462 F. Supp. 725 (D.D.C. 1978), aff'd, 636 F.2d 738 (D.C. Cir. 1980).

171. See Smith v. Board of Education, 844 F.2d 90 (2d Cir. 1988).

172. Id. at 94.

173. The free exercise claim made by those desiring that the practice be reinstated appears weak. See Lundberg v. West Monona Community School District, 731 F. Supp. 331 (N.D. Iowa 1989); DuPuy, supra note 7, at 352-55.

174. Weist v. Mt. Lebanon School District, 320 A.2d 362, 367 (Pa. 1974), cert. denied, 419 U.S. 967 (1974) (Roberts, J., concurring).

175. Id.

176. Id. (citing Abington School District v. Schempp, 374 U.S. 203 [1963]).

177. 731 F. Supp. 331 (N.D. Iowa 1989).

178. Id. at 334-35.

179. Id. at 337. Whether the court was accurate in its determination is perhaps arguable. The forum could be characterized as a limited public forum. However, because the event is conducted on school grounds, using its facilities, and because the school authorities have the final say as to what will be included in the ceremony, such an assertion may be difficult to maintain. See Cornelius v. NAACP Legal Defense & Educational Fund, 473 U.S. 788, 805 (1985); Perry Education Association v. Perry Local Educator's Association, 460 U.S. 3745-46 (1983) for a discussion of the various types of forums.

180. Id. at 338.

181. 484 U.S. 260 (1988).

182. Lundberg, 731 F. Supp. at 338.

183. See Weisman v. Lee, 728 F. Supp. 68 (D.R.I. 1990) (the fact that two teachers planned the ceremony was one factor influencing the holding); Stein v. Plainwell Community Schools, 610 F. Supp. 43, 45 (W.D. Mich. 1985), rev'd, 822 F.2d 1406 (6th Cir. 1987) (Portage High School gave their students the task of organizing the ceremony); Grossberg v. Deusebio, 380 F. Supp. 285, 287 (E.D. Va. 1974) (where students planned the ceremony and even funded most of it). Some courts do not find this dispositive. See Berlin, supra note 21, at 9, where the normal routine was for a ministerial alliance to choose the speaker. Contra Jager v. Douglas County School District, 862 F.2d 824, 831 (11th Cir. 1989), cert. denied, 109 S. Ct. 2431 (1989) (court noted that when students choose, there is no potential entanglement). Other courts have found it appropriate for a student to consult with a school administrator and suggest speakers and then

let the administrator make the final decision, even when the principal disagrees with the student and chooses another speaker. *Sands v. Morongo Unified School District*, 262 Cal. Rptr. 452, 454-55, *pet. for review granted*, 264 Cal. Rptr. 683, 782 P.2d 1139 (1989). Other courts have found no violation when the school board chooses the speaker. *Weist v. Mt. Lebanon School District*, 457 Pa. 166, 320 A.2d 362, 363 *cert. denied*, 419 U.S. 967 (1974); *Graham v. Central Community School District*, 608 F. Supp. 531, 532-33 (S.D. Iowa 1985).

184. See *Berlin v. Okaloosa County School District*, No. PCA-87-30450-RV (N.D. Fla. March 1, 1988) (WESTLAW 85937) at 3 ("No effort is made by the school's officials to control the content of the invocations.").

185. *Marsh v. Chambers*, 463 U.S. 783, 792 (1983) (Court emphasized that opening prayer is not a proselytizing activity); *Jager*, 862 F.2d at 831 (court noted that because the school did not monitor content, the threat of entanglement was lessened). In *Stein*, the district court, applying *Lemon*, noted that the administration had suggested that the minister keep the prayer brief and nondenominational. The court did not see this as monitoring the content. *Stein*, 610 F. Supp. at 45. This court found it important that neither the school nor the senior class representatives previewed the prayer to assess its content. If the school wanted to follow the holding in *Stein*, it would have to advise the speaker to delete all references to Christian Deity or any other references that would identify the prayer with a particular religion not consistent with the American civil religion. In advising the speaker in this way, however, the risk of entanglement is heightened. If the case is analyzed under a *Lemon* standard, such advice might render the prayer unconstitutional. Furthermore, as noted before, the school should not look to content even under the *Marsh* standard applied by the *Stein* court.

186. *Wood v. Mt. Lebanon Township School District*, 342 F. Supp. 1293, 1295 (W.D. Pa. 1972).

187. See *Kay v. David Douglas School District*, 79 Or. App. 384, 719 P.2d 875 (1986), *rev'd on other grounds*, 303 Or. 574, 738 P.2d 1389 (1987), *cert. denied*, 484 U.S. 1032 (1988) (key fact in case was that teachers read the invocation). *Contra Sands*, 262 Cal. Rptr. at 455.

188. *Jager*, 862 F.2d at 831 (court focused on fact that Christian ministers are primary speakers). In *Sands*, the court noted that the students had chosen a Protestant preacher for the invocation and a Catholic priest for the benediction. The court also noted that the same Protestant minister had been giving the invocation for the past nine years, yet the court did not find that offensive. *Sands*, at 455. In *Marsh*, the Court held that the continued appointment of a clergy from a particular denomination did not threaten establishment. *Marsh*, 463 U.S. 787 at 793-94 (1983). See also Connecticut, *supra* note 28, at 162.

189. See *Jager*, 862 F.2d at 834.

190. *Id.*

191. See *Bogen v. Doty*, 598 F.2d 1110, 1114 (8th Cir. 1979).

192. *Id.* at 1112. However, in *Stein* the audience was requested to stand, and the court did not discuss this. *Stein*, 822 F.2d at 1411 (Wellford, J., dissenting).

CHAPTER EIGHTEEN: *The Open Society*

1. 323 U.S. 516 (1945).
2. *Id.* at 543.
3. *Id.* at 530.
4. 308 U.S. 147 (1939).
5. *Id.* at 163.
6. 408 U.S. 169 (1972).
7. *Id.* at 183.

BIBLIOGRAPHY

Adams and Emmerich. "A Heritage of Religious Liberty." 137 *University of Pennsylvania Law Review* 1559 (1989).

Annotation. "Schools—Use for Religious Purposes." 79 *A.L.R.* 2d 1148.

Antieau, Chester James, *et al*. *Freedom from Federal Establishment: Formation and History of the First Amendment Religion Clauses*. Milwaukee: Bruce, 1964.

Ares. "Religious Meetings in the Public High School: Freedom of Speech or Establishment of Religion?" 20 *University of California-Davis Law Review* 313 (1987).

Arons, Stephen. *Compelling Belief: The Culture of American Schooling*. New York: McGraw Hill, 1983.

Arons and Lawrence. "The Manipulation of Consciousness: A First Amendment Critique of Schooling." 15 *Harvard Civil Rights-Civil Liberties Law Review* 309 (1980).

Bainham. *Children, Parents and the State*. 1988.

Bainton, Roland H. *The Travail of Religious Liberty*. Hamden, Conn.: Shoestring Press, 1971.

Barnett, J. *The American Christmas: A Study in National Culture*. New York: Macmillan, 1954.

Bergh, Albert Ellery, ed. *The Writings of Thomas Jefferson*. Vol. XVII. Washington, D. C.: The Thomas Jefferson Memorial Association, 1907.

Beshoner. "Home Education in America: Parental Rights Reasserted." 49 *Missouri Law Review* 191 (1981).

Bigelow, John. *The Life of Benjamin Franklin, Written by Himself*. Philadelphia: J. B. Lippincott, 1916.

Black. "The Bill of Rights." 35 *New York University Law Review* 865 (1960).

Bloom. "A Successful Jewish Boycott of the New York City Public Schools—Christmas 1906." 70 *American Jewish History* 180-88 (December 1980).

Bloustein. "Privacy as an Aspect of Human Dignity: An Answer to Dean Prosser." 39 *New York University Law Review* 962 (1964).

Boston. "Time Out for Religion." 43 *Church and State* 128 (1990).

Braveman, M. *The December Dilemma*. American Jewish Committee, 1986.

Bredemeir, Harry C. and Rubard M. Stephenson. *The Analysis of Social Systems*. New York: Holt, Rinehart, and Winston, 1962.

Bremner, Robert H., ed. *Children and Youth in America: A Documentary History. Vol. II.* Cambridge, Mass.: Harvard University Press, 1971.

Brown, Windsor. *The Secularization of American Education.* New York: Russell & Russell, 1912, 1967.

Burkholder. "Religious Rights of Teachers in Public Education." 18 *Journal of Law & Education* 335 (1989).

Calhoun, Arthur. *A Social History of the American Family from Colonial Times to the Present.* New York: Arno Press, 1973.

Casenote. "Christmas Carols in School Assemblies May Be Constitutional." 31 *Mercer Law Review* 627 (1980).

Casenote. "New Guidance from the Eighth Circuit on the Scope of Permissible Religious Accommodation in Public Schools." 49 *University of Missouri at Kansas City Law Review* 219 (1981).

Choper. "The Religion Clauses of the First Amendment: Reconciling the Conflict." 41 *University of Pittsburgh Law Review* 673 (1980).

———. "Religion in the Public Schools: A Proposed Constitutional Standard." 47 *Minnesota Law Review* 329 (1963).

Coleman, James. *The Adolescent Society.* New York: Free Press of Glencoe, 1961.

Commager, Henry Steele. Preface for *McGuffey's Fifth Eclectic Reader*, as cited in John Whitehead, *The Freedom of Religious Expression in Public Universities and High Schools.* 2d ed. Westchester, Ill.: Crossway Books, 1986.

———, ed. *Documents of American History.* New York: Appleton-Century-Crofts, Inc., 1949.

Comment. "Ceremonial Invocations at Public High School Events and the Establishment Clause." 16 *Florida State University Law Review* 1001 (1989).

Comment. "Constitutional Law—Religious Exercises in Public Schools." 20 *Arkansas Law Review* 320 (1967).

Comment. "Damned if You Do, Damned if you Don't: Religious Shunning and the Free Exercise Clause." 137 *University of Pennsylvania Law Review* 271 (1988).

Comment. "Humanistic Values in the Public School Curriculum: Problems in Defining an Appropriate 'Wall of Separation.'" 61 *Northwestern University Law Review* 795 (1966).

Comment. "Invoking the Presence of God at Public High School Graduation Ceremonies: *Graham v. Central Community School District.*" 71 *Iowa Law Review* 1247 (1986).

Comment. "A Non-Conflict Approach to the First Amendment Religion Clauses." 131 *University of Pennsylvania Law Review* 1175 (1983).

Comment. "The Released Time Program in Public Schools." 10 *Baylor Law Review* 292 (1950).

Comment. "*Stein v. Plainwell Community Schools*: The Constitutionality of Prayer in Public High School Commencement Exercises." 22 *Georgia Law Review* 469 (1988).

Comment. "Students' Constitutional Rights in Public Secondary Education." 14 *Washburn Law Journal* 106 (1975).

Comment. "The Constitutionality of Christmas Programs in Public Schools— Should the United States Supreme Court Modify Its Interpretation of the

Establishment Clause?" 11 *Southern Illinois University Law Journal* 1233 (1987).

The Compact Edition of the Oxford English Dictionary. Vol. I. London: Oxford University Press, 1979.

Cooley, Thomas M. *The General Principles of Constitutional Law in the United States of America.* Boston: Little, Brown and Co., 1898.

Cord, Robert. *Separation of Church and State: Historical Fact and Current Fiction.* New York: Lambeth Press, 1982.

Cremin, Lawrence. *The American Common School.* New York: Columbia University Press, 1951.

_____. *American Education: The Colonial Experience, 1607-1783.* New York: Harper & Row, 1970.

Cubberly, Ellwood. *The History of Education.* New York: Houghton Mifflin Co., 1920.

Dash, Samuel, *et al. The Eavesdroppers.* New York: Da Capo Press, 1971.

Davis, William T. *History of the Town of Plymouth.* Philadelphia: J. W. Lewis & Co., 1885.

Dawson, W. *Christmas: Its Origin and Associations.* London: Elliot Stock, 1902.

Declaration of Independence. Reprinted in *Organic Laws of the United States. U.S. Code* at xxxi. (1976).

Dent. "Religious Children, Secular Schools." 61 *Southern California Law Review* 863 (1988).

Dewey, John. *A Common Faith.* New Haven, Conn.: Yale University Press, 1934.

_____. *Individualism, Old and New.* New York: Capricorn Books, 1962.

_____. "Individuality and Experience." *Journal of the Barnes Foundation* (1926). In *John Dewey on Education: Selected Writings.* Ed. Reginald D. Archambault. New York: Random House, 1964.

_____. "My Pedagogic Creed." *John Dewey on Education: Selected Writings.* Ed. Reginald D. Archambault. New York: Random House, 1964.

_____. *The Public and Its Problems.* New York: Henry Holt and Co., 1927.

Diamond. "The First Amendment and Public Schools: The Case Against Judicial Intervention." 59 *Texas Law Review* 477 (1981).

Diliberto. "Federal and State Constitutionality of Baccalaureate Services in the Public Schools." 15 *Ohio Northern University Law Review* 522 (1988).

Documents Illustrative of the Formation of the Union of American States, 1927.

Dreisbach, Daniel L. *Real Threat and Mere Shadow: Religious Liberty and the First Amendment.* Westchester, Ill.: Crossway Books, 1987.

Dupuy. "Religion, Graduation, and the First Amendment: A Threat or A Shadow?" 35 *Drake Law Review* 323 (1985-86).

Eastland, Terry. "In Defense of Religious America." *Commentary,* June 1981.

Elkind, David. "The Child's Conception of His Religious Denomination, I: The Jewish Child." 99 *Journal of Genetic Psychology* 209 (1961).

_____. "The Child's Conception of His Religious Denomination, II: The Catholic Child." 101 *Journal of Genetic Psychology* 185 (1962).

_____. "The Child's Conception of His Religious Denomination, III: The Protestant Child." 103 *Journal of Genetic Psychology* 291 (1963).

_____. *The Hurried Child: Growing Up Too Fast Too Soon.* Reading, Mass.: Addison-Wesley Publishing Co., 1981.

Elliott, Ian, ed. *James Madison, 1751-1836.* New York: Oceana, 1969.

Farber and Nowak. "The Misleading Nature of Public Forum Analysis: Content and Context in First Amendment Adjudication." 70 *Virginia Law Review* 1219 (1984).

Fink. *Evaluation of Commencement Practices in American Public Secondary Schools.* 1940.

Fitzpatrick, John C. *George Washington Himself.* Indianapolis: Bobbs-Merrill, 1933.

———, ed. *The Writings of George Washington.* Washington, D.C.: United States Government Printing Office, 1932.

Foner, Philip S., ed. *Basic Writings of Thomas Jefferson.* New York: Willey Book Co., 1944.

Freeman. "The Supreme Court and First Amendment Rights of Students in the Public School Classroom: A Proposed Model of Analysis." 12 *Hastings Constitutional Law Quarterly* 1 (1984).

Gales and Seaton, eds. 1 *Annals of Congress* 1834.

Giannella. "Religious Liberty, Nonestablishment, and Doctrinal Development: Part I. The Religious Liberty Guarantee." 80 *Harvard Law Review* 1381 (1967).

———. "Part II. The Nonestablishment Principle." 81 *Harvard Law Review* 513 (1968).

Goodsell, Willystine. *A History of the Family as a Social and Educational Institution.* New York: Macmillan, 1915.

Gottlieb. "In the Name of Patriotism: The Constitutionality of 'Bending' History in Public Secondary Schools." 62 *New York University Law Review* 497 (1987).

Gow, Kathleen M. *Yes, Virginia, There Is Right and Wrong!* Toronto: John Wiley and Sons Canada Ltd., 1980.

Greenawalt. "Religion as a Concept in Constitutional Law." 72 *California Law Review* 753 (1984).

Gross, Martin L. *The Brain Watchers.* New York: Random House, 1962.

Gunn, M. *A Guide to Academic Protocol.* New York: Columbia University Press, 1969.

Hafen. "Developing Student Expression Through Institutional Authority: Public Schools as Mediating Structures." 48 *Ohio State Law Journal* 663 (1987).

———. "Hazelwood School District and the Role of First Amendment Institutions." 1988 *Duke Law Journal* 685 (1988).

Harmin, Merrill, *et al. Clarifying Values Through Subject Matter.* Minneapolis: Winston Press, 1974.

Hirschoff. "Parents and the Public School Curriculum: Is There a Right to Have One's Child Excused from Objectionable Instruction?" 50 *Southern California Law Review* 871 (1977).

Howe, Mark DeWolfe. *The Garden and the Wilderness: Religion and Government in American Constitutional History.* Chicago: University of Chicago Press, 1965.

Hunt, Gaillard, ed. *The Writings of James Madison, Volume V, 1787-1790.* New York: G. P. Putnam's Sons, 1904.

Hunter. "Curriculum, Pedagogy, and the Constitutional Rights of Teachers in Secondary Schools." 25 *William & Mary Law Review* 1 (1983).

Ingber. "The Marketplace of Ideas: A Legitimizing Myth." 1984 *Duke Law Journal* 29 (1989).

———. "Religion or Ideology?: A Needed Clarification of the Religion Clauses." 41 *Stanford Law Review* 233 (1989).

Kahan. "Jewish Divorce and Secular Courts: The Promise of Avitzur." 73 *Georgetown Law Journal* 193 (1984).

Kauper. "Prayer, Public Schools and the Supreme Court." 61 *Michigan Law Review* 1031 (1963).

Kent, James. *Commentaries on American Law*. Vol. II. Boston: Little, Brown, 1858.

Kessler. "Locke's Influence on Jefferson's 'Bill for Establishing Religious Freedom.'" 25 *Journal of Church and State* 231 (1983).

Knicely, James. *Discrimination in the Public Forum Generally*. Charlottesville, Va.: The Rutherford Institute, 1989.

Koch, Adrienne and William Peden, eds. *The Life and Selected Writings of Thomas Jefferson*. New York: Random House, 1944.

Kohlberg, Lawrence, *et al*. *Moral Stages: A Current Formulation and a Response to Critics*. Basel: S. Karger, 1983.

Kohlberg and Mayer. "Development as the Aim of Education." 42 *Harvard Educational Review* 449 (1972).

Kurland. "The Supreme Court, Compulsory Education, and the First Amendment's Religion Clauses." 75 *West Virginia Law Review* 213 (1973).

Lapidus, Edith J. *Eavesdropping on Trial*. Rochelle Park, N. J.: Hayden Book Co., 1974.

Lawrence. "The Manipulation of Consciousness: A First Amendment Critique of Schooling." 15 *Harvard Civil Rights-Civil Liberties Law Review* 309 (1980).

———. "Education for Self-Government: Reassessing the Role of the Public School in a Democracy." 82 *Michigan Law Review* 810 (1984).

Laycock. "Equal Access and Moments of Silence: The Equal Status of Religious Speech by Private Speakers." 81 *Northwestern University Law Review* 1 (1986).

———. "Toward a General Theory of the Religion Clauses: The Case of Church Labor Relations and the Right to Church Autonomy." 81 *Columbia Law Review* 1373 (1981).

Leedes. "Pigeon Holes in the Public Forum." 20 *University of Richmond Law Review* 499 (1986).

Levin. "Educating Youth for Citizenship: The Conflict Between Authority and Individual Rights in the Public School." 95 *Yale Law Journal* 1647 (1986).

Lewis, C., ed. *A Calendar of Religious Holidays and Ethnic Festivals, September 1988 to August 1990*. National Conference of Christians and Jews.

Lewis, C. S. *The Abolition of Man*. New York: Macmillan, 1947.

Lines. "Excusal from Public School Curriculum Requirements." 5 *Education Law Reporter* 691 (1982).

Lipscomb, Andrew A., ed. *The Writings of Thomas Jefferson*. Vol. XIX. Washington, D. C.: The Thomas Jefferson Memorial Association, 1905.

Lupu. "Where Rights Begin: The Problem of Burdens on the Free Exercise of Religion." 102 *Harvard Law Review* 933 (1989).

Made, Robert Douthat. *Patrick Henry: Patriot in the Making.* Philadelphia: J. B. Lippincott, 1916.

Madison, James. *Letters and Other Writings of James Madison, Fourth President of the United States.* New York: R. Worthington, 1884.

Malone, Dumas. *Jefferson the Virginian.* Boston: Little Brown, 1948.

Mawdsley. "Parental Rights and Public Education." 59 *Education Law Reporter* (May 1990).

McConnell. "Accommodation of Religion." 1985 Supreme Court Review 1 (1985).

———. "The Origins and Historical Understanding of Free Exercise of Religion." 103 *Harvard Law Review* 1409 (1990).

McGuffey's Newly Revised Rhetorical Guide. Cincinnati: Winthrop B. Smith and Co., 1953.

McKown, H. *Commencement Activities.* 1931

Mead, George H. *Mind, Self, and Society from the Standpoint of a Social Behaviorist.* Ed. Charles W. Morris. Chicago: University of Chicago Press, 1967.

———. *Movements of Thought in the Nineteenth Century.* Chicago: University of Chicago Press, 1936.

Meade, Robert D. *Patrick Henry: Patriot in the Making.* Philadelphia: J. B. Lippincott, 1957.

Menendez, A. *The December Dilemma: Christmas in American Public Life.* Silver Spring, Md.: Americans United for Separation of Church and State, 1988.

Merel. "The Protection of Individual Choice in Religion: A Consistent Understanding of Religion Under the First Amendment." 45 *University of Chicago Law Review* 805 (1978).

Mill, John Stuart. "On Liberty." From R. B. McCallum, ed. *On Liberty and Considerations on Representative Government.* New York: Macmillan, 1947.

Milton, John. *Areopagitica.* Cambridge: Cambridge University Press, 1918.

Mitchell. "Secularism in Public Education: The Constitutional Issues." 67 *Boston University Law Review* 603 (1987).

Moore. "The Supreme Court and the Relationship Between the 'Establishment' and 'Free Exercise' Clauses." 42 *Texas Law Review* 142 (1963).

Moravia, Alberto. *Man as an End: A Defense of Humanism.* Trans. B. Wall. Westport, Conn.: Greenwood Press, 1976.

Morgan, Joy Elmer, ed. *Horace Mann: His Ideas and Ideals.* Washington, D.C.: National Home Library Foundation, 1936.

Moshman, David. *Children, Education, and the First Amendment: A Psycholegal Analysis.* Lincoln, Nebr.: University of Nebraska Press, 1989.

Mosier, Richard D. *Making the American Mind: Social and Moral Ideas in the McGuffey Readers.* New York: King's Crown Press, 1947.

Moskowitz. "The Making of the Moral Child: Legal Implications of Values Education." 6 *Pepperdine Law Review* 105 (1938).

Murphy. "Access to Public School Facilities and Students by Outsiders." 16 *School Law Bulletin* 9 (Winter 1985).

_____. "The Prior Restraint Doctrine in the Supreme Court: A Reevaluation." 51 *Notre Dame Lawyer* 898 (1976).

Neill, A. S. *Summerhill: A Radical Approach to Child-Rearing.* New York: Hart Publishing Co., 1960.

Nimmer, M. *Nimmer on Freedom of Speech.* New York: Matthew Bender, 1984.

Note. "An Establishment Clause Analysis of Graduation Ceremony Invocations: *Stein v. Plainwell Community Schools.*" 21 *Connecticut Law Review* 133 (1988).

Note. "*Bowen v. Kendrick*: Establishing a New Relationship Between Church and State." 38 *American University Law Review* 953 (1989).

Note. "Defining 'Religion' in the First Amendment: A Functional Approach." 74 *Cornell Law Review* 532 (1989).

Note. "*Delconte v. State*: Some Thoughts on Home Education." 64 *North Carolina Review* 1302 (1986).

Note. "Developments in the Law—Religion and the State: II. The Complex Interaction Between Religion and Government." 100 *Harvard Law Review* 1606 (1987).

Note. "Education and the Court: The Supreme Court's Educational Ideology." 40 *Vanderbilt Law Review* 939 (1987).

Note. "Freedom and Publication: The Need for New Standards." 50 *Notre Dame Law Review* 530 (1975).

Note. "Invocations and Benedictions—Is the Supreme Court 'Graduating' to a Marsh Analysis?" 65 *University of Detroit Law Review* 769 (1988).

Note. "Permissible Accommodations of Religion: Reconsidering the New York 'Get' Statute." 96 *Yale Law Journal* 1147 (1987).

Note. "Public Forum Analysis After *Perry Education Association v. Perry Local Educator's Association*—A Conceptual Approach to Claims of First Amendment Access to Publicly Owned Property." 54 *Fordham Law Review* 545 (1986).

Note. "Reconceptualizing Establishment Clause Cases as Free Exercise Class Actions." 98 *Yale Law Journal* 1739 (1989).

Note. "Reinterpreting the Religion Clauses: Constitutional Construction and Conceptions of the Self." 97 *Harvard Law Review* 1468 (1984).

Note. "Religious Expression in the Public School Forum: The High School Student's Right to Free Speech." 72 *Georgetown Law Journal* 135 (1983).

Note. "Religious-Holiday Observances in the Public Schools." 48 *New York University Law Review* 1116 (1973).

Note. "Religious Liberty in the Public High School: Bible Study Clubs." 17 *John Marshall Law Review* 933 (1984).

Note. "Religious Rights of Public School Teachers." 23 *University of California-Los Angeles Law Review* 763 (1976).

Note. "Secular Humanism in Public School Textbooks: Thou Shalt Have No Other God (Except Thyself)." 63 *Notre Dame Law Journal* 358 (1988).

Note. "State Indoctrination and the Protection of Non-State Voices in the Schools: Justifying a Prohibition of School Library Censorship." 35 *Stanford Law Review* 497 (1982).

Note. "Teaching Inequality: The Problem of Public School Tracking." 102 *Harvard Law Review* 1318 (1989).

Note. "The Constitutional Dimensions of Student-Initiated Religious Activity in Public High Schools." 92 *Yale Law Journal* 499 (1983).

Note. "The Constitutionality of the 1972 Amendment of Title VII's Exemption for Religious Organizations." 73 *Michigan Law Review* 538 (1975).

Note. "The Constitutionality of Student-Initiated Religious Activity in Public Schools." 92 *Yale Law Journal* 449 (1983).

Note. "The Constitutionality of Student-Initiated Religious Meetings on Public School Grounds." 50 *University of Cincinnati Law Review* 740 (1981).

Note. "The Establishment Clause and Its Application in the Public Schools." 59 *Nebraska Law Review* 1143 (1980).

Note. "The Free Exercise Boundaries of Permissible Accommodation Under the Establishment Clause." 99 *Yale Law Journal* 1127 (1990).

Note. "The Myth of Religious Neutrality by Separation in Education." 71 *Virginia Law Review* 127 (1985).

Note. "The Right of Public High School Students to Conduct a Prayer Group on Public School Premises During Student Activity Period." 10 *Thurgood Marshall Law Journal* 449 (1985).

Note. "Toward a Constitutional Definition of Religion." 91 *Harvard Law Review* 1056 (1978).

Nowak, John, et al. *Hancock on Constitutional Law*. St. Paul, Minn: West Publishing Co., 1983.

Packard, Vance Oakley. *The Naked Society*. New York: D. McKay Co., 1964.

Padover, Saul K., ed. *The Complete Jefferson*. New York: Duell, Sloan & Pearce, Inc., 1943.

——. *Jefferson*. New York: Harcourt-Brace, 1942.

Paulsen. "Religion Equality and the Constitution: An Equal Protection Approach to Establishment Clause Adjudication." 61 *Notre Dame Law Review* 311 (1986).

Pevar. "Public Schools Must Stop Having Christmas Assemblies." 24 *St. Louis University Law Journal* 327 (1980).

Pfeffer. "The Supremacy of Free Exercise." 61 *Georgetown Law Journal* 1115 (1973).

Piaget, Jean. *Six Psychological Studies*. Ed. David Elkind. New York: Random House, 1968.

Piele and Pitt. "The Use of School Facilities by Student Groups for Religious Activities." 13 *Journal of Law and Education* 197 (1984).

Postman, Neil. *The Disappearance of Childhood*. New York: Delacorte Press, 1982.

Prosser. "Privacy." 48 *California Law Review* 383 (1960).

Recent Developments. "The Constitutionality Under the Religion Clauses of the First Amendment of Compulsory Sex Education in Public Schools." 68 *Michigan Law Review* 1050 (1970).

Records of the Governor and Company of Massachusetts Bay in New England. Vol. II. 1647.

Reichley, J. *Religion in American Public Life*. Washington, D. C.: The Brookings Institution, 1985.

"The 'Released Time' Cases Revisited." 83 *Yale Law Journal* 1202 (1974).

Rice. "Conscientious Objection to Public Education: The Grievance and the Remedies." 1978 *Brigham Young University Law Review* 847 (1978).

Rousseau, Jean-Jacques. *Emile, or On Education.* Trans. Allan Bloom. New York: Basic Books, Inc., 1979.

Schauer. "Fear, Risk and the First Amendment: Unraveling the 'Chilling Effect.'" 58 *Boston University Law Review* 685 (1978).

Schwarz. "No Imposition of Religion: The Establishment Clause Value." 77 *Yale Law Review* 692 (1968).

Sheard, K. *Academic Heraldry in America.* Marquette, Mich.: Northern Michigan University Press, 1962.

Sherry. "Republican Citizenship in a Democratic Society." 66 *Texas Law Review* 1229 (1988).

Shiffrin. "Government Speech." 27 *UCLA Law Review* 565 (1980).

Shirer, William. *The Rise and Fall of the Third Reich.* New York: Simon and Schuster, 1980.

Skinner, B. F. *About Behaviorism.* New York: Knopf, 1974.

———. *Beyond Freedom and Dignity.* New York: Knopf, 1972.

Smith. "Constitutional Rights of Students, Their Families, and Teachers in the Public Schools." 10 *Campbell Law Review* 353 (1988).

———. "Symbols, Perceptions, and Doctrinal Illusions: Establishment Neutrality and the 'No Endorsement' Test." 86 *Michigan Law Review* 266 (1987).

Smith and Hayes. "A Christmas Carol Revisited: Humbug in the Sioux Falls Schools." 24 *St. Louis University Law Journal* 359 (1980).

Snyder, P. *December 25th.* New York: Dodd, Mead & Co., 1985.

Stern, Mark. *Religion and the Public Schools: A Summary of the Law.* American Jewish Congress, September 1989.

Stone. "The Equal Access Controversy: The Religion Clauses and the Meaning of 'Neutrality.'" 81 *Northwestern University Law Review* 168 (1986).

Story, Joseph. "Commentaries on the Constitution of the United States." Ed. John Nowak. Durham, N. C.: Carolina Academic Press, 1987.

Strossen. "A Framework for Evaluating Equal Access Claims by Religious Groups: Is There a Window for Free Speech in the Wall Separating Church and State?" 71 *Cornell Law Review* 143 (1985).

———. "'Secular Humanism' and 'Scientific Creationism': Proposed Standards for Reviewing Curricular Decisions Affecting Students' Religious Freedom." 47 *Ohio State Law Journal* 333 (1986).

Teitel. "When Separate Is Equal: Why Organized Religious Exercises, Unlike Chess, Do Not Belong in the Public Schools." 81 *Northwestern University Law Review* 174 (1986).

———. "The Unconstitutionality of Equal Access Policies and Legislation Allowing Organized Student-Initiated Religious Activities in the Public Schools: A Proposal for a Unitary First Amendment Forum Analysis." 12 *Hastings Constitutional Law Quarterly* 529 (1985).

Toms and Whitehead. "The Religious Student in Public Education: Resolving a Constitutional Dilemma." 27 *Emory Law Journal* 3 (1978).

Tribe, Laurence. *American Constitutional Law.* 2d. ed. Mineola, N. Y.: The Foundation Press, 1988.

———. *American Constitutional Law.* Mineola, N. Y.: The Foundation Press, 1978.

Tushnet. "The Constitutionality of Religion." 18 *Connecticut Law Review* 701 (1986).

U. S. Congress. Hearings on S.815 and S.1059 Before the Senate Committee on the Judiciary. *Equal Access: A First Amendment Question.* 98th Cong., 1st sess., 1983.

Van Geel. "The Search for Constitutional Limits of Government's Authority to Inculcate Youth." 62 *Texas Law Review* 197 (1983).

Vitz, Paul C. *Religion and Traditional Values in Public School Textbooks: An Empirical Study.* Washington, D. C.: National Institute of Education, 1985.

Warmflash. "The New York Approach to Enforcing Marriage Contracts: From Avitzur to the 'Get' Statute." 50 *Brooklyn Law Journal* 229 (1984).

Warren and Brandeis. "The Right of Privacy." 4 *Harvard Law Review* 193 (1890).

Webster's New Collegiate Dictionary. Springfield, Mass.: G. & C. Merriam Co., 1975.

Welch. "The State as a Purveyor of Morality." 56 *George Washington Law Review* 540 (1988).

Whitehead, Alfred North. *The Aims of Education and Other Essays.* New York: Macmillan, 1959.

Whitehead, John. *Home Education Reporter.* Charlottesville, Va.: The Rutherford Institute, 1990.

———. "Accommodation and Equal Treatment of Religion: Federal Funding of Religiously-Affiliated Child Care Facilities." 26 *Harvard Journal on Legislation* 573 (1989).

———. "Avoiding Religious Apartheid: Affording Equal Treatment for Student-Initiated Religious Expression in Public Schools." 16 *Pepperdine Law Journal* 229 (1989).

———. *The Freedom of Religious Expression in Public Universities and High Schools.* 2d ed. Westchester, Ill.: Crossway Books, 1986.

Wilbur, William H. *The Making of George Washington.* 2d ed. Daytona Beach: Patriotic Education, Inc., 1973.

Williams, Joyce Wolfgang, and Marjorie Stith. *Middle Childhood: Behavior and Development.* New York: Macmillan, 1974.

Wilson, J. O. *Public Schools of Washington.* Vol. I. Records of the Columbia Historical Society (1987).

Wittmer, Joe and Robert D. Myrick. *Facilitative Teaching: Theory and Practice.* 2d ed. Minneapolis: Educational Media Corp., 1980.

Wolff, Robert Paul. *The Poverty of Liberalism.* Boston: Beacon Press, 1968.

Wood, James, ed. *Religion and State: Essays in Honor of Leo Pfeffer.* Waco, Tex.: Baylor University Press, 1985.

Woodruff. "Religious Holidays and the Public Schools." 16 *Religion and Public Education* 123 (Winter 1989).

The Writings of Thomas Jefferson. Mem. ed. 1904.

Yodof. "Library Book Selection and the Public School: The Quest of the Archimedean Point." 59 *Indiana Law Journal* 527 (1984).

Yodof, Mark. *When Government Speaks: Politics, Law, and Government Expression in America.* Berkeley: University of California, 1983.

INDEX OF CASES

309

GENERAL INDEX

ABOUT THE AUTHOR

An author and an attorney specializing in constitutional law, *John W. Whitehead* serves as president of The Rutherford Institute, headquartered in Charlottesville, Virginia. He has successfully litigated many constitutional law cases.

Mr. Whitehead has taught constitutional law and courses on the First Amendment. He has also lectured at various law schools throughout the United States.

Mr. Whitehead has served as counsel to many organizations and as counsel *amicus curiae* in numerous cases before the United States Supreme Court and various United States Circuit Courts. He is a member of the bars of the Supreme Courts of Virginia and Arkansas; the United States Supreme Court; the United States Courts of Appeals for the Fourth, Fifth, Seventh, and Ninth Circuits; and various United States District Courts. He has also been appointed Special Assistant Attorney General for the State of Louisiana.

The author of fourteen books and coauthor of others, he has also published articles in legal journals. These include, for example, *The Religious Student in Public Education: Resolving a Constitutional Dilemma*, 27 Emory Law Journal 3 (1978) and *Avoiding Religious Apartheid: Affording Equal Treatment for Student-Initiated Religious Expression in Public Schools*, 16 Pepperdine Law Review 229 (1989).

Mr. Whitehead is a member of the American Trial Lawyers Association and numerous honorary societies. He is included in *Who's Who in American Law*, *Who's Who in the World*, *The International Who's Who of Intellectuals*, and other listings.

THE RUTHERFORD INSTITUTE

The Rutherford Institute is a civil liberties legal and educational organization that defends religious persons whose constitutional rights have been threatened or violated.

The Institute has assisted schools, teachers, parents, students, and others in the pursuit of a better understanding of constitutional principles as they operate in public education.

For example, the Institute successfully defended a Florida sixth grader after school officials confiscated the New Testaments that she had handed out to classmates after her book report on the Bible. That action, followed by interrogation and harassment of the student by school officials, sparked a lawsuit against the school district for violating her First Amendment rights. The Institute obtained a court order that protected the student's right to exercise her freedom of speech at school.

The Institute filed a suit on behalf of several high school students in Colorado when school authorities prohibited the students from distributing on school grounds copies of a free nonstudent newspaper which contained mainly religious articles. A federal court invalidated the school policy.

In California, Institute attorneys achieved another victory when a school board agreed that a high school junior had the constitutional right to pass out pamphlets on school property. As another concession, the school district agreed to set up orientation workshops to educate teachers and administrators on students' rights to free speech.

In Pennsylvania, the Institute defended the rights of several junior high students to distribute copies of a non-student religious periodical on school grounds. The court upheld the rights of the students to distribute the literature on school grounds and required that further restrictions by the school authorities on such distribution be content-neutral.

In addition to defending the freedom of religious expression in the public schools, Institute attorneys also participate in legal action to protect other vital constitutional rights. The Institute has established a network of state, regional, and international chapters to defend vital liberties.

To educate the public on priority issues, the Institute's Law Center publishes numerous books and papers and provides educational training programs. Legal research resources are also made available to assist attorneys involved in First Amendment litigation.

Address: The Rutherford Institute, P. O. Box 7482, Charlottesville, VA 22901-7482, (804) 978-3888.